BAND OF ANGELS

Also by Kate Cooper

The Virgin and the Bride
The Fall of the Roman Household

BAND OF ANGELS

THE FORGOTTEN WORLD OF EARLY CHRISTIAN WOMEN

KATE COOPER

The Overlook Press
New York, NY

This edition first published in hardcover in the United States in 2013 by
The Overlook Press, Peter Mayer Publishers, Inc.

141 Wooster Street
New York, NY 10012
www.overlookpress.com
For bulk and special sales, please contact sales@overlookny.com.
or write to address above

First published in Great Britain by Atlantic Books in 2013

Cataloging-in-Publication Data is available from the Library of Congress

Manufactured in the United States of America
FIRST EDITION
ISBN: 978-1-4683-0740-5
1 3 5 7 9 10 8 6 4 2

Margaret Robb Shook Cooper (1925–2012)
Mary Louise Shook Wilkinson (1919–2001)
In memoriam

Contents

Preface

In the house where we lived when I was a child, my bedroom was a tiny room at the top of the stairs. It had space for only a bed and a little table, but it holds a luminous place in my memory. It was there that my mother and I engaged in long talks about serious questions. We debated whether the Narnia children could really be friends with a lion, and whose fault it was that Juliet and Romeo did not live happily ever after.

One of these talks took place not long after the death of my grandmother, my mother's own mother. With the fierce and selfish love of small children everywhere, I had seen the wider principle behind this first exposure to death. A thing that could happen to my grandmother, I reasoned, could also happen to my mother, the indispensable person around whom the whole universe seemed to revolve. I never entirely recovered from the shock of that thought.

In retrospect, I admire the simplicity with which my mother spoke to this terrible awakening. She had recently discovered a secret, she told me. The love that bound her to her mother, she now knew, was strong enough to unite them in death as it had in life. Her mother was still with her, and would remain with her always. By a wonderful chain of connection, I too was bound in with them, and the love between us was a thread that could not be broken. One day, I would follow them both – my grandmother and my mother – to a place beyond our imagining, where they would be waiting for me. I was not to worry, she told me, about what it meant to say that such a place existed. No one knew much about it, but the details were beside the point. The thing to remember was that love is more powerful than death.

I recognize now that the whole conversation, as it unfolded in my bedroom, was an act of bravura on my mother's part. It was a gambit, at the end of a long day, to untangle a child from the day's worries and to set her on the path towards sleep. At the same time, it was an attempt to tame the pain of loss, the loss that she felt as a daughter whose own mother had died. By finding the connection between her own mother's life and that of her child, she was able to find a place for her grief in the coming and going of generations. In trying to settle a restless child, she had tested the limits of her own understanding of the world, and this had allowed her to glimpse a luminous truth.

Years later, when her grandchildren came into the world, my mother remained fascinated by the connection she had seen between the waxing and waning of life. As she neared her own death, she became more and more certain that her own departure from this life was a necessary and fitting end to the role she had played bringing new life into the world. To the end, she maintained that the flow of time and the handing on from generation to generation are what make life what it is, and it is good.

My mother grew up in the Deep South during the Great Depression, and along with a legacy of plain-spoken wisdom handed from mother to daughter, she was heir to a great southern patrimony of story-telling. When I was a child, the fact that she was a teller of tales seemed to be the most natural thing in the world. To an unsuspecting ear, the telling of stories never seemed to follow a plan. It seemed to happen in conversation quite naturally. Stories welled up at just the moment when they were needed, to help make sense of a problem or situation in our own lives that was being talked about. They were a tool to think with. Remembering how earlier members of our family had met similar challenges was a way of keeping their memory alive.

Yet there was a logic to how the stories came up in conversation. The cycle of family stories was a kind of storehouse of hopeful thinking and advice on how to cope with difficult situations. Stories about the Depression tended to involve low-cost fun at family parties. The more painful stories were angled to highlight the generosity and courage of earlier generations, or to call attention to examples worth imitating. It was as if the women of our family had sent a message in a bottle down the stream of time, to tell us what they had learned about the world.

Many of my mother's stories were from her own childhood, but others reached back further, to her grandmother's youth during the Civil War and Reconstruction. Perhaps because they were handed from mother to daughter, the stories tended to revolve around the women of the family. As daughters and granddaughters remembered them, our foremothers formed a parade of heroines set against a kaleidoscope of changing circumstances. They had shown spirit in the face of great and small tragedies. Babies and children, including two of my mother's own siblings, had died of fever. Husbands, sons, and brothers had been killed in war, or – worse – by the lawless vigilante groups who ruled isolated rural communities during the Reconstruction. The widows in my family had not fainted in drawing rooms. They had worked tirelessly, in the face of illness and other dangers, to protect and sustain the lives of those who depended on them.

It was a landowning family, so they had responsibility not only for children but for a community of male and female dependants. Some of the stories celebrated the leadership of the family's matriarchs, often in difficult circumstances. Others remembered the pluck of women who had worked long hours in the households of my family's history: servants and, in my great-great grandmother's time, slaves. It was not all sweetness and light. A frequent moral was that the person in charge in any situation was not necessarily the one who had the most common sense. Even our heroines had had failings: the fact was acknowledged with affectionate laughter, but not dwelt upon. For the most part, the stories tended to idealize their protagonists, and to encourage the idea of making the best of a bad lot.

I do not remember when or how it was that I became aware that the fearlessness of our family heroines was bound up with their religious faith. It seemed clear that theirs was a god from whom they could draw extraordinary strength. Yet there was a paradox here. These women had lived in nineteenth- and early twentieth-century Alabama, an environment known not only for its spirited women, but also for its men-folk's tendency to impute inferiority to the 'weaker' sex. To the untrained eye it looked as if the Church had tended to be on the side of the men. If one reads the standard histories, the world of my great-grandmother was one in which wives were subject to their husbands, children were seen but not heard, and the Bible was used to keep the women and children in their place.

But the world of stories handed down from mother to daughter was somehow different to the world of the standard histories. It was a parallel universe, one in which female good sense would always have its day, and the opinions of fathers, husbands, and the clergy were taken with a grain of salt. In reality, our heroines had had to hold their ground repeatedly in the face of male arrogance. But if this fact was acknowledged in the world of stories, it was thrown off with a wry observation about men's inability to perceive the superiority of women. In my mother's day, the joke was that Fred Astaire was the greatest dancer in the world, but Ginger Rogers did everything Fred did backwards, and with high heels on.

There were one or two skeletons in the family closet where the men-folk were concerned. Certain husbands and sons had caused pain and suffering to their wives and mothers. But for the most part, these unedifying characters were quietly written out, except where their failings offered a valuable moral lesson. I realize now, remembering how the aunts and matriarchs talked, that there were two versions of the family's history. In one, the men strode about doing important things, and the women were barely in view. But the women's version paid equally scant attention to the men. If men had more power than women, this did not mean they were more important.

It did not occur to me at the time as something unusual, but my mother and her sister had quite a distinctive way of reading the

Bible. The Bible stories that came up again and again in conversation were those in which Jesus defended the weak or put the arrogant in their place. He had been a great teacher, and yet his message was marvellously simple. It seemed to boil down to loving one's neighbour and trying not to think too much about one's own importance.

The most troubling of the stories of Jesus was about his visit to two sisters, one called Mary, like the mother of Jesus, and the other Martha. Martha seemed to be like my own mother's sister, older and more responsible. When Jesus came to visit their house, Martha organized hospitality not only for him but for the rag-tag entourage who accompanied him. Mary, by contrast, was like my mother: younger, somewhat impetuous, willing to talk all day about ideas and a bit resentful when asked to get back to the 'women's work'. In the story, Mary sat at the feet of Jesus drinking in his marvellous preaching while her sister Martha saw to food and drink for the visitors. Martha became agitated about this, and mentioned it to Jesus. But instead of asking Mary to help her sister, Jesus told Martha that Mary should be praised for caring more about his preaching than about giving him supper.

This surprising answer was the subject of much debate when I was growing up. Should we be delighted that Jesus had taken up for the sister who could not quite manage to do what was expected of her, or should we be irritated at his willingness to take for granted the 'woman's work' of feeding him and his disciples? The story left an unsolved problem hanging in the air, and this made it interesting.

Curiously, the boys and men in our world seemed to hear the story differently. For them, the story was simpler. Their attention was captured by Mary's desire to be close to Jesus, but not by Martha's shock at a guest who was prepared to belittle her hospitality even as he accepted it. We found it odd and somehow reassuring that the Bible story held a message – a little thorn of moral difficulty – that only the women seemed to 'get'.

I learned much later, when I became a historian, that there is a reason for these 'secret messages' to one group of readers or another in the Bible. Most historians now believe that many biblical narratives did not originate with a single writer. Rather, many of the books, such as the Gospels which tell the story of Jesus, were a collective effort. At first, stories were handed down orally from parent to child, or teacher to disciple. Later, as the people who had known Jesus began to grow old and die, writers collected the stories they could find from trusted storytellers and wrote them down. Sometimes the stories carry traces of the differing viewpoints of earlier storytellers, and this is especially significant where stories involving women are concerned.

In the ancient world, the task of caring for the very young and the very old fell to women, and this meant that they were often involved in handing on stories from one generation to the next. Some male writers complained that female storytellers were more influential than they ought to be, but for the most part the influence of women on the young was seen as an unremarkable fact.

Of course, the best known of all the Christian stories involves a woman: it is the story of Mary, the virgin from Galilee, and the Angel who tells her that she will have a child, the Son of God. But surprisingly, the story of Mary and the Angel was not widely known among the earliest Christians. There are four Gospels in the New Testament, but only the Gospel of Luke tells the story of Mary and her child's miraculous birth. The other three Gospel writers were fascinated by the life and death of Jesus of Nazareth, but they were not interested in – or possibly they did not know about – his mother's encounter with the Angel in Nazareth or his birth in a manger in Bethlehem.

It is a curious fact: only one of our four earliest sources for the life of Jesus tells what is perhaps the greatest of the stories of early Christianity. How could the other three writers have missed such a prize? The most likely answer is that they did not know that version of the story. But it is also possible that it simply did not 'speak' to them as they tried to find a pattern in the stories and sayings they had inherited. Each storyteller would develop the aspects of the inherited tradition that were most useful to his or her own community, relying on the inspiration of the spirit to make sense of it all.

Stories have a life of their own, and if you listen closely enough to a story, you can learn something invaluable about the people who told it, and the people to whom it was told. Early Christianity was a movement built on stories, and those stories were mostly about relationships – sometimes relationships between human beings, and sometimes between a human being and his or her god. The stories were charged with an electricity that was meant to change people's lives. They were aimed at encouraging specific qualities in the listener: generosity, forbearance or simple common sense.

My own experience as a parent has led me to appreciate how a teller will bring out aspects of a story that seem to speak to a given situation. Parents use stories to steer children's behaviour and, over time, the uses to which the stories are put come to influence how they are remembered. Stories become part of the fabric of family relationships. As a parent, you want to show a beloved child how to get along in the world, and you are conscious, as you retell a familiar story, of how it might help the child to make sense of things. Some stories encourage the skill of finding hidden possibilities in a difficult situation. Others suggest that there is no point in dwelling on problems about which nothing can be done. Often, in telling a story, a parent will try to downplay plot developments which could lead the child to imagine that hard work and honesty have no value. Virtue will somehow be rewarded, even if not in the way one might have hoped for.

It is part of the logic of storytelling to celebrate the good and condemn the wicked. Yet at the same time, the good should not demand too much credit for their virtue. Early Christian stories return to this point again and again. Take the sisters Mary and Martha in the Gospel of Luke, for example. Jesus does praise Martha, the generous sister who hosts his entourage – but only within limits. When Mary sits and listens raptly to the words of Jesus rather than helping to care for the guests, Jesus wants Martha to praise her sister's attentiveness rather than finding fault with her impracticality. The same is true in the story of the Prodigal Son. The virtuous brother who makes every effort to please his father is given measured praise. But the father holds up the reckless brother who is now trying to rebuild his relationship with his family as a model of whole-hearted repentance.

It is an axiom of modern social psychology that the stories that tend to get repeated are the ones that somehow have the potential to strengthen the communities in which they are told, or to enhance the relationship between the teller and the hearer. This principle seems to be reflected in the stories that were handed down from the community around Jesus. Again and again, early Christian stories suggest that virtue is not enough. The lives of families and communities can only really flourish where virtue takes second place to love.

Looking back, I realize that my mother's efforts to soften my understanding of death were not immediately successful. I was a sleepless child, troubled by dreams. I remember one terrible dream – I believe it happened only once – in which my mother was sitting on a bed, not my own. It was clear, in the way that one knows things in dreams without being told them, that she was dying. The main action in the dream was that my father was trying to take me away, and I was struggling with all my power to keep my eyes on her. I knew that I was not strong enough to hold on for long. The dark certainty that I would lose her one day never left me after that. I suppose it was my first step away from childhood.

I think it must have been around this time that my mother's sister gave me one of my treasured childhood possessions, a drawing of a child at prayer, to hang over my bed. Below the picture was a little text which was meant to get me started as I said my own prayers at bedtime. I did not notice until years later that the little text was aimed straight at the heart of my new fear. It taught me to ask God to keep watch over my family while I slept, and encouraged me to trust that someone more powerful than myself would take care of my mother. I only came to understand the meaning of this gift years later, as I sat by my mother's bed in that other bedroom where she died. By then, she had lived a long and fruitful life, and it was a blessing to be with her in the quiet moment when life ebbed away. My mother's older sister had died years earlier, but her love was a luminous presence with us during my mother's last hours, for it was she who had taught me to call on God to protect my mother when I could not.

I don't think any living person is entirely sure what it means to commend a dying person into God's care. Different traditions have different ways of understanding this act of helping a human life to return peacefully to the realm of the unknown, and none of them is foolproof. But it makes all the difference, at a death-bed, to be at peace with the idea that each of us will ultimately make this journey. Among the gifts which my mother and her sister gave me during their long lives, one of the most precious was showing me how to lose them when the time came. With this, they converted an abstract theological proposition into a simple, unchallengeable fact: love is stronger than death.

I have come to see that what gives staying power to any tradition of religion or philosophy is the quality of what it offers at those moments when you brush up against the limit of our understanding – or you have to try to make sense of things for a sleepless child who appears at the top of the stairs. A tradition is a collective memory of inspired coping with these moments. Its real value is in how it allows the parents and children of each generation the chance to learn from the inspirations and failures of those who went before, and to leave a trace for those who will come after.

I want to stop to underline this point, because modern discussions about religion are often based on a misunderstanding of what the great religions are really about. Modern people tend to talk about religion as being primarily about doctrines and 'beliefs', but this doesn't make any sense as a way of approaching the ancient world. When the earliest Christians spoke of faith – *pistis* in Greek – they were not talking about whether or not something exists. For the early Christians, faith wasn't about whether a God existed – theirs was a world full of gods, good and bad. For them, it was about *which* god one accepted as one's own. *Pistis* was a relationship of trust and even love – more similar to the English 'faithfulness' or 'loyalty' than to 'faith' in our modern sense of 'belief'.

To explain what they meant by *pistis*, early Christian preachers sometimes took the relationship between a husband and wife, or a parent and child, as an example. The idea was that the God of the Christians was a loving God, and that loyalty to him meant something different than did loyalty to the other gods of the ancient world, so many of whom were known to be cruel or capricious. *This* God was one who so loved the world that he promised to change the lives of his followers, and to offer a new way of thinking about their lives and their relationships. His faith was not a collection of 'beliefs', it was a way of life.

To the modern world, the role of women in shaping the early history of Christianity is largely unknown. Part of the reason for this is a general problem about historical documents. The ones that get preserved tend to be about matters of institutional interest – who should have formal institutional roles, for example – and the informal happenings of daily life rarely get a look-in. Yet it was precisely the small-scale acts of seemingly unimportant people that allowed Christianity to snowball into an empire-wide spiritual revolution.

The earliest Christians were village people and traders from the remote provinces of a great empire, people who thought of themselves as nobodies and who never expected to become players on the historical stage. They prayed together not in buildings called churches but in one another's homes, often sharing a communal meal of thanksgiving. Part of the genius of the early Christian missions was that they put the invisible rhythms of family life and hospitality to new use, as the framework to spread the faith.

How can we gain access to this forgotten aspect of the early

Christian story? Part of the historian's job is to read between the lines. Most historical sources skim over matters that the writers did not see as particularly important, and the world of women often fell into this category. So the story depends largely on glancing references. At times, you feel as if you are an Arctic explorer, trying to judge an underwater landscape on the basis of little more than the tips of the icebergs that are visible above the surface.

More substantial stories about women do survive from the early period, but it is not always clear whether they are truth or pious fiction. Only with the third century do we begin to have sustained evidence for the lives of identifiable historical women, and it is not until the end of the fourth century that we have such evidence in abundance. In their own way, the heroines of legend are as interesting as the real historical women. The stories that were told about them carry valuable clues about what life was like for women in a given place and time. Sometimes, there is reason to suspect that the meaning of a story changed over time, for example when a tale originally told by women fell into men's hands and was written down. Each source poses its own difficulties, and each needs to be handled with care.

Over the years I have had the opportunity to cross-examine the sources, using one text to consider what another might be leaving out, and as a result I no longer find their gaps and silences as daunting as I did when I first started. So when we meet figures whose historical reality is in doubt, I have tried to clarify how their story sheds light on the world of women as the storytellers knew it – the landscape they expected the readers and listeners of their own day to recognize. But in the end, this book remains an exercise of the imagination. It is an attempt to reconstruct a lost story from fragments, a series of portraits seen through a glass darkly.

My decision to become a historian was formed, many years ago, during a memorable summer when I was a student. One of our professors had persuaded the Dean to sponsor a travelling seminar in Greece, visiting the cities where the Apostle Paul had preached. He argued that the best way to understand the pastoral problems that had shaped early Christian thought was by acquainting ourselves with life in the first-century cities.

It was to the Corinthians that the Apostle Paul addressed his most passionate letters of advice – they were a troublesome lot – and when we arrived in Corinth this fact lent excitement to our visit. Exploring the ruins, we were delighted by the idea that we might be standing on the same worn pavements where the Corinthians of Paul's day had quarrelled about everything and nothing at all.

I remember vividly a conversation late one afternoon, as the slanting light began to turn from gold to a powdery deep blue. We were in the ruins of a first-century house. Many of the disputes in early Christian Corinth had revolved around table fellowship – who could eat with whom, and what kind of food they could share – so when we reached the dining room a conversation about those issues bubbled up, quite naturally. The women in our group thought we should try to find out where the food had been cooked, and by whom. As we threw out our ideas and suggestions, our teacher presided over our deliberations as both referee and muse, and yet he had a lovely humility about the questions he had never thought to ask. He encouraged those of us who thought women must have played an important role in those early debates. Why would they not have, when the debates were fundamentally about family life and hospitality? In those days it was unusual to hear a distinguished male biblical scholar talk earnestly about kitchens and food preparation, and this only added to the charm of it all.

I have tried, in the chapters that follow, to convey some of the excitement of that afternoon in Corinth – to offer, to the best of my ability, a similar invitation to visit a forgotten world in the company of a sure-footed guide. So our story begins in Corinth, with the Apostle Paul and the early house-churches. It then moves forward to the later first century, when the Gospels were written to preserve the memory of the life and death of Jesus, though these events had in fact taken place before Paul's time. Then the story picks up speed, continuing forward across four centuries as the Christian movement spread outwards and upwards into all levels of ancient society. By the story's end, Christianity had become the religion of emperors and – as we shall see – of empresses.

It was during my mother's last illness that I began writing this book, and I knew from the beginning that she would not see it in its final form. Even after she was gone I found that I somehow still wanted to think of her, rather than anyone else, when I imagined the book's reader. Partly it was a desire to write the kind of book that she and my aunt would have wanted to read. I used to comb the bookshops every year around the time of their birthdays, looking for something to feed their interest in the women of the past, and it was often hard to find something that was just right. And I suppose it also seemed to me that if I could keep her in mind as I wrote, the mere fact of writing could be a kind of imaginary gift to send after her when she had gone. So here it is, a message in a bottle, ready to float out onto the water.

I stll remember her delight when I came home from that long-ago summer filled with the stories of my visits to first-century kitchens. She was far more certain than I was, then, that my desire to become a historian would bear fruit. You could feel it in the way she listened – ever the mother, she was trying, by her encourage-ment, to conjure into life the hoped-for future version of her precious child. Her delight and her faith – in the people she loved and in the power of the imagination – are a legacy that connect her to the women of earlier generations, and to those of the generations to come. Faith, hope, and love: these three remain. In what follows we will meet them again and again.

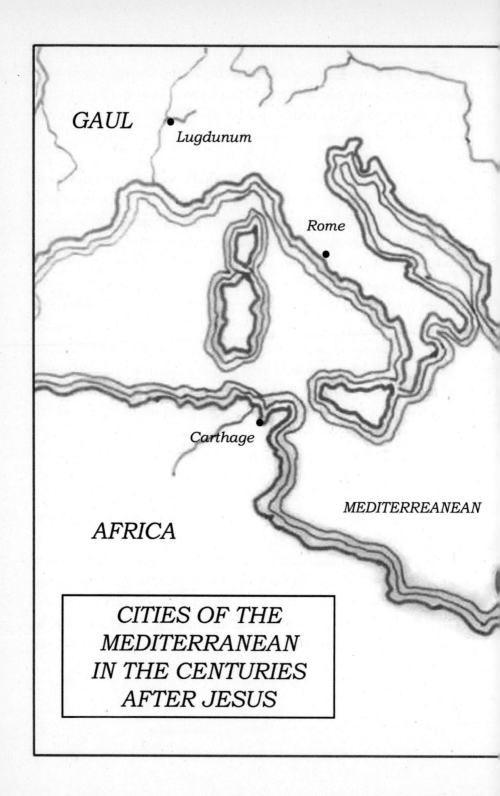

GAUL

• *Lugdunum*

Rome
•

Carthage
•

MEDITERREANEAN

AFRICA

CITIES OF THE
MEDITERRANEAN
IN THE CENTURIES
AFTER JESUS

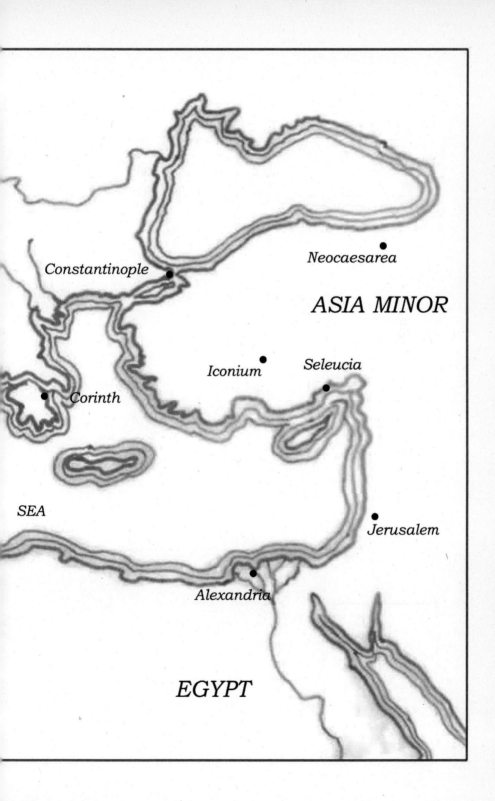

BAND OF ANGELS

1

LOOKING FOR CHLOE

Our evidence for early Christian women begins with a missing person. We know almost nothing about her, only her name – Chloe – and the fact that she had a house, probably in the Greek city of Corinth, in the first century. But her absence is significant, because she seems to have been involved, somehow, in the dispute that gave rise to Christianity as a world religion.

Of course, the familiar story of Christianity begins with another woman, the Virgin Mary, and the visit by an Angel who announced that her child would be the Son of God. But none of the sources that have come down to us were written in Mary's own day. It was only years later, when the people who had known her son had begun to grow old and die that the stories of those early days began to be collected and put into writing in the Gospels, the early collections of the stories and sayings of Jesus.

The first surviving Christian texts were written in the fifties of the first century, after the death of Jesus in the thirties but well before the writing of the first Gospels in the seventies. They are not histories; rather, they are the working correspondence of Paul of Tarsus, a Jewish tent-maker who was travelling in Greece and Asia Minor – modern Turkey. Paul's letters, which survive in the New Testament, are a testament to his relationships with women and men in the cloth trade in the early Christian missionary movement. Frequently, he speaks warmly of women who helped him and even paid his way.

The most emotionally intense of Paul's letters is known to posterity as the First Letter of Paul the Apostle to the Corinthians. Written to his followers in the port city of Corinth, it seems to be the product of a crisis in the Corinthian community which forced him to think searchingly about what was really important. It is a manifesto for a new way of thinking about human relationships.

The trigger for Paul's distress seems to have had something to do with how women in the community were behaving, and this means that the search for Chloe may hold the key to a deeper understanding of Paul's conflict with the Corinthian Christians. Certainly, trying to see her more clearly can help us to perceive the roles and possibilities that were open to women in the early Christian communities. The elusive Chloe offers a starting-point for the thought-experiment of trying to see the world through early Christian women's eyes.

Paul mentions at the beginning of his letter that people from Chloe's household have complained to him: this is his reason for writing. As the founder of the infant Christian community at Corinth, he is clearly disturbed by the report that things there are not as they should be. What is less clear is what role Chloe is playing in the situation. Here is the single mention of Chloe in Paul's letters:

> I appeal to you, brothers and sisters, in the name of our Lord Jesus Christ . . . that there be no divisions among you, but that you be perfectly united in mind and thought. My brothers and sisters, some from Chloe's household have informed me that there are quarrels among you. (1 Corinthians 1: 10–11)

In the end, the rumours from Chloe's house will spur Paul to do some of his deepest thinking. In First Corinthians, he puts forward a new vision of the Christian community as the Body of Christ, a single emotional organism made up of individuals who undertake to trust one another completely. His agitation about the trouble in Corinth turns out to have far-reaching consequences, because the future of Christianity will be shaped by this vision of the community as one body with many members, all equal even if each plays a different role.

But who was Chloe? He tells us very little about her. Of course, the people to whom he is writing already know who she is. But Paul's silence also implies, quite firmly, that he does not have anything good to say about her. In general, when Paul mentions people in his letters he does so with a greeting, or a brief word of praise for what they have done for the community. With Chloe, he gives us only her name. An educated guess at Chloe's identity turns up two possibilities.

The first is that she is a prosperous pagan householder, not herself a member of the Christian community but a figure of respect – or fear – in the lives of the Corinthian faithful. On this reading, the complainers in Chloe's household are her slaves or servants, and there is no particular criticism of her implied in the fact that Paul doesn't greet her. She is simply not part of the Christian circle, and not a party to the dispute among the Corinthian Christians.

But there is a darker alternative. Many historians have taken the view that Chloe is the leader of a Christian community in Corinth. If this is the case, the people whom Paul identifies as coming from her household are members of a house-church which meets in her home. Of course, it is possible that Chloe and Paul are allies: many scholars believe that it was Chloe herself who sent messengers to Paul to alert him of the trouble in Corinth. But it is equally possible that Chloe is one of Paul's rivals. Perhaps some of her followers have gone behind her back to Paul, the absent founder of the community, with complaints about what is happening in her house.

If Chloe was a Christian in a position of responsibility, the host of a house-church or a missionary colleague, the fact that Paul mentions her without sending greetings or adding a word of praise constitutes quite a noticeable slight, whether they had fallen out or not. Did they know one another well? Was she the leader of a faction which had begun to move in a direction Paul did not like? It may be wrong to accuse Chloe of stirring up trouble among the Corinthians, but it is clear that someone did, and it is also obvious that one or more women were involved.

To judge from Paul's letter, many of the complaints coming from Chloe's household are about the behaviour of women in the group. Other points of dispute concern domestic questions and romantic relationships. Finally, there are painful rivalries about leadership. Whom should others listen to? Who is in charge? If a woman is in charge, questions of this kind can become especially pointed.

Even if it is impossible to give a firm answer to the question of Chloe's identity, the 'Chloe question' is a problem to conjure with, a capsule version of the wider problem historians face in tracing early Christian women. Often, the evidence tells us just enough to know that women were present, but not quite enough to see where they fit in. This is partly because ancient writers were worried about women's modesty. In ancient Mediterranean society, even mentioning a woman's name could sometimes be taken as an insult, since quiet dignity and self-effacement were highly prized virtues for women. But there is also reason to think that women began to disappear from early Christian history as it began to be written.

In the earliest churches women played a central and visible role, but things changed over time. The movement grew, and the first tendrils of an enduring institution began to emerge. By the fifth century the Church would develop into an institution durable enough to outlast the Roman Empire, although in the first century all this was far in the future.

As the men began to establish institutional roles, in the second and third centuries, the women continued for the most part to put their time and energy into ongoing efforts of caring and community-building. Even if their contribution was recognized as essential, to the eyes of later historians it seemed unchanging and unremarkable, and it often went unmentioned. Until very recently, historians saw it as their task to trace the organizational roots of institutions rather than the daily lives of ordinary people.

The things that knit a community together are often ephemeral: shared meals and festivals, family gatherings, weddings and funerals. Staging the happenings that make a community feel like a community takes work, but when done well, the work is largely invisible. It might be on the small scale of offering refreshment to a neighbour, or the larger scale of feeding a village. In either case, it is an effort

focused on the here-and-now. Leaving monuments for ʲ
not usually on the agenda when one is cooking for comp

There is an irony here. Self-effacing acts of community
are exactly what Paul of Tarsus asked not only womer   ....
Christians to do. He was not at all interested in future historians.
To the contrary, he believed that Jesus of Nazareth had been the
long-awaited Messiah of Israel, and that his coming was a sign that
the end of the world was near. Paul wanted his followers to reorganize their lives around a new ideal of love and spiritual unity,
so that they would be at peace with themselves and one another
when the end came. Essentially, he was asking the men in his
community to be more like the women – or, at least, more like an
ideal of self-forgetful feminine virtue.

But the end never came. Instead, Paul's letters became the foundation for a 2,000-year institution, one which would make an incalculable
difference to history. The letters have been read and reread over the
centuries by successive generations, each scholar searching with new
eyes for advice on how to build a Christian community.

Chloe's Sisters: Prisca, Phoebe, and Junia

It was around the year 55 that Paul addressed his first letter to
Corinth. We know that there was a crisis: Paul's informants from
Chloe's household had let it be known that the community there
was beginning to unravel. They themselves were trying to remain
loyal to what Paul had taught them during his stay, but they were
troubled by the choices that others had begun to make.

Biblical scholars tend to think of the Apostle Paul as a man's
man, and it is true that he refers to men frequently in his letters.
But he forged close working relationships with women as well, some
of them during his time in Corinth. In fact, it was there that he
established many of his most valued relationships.

5

Prisca was perhaps the closest to Paul, but we know very little about her. When Paul arrived in Corinth, he sought a household of like-minded individuals in the textile trade with whom he could live and work. By a stroke of good fortune, he joined the household of Prisca and Aquila. The Book of Acts, written around the end of the first century by one of Paul's followers, makes it clear that his hosts in Corinth had a nomadic lifestyle similar to his own.

> There he met a Jew named Aquila, a native of Pontus, who had recently come from Italy with his wife Priscilla, because Claudius had ordered all the Jews to leave Rome. Paul went to see them, and because he was a tentmaker as they were, he stayed and worked with them. (Acts 18: 2)

Prisca and Aquila quickly became indispensable supporters. For a while, the three travelled together – it was in their company that, some months afterwards, Paul left Corinth for Ephesus, where he would write his First Letter to the Corinthians.

Later, he would return to Corinth alone, and Prisca and Aquila returned to Rome. Tradition records that Paul eventually followed them there. During his last stay in Corinth he sent a letter to the Roman community which called attention to what Prisca and Aquila had done for him: 'Greet Prisca and Aquila, my fellow workers in Christ Jesus. They risked their lives for me. Not only I but all the churches of the Gentiles are grateful to them.' (Romans 16: 3–4)

The very fact that Prisca is mentioned first in Paul's greeting to the couple means she was important to Paul in her own right. Ancient writers often referred to a married couple by the man's name only, so the choice to name Prisca, and to put her name first, is significant.

Prisca was by no means the only woman Paul worked with. In fact, he seems to have benefited from a network of female supporters who were unusually independent by comparison to many of their contemporaries. The key to these women's independ-ence has to do with both wealth and legal status: they seem to have been citizens of cities that granted unusually generous property rights to women.

In the ancient Mediterranean, most cities had their own laws, so the rights of citizens would vary from city to city. But citizenship was often complicated by the patchwork history of how the different cities had been conquered by Rome.

In Paul's day, the Greek-speaking city of Corinth was a Roman administrative centre, governing Achaea, the southern part of Greece. It was a city with a turbulent history. Two centuries earlier, in 146 BC, the Romans had captured two of their most threatening rival cities, Corinth and Carthage. Both were strategically located seaports: Carthage just across from Sicily in what is now Northern Tunisia, at the bottleneck between the Eastern and Western Mediterranean, and Corinth on the isthmus linking the Adriatic and the Aegean, controlling sea trade between Asia and Europe.

The Roman conquerors had treated both Carthage and Corinth harshly. Normal Roman policy on annexing a territory was to leave as much as possible undisturbed, but these cities were too important. So the Romans destroyed both of them completely, only re-founding them a century later as Roman colonies when Julius Caesar was establishing new centres to administer what was now a Mediterranean-wide Roman Empire. By the time Paul arrived in Corinth, in the early fifties, this crisis was long past, and Corinth's status as a Roman colony had become an advantage. Normally, the citizens of each city conquered by the Romans were allowed to follow their own laws and traditions. The citizens of Rome enjoyed additional rights under Roman law, because theirs was the conqueror's city, and Roman law was the conqueror's law. In the provincial cities, a fortunate few were granted Roman citizenship in addition to that of their native city. Paul himself was one of these: a Greek-speaking Jew from Tarsus, but nonetheless a citizen of Rome, a city he had never seen. In the provinces, Roman citizens were an elite with respect to the law – even if, like Paul, they were not particularly rich.

Where women were concerned, the citizenship question was

especially important. The status and independence of women under the different legal systems varied greatly, and Roman women enjoyed unparalleled legal independence. Colonies such as Corinth and Philippi modelled their citizen rights on those of Rome, and this helps to explain why the women of Corinth were comparatively independent, and thus in a position to adopt new habits and ideas. Their citizen status allowed them to own property and businesses in their own right, and they were used to juggling the sometimes diverging demands of a complex identity.

The closing chapter of Paul's letter to the Romans, written during his last stay in Corinth, mentions a number of female leaders as co-workers in their own right, rather than alongside their husbands. Phoebe, from Cenchreae, the harbour belonging to Corinth, must have been an independent woman of means, for Paul calls her his patron. It was Phoebe who carried the letter to Rome. Paul adds, in the closing passage of the letter, a request to the Roman community to offer her any help she may need.

> I commend to you our sister Phoebe, a supporter (*diakonon*) of the church in Cenchreae. I ask you to receive her in the Lord in a way worthy of his people and to give her any help she may need from you, for she has been a patron (*prostatēs*) of many people, including me. (Romans 16: 1–2)

What did it mean for a woman to be a *prostatēs*? A cluster of first-century inscriptions discovered by a French archaeological team in Corinth in 1954 offers an answer. In these inscriptions, Junia Theodora, a propertied Roman citizen who had come across the Aegean to Corinth from Lycia in Asia Minor, is hailed as a *prostatissa* by the citizens of the Lycian League, an organization to promote the interests of the cities of Lycia. The Lycians thank Junia for opening her house to them as guests when their affairs brought them to Corinth, the gateway for ships sailing west to Rome from the Eastern Mediterranean. They commend her for acting on behalf of the Lycian cities in numerous matters. This might have been negotiating trade access for the Lycian ships in the important port of Corinth, or cultivating political patronage on behalf of the federation with contacts in Rome. Each of the five city councils passed a motion to commend Junia in gratitude for her benefactions.[1]

There is no way of discovering whether Phoebe was as powerful as Junia Theodora, but it is not impossible, since we know that she herself travelled to Rome. Many versions of the English Bible translate the term *diakonon* as 'deacon', while others translate it as 'servant'. In the first-century context, the term is often used to speak of individuals who organize practicalities and provide resources, often out of their own means. In the later centuries, it would evolve into an ordained role for both men and women.[2]

In addition to Phoebe, Paul mentions a certain Mary – 'Mary, who worked very hard for you' – and sends greetings to a cluster of women whom he seems to have known as a team. 'Greet Tryphaena and Tryphosa, those women who work hard in the Lord. Greet my dear friend Persis, another woman who has worked very hard in the Lord.' Still others are known to Paul through family groupings: 'Greet Rufus, chosen in the Lord, and his mother, who has been a mother to me, too', and again, 'Greet Philologus, Julia, Nereus and his sister, and Olympas, and all the Lord's people who are with them.'

A curious second-century source known as the *Acts of Paul and Thecla* remembers one of these women, Tryphaena, and supplies a vivid back-story for her. She is quite an exotic character, a cousin of the Roman emperor and queen of a minor Eastern kingdom, who comes to the aid of one of Paul's companions while he and his followers are in south-western Asia Minor. But there is no way of knowing whether the tale preserves a sliver of memory about one of the richer women of the Roman community or whether it is a pure invention.

Paul clearly found a special affinity with the women of the trading communities of the Aegean. The women were diverse and played different roles according to their circumstances. On the one hand, there were the independent business women like Phoebe, who were in a position to act as patronesses for the new community: making resources available, mobilizing business contacts to offer support, and strengthening networks when they travelled. On the other hand, there were women like the mother of Rufus, whose position in family groupings meant that they could be invaluable in community-building and networking for the faith.

And there is one more important woman – Junia – in Paul's letter to the Romans. There is no real reason to think she is the same Junia who was praised by the Lycians, although it is not impossible. Paul's Junia has been subject of debate for a different reason. Towards the end of his letter, Paul refers to her as an apostle: 'Greet Andronicus and Junia, my relatives (*suggeneis*) who have been in prison with me. They are outstanding among the apostles, and they were in Christ before I was.' This passage has shocked some historians. They imagine the earliest churches anachronistically, as established institutions, with apostles as institutional officers, and they find it hard to imagine that a woman would have played such a role. But such formal arrangements were a long way in the future, and Christian leadership was far more flexible in these early communities than it would become in later centuries.[3] Ancient readers had no trouble accepting that Paul would describe a woman as 'outstanding among the apostles'. In a sermon on Paul's letters, for example, the fourth-century bishop John Chrysostom imagined Junia and Andronicus as a married couple like Prisca and Aquila. To Chrysostom, missionary work was a fitting ministry for couples. He also saw it as perfectly natural that Paul should honour the contributions made by both men and women, rather than hiding the women behind the men.

A Network of Friends and Family

Paul's greeting to Junia and Andronicus holds another important and largely neglected clue to how women contributed to the early

Christian movement. Paul mentions that they were members of his own family – and in doing so he makes it clear that other members of his own family were already members of the Jesus movement at the time he converted – 'they were in Christ before I was'. It seems surprising to imagine that the most influential of the early Christian missionaries had joined the new faith in the context of a family gathering, but it makes perfect sense. Was Paul a younger relative, who grew up on the fringes of the movement but did not join until adulthood? Or was he perhaps a sceptic, who had waited to join the movement until he was convinced?

The Book of Acts tends to support the latter view, even though its story of Paul's conversion passes over the family connection altogether. In Acts, Paul begins as an enemy of the Christians, but as he travels along the road to Damascus he is struck by a vision from heaven. The writer of Acts is looking back with hindsight, remembering a revered teacher. He may not have remembered the family connection which Paul himself mentions, or he may have wanted to downplay anything that might make Paul look like a follower rather than a leader.

Modern sociologists faced with a religious movement that is spreading quickly would expect to find just this kind of spontaneous spread through friendship and family networks. Fieldwork-based study of modern groups shows that the most effective way to circulate ideas and suggestions is through families and informal social networks – this is the pattern behind 'viral' marketing. The importance of networks is especially well documented for religious ideas.

In the 1980s, a series of influential studies began to 'track' the missionary leaders of the new religious movements that were achieving explosive growth in the United States. They found that the most successful groups used social networks, rather than one-off events such as preaching to crowds, as the central strategy for attracting new members. Though unspectacular and informal, the quiet chat among friends is a far more effective vehicle for spreading ideas than a splashy public event. In fact, studies have demonstrated that the 'success rate' of missionary encounters that take place in the home of a friend or family member is five hundred times higher than encounters in an institutional setting or a public place. This makes sense: people are more likely to be influenced by trusted friends than by strangers about whom they know nothing.

Word-of-mouth networks are outstandingly effective for another reason as well. In a social network, each new convert has the opportunity to multiply the network's reach by sharing the message with others who may pass it on yet again. A successfully networked idea will tend to pick up speed as it travels, because if each person passes it on to two or three others, its reach will expand exponentially. Thus a network of family and friends can achieve a kind of growth that is almost impossible by other means. If each member of a movement attracts a total of two or three new members across a lifetime, a mechanism similar to compounding interest will take effect. The sociologist Rodney Stark has argued that if the early Christians were able consistently to sustain a growth rate of 40 per cent per decade, with each member of the movement attracting roughly one new member every twenty years, the membership could have grown from dozens after the death of Jesus to reach the thousands in the second century, before tipping dramatically into the millions by the third.[4]

The ancient evidence tends to fit well with this network-based model of conversion. The Christian communities of the first centuries have long been referred to as 'house churches' because during the early centuries when their group had no legal status and could not own institutional property Christians met in one another's homes. The importance of women in the early missions seems to have grown quite naturally out of their central position in households and families. Christian ideas were a natural fit for a relationship-based growth strategy, since they were so often aimed at making relationships stronger, and this in turn must have strengthened the relationship networks that carried them. It is a variant of the principle that bedtime stories often involve characters who grow drowsy: ideas about how friends and family can get along better are a natural topic for conversations among friends and families.

There is another surprising fit between network theory and what we know about Christianity's dramatic growth, and this is Paul's position in a network of travelling traders and craftsmen. It is no accident that the most influential of the early missionaries was a tent-maker. Paul's travels around the Mediterranean were funded – and perhaps partly motivated – by his work in the linen trade. As he circulated around the network of Jewish and other like-minded linen merchants in the Eastern Mediterranean, he was able both to benefit from and to strengthen whatever relationships already existed between individuals and families in the different cities.

As it happens, even what *kind* of tents Paul made probably helped his work as a missionary. Scholars have debated whether Paul made the large leather tents used for travel – especially by the military – or lighter tents in linen. Linen tents and awnings were everywhere in the ancient world, used by everyone from peddlers to Roman emperors to give shade to anything from market-stalls to the upper seating tiers of amphitheatres. (Pliny tells us, for example, that Julius Caesar paid for linen awnings to provide shade for the entire Roman Forum.[5])

Recently, historical opinion has swung in favour of the linen, and this fits with what we know about his work as a missionary. The linen trade was built around just the kind of people who seem to have made up the communities where Paul settled: independent craftsmen, traders and small-business owners. Indeed, Paul's first contacts in the cities he travelled to were traders in the textile industry. Working closely with cloth merchants put him in daily contact with women and men whose livelihood depended on their ability to build up networks of trust, in order to support both small and large family businesses.

The leather tents, by contrast, were produced by large firms employing dependent factory workers, often under contract to the military. It seems fairly clear that a restless and independent-minded travelling preacher would not have been a particular asset to this kind of enterprise. But the cloth trade was just the place for an independent artisan who was willing to travel. He could make himself indispensable to small family businesses by helping them to build up relationships with traders in other cities, expanding their network of suppliers and opening up new markets for their products.

Each trading family had contacts in other cities around the Mediterranean. In Corinth, Paul met Prisca and Aquila, tent-makers from Rome, while in Philippi he met Lydia, a purple-seller from Thyatira, an important centre for weaving and dyeing on Asia Minor's west coast. Paul himself was from Tarsus of Cilicia, a port on the south coast of Asia Minor known for its importance in the linen trade as well as the fame of its rhetorical schools. (In fact, Paul seems to have had a hand in both of his city's most famous pursuits. His spellbinding qualities as a speaker are legendary, so it would not be surprising if he had spent his childhood listening to the city's famous orators.)

Long after Paul's death, Luke the Evangelist remembered Paul's first meeting with Lydia, the purple-seller. As Luke tells the story in his Book of Acts, when Paul reached Philippi she was the first of the local business-owners to adopt him as a protégé.

> On the Sabbath we went outside the city gate to the river, where we expected to find a place of prayer. We sat down and began to speak to the women who had gathered there. One of those listening was a woman from the city of Thyatira named Lydia, a dealer in purple cloth. She was a worshipper of God (*sebomen ton theon*). The Lord opened her heart to respond to Paul's message. When she and the members of her household were baptized, she invited us to her home. 'If you consider me a believer in the Lord,' she said, 'come and stay at my house.' And she persuaded us. (Acts 16: 13–15)

Even Acts, whose account of Paul's missions tended to focus on the men, remembers Paul's encounter with Lydia as a turning-point. It was with a woman of means who owned a trading house in the port, and a group of women gathered for prayer on a riverbank, that

Paul's mission to Greece – and thus the history of Christianity in Europe – found its first footing.

Lydia, the Purple-Seller: An Independent Woman

Independent women of property played an important role in supporting Paul's communities, and the cosmopolitan port cities of Philippi and Corinth were a natural place to find them. Luke's story of Lydia, the purple-seller, tells us three very important things about how Paul's relationships with women of this kind were remembered.

First, that Paul the Apostle was a man who sought out women, and who knew how to accept their help. Second, that Lydia, like Paul, was in the cloth trade; as a purple-seller she was far more prosperous than a humble tent-maker, so in acquiring her patronage he acquired an invaluable ally. The third is equally important in a different way: Lydia was remembered as a *theosebēs*, a 'worshipper of God' or 'God-fearer'. This was the name first-century Jewish writers used for a Gentile who was interested in Judaism. It is one of many cases in the New Testament where a phrase that sounds vague to a modern ear actually means something quite specific. The God-fearers were important for Paul, because they had connections in both the Jewish community that he had come from, and in the Gentile community that he was trying to reach. They were a group who would prove invaluable in helping to carry Paul's message out into the wider world.

Paul's decision to carry the Gospel beyond the Jewish community, to the Gentiles, would secure its future. At the death of Jesus his followers were a fringe group within Judaism; under Paul's leadership they rapidly became a multicultural movement which could speak to history in its own right. Paul did not know it at the time, but in his travels he was establishing what would become one of the great world religions. It is a paradox that this man, who would change history, believed that history was about to end.

By the time he wrote to the Corinthians, Paul was a hardened traveller. Over a decade earlier, he had left Jerusalem, where he had made a career as an expert in Jewish law. Since then he had circulated among the cities of Greece and Asia Minor, practising his trade and preaching to both Jews and Gentiles, to warn them that the end of the world was coming. He was certain that this was good news, for there had been a sign from heaven: a miracle-worker from Galilee had been resurrected from the dead. Jesus of Nazareth was the long-awaited Anointed One, known in Greek as the *Christos*, the Christ, in Hebrew as the *masiah*, the Messiah – both words simply mean 'anointed'. The death and resurrection of Jesus were a radiant sign to humanity, an invitation to live a life transformed by God's love.

As a Pharisee, Paul knew that the foundation of the life of Jews in Israel – now a cluster of Roman provinces including Judaea and Galilee – had always been the covenant or sacred pact between God and Abraham. The story of the covenant was an ancient tradition about the intensity of love, how the love within human families both strengthened and competed with the love between humanity and God. It was recorded in the Book of Genesis that Abraham had been willing to sacrifice his most precious human relationship, with his long-awaited son Isaac, to show that he would give up everything for God. But God had spared him the sacrifice.

In the mid first century, when Paul was writing, the Jewish faith had three key components. First, there was the Great Temple in Jerusalem. Up to the year 70, blood sacrifice of animals was conducted in the Temple to atone for the sins of Israel, though the Temple would be destroyed by the Roman army at the end of the Jewish Wars of 66–70. Second, there were the synagogues. 'Jew' or 'Judaean' – *iudaios* – is the Greek name for the inhabitants of Judaea, the region around Jerusalem, but in the first century, most 'Judaeans' lived elsewhere. Many lived in the Diaspora, the network of ex-patriate communities scattered around the Mediterranean. The *synagogai* or synagogues – literally 'gathering-places' – provided a focus for the Diaspora communities. Women presided over the third key centre of Jewish practice, which was the household.

Ancient Judaism was based on a family partnership. Many of the commands of Jewish teaching – like keeping the Sabbath – applied to both men and women. But for others, there was a division of labour between the sexes. Studying the Torah as it was recorded in the Scriptures was largely restricted to men, while mothers instructed their daughters in the routines of domestic Torah observance. Kosher cleaning and cooking involved rules and traditions that were handed down like the jewellery belonging to a beloved grandmother, a treasured possession to be cherished within a family along with a heritage of stories, ideas, and values.[6]

So a female God-fearer like Lydia was in a delicate position as she made the acquaintance of the ancient Jewish traditions. She would need a female sponsor if she meant to make any real progress with understanding what the God of Israel meant to women. In all likelihood, she had friends and acquaintances in Philippi's Jewish community through her work in the cloth trade. We have already seen that in an era where there was no strict division between households and workplaces, the relationships of trust that developed between long-standing trading partners were often reinforced by shared religious convictions. The converse is also true. In cosmopolitan Philippi, if Lydia became interested in Jewish ideas, it is probably because she had had friends in the lively community of Jewish women there who spun, wove, and sold cloth.

Lydia's own business traded the rare purple dye that had coloured the robes of kings and emperors since the time of the Phoenicians. Purple was extremely expensive, and traders in purple were prosperous. They were people of importance not only for this reason, but also because to be successful they had to have built strong relationships in the shipping industry so that their wares could move safely and swiftly around the Mediterranean. When Lydia converted 'with all her household' to the new movement, she brought substantial resources – and probably numbers – to the cause.[7]

Modern readers may be surprised to find a woman in charge of such an enterprise 2,000 years ago, but an ancient reader would not have been. Like Corinth, Philippi was a Roman colony, so it was not unusual to find independent citizen women there. Lydia was from Thyatira rather than Philippi, but she is likely to have been a citizen of Rome or one of Rome's colonies, since she was conducting business in her own name. She may have been a widow or an unmarried heiress heading a household of her own.

It is not impossible that she was married: under Roman law, her husband would have no legal control over her property. In a citizen household, the husband and wife belonged to two legally distinct families – in many ways, it was as if they were living parallel lives under the same roof. The Roman principle was that a father had undisputed authority over his children by marriage, and this limited the rights that other people could exercise over them. A mother, for example, had limited rights – the father would have undisputed custody of any children born in wedlock if the marriage were to end. The wife, meanwhile, remained part of her father's family rather than joining her husband's, so her position was as a kind of hinge between the two families.[8]

If a wife had substantial property or business interests, she was required by law to hold them independently of her husband in order to protect the interests of her own family. These might include farms, factories, trading concerns, or urban apartment blocks. A less wealthy wife might run her own tavern or her own bakery out of premises that she owned or rented independently of her husband. The financial independence of propertied women meant that a woman who chose to support a cause could do so from her own resources whether or not she had a husband, and – if she did – whether or not the husband agreed with her.

Of course, it was to a wife's advantage to cultivate a successful partnership with her husband. A married woman who wished to defy her husband could only do so if her relatives and business associates offered solid support, and it was never a pretty business. Essentially, it was not in her interest to challenge his position unless she was clearly on the side of right. Moral authority and the ability to cultivate networks of support were indispensable. In principle, a married woman could draw on the help of her husband's family and of her own relatives, as well as of her husband himself. Men had far greater access to public office and politics, and as a result most women had the habit of channelling things through their husbands, male relatives, or other male allies. We often hear in early Christian sources of husbands and wives working together on behalf of the church, and when one hears of a married couple at work, it is often worth asking whether the husband was acting as a 'cover' for an energetic wife.

In trading families women were often at the centre of things, and this is what allowed them to play such an important role in the early Christian movement. Yet in order to understand the significance of women's contribution, it is necessary to understand that there was no Church in antiquity, in the institutional sense. The movement was a patchwork of independent communities, and in the early years, the communication networks and leadership patterns were characterized by improvisation. When a person converted, he or she would have to find a new place in a changing social constellation of viewpoints and loyalties.

For the most part, the existing relationships in communities became the basis for what happened when Christian ideas were introduced. Mediterranean society was based on village and family groupings, and what allowed both women and men to acquire authority in these groups was the simple fact that other people were willing to listen to them.

During the long centuries when the churches had no legal status, property-owners and travelling teachers were each central to the survival of the movement. The ordained offices of bishop, presbyter, and deacon did not begin to develop into recognizable roles until the late first century, and it was centuries before they took the form in which we know them in the modern world. (The term 'presbyter', for example, simply means 'elder'.) In the early years, relatively prosperous householders who could offer meeting spaces and other resources from their own private means were among the most important of the 'elders' because of the assistance they could give to the group and to its individual members. If they did so with humility and good grace, this would be viewed as the result of generosity rather than self-importance, and the fact that they were rich would not be held against them.

So a business-owner like Lydia could expect to play an important role in the new movement. A prosperous trader who takes a travelling preacher as a protégé is not likely to do so without becoming involved in the cause. If she helped with shelter and financial support, she was probably involved in other ways. The same is true, in turn, of the mysterious Chloe, whose household was the source of the rumours Paul heard from Corinth. If Chloe's household joined Paul's group at the request of their mistress – in the same way that those from Lydia's household did – then she was a person of standing among the faithful in Corinth.

We still do not know where Chloe stood with respect to the Corinthian Christians. If she was simply the mistress of a household in which a few servants had joined the new movement, she may not even have been aware of the movement's existence. On the other hand, if she was the host of a Christian community meeting in her house, she was a respected member of the community, and even a leader.

So the question to consider, as we turn to Paul's First Letter to the Corinthians, is whether his sometimes acerbic comments about women in the congregation reflect an attempt to help a female colleague who has lost control, a covert irritation at a female rival – or whether the powerful woman in the background is simply a woman in whose house some of his followers are living or working. It is probably an unanswerable question, but sometimes an unanswerable question can be a useful tool.

2

THE GOSPEL OF LOVE

For Paul, Corinth was a place of great importance, where he had met friends with whom he would share his work for the rest of his life. But the group he had lived with at Corinth was a transient community. As he wrote his First Letter to the Corinthians from Ephesus, across the Aegean on the western coast of Asia Minor, many of those he had known in Corinth were now elsewhere, whether because of business commitments or to carry the word about Christ and the coming end of the world.

Paul's friends Prisca and Aquila, who had been his hosts in Corinth, were with him in Ephesus. His closing words in the letter include a greeting from both of them, but this companionship was only temporary. They would return to Rome and he would resume his travels, stopping in each city long enough to create a community, and then moving on. When things began to seem too comfortable, it was be a sign that he was no longer needed. The periods of living and working with close friends were a source of warmth in a way of life that must often have seemed bleak.

By the time Paul wrote the First Letter to the Corinthians, there was bickering in the Corinthian community over who was in charge. Chloe's people complained that something had gone wrong: the trouble may have had its origins in events that took place while he was still there, or in growing pains at the time of his departure. Or perhaps the leaders who tried to carry his work forward were not up to the task. One can feel Paul's disappointment in the letter. He seems to think that someone has twisted the message of his preaching, though it is also possible that his own thoughts are changing too quickly for his friends to keep up. In the letter, he makes a bold emotional play: it is crushing to learn that the Corinthians have not engaged deeply enough with his ideas to be able to live by them while he is away.

The crux of the Corinthian conflict, as Paul sees it, is a question of accountability. Some members of the group are behaving strangely, but more worryingly they are arguing that their superior grasp of religious truth gives them authority to despise convention. Other members of the community are understandably agitated, as much by the self-importance as by the eccentric behaviour. Paul seems less worried about the actual behaviour than about the lack of concern for the feelings of others that it reveals. Paul's view is that individuals cannot flourish if they try to do so at the expense of the greater good. For example, the idea that some people think of them-selves as more enlightened yet see this as licence to behave in a way that is making other people anxious. Paul warns that a spiritual revelation has no value if it does not lead to greater compassion. The 'enlightened' ones have missed the point.

Modern scholars have spilt a great deal of ink in trying to under-stand what motivated the troublemakers in Corinth. Some members of the community were eager to attain spiritual enlightenment or *gnosis*, the Greek word for 'knowledge'. Among the 'gnostics', some argued that those who had reached the state of enlightenment should no longer be bound by the traditional rules of society. This may have been an honest attempt to push ahead with Paul's own idea of a new life in Christ. Members of the community were relying on word of mouth for their information about Paul's teaching after he left, so it would be quite natural if there were debate over what he had actually taught, or about how he would react to new ideas.

Many of the people he felt betrayed by were women, and it is to them that some of his most anguished comments were aimed. Readers often miss the fact that Paul's First Letter to the Corinthians, with its passionate arguments about the nature of human love, was a volley in an ongoing relationship drama between a male leader and a group of deputies that included a number of spirited women. In all likelihood, Paul was somewhat taken aback that the bond he had developed with the women of the group had not been strong enough to keep them from experimenting in ways that disturbed him once he had left.

The most successful missionaries are people who can understand the concerns of a wide variety of people in the communities they visit, and Paul seems to have had this quality. As a missionary, he constantly found himself as a guest in the houses of people he barely knew, usually traders or comparatively prosperous villagers who had a bed to spare, and could afford to offer a meal to a guest. He was frequently dependent on the kindness of strangers, and thrust, as a result, into the domestic and business intimacies of his hosts.

This position as an outsider in successive households allowed Paul to notice things other men did not. In every household there was a constant stream of activity centred on care-giving and hospitality, which the men mostly turned a blind eye to as 'women's work'. Among these tasks were those of caring for weaker family members and reminding the stronger to remember the needs of the weak. As the ones entrusted with this work, the women may have been sensitive to the challenges Paul faced as a missionary. At the same time, their position in a man's world involved a difficult balancing act. The challenges they faced gave them both the motive and the skill to collaborate productively with a sympathetic visitor. One can see in the letter what it was about Paul that made so many people love him. Here was a man who was not afraid of emotional honesty.

Paul had brought a gospel, an *evangelion* (the word literally means 'good news', though the force of the Greek is captured better by 'message from heaven'). Both women and men were now invited to live *en Christō* – 'in Christ' – and to understand themselves in a new way, as part of the 'body of Christ'. They should give little thought to what separated them; rather, they should train their hearts on what they had in common. The life of the spirit would allow them to reach beyond the roles and social identities they had inherited.

It was an invitation to live each day as if it were the last. Paul did not want his friends to worry too much about negotiating arrangements in the community, or even in their own families. The whole basis of reality was changing, and this meant that plans for the long term were misguided: 'Because of the present crisis, I think that it is good for a person (*anthrōpoi*) to remain as he is. Are you pledged to a woman? Do not seek to be released. Are you free from such a commitment? Do not look for a wife.' (1 Cor. 7: 26–27)

These prescriptions about marriage and family life have often been read as if Paul intended to found a new value system based on ambivalence towards love and sex, but nothing could be further from the truth. What he means here is that plans for the future are irrelevant, because the end of time is at hand. 'But if you do marry, you have not sinned; and if a virgin marries, she has not sinned. But those who marry will face many troubles in this life, and I want to spare you this. What I mean, brothers and sisters, is that the time is short.' (7: 28–29) The Corinthians must prepare to lose the things they love. But they should not grieve: attachments here on earth are only a dim reflection of a love that is deeper and more permanent.

This was a profound statement but it reflected a harsh practical reality. Ancient families living centuries before the invention of antibiotics faced a daunting mortality rate. A sudden fever could carry off any member of a household within hours. This was all the more true in a harbour city like Corinth, where each new boat brought pathogens against which the local population had yet to build up resistance. This meant that human bonds were even more fragile than they are for modern people. The bonds of love and family carried with them the constant threat of loss. Paul's idea that each human relationship reflected a more permanent bond with God would capture the imagination of later generations of Christians. It must have been electrifying to the inhabitants of a first-century seaport.

The problem to which the Apostle turns next is one of special interest to the women. It concerns the domestic Torah, the eating habits of the community's families. Some members of the community – probably those who grew up as pagans – argue that the new community should not require its members to follow Jewish food laws. In the first century, these laws were a 'hot' issue in Jewish communities. The group of rabbis known as Pharisees in Paul's day advocated a stringent interpretation of the food prohibitions recorded in the Hebrew Bible. Practices like maintaining a strict division between meat and milk would become the basis for the laws of *kashrut* or kosher observance as it is still practised today in Orthodox Judaism. But at the time, they were novel and controversial.

From Paul's perspective, the important point is that more funda-mental traditions of the Jewish community were being challenged. Some members claim that they do not need to respect the ancient prohibition against eating meat that has been sacrificed to idols, that is, to the gods of another faith. In all likelihood, the meat-eaters are defending an ancient habit of pagan families, who would supple-ment their largely vegetarian diets by attending the great outdoor feasts that followed an animal sacrifice. The richer priestly families would sponsor communal barbecues at which the sacrificed animals would be roasted and served to the crowd, an opportunity for the poor to fill their bellies and for both rich and poor to celebrate the collective life of the community.[1]

For Paul, the problem was not so much that the meat had been sacrificed as that a certain group's insistence on eating it was causing distress. People who were trying to observe the Jewish custom found it disturbing to be told that the custom was only for fools.

Women must have been involved in this dispute, since Jewish tradition placed strong emphasis on a woman's role in staging the domestic rituals around food. Another conflict concerns the women more directly. Paul writes that he has heard that some women, when speaking in the spirit during sessions of collective prayer, are refusing to wear headscarves. Again, others have been gossiping about it, and it is their disquiet that Paul really cares about. In order to shame the offenders, Paul offers a somewhat irritable theological justification for the traditional custom of head-covering for women.

> [T]he head of every man is Christ, and the head of the woman
> is man, and the head of Christ is God. Every man who prays or
> prophesies with his head covered dishonours his head. But every
> woman who prays or prophesies with her head uncovered dishon-
> ours her head. (1 Cor. 11: 3–5)

Here, he is going out of his way to make the women who have
refused to cover their hair feel uncomfortable. But he is not particularly interested in their hair. Rather, he is furious that certain
members of the community are causing unnecessary friction by
acting in a way that he thinks is pointless and self-important.

Yet Paul's irritable tone here should not mislead us into thinking
that he is against women prophesying or holding spiritual authority.
He has already made it clear that he expects the end of the world
within his lifetime, and he has no real interest in distinctions of
earthly status.

It is in this light that we should read his argument that women
should not make a fuss about challenging the ancient custom of
veiling their heads. The distinctions of sex are of this world rather
than the next, but it is wrong to show contempt for those distinctions if in doing so one causes distress to others. The issue, in Paul's
eyes, is not important enough to justify the amount of distress it is
causing. And it is this that he finds unacceptable.

One would dearly love to know whether those who complained
about the women prophets were themselves female. This would fit
with what we know about modern debates over the veiling of women,
where it is often women themselves who argue most passionately
to defend traditional customs. It seems likely that Paul has been
drawn into a debate between two factions of women.

Now Paul reveals the foundation of his idea that unity is more
important than the points being quarrelled over: the squabbles are
an insult to Jesus himself. On the night before he died, Paul tells
his listeners, Jesus had told his disciples that when they prayed over
bread and wine he would be there with them. It was already a

well-known story in Paul's day – it was to be re-told in the Gospels of Matthew, Mark, and Luke – but Paul makes it his own.

> For I received from the Lord what I also passed on to you: the Lord Jesus, on the night he was betrayed, took bread, and when he had given thanks, he broke it and said, 'This is my body, which is for you; do this in remembrance of me.' In the same way, after supper he took the cup, saying, 'This cup is the new covenant in my blood; do this, whenever you drink it, in remembrance of me.' For whenever you eat this bread and drink this cup, you proclaim the Lord's death until he comes. (1 Cor. 11: 23–26)

It is simply unbearable that the Corinthians should allow petty quarrels to interrupt the precious moments of communion among those who share the memory of Jesus.

In order to address this heartlessness, Paul will reach beyond himself, in the next few dozen lines of his text, to find something entirely breathtaking. Whether by inspiration or sheer force of will, he allows his irritation to burn away, to be replaced by a new way of thinking about what binds human beings to one another. For a brief, luminous moment, he will carry his listeners to the threshold of a new way of seeing, inviting them – pleading with them – to grasp that they are really only themselves when they are at peace with one another. The words he conjures to try to convey his message of love to the Corinthians will endure as arguably the most important in Western literature.

Certainly, as Paul wrote the twelfth and thirteenth chapters of his First Letter to the Corinthians, he had no way of knowing how priceless a legacy he was leaving to the Christians of future centuries. He was a man who honestly thought that the world was about to end. So, as we read what he says next, we must try to think of him only as someone trying to solve a problem, as a man troubled by the pointless quarrelling of beloved friends.

Paul begins his all-or-nothing assault on the mean-spiritedness of the Corinthians by limbering up with a thought-exercise, an exploration of what Jesus meant by saying 'this is my body'. This saying, Paul tells the Corinthians, is a window into a new dimension of reality. Christ's body is not only the food and wine that the faithful eat and drink when they are together. The community itself is Christ's body. This is why unity among them is so important, and why it is so wrong for anyone to try to stand out at the expense of the others.

> Just as the body, though one, has many parts, but all its many parts form one body, so it is with Christ. For we were all baptized by one Spirit so as to form one body – whether Jews or Gentiles, slave or free – and all were made to drink of one Spirit. (1 Cor. 12: 12–13)

Paul wants the Corinthians to understand that their unity makes them part of something greater. The Messiah has embraced them within his own person, the Body of Christ.

> And so the body does not consist of one part but of many. Now if the foot should say, 'Because I am not a hand, I do not belong to the body,' it would not for that reason stop being part of the body. And if the ear should say, 'Because I am not an eye, I do not belong to the body,' it would not for this reason stop being part of the body. If the whole body were an eye, where would the sense of hearing be? If the whole body were an ear, where would the sense of smell be? But in fact, God has placed the parts in the body, every one of them, just as he wanted them to be. If all were one part, where would the body be? As it is, there are many parts, but one body. (1 Cor. 12: 14–20)

The reason it is wrong for individuals to try to stand out against the group is not only that arrogance is destructive. It is that it reveals a fundamental misunderstanding of the life in Christ.

There is something far greater at play here than the spiritual insight of a single individual: 'The eye cannot say to the hand, "I don't need you!" And the head cannot say to the feet, "I don't need you!" On the contrary, those parts of the body that seem to be weaker are indispensable.' (1 Cor. 12: 21–22) Paul wants to persuade his listeners to set aside their power-games over who will be seen as important. 'If one part suffers, every part suffers with it; if one part is honoured, every part rejoices with it.' (1 Cor. 12: 26) Together, each of the Corinthians is infinitely greater than he or she would be alone. His moral is that those who take up these roles should place their hope not in themselves but in the body that is the sum of their individual parts. Paul wants the Corinthians to take the idea and test it, by living with it and putting it into practice in their own lives.

What he does next, however, is entirely unexpected. Reaching for a way to make it clear why any member's craving to stand out from the group is so painfully wrong-headed, he changes key. In rapturous, almost hallucinatory prose, Paul shows that what is missing is love. It is their failure to love one another that has caused the Corinthians to fail as a community. For a moment, Paul stops railing against them, and turns inward, to consider how he too may have failed.

> If I speak in the tongues of men or of angels, but do not have love, I am only a resounding gong or a clanging cymbal. If I have the gift of prophecy and can fathom all mysteries and all knowledge, and if I have a faith that can move mountains, but do not have love, I am nothing. If I give all I possess to the poor and give over my body to the flames but do not have love, I gain nothing. (1 Cor. 13: 1–3)

Listen closely as he begins to explain what love is. The words have become almost too familiar over the centuries. But Paul is framing out a bold and unexpected idea.

Love is patient, love is kind. It does not envy, it does not boast, it is not proud. It does not dishonour others, it is not self-seeking, it is not easily angered, it keeps no record of wrongs. Love does not delight in evil but rejoices with the truth. It always protects, always trusts, always hopes, always perseveres. (1 Cor. 13: 4–6)

What Paul wants his listeners to know, here, is that love embodies precisely that quality of permanence that is called for when 'the form of this world is passing away'. Love is the substance of the new life in Christ. This is not only a question of ethics; it goes deeper than that. Love is stronger than time or death, a window into a deeper reality. 'Love never fails. But where there are prophecies, they will cease; where there are tongues, they will be stilled; where there is knowledge, it will pass away.' (1 Cor. 13: 8) Love is the closest human beings can come to the mysterious oneness of eternity.

And this is the final point: the self-important attempts at 'knowledge' that have been stirring up so much trouble are the painful stumblings of children pulling away from an infinitely patient and infinitely loving parent.

When I was a child, I talked like a child, I thought like a child, I reasoned like a child. When I became a man, I put the ways of childhood behind me. For now we see only a reflection as in a mirror; then we shall see face to face. Now I know in part; then I shall know fully, even as I am fully known. (1 Cor. 13: 11–12)

All the talk by the Corinthians about their superior understanding of spiritual matters is now revealed as a sign of painful failure. What God has given to human beings, in Christ, is far more than the small-minded Corinthians can see. Their competition over spiritual knowledge is painfully misguided. The deeper human need is not to know but to be known. Finally, Paul draws to a close. 'And now these three remain: faith, hope and love. But the greatest of these is love.' (1 Cor. 13: 13) The listener has been carried, up to now, by the prose rhythms of the gifted preacher. As the waves of sound and image come to rest, the ear is vividly aware of the fact that this was a letter written to be read aloud. One feels the pause deeply when he reaches his stopping-point. Yet – almost unbelievably – he wants to go further.

Paul has captured his listeners and he has dazzled them; now he wants to drive his message home. He wants his vision of the power of love to have practical consequences – to change the life of the Corinthian community. To underline his point, he stages an anti-climax. From the lyrical height of his meditation on love, he makes a sharp turn into the dull routine of community-building. The transition is jarring, almost flat-footed – unexpected in a man who can speak with the voice of an angel. But Paul wants this feeling of deflation for his listeners. He wants them to grasp a deeper point, that the practicalities are the embodiment of a spiritual principle. This is the insight he has been aiming at through the course of the whole letter. When the group meets, he wants the Corinthians to see that the whole community is lifted up, rather than allowing single individuals to find recognition at the expense of others. These questions of order and mutual care are the heart of the matter, and to solve them will require a change of heart.

An Ambiguous Legacy for Women?

In his discussion of how the community should treat one another when they pray together, there is a difficult passage about women, which requires careful examination.

As in all the congregations of the Lord's people, women should remain silent in the churches. They are not allowed to speak, but must be in submission, as the Law says. If they want to

> inquire about something, they should ask their own husbands
> at home; for it is disgraceful for a woman to speak in the church.
> (1 Cor. 14: 34–35)

Scholars have found different ways to cope with these verses, which seem to contradict Paul's earlier discussion of women prophets in the congregation. Some have suggested that the verses were added by a later editor, while others have tried to reconcile them with what Paul says elsewhere.

The second approach suggests that what the writer intends here – whether it is Paul or someone else – is not to exclude women from prophecy, but to address the question of whether or not listeners should be allowed to talk amongst themselves. On this view, when the writer says 'it is disgraceful for a woman to speak' he is talking of conversational speech, not prophecy – this is in fact a fair reading of the Greek. If this view is correct, the writer doesn't mean that female *prophets* should remain silent – he means that *listeners* should listen quietly while the prophets prophesy. This way of reading the lines allows them to fit, more or less, with the general theme of the passage, although it remains to explain why his complaint about chattering is aimed at women, when the rest of the chapter seems to be aimed at both women and men. Were the female listeners more disrespectful than the men? Were the prophets they were interrupting also women? Were women evaluating each other's performance, instead of listening for the voice of the Spirit?

The early manuscripts show that already in antiquity scholars were worried about these verses. They appear in only some manuscripts of Paul's text, which means that certain copyists suspected they were not by Paul and tried to correct the mistake by omitting them. Many modern scholars believe the verses were originally a marginal note made by an early reader. On this hypothesis, later copyists mistook the note for a part of Paul's text that an earlier copyist had missed, and then added it in, in the margin. It is certainly possible that the passage was the irritated comment of an early reader who thought that Paul had been too encouraging to women, or who was worried that Paul's encouragement could be taken as an excuse for women getting out of hand.[2]

Some readers have felt that there is an element of misogyny here, or at least of particular impatience with women. My own sense is that if Paul is impatient with women, it is because he thinks women, more than anyone, ought to understand what he is getting at. He could easily expect that in talking about how the individual should make sacrifices for the greater good of the community, he was saying something that women would understand.

In both the Jewish and Roman traditions, women had always been in a position that was powerful but also vulnerable. Paul worked very closely with women, and he was well aware of their special role in caring for children and the aged. He could easily expect them to see why the needs of the wider group should be addressed before the demands of any single individual. So he may have felt it as a betrayal if some of the Corinthian women insisted on calling attention to themselves in a way that was causing seemingly unnecessary anxiety to others.

In fairness, we have to ask whether a double standard was being operated against women in these communities. In many early Christian sources, if a man behaves stupidly it is because he is a fool, while if a woman does so it is seen as typical of her sex. Many readers will wonder why women were so passionate in working for a cause that seems often, on the face of it, to have taken an unnecessarily demeaning tone in speaking of women. From the story of Eve in the Book of Genesis to the Whore of Babylon in the Book of Revelation, the Christian scriptures are littered with alarming portrayals of women as temptresses.

Yet I have often wondered why, if women played such an influential role in early Christian communities, they did not try harder to rid the growing movement of an element which can only have seemed unsavoury from their point of view. Some historians have tried to 'explain away' this problem, by suggesting that the Jewish and Graeco-Roman cultures out of which Christianity grew were equally misogynistic, or even more so. On this reading, early Christian women simply had to make the best of a bad lot. Other scholars think that misogyny was difficult to dislodge because it was seen as useful: the men-folk were attached to it not out of hatred for women, but as a vehicle for male bonding, a means of defining an idea of male collective interest that bound the men of different families together in an interest group. My own view is that both of these have some truth to them, but there is also another factor at play.

There is a paradox in the way women were viewed in ancient Mediterranean society: they were seen as both more virtuous and more dangerous than men. From Homer and Virgil to the Book of Genesis, ancient writers agreed that women's influence on men could be dangerous and unpredictable, because seeing behind a woman's charm to tell whether she was using her powers of persuasion for good or evil was a skill many men did not possess. Ancient men were conscious that their reason was often compromised when they were dealing with women, and this made them nervous. A good woman could inspire a man to reach beyond himself for a good cause, but a woman who wanted to lead him astray could do so more easily than could another man.

For women, the paradox captured an equal and opposite social fact. However powerful they were, women tended to live with men who had more power than they did. They often found themselves in a position where they needed to enlist the help of men to get something done, and it was a well-known fact that men often responded to perfectly reasonable requests from a woman in a way that made no sense. Men could behave like over-sized children: they were powerful, but they tended to thrash about in a way that was irrational and volatile. Whatever a good woman's efforts to keep things moving smoothly, where men were involved there was always an element of unpredictability.

More irritatingly, men seemed to be almost entirely unable to recognize female intelligence, and they appeared to have no instinct for telling the difference between virtue and charm. They often dismissed the efforts of honest women and encouraged the dishonest, who were poised to take advantage of their weakness. This led to tension among the women. Some women were happy to take the short-cut of treating men as irrational and simply trying to get round them, but others saw that this kind of behaviour made it even more difficult for an honest woman to gain men's trust, and found it despicable. Faced with the easy success of the short-cut takers, the champions of virtue found themselves in the curious position of trying to warn men not to listen to other women. Disturbingly, they often found themselves in agreement when men complained about the treachery of their sisters.

This put the honest women in an exasperating position, but in the early Christian communities their exasperation was put to good use. It is a principle of modern social theory that people who are willing to work against a disadvantage are very good for the vitality of the wider group they belong to. Sociologically speaking, this makes perfect sense. Modern social research has shown that asking new members to make seemingly pointless sacrifices is a classic tactic of groups that are able to achieve an unusually high growth rate. What makes an emerging group really begin to 'take off' in terms of growth is not the *number* of converts the group is able to attract, but the *quality* of the people who join. Some people are motivated rather than paralysed by the sense of working at a disadvantage, and these people are the holy grail of recruitment. One of the ways groups can fish for them is by letting it be known that group membership is not for the faint-hearted. The most able recruitment specialists have an intuitive sense of how to use this strategy to test the energy, skills, and commitment of potential members of a group.

This kind of disadvantage – known in sociological terms as a stigma – can be the by-product of circumstance, or it can be accidental. But to do its job, it has to be set at just the right level. It must be onerous enough to deter 'fellow travellers' – people who want to benefit from what the group has to offer, but who have little to contribute themselves. Generally, the group is better off without these members: in the short run, they will add to the numbers, but in the long run they will dilute the group's sense of purpose and slow down its growth. At the same time, the stigma cannot be too strong – in that case it will put off the more valuable people the group wants to attract.

The convert every group hopes for is the kind of energetic soul who will quickly become indispensable. On the whole, these people have a high tolerance for setbacks. Making sacrifices for a cause only convinces them more deeply of its value. The effect of a properly calibrated stigma on this kind of convert will be energizing. If a negative stereotype is put forward, he or she will try to disprove the stereotype.

Try to imagine the ideal convert from the point of view of the missionary who is trying to find her in a crowd. She is a star at building networks of influence and at motivating friends and family to get involved. She already has a wide network of both male and female contacts, and she is the kind of woman that both men and women tend to listen to. She is someone who tends to dismiss obstacles, or to compensate for them by means of superior performance.

This ideal convert is even more valuable to the group if she is not particularly interested in gaining recognition for her labour. Genuine altruism is a priceless characteristic in religious leaders, and it is difficult to screen for. But warning someone in advance that they will not receive full credit for their efforts is a good place to start. In all likelihood, the supporting players will all quietly shuffle offstage when the challenge is set, leaving only the star to face the audience. Before long, she herself will begin recruiting others. As long as she herself remains in play, the company can include as many bit players and character actors as her charisma will support.

Such a figure only comes along rarely. Paul may have found more than one of them during his travels, but it is difficult to single them out. Prisca and Junia, Phoebe and Mary, Tryphena and Tryphosa: surely there is a star here somewhere. But when we scan through the list of fellow workers Paul included in his letter to the community in Rome, we are essentially in the same position that Paul was in when he first met them. Faced with a crowd of possible stars, we want to find a way to discover more about them.

To the historian, this is frustrating, because we don't have the opportunity Paul did to ask questions and hear a living answer. Our sources are infuriatingly thin. But in a way, this is fitting. The semi-anonymity of Paul's women expresses perfectly one of Paul's most beloved ideas – that recognition for each individual is less important than the part she or he plays, often invisibly, in the Body of Christ.

What would Chloe have made of all this, if she were a colleague with whom relations had broken down, or perhaps even the leader of the faction who were causing trouble in Corinth? The irony is that if she found Paul's arguments persuasive, and discovered a way to restore harmony in the community, it might well have gone unrecorded. It is a bittersweet fact: if we know very little about the women of Paul's circle, it may in part be that they followed his advice and put their energies into the well-being of the group rather than leaving a record of their own importance.

The Gospel of Love

We do not know how things turned out in Corinth. We know that Paul returned to the city at least twice – his Letter to the Romans was written during the third visit. We know that the Corinthians saw the value of Paul's first letter to them, for it was saved, and copies were made to pass on to other churches, which is how it has survived to be handed down through time. Paul wrote two further letters to the Corinthians, though only one, the third, has survived. Confusingly, it is preserved as the Second Letter to the Corinthians, because the second was already lost in antiquity. It attests that the dispute was still not settled after repeated efforts, but what happened after it was written is unknown.

In the end, Paul's letters would remain as the earliest Christian writings to survive. Jesus himself had left no writings to guide his followers, only a legacy of sayings which they had tried to learn by heart. A decade or so after the death of Jesus, when Paul became involved with the community, its future was unclear. It was Paul himself who would make the difference. His reinterpretation of the ancient traditions of the Hebrew Bible in fresh, intensely emotional terms was something that even someone without a Jewish background could respond to.

In his other letters, Paul shows how his view of God's love is built on the ancient traditions reaching back to the Book of Genesis. God had tested Abraham by asking him to sacrifice his son Isaac, and Abraham's willingness to give up everything he loved was the basis of his covenant with God. Now, in Jesus of Nazareth, God himself had offered his own Son as a sacrifice, to mark the fulfilment of his covenant with Abraham.

But in the First Letter to the Corinthians, the emphasis is not on the ancient story – it is on the underlying emotional reality of the here and now. Paul's restless life as a missionary has allowed him to share, for a time, in the domestic intimacy of other people's families, but always without entirely being at home. He understands better than most what it costs to give up what one loves. What he wants his friends to feel is the intensity of God's love for humanity, a love strong enough to account for God's willingness to give up his own Son.

Towards the end of his letter to the Corinthians, Paul strives to encapsulate the pith – in its earliest surviving version – of what would endure as the core of the Christian Gospel.

For what I received I passed on to you as of first importance: that Christ died for our sins according to the Scriptures, that he was buried, that he was raised on the third day according to the Scriptures, and that he appeared to Peter, and then to the Twelve . . . and last of all he appeared to me also. (1 Cor. 15: 3–5, 8)

He is trying to capture, here, his flash of understanding. He has seen that the story of Jesus is not simply about the teachings of a provincial miracle-worker, but about God's love of the world. Jesus was born just for this: to die and be raised from the dead as a sign of God's love.

Paul was a Pharisee, and his vision of community had its roots in the heritage of first-century study of the Torah, a quintessentially masculine tradition. But in his letters, one can hear that he is doing something unexpected with the scriptural tradition he has inherited. There is a breathtaking emotional intensity in his letters, a willingness to find, in the mundane practicalities of daily life, a window into the infinite. The profound connection between the seemingly trivial difficulties of family life and the greater life-and-death questions is a new sound in ancient literature, and it is one which will be picked up and amplified by the greatest of Paul's followers, the gifted writer who, after Paul's death, will write the Gospel of Luke. Yet in Paul's letters we can hear something more than his own genius: an echo of female voices, of conversations over the years with the women of the Aegean cloth trade who were his close collaborators. During this long fellowship, the apostle has not only been talking to women: he has been *listening*.

3

THE GALILEAN WOMEN

One of the Gospel of Luke's most memorable stories captures a scene that could have come straight from Paul's letters, though there is every reason to think it reaches back to the time of Jesus and his disciples. It concerns Mary and Martha, two sisters from the village of Bethany, east of Jerusalem at the edge of the Judaean wilderness.

As Jesus and his disciples were on their way, he came to a village where a woman named Martha opened her home to him. She had a sister called Mary, who sat at the Lord's feet listening to what he said. But Martha was distracted by all the preparations that had to be made. She came to him and asked, 'Lord, don't you care that my sister has left me to do the work (*diakonein*) by myself? Tell her to help me!'

'Martha, Martha,' the Lord answered, 'you are worried and upset about many things, but only one thing is needed. Mary has chosen what is good, and it will not be taken away from her.' (Luke 10: 38–42)

The story has proved a talking-point for women across the centuries. What kind of distinction is Jesus making between the differing gifts of the two sisters? Did Jesus value Martha's generosity, or did he take it for granted? In speaking up for Mary, did he or did he not want to indicate that women who sought a place among the Apostles should be welcomed?

At its most basic level, the story calls attention to the value Jesus places on the spiritual contribution of women. Mary's dedication to Jesus and his teaching must be respected. In a first-century Jewish society where the study of Torah was reserved for boys and men, for the rabbi Jesus to state firmly that 'it will not be taken away from her' is a powerful act. While the other Gospel writers either did not know the story or missed its importance, Luke gives us a Jesus who wants to change the place of women in the spiritual landscape. His explicit statement has been invaluable to queens, abbesses, and younger sisters across two millennia. Luke sends a clear message that Jesus welcomed women to his circle of disciples.

And yet Martha's role in the story has been sorely misunderstood. Look closely at the way the story is introduced – 'he came to a village where a woman named Martha opened her home to him'. Martha is not a servant or merely someone's daughter: the story takes place in her own house. Martha, in fact, is one of a group of strong women who are present in Luke's Gospel but often go unnoticed. These are the women of property who supported the fledgling Christian movement from their own resources.[1] It isn't clear on what basis Martha of Bethany was able to maintain her own household. Jewish law did not allow women as much independence as Roman law – in principle, a woman's property was transferred from father to husband at the time of marriage. But many families in Roman-period Judaea seem to have found a way to allow their daughters to inherit property in their own name rather than through fathers or husbands.

By a curious accident, the personal papers of an early second-century Jewish heiress living near the Dead Sea have survived. They were discovered in 1960 after lying hidden in a cave since the 130s, when the unstable atmosphere of the Bar Kokhba revolt led their owner, Babatha, to hide them. Babatha was a widow who had remarried. Her new husband remained married to his first wife, Miriam. Though Roman law allowed only one wife to a husband, Jewish law, like modern Islamic law, allowed men to take multiple wives. Babatha was a junior wife in an emphatically non-Roman arrangement, but she owned property in her own right, in a way that seems to reflect Roman rather than Jewish law – in Jewish law of the period, a husband controlled his wife's property. Among her holdings were a number of date orchards. Her tax documents show that she acted independently of her husband in legal and financial matters, even lending him money at interest, by a documented loan.[2]

Martha was probably not a property-owner at Babatha's level, but she was prosperous enough to host a miracle-worker's entourage. The Mishnah, a revered collection of the sayings of first- and second-century rabbis compiled at the beginning of the third century, surveys a woman's domestic duties in the Jewish households of Roman Palestine, noting, at Mishnah Ketubot 5.5, that in the more prosperous households, the mistress of the household would be exempted from much of the practical work.

These are the labours that a wife does for her husband: she grinds, and she bakes, and she launders; she cooks, and she nurses her child; she tends the bedding and she works in wool.

If [the wife] brought one household slave [when she married], then she does not grind and she does not bake and she does not launder.

[If she brought] two, then she does not cook and she does not nurse her child.

[If she brought] three, then she does not tend to the bedding and she does not work in wool.

[If she brought] four, then she may sit upon a chair of leisure.[3]

Since Martha and her sister were involved in seeing to their guests themselves, the number of slaves was probably low, but this is not certain.

Luke's own community included women of property, and this influenced his way of imagining Martha. The passage has often been read as dismissing her practical contribution, but this is incorrect. The story of Mary and Martha is not the tale of a refusal by Jesus to support a woman struggling in a neglected role. Rather, Jesus corrects a head of household who he thinks is pushing a dependent family member too hard. Once we understand that Martha held a position of authority, the story makes a different kind of sense. It seems to be aimed at the church leadership of Luke's own day, reminding them to honour a variety of gifts among the faithful.

The story of Martha and Mary was probably first told to a mixed group of family and friends in a domestic setting. In the first century, what passed for a formal church service was a home-spun affair, a communal meal offered in the main room or courtyard of a family dwelling. The elders of the community would say prayers before the meal, and sometimes one of the elders would tell stories of the early days. Each community maintained its own isolated island of fellowship and prayer, and occasionally, a travelling teacher would visit, telling stories and saying prayers that linked the little island to a wider fellowship.

So we can imagine listeners gathered around a storyteller in a front room or a courtyard, just as the disciples in the story had gathered around Jesus. As the story unfolds, there is a natural sympathy for the disobedient sister's desire to find a place with the listeners. Mary's desire to hear Jesus speak means that someone who is listening to her story has something important in common with her. So the listener will be relieved to hear it when Jesus says that Mary has chosen the greater part.

But like the disciples in Bethany, the people listening to the story are gathered in someone's house, and that someone, like Martha, has a special position by virtue of playing host. The host may or may not be a woman, but she or he is by definition a respected individual who has access to friendship networks and material resources. How does the exchange between Martha and Jesus sound to this person's ears, and to the ears of others, when this person is in the room?

Modern readers often fail to notice that one of the most interesting things about Jesus's rebuke to Martha is the curious position of the storyteller as she or he relates it. Even in the late first century, when the Gospel stories began to be written down, most people encountered them in an oral setting. Only a fraction of the community could read or write, so the Gospels were written to be read aloud.

So as we read the Gospel of Luke, we should imagine that we are in an early house-church, listening, along with a small group of friends. The reader is a respected member of the community because of the simple fact that she or he can read, and has become all the more so from taking on the task of reading to the group from the precious handwritten Gospel. Unless the reader is also the host of the group, she or he is a guest in someone else's house, a fact which adds drama to the story of that earlier guest – Jesus himself – who criticized his hostess.

The Mary and Martha story has been read over the years as failing to value the practical contribution of the Marthas of the world, but this is not quite right. In fact, the story illustrates the growing pains of a movement which can only survive if the Marthas – the established householders on whom the movement depends – are able to wear their authority lightly. Part of the job of the wandering teachers is to remind the householders not to become too taken with their own importance.

And yet, at the same time, Luke is also exploring the concerns of the women like Martha who shouldered responsibility for the fledgling movement. He stops to consider the resentment they would feel if they began to suspect that their generosity, or their work of organizing and providing, was being taken for granted. One has the feeling that he has been watching the women around him and noticing their concerns. Luke's Jesus wants the women to rise above these anxieties, but he does not intend to take their contribution for granted.

Theologians have long debated whether the Gospel of Luke could have been written by a woman. It certainly isn't impossible; the early Church produced more than its share of female writers. The Gospel was clearly written by a person who could think about the community around Jesus from both the male and the female point of view.

If the author was a man, he took heed of what the women around him were thinking.

Like all the Gospel-writers, Luke is careful to show that Jesus paid attention to the problems that the listeners of his own day can be expected to care about. Luke's Jesus sees that women run the risk of being cast as supporting players in the community, attending to practical matters rather than joining the men in asking questions and debating ideas. This is not something he wants to encourage. Rather, Luke's Jesus wants to make it clear that if a woman makes the choice made by Mary, joining with men in listening to their teacher: 'she has chosen the good: it will not be taken away from her'. Hospitality, material support, and organizing are to be valued. However, he reminds us, these gifts cannot take the place of attention to Jesus himself and his message of love, which is the *raison d'être* of the new community.

Finally, we should notice the frank and easy relationship between Martha and Jesus. Luke takes it for granted that powerful women will not hesitate to make their concerns heard. Martha is asked to set aside her grievance when she raises it, and in asking her to do so Jesus does not spare her ego. But his frank criticism is a sign of respect. In Luke's Gospel, Jesus is never unkind to the weak. He treats Martha with humiliating honesty, just as he would treat the male disciples.

A Child is Born

When a powerful story addresses the problems of women and families it makes sense to imagine that it was first told in a family setting. Stories and ideas that encourage useful behaviour that is relevant to the listener's situation are more likely than others to gain wide distribution. The logic here is obvious: stories that involve a restless child settling down and going to bed are more likely to circulate as bedtime stories than tales of a child getting up repeatedly in the night.

Luke's stories often revolve around women and families, and this probably reflects both Jesus's ministry and Luke's own missionary environment. Yet many of the stories of family life in Luke's Gospel are unique to him – they appear nowhere else in the early tradition. We can build up a profile of his interests and sensibilities. Some of his stories take a female point of view or focus closely on women: one thinks here of the stories surrounding Mary, the mother of Jesus, and her role in the birth and death of her son. Others highlight family dynamics that may or may not involve women. It is Luke who gives us the two great stories of sibling rivalry in the New Testament, and while the story of Martha and Mary of Bethany, involves women, the other, the parable of the Prodigal Son, is about two brothers. The bright thread that connects the stories told only by Luke is the idea, as disarming now as it was 2,000 years ago, that the power of God is at work in the ordinary lives of ordinary families.

Paul had written in the fifties and sixties, and he is the first of the Christian leaders whose own writings survive. For Jesus, Mary, and the earliest disciples, we have only sayings and stories handed down orally and recorded by a later generation. In all likelihood Paul had long been dead when the Gospels, the late first-century sources that tell the story of Jesus of Nazareth and his disciples, began to be written. Paul seems to have died in the late sixties, while the Gospels were written in the decades after the destruction of Jerusalem in the year 70.

At the beginning of his Gospel, Luke tells us that he has inherited eye-witness stories that are in danger of dying out. Those who knew Jesus and his disciples have now reached old age. Luke tells us that he has inherited stories from those who knew Jesus, and he is worried that the stories will be distorted in the retelling as time passes if they are not recorded carefully and accurately. There is a widespread view among scholars that in writing the 'Gospel according to Luke', our writer is handing down the memories of an earlier teacher who was called by that name; if that is the case then our writer may have had a different name altogether. By the end of the second century, the writer was believed to be a doctor called Luke; a number of first-century letters, including Paul's letter to Philemon, refer to a person by this name.[4]

Unlike the other evangelists, Luke gave his Gospel a sequel, the Acts of the Apostles, which picks up the story of the disciples after the death of Jesus to explain how Paul joined the group and carried the Gospel out of Judaea and as far as Rome. Acts tells part of its story from the point of view of one of Paul's travelling companions.

Fortunately, the question of the writer's name does not affect the historical value of what the Gospel tells us about women and families. For convenience, we will follow the ancient tradition of referring to the Gospel's writer as Luke, rather than the more cautious 'author of the Gospel according to Luke', and to saying 'he' and 'him', though there is no decisive evidence for the writer's gender.

Each of the surviving Gospels has its own way of telling the story of Jesus, and this was certainly true of Luke. He was heir to traditions about the Galilean miracle-worker's life and death that reached back to the time before Paul, many back to Jesus himself. Yet Luke's Jesus does and says things that develop ideas we have already met in Paul's letters. Paul's thought has become the lens through which Luke sees the story of Jesus.

The birth of Jesus illustrates the differences among the Gospels dramatically. Two – Mark and John – leave it out altogether. The Gospel of Matthew opens with a long discussion of the child's human step-father Joseph's descent from Abraham through David and then offers a very brief discussion of the events surrounding Jesus's birth, told with a focus on Joseph and beginning with Joseph's worries when he hears that his bride is pregnant. Matthew's story of the birth of Jesus is aimed at establishing the baby's credentials as the Messiah whose coming had been foretold by the prophets. Matthew gives us no Annunciation to Mary by the Angel, no visitation between Mary and her kinswoman Elizabeth, no manger, and no shepherds. Instead, an angel appears to Joseph to reassure him that the baby is indeed of the Holy Spirit, and his wife's pregnancy the fulfilment of the scriptures. Matthew skips the birth itself and goes directly to the three wise men following the star that announces the arrival of the Messiah. It is only Luke who tells anything that resembles the familiar Christmas story.

These differences are entirely understandable. Each of the Gospel-writers was a person with distinctive interests and gifts, and each had his own way of making sense out of the shared traditions about Jesus that had been handed down. This was not a question of dishonesty or 'spin'. Each writer was familiar with a different collection of traditional stories. When two storytellers remember the same story, they often do so in a way that reflects their own interests and concerns and, over time, variations develop. Since ancient readers believed that the Gospel-writers were divinely chosen and inspired, these variations were prized as the work of the Spirit who spoke through the storytellers.

If we pay close attention to how Luke tells the story of the Incarnation, we see that it is not only the birth of a Messiah, but something more human. Luke gives us a family drama involving flesh-and-blood women and men making hard decisions and personal sacrifices. Here is how he tells the story of the Annunciation:

> The angel went to her and said, 'Greetings, you who are highly favoured! The Lord is with you.' Mary was greatly troubled at his words, and wondered what kind of greeting this might be. But the angel said to her, 'Do not be afraid, Mary, you have found favour with God. You will conceive and give birth to a son, and you are to call him Jesus. He will be great and will be called the Son of the Most High. The Lord God will give to him the throne of his father David, and he will reign over Jacob's descendants forever; his kingdom will never end.'
>
> 'How will this be,' Mary asked the angel, 'since I am a virgin?'
>
> The angel answered, 'The Holy Spirit will come on you, and the power of the Most High will overshadow you. So the holy

one to be born will be called the Son of God. Even your relative Elizabeth is going to have a child in her old age, and she who was said to be unable to conceive is in her sixth month. . .'

'I am the Lord's servant,' Mary answered. 'May your words to me be fulfilled.' Then the angel left her. (Luke 1: 28–36, 38)

What happens next is unique to Luke's Gospel: the story is told from the woman's point of view. Joseph does not figure at all in Mary's initial reaction, and we never hear his views on the pregnancy. When Mary discovers that she is with child, she turns to another woman, her kinswoman Elizabeth. Providentially, Elizabeth is also carrying a baby, the future John the Baptist.

At that time Mary got ready and hurried to a town in the hill country of Judea where she entered Zechariah's home and greeted Elizabeth. When Elizabeth heard Mary's greeting, the baby leaped in her womb, and Elizabeth was filled with the Holy Spirit. In a loud voice she exclaimed, 'Blessed are you among women, and blessed is the child you will bear! But why am I so favoured, that the mother of my Lord should come to me? As soon as the sound of your greeting came to my ears, the baby in my womb leaped for joy.' (Luke 1: 39–44)

It is Elizabeth who first recognizes the enormity of what Mary has agreed to do. Even before the birth of Jesus, Elizabeth sees that he will be one to be called Lord, and she offers her benediction – 'Blessed are you among women'. Her own son, John the Baptist, will prepare the way for Jesus when both of them reach adulthood. The kinship and friendship between the mothers will be handed on to the sons.

And it is to Elizabeth – not to the Angel – that Mary delivers the Magnificat, her speech of acceptance for the role she has been offered in history.

My soul glorifies the Lord,

and my spirit rejoices in God my Saviour.

For He has been mindful of the humble estate of his servant.

From now on all generations will call me blessed.

(Luke 1: 46–48)

Mary's words, 'my soul glorifies the Lord', have been handed down through history as one of the great prayers of the medieval Church, the Magnificat. Mary is no theologian in an academic sense. But as Luke tells the story, she and Elizabeth are the first theologians of a new faith. Their gift is an intrepid willingness to look for God's purpose in their own and one another's lives. If they are blood kin, they are also kindred spirits, helping to build up one another's strength and courage.

In ancient literature, a hero or heroine is often uprooted from his or her natural circumstances and must find a new identity in an unfamiliar landscape. Luke's vision of Mary fits this pattern: she is repeatedly in movement during her pregnancy. He tells us that after the visit to Elizabeth in the Judaean hills, Mary made a second journey to Judaea, this time to Bethlehem, with her husband Joseph.

As Luke tells the story, the Bethlehem journey was a result of real-life pressures. Periodically, the Roman colonial power in Judaea ordered a census of the population to be made, and this meant that individuals from all walks of life were required to return to the district where they were registered. Just before Jesus was born, Mary and her husband had to travel from Nazareth in Galilee, where Joseph worked as a carpenter, to Bethlehem in Judaea, his ancestral home. Luke tells us that it was because of the inconveniently timed requirement of the Roman authorities that Jesus came to be born in a stable, 'because there was no room at the inn' during his parents' journey. But there was also a question of destiny. An ancient prophecy had foretold that the Messiah, or anointed king of the Jews, would be born in Bethlehem.

It is near Bethlehem that the Angel of the Lord appears to the shepherds keeping watch by night. Here, too, Luke singles out Mary as the one who tries to make sense of what God has done.

> The shepherds said to one another, 'Let's go to Bethlehem and see this thing that has happened, which the Lord has made known to us.' So they hurried off and found Mary and Joseph, and the baby, who was lying in the manger. When they had seen him, they spread the word concerning what had been told them about this child. And all who heard it were amazed at what the shepherds said to them. But Mary treasured up all these things and pondered them in her heart. (Luke 2: 15–19)

Luke closes the scene with an image of the child's mother holding on to what she has heard and trying to make sense of what is to become of her child. He sees, far more clearly than do the other evangelists, that Mary's courage, and her willingness to try to make sense of the destiny of her child, is the foundation for what will become Christianity.

One of Luke's particular gifts as a writer is this ability to see how God speaks to, and through, women. Later writers have sometimes made light of Luke's interest in women, by arguing that a story like the Visitation between Mary and Elizabeth is only 'really' there because Luke wants to explain the close ties between Jesus and John the Baptist. Luke had inherited his stories, so the fact that so many of them concern women probably means that he had access to traditions handed down by women. Like the people he wrote about, Luke was raised in an ancient Mediterranean society where men and women's social lives were largely separate. We know that he was a follower of the Apostle Paul, and that Paul had worked closely with female leaders in his missionary work, including women like Junia who had been involved in the movement before he joined. So Luke may well have been acquainted with women who had received stories through a chain of female storytelling. And of course, he may well himself have had close working relationships with women. An unsympathetic writer could easily have suppressed the stories that tell us about the distinctive pressures that women faced, but Luke chose not to.

Yet it is certainly true that Luke had his own way of re-casting the traditions he had received. Even the language his Gospel was written in imposed a certain distance. Mariam of Nazareth was a speaker of Aramaic, yet the stories about her and her son Jesus came to be told in Greek. Aramaic was the language of the Near East in the Roman period, while Greek, the language of Plato and Alexander the Great, was an international language like English today, used by Jews and Gentiles alike throughout the Mediterranean. So the Aramaic Mariam became the Greek Maria. Her story had found a vessel that could carry it out into the wider world.

A Woman of Spirit

Like many heroines of ancient literature, Mary was a village-dweller from a distant province of the Roman Empire. She was barely of marriageable age, still a child by modern reckoning. Today the Virgin Mary can sometimes appear to be a mute and passive figure – a candy-coloured goddess on a pedestal – but the unmarried teenager of Luke's Gospel is a different kind of heroine altogether.

When she hears the news that God has chosen her to play a physically and emotionally dangerous role in history, Mary reacts not with confusion or reluctance, but with swift acceptance. To any of her contemporaries who heard about this for the first time, the young woman's acceptance would have seemed surprising, almost shocking. For an unmarried woman in first-century Galilee, a pregnancy of any kind would be frightening news, even if the child were wished-for and the identity of the child's father was not in doubt.

Consider Mary's youth. In first-century Galilee, the age of marriage for women was probably around twelve. Giving birth itself was both more and less terrifying to Mary than to the modern reader. In one sense it was less so, since Mary grew up in the kind of village where families shared their cottages with livestock. Ancient tradition held that Mary's father Joachim was a shepherd, and that the Angel appeared to Mary in late March – lambing time. To a shepherd's child, the arrival of new life was the most natural thing in the world. Renaissance artists imagined her reading a book when the Angel came, but it would have been closer to the truth to picture her keeping vigil with a labouring ewe.

At the same time, pregnancy in first-century Galilee was far more dangerous than it is today. A first pregnancy carried a high risk of death in childbirth. Should the mother survive, the infant might not: the rate of infant mortality in the ancient world was daunting. Miscarriages and stillbirths were frequent. As many as 30 per cent of babies born alive could be expected to die in the first year of life. Of those who reached their first birthday, a similar percentage would fail to survive to adulthood. In a pre-industrial village society where healthcare was far more limited than in the poorest of modern nations, a woman's work of raising children meant that she was constantly on the frontlines in the battle against death and disease. To bring a child into the world was to live with the constant shadow of death.[5]

Mary's unexpected pregnancy brought other fears as well. A girl of her social class and religious upbringing would be anxious to secure the economic and social security a husband could offer. If she was betrothed, as Mary was, an illegitimate pregnancy carried with it the threat that that she would lose her promised marriage. This was an alarming prospect. If her husband-to-be was willing to stand by her, they could brave it out. But if not, a second offer was unlikely for a bride who had given away her claim to respectability, and the economic consequences of not marrying were potentially catastrophic. So Mary's courage was no small matter.

Faced with a strange and fearful challenge, the shepherd's daughter finds poetry: 'My soul glorifies the Lord and my spirit rejoices in God my Saviour'. In Luke's telling, Mary's acceptance of her destiny stands as a powerful act of the imagination. Her song of praise is a manifesto, a bold statement that the power of God does not belong to people of worldly importance. Luke wants us to see the infinite potential of those moments when a person steps away from safety and into the unknown.

By reminding his audience that his story is set in the hard-scrabble world of subsistence farming in Galilee, and training his focus on a lowly heroine, Luke underlines the idea that no challenge is too great for even the most insignificant person, if that person has trust in God. He is passionately committed to the idea that people's lives can be transformed by seemingly impossible challenges. Early Christian writers often tried to convey the idea of the power of God by telling the story of courageous women. The theory seems to have been that if women were weaker than men, their courage was all the more remarkable. Repeatedly in early Christian literature, very young heroines – children by our standards – will discover a blazing fierceness of purpose when faced with the impossible.

Women are everywhere in the Gospel of Luke, once you begin to look for them. But it is not only that there are women: it is often a specific *kind* of woman. Luke's women, like Mary of Nazareth or Mary and Martha of Bethany, find themselves in comparatively exposed positions. They are women without husbands, female heads of household and business-owners, or daughters faced with circumstances their parents could not be expected to understand.

We already know that the genuinely independent women – the heads of household and business-owners – played a critical role in the early Christian communities. Women in this situation were perhaps more likely to develop strong networks outside the household than were the women who played the 'invisible' roles of wife and mother within the family. But the 'invisible' women whose lives were entirely bound up in family life were important in a different way. In ancient Mediterranean society, women passed at an early age from childhood to marriage. At the subsistence level of the

Galilean villager, wives and mothers shouldered demanding responsibilities in caring for the vulnerable – for children and the elderly.
They were often economically and legally dependent on their male
kin, and they tended to enjoy far less freedom to follow their own
interests than did men of the same status. Village women were
perfectly suited as heroines for stories about finding the hidden
possibilities in a difficult situation.

Luke celebrates the willingness of the village women of Galilee
and Judaea to take risks and make sacrifices. The circle of women
who gathered around Mary and her son Jesus appear frequently in
his Gospel, and if one of his themes is their courage, another is the
link between their courage and their sense of community. His heroines are not afraid to rely on the friendship of other women. If Mary
was able to rejoice in the role laid out for her by the Angel, it was
due in no small part to the strength that she found in the friendship of her kinswoman.

A Story of Love and Loss

Luke's way of telling Mary's story is not simply a thoughtless handing
on of tradition – it reflects his own values and choices. To appreciate
this, we can compare his Gospel to an apocryphal source from the
second century, the Infancy Gospel known to scholars as the
Protevangelium of James, which tells the story of Mary's unexpected
pregnancy from an entirely different point of view. Where Luke is
interested in moral courage and hidden potential, the Infancy Gospel
offers an exercise in magic realism. Its vision of Mary's childhood
is characterized by colourful detail and a touch of comedy.

The Virgin is pictured as an unusual girl whose elderly parents,
recognizing her supernatural gifts, send her to the Temple of
Jerusalem to be raised by the temple priests and virgins. This otherworldly childhood prepares her for what was to come: 'Mary dwelt

in the temple of the Lord, and was nurtured there like a dove, and she received food from the hand of an angel.'[6]

When the child turns twelve, the priests decide that she should marry, and they settle on Joseph to care for her and be her husband. In the Gospel of Luke, Joseph's age isn't mentioned, but in the Infancy Gospel he is an elderly widower, which lends a note of comedy to his worries that Mary may be in love with someone else. After the betrothal, she goes to stay with Elizabeth, and when the elderly Joseph comes to visit his fiancée, he is horrified to find that she is clearly expecting a baby. Our writer takes a nosy interest in Joseph's distress when it seems obvious to everyone that Mary has fled into the arms of a younger and more attractive suitor. When Joseph accepts the girl's story that her pregnancy is the result of a miraculous visit by an angel, he seems to have been cast in a stock comic role, that of the husband too foolish, or besotted, to perceive that his wife has betrayed him. But of course the irony is that it was God, not a human rival, who is the father of the child. In the end Joseph executes with dignity the humiliating task of convincing the temple authorities to believe the story about his young wife's visitation by with an angel. After a series of scenes delighting in Joseph's humiliation, Mary's virginity is established to the satisfaction of all, and the baby is born in a cloud of dazzling light.

The Infancy Gospel is set in a world where anything can happen: the miraculous and the ridiculous can be found side by side. Although the elements of Mary's story overlap quite a bit with those in the Gospel of Luke, the two writers are trying to do very different things indeed with the material they have to hand.

The comic nosiness of the Infancy Gospel makes one notice how much emotional realism one finds in Luke. When he tells the story of Mary and Joseph, it is a tale of individuals struggling to fulfil their destiny, and at the same time of a human family struggling to cope with the real-life pressures of raising an unexpected child. For Luke, it is important that the marriage and family of Mary and Joseph do not go according to plan. A child comes at a time when its arrival can cause only anxiety; the child is not Joseph's; both the child's mother and his earthly stepfather must find a way to care for him. Mary and Joseph are the first of many whose lives will be transformed by the simple act of accepting the unexpected, of being ready and willing to take up the daunting task that is set before them.

It is no accident that Luke begins with the birth of a baby, for it is a story about the infinite value of a single human being. The idea is captured perfectly by the hope and anxiety of a new mother. The story opens with a young woman, herself still barely out of childhood, and her promise to bear and nurture a child who will play a mysterious and far-reaching role in human history. Luke knows women well enough to spot Mary's musing over her unborn child's future. Her baby is a person of potentially infinite importance. In this, he is like every child in its own mother's eyes, and Mary, musing and worrying, is like every other mother.

Mary will watch her son grow, and she will worry over him; like every other child, he will be unique, he will say things that no one else ever said and do things that no one ever did before. And then, like so many other mothers of sons in restless colonial districts, she will lose him. He will find himself in trouble with the authorities; he will be too proud to save himself; the authorities will take him into custody and execute him as a criminal. His mistake, shared by other bright boys from other villages, will be to let his actions be misunderstood, to let himself be seen as of an enemy of the Roman state.

Mary will share the tragedy of every mother who has ever lost a child. Luke does not suggest that Mary knows her child's fate, but he knows, and he is aware that most of his audience know as well. It is an understatement to say that the story does not have a conventional happy ending. Yet it is not, finally, a story only of loss. In the end, the story of Mary's son is a story about the power of love. The love that shines through in her son's kindness to strangers is a powerful force; it is the power through which God has chosen to change the world. Luke knows, as he writes, that Jesus came to earth not to die, but to bring a message from his Father, that love is more powerful than death.

Mary will see quickly that her son has unusual qualities. When he is still a baby, his parents travel to Jerusalem to make a sacrifice of thanksgiving at the temple. It is a visit just like any other Jewish family would make, but the elders at prayer in the Temple Court recognize the baby as a child sent by God. The prophetess Anna foretells great things for the boy, but the venerable Simeon has both good and bad news. He hails the baby as the Messiah, the Anointed One who will save Israel. But then he turns to the boy's mother and warns that the story will have a painful outcome.

During his twelfth year, on the way home from the family's annual journey to Jerusalem for the Passover, Jesus slips away from the crowd of relatives making their way together. His parents hardly notice at first:

Thinking he was in their company, they travelled on for a day. Then they began looking for him among their relatives and friends. When they did not find him, they went back to Jerusalem to look for him. After three days they found him in the temple courts, sitting among the teachers, listening to them and asking them questions. Everyone who heard him was amazed at his understanding and his answers. (Luke 2: 44–47)

If Jesus expects to receive praise for having shown himself so at ease among the men of religion, he has yet to contend with his mother, who treats him like a normal human child. 'When his parents saw him, they were astonished. His mother said to him, "Son, why have you treated us like this? Your father and I have been anxiously searching for you."' (Luke 2: 48) This is the first foreshadowing of the fact that he will not remain with them always, and he is unapologetic. '"Why were you searching for me?" he asked. "Didn't you know I had to be in my Father's house?" But they did not understand what he was saying to them.' (Luke 2: 49–50) The boy calls attention to his disturbing future, but those around him are not yet ready. Luke closes the story with his mother's attempt to draw sense from the episode: 'Then he went down to Nazareth with them and was obedient to them. But his mother treasured all these things in her heart.' (Luke 2: 51)

Mary would remain with Jesus throughout his life on earth. This fits the typical pattern of ancient village life: kin were the core of an individual's personal network, the source of information and manpower when they needed to get something done. A man's female kin were an asset in this kind of society: they could quietly see to it that other women's sons and husbands delivered on promises; they could offer hospitality to visitors and visit other households to ask for help or to strengthen bonds of trust. When Jesus became a rabbi, Mary was to lead a group of his followers – Luke calls them 'the women who followed him from Galilee' – who appear at critical points in his story. The women stand as examples of exemplary readiness to contribute to his work, and of exemplary willingness to grapple with the meaning of his life, death, and resurrection.

The Women from Galilee

When Luke comes to tell of the ministry of Jesus, he is especially interested in families. Once Jesus has reached adulthood, he returns to Galilee after baptism at the hands of Elizabeth's son John the Baptist and forty days in the wilderness. Around the age of thirty, he begins teaching in the synagogues, first at Nazareth and then at Capernaum, a fishing village on the northern shore of the Sea of Galilee. He acquires his first disciple when a young married man, Simon, invites him into a house where someone is ill.

Jesus left the synagogue and went to the home of Simon. Now Simon's mother-in-law was suffering from a high fever, and they asked Jesus to help her. So he bent over and rebuked the fever, and it left her. She got up at once and began to wait on (*diakonei*) them. (Luke 4: 38–39)

It is in the context of this domestic healing that we first hear of Simon, who as Simon Peter will become Jesus's principal disciple. He is a normal married villager who has responsibility for his wife's mother.

Later tradition would remember Simon Peter as the prince of the Apostles and the first bishop of the city of Rome, so it is pertinent to ask where he fits into the map of households and family life that we are beginning to build up. We can begin with his house. Capernaum was excavated by a German team beginning in 1905, and special attention was paid to a stone house near the sea-front which an ancient tradition identified as the house of St Peter. Around a substantial courtyard – six metres by six metres – smaller bedrooms and utility rooms were arranged in an irregular pattern that seems to have grown over time. In the fifth century, the house was razed and a church to St Peter was built over its foundations.

There is no way to be sure that the house was Peter's, but if it was, it may shed light on what singled him out as someone who could play a leadership role among the Galilean men. The family who lived in the house were comparatively prosperous among the fishing families of the village. Their courtyard was not massive, but it could accommodate two or three dozen people if it had to. If the house was indeed Peter's, the fact that he had a meeting-space at his disposal goes a long way to explaining how he got his start.

Another of his assets may have been the women in his family. Little is known about his wife, but ancient tradition holds that he had a daughter, who grew up to become St Petronilla. Again, this can't be proved, but it shows that the early communities thought of him as a family man. And of course we know from the passage above that he had a mother-in-law.

It is telling that the first thing the mother-in-law does when Jesus heals her is to serve Jesus and his disciples. The Greek word Luke chooses to describe this act is *diakonizō*. It refers to people who provide things to others, whether modest domestic hospitality or large-scale works of charity. It is an important choice, because the term *diakonos* – which originally meant 'supporter' – was already being used informally in Luke's day, and would eventually designate an ordained leadership role.

Luke uses the word *diakonizō* frequently to characterize women's role within the community, and this reflects his sense of how communities work. In first-century Galilee and Judaea, the role of women revolved around hospitality and the work of caring, whether for children, for the sick, or for the elderly. The dedicated women who gathered around Jesus were, in all likelihood, already the providers of nursing and charitable work in the community. Ancient tradition held that Luke had been a doctor, and though we don't have firm evidence to confirm that it is true, we can certainly see why people thought so. Just as Paul worked closely with women in the cloth trade, so Luke could have worked with them in the care of the sick. This could account for why he sees the importance, in the stories about women, of aspects that one might not expect a man to notice.

One of the things Luke has noticed is women's need to make it known that they are reluctant to be the centre of attention. Female virtue in ancient Judaean society was closely associated with a kind of social invisibility. The idea that womanly influence could be dangerous was well established. The story of Adam and Eve from the Book of Genesis was told repeatedly: Eve had persuaded Adam to eat the forbidden fruit of the Tree of Knowledge, with the result that both were expelled from the Garden of Eden. Women's voices – their thoughts and ideas – were often judged against a more critical standard than were those of the men. This may account for why Luke casts the women around Jesus in roles that are recognizably useful but do not attract too much attention.

Luke also has his own reasons for stressing the women's humility. He wants to suggest that the women are able to show Jesus a loyalty and a humility that is beyond the spiritual maturity of the male disciples, whose tendency to fail Jesus – and even to betray him – is a theme of all the Gospels. To be fair, Luke probably isn't saying that women are more spiritually mature than men. Rather, he is using them as a foil to point up the men's weaknesses.

But this does not take away the fact that Luke sees the frustrations women face, including the constant discipline of being quietly useful while others crowd in to take the more obviously attractive roles. Furthermore, he remembers Jesus as a teacher who was willing to recognize the value of women's contribution. Working in partnership with a man also protected the women from being bothered by other men who resented their independent activity or simply wanted to meddle. For the women of Galilee, Jesus was invaluable as a sympathetic male focal point around which their activity could be organized. The presence of such a person in their midst would have been a godsend even if the man in question had not been a miracle-worker.

The thread of women's loyalty to Jesus is woven into the larger story of his concern for the poor and the powerless. His Sermon on the Plain preserves many of the same sayings of Jesus as Matthew's better-known Sermon on the Mount, but Luke draws a different moral from the shared material. When he comes to present the greatest of the sayings, the blessings known as the Beatitudes, he remembers them in a form that highlights how Jesus cares for the needy. Matthew remembers Jesus as saying 'Blessed are those who hunger and thirst for righteousness' (Matthew 5: 6), but Luke records the saying as simply, 'Blessed are you who hunger now' (Luke 6: 21). His Jesus adds a warning: 'But woe to you who are rich, for you have already received your comfort. Woe to you who are well fed now, for you will go hungry.' (Luke 6: 24) The original saying of Jesus had probably been 'blessed are the hungry', but Luke and Matthew remembered it in ways that reflected their own interests.

Both Matthew and Luke follow up the Beatitudes with Jesus's ethical sayings about loving one's neighbour. But Luke takes the opportunity to develop the point by including a saying that Matthew knows, but does not use here: 'Do to others as you would have them do to you.' (Luke 6: 31) By inserting this saying, Luke gives new meaning to the passage which follows, where Jesus says, 'If you love those who love you, what credit is that to you? . . . And if you do good to those who are good to you, what credit is that to you?' (Luke 6: 32–33)

Luke is building in this section towards the painful fact that Mary will lose her son, but also that he will be restored to those who love him after his death. And yet he also wants to make a simpler point, that Jesus saw and valued the bonds of love and mutual care within families. Two of the miracles from this section of his Gospel explore the theme of the power of love against death through extreme cases of miraculous healing, in which a dead family member is brought back to life.

In the first of these stories, Jesus and his disciples encounter a widow whose only son's dead body is being carried out of his village for burial. Luke knows that in Galilee a woman of the lower classes who has neither husband nor son is in a socially and economically vulnerable position. In losing her son, the widow of Nain has lost both an important human relationship and also her protector against intimidation and mistreatment. When Jesus sees the widow, he tells her not to weep, and then turns to the body laid out on the bier and commands him to arise. Luke seems to see the miracle as a gesture of kindness to the bereaved mother, rather than to the man himself: 'The dead man sat up and began to talk, and Jesus gave him back to his mother.' (Luke 7: 15)[7]

The second resurrection miracle involves a young woman, and here again, Jesus shows compassion for a parent's anxiety at the prospect of losing a child. The distraught father seeks Jesus out as he is returning from casting out demons from a herd of swine at Gerasa. 'Then a man named Jairus, a synagogue leader, came and fell at Jesus' feet, pleading with him to come to his house, because his only daughter, a girl of about twelve, was dying.' (Luke 8: 41–2)

A curious healing takes place along the way as Jesus walks with Jairus and the disciples towards the man's house. A woman steals up behind him to touch his cloak. He stops the group, and asks, 'Who touched me?', and the woman comes forward to tell him that she was ill, but the touch has cured her. Now Jesus gives his blessing: 'Daughter, your faith has healed you. Go in peace.'(Luke 8: 41) It is a digression, offering an illustration of the power of the woman's faith.

While Jesus and his companions stand with the woman, a messenger comes to Jairus to tell him bad news. '"Your daughter is dead," he said. "Do not bother the Teacher anymore." But Jesus on hearing this answered him, "Do not fear; only believe, and she will be well."' The lesson of the woman who touched his cloak is now made clear: it is faith that has the power to heal the child. So Jesus and Jairus continue to the house, where they find the family in great distress.

> . . . all the people were wailing and mourning for her. 'Stop wailing,' Jesus said. 'She is not dead but asleep.' They laughed at him, knowing that she was dead. But he took her by the hand and said: 'Child, get up.' Her spirit returned, and at once she got up. (Luke 8: 52–55)

Again, Jesus restores a dead child to its parents – in this case a young girl rather than a grown man – and along with the child, he restores the hopes that the parents have invested in a new life. Luke is laying emphasis, here, on the fragility of a parent's love for a child in the face of death. At the same time, he is underlining the power of faith to work miracles.

An earlier story in Luke's Galilean section seems to take place while Jesus is still in Nain, not long after healing the widow's son. He preaches to the crowds there, and one of the local rabbis invites Jesus to a meal in his home. Somehow a woman notorious for her sins becomes aware that Jesus is visiting, and enters the house with a flask of ointment. 'As she stood behind him at his feet weeping, she began to wet his feet with her tears. Then she wiped them with her hair, kissed them, and poured perfume on them.' (Luke 7: 38) Luke reports her behaviour without comment; bathing and anointing the feet of guests was a standard gesture of hospitality at the time.

The rest of the story focuses on the confused reaction of the host, and Jesus's own attempt to draw a moral from the incident. When Jesus allows the woman to anoint him, the rabbi takes it as a sign that he must be a charlatan, on the understanding that a genuine religious teacher would avoid contact with a woman known for her sins. But Jesus corrects the man by telling a story:

'Two people owed money to a certain money-lender. One owed him five hundred denarii, and the other fifty. Neither of them had to money to pay him back, so he forgave the debt of both. Now which of them will love him more?'

Simon replied, 'I suppose the one who had the bigger debt forgiven.'

'You have judged correctly,' Jesus said. (Luke 7: 41–43)

The moral, of course, is that whatever the woman's past, the important thing is the dedication she has shown to Jesus himself.

'Therefore I tell you, her many sins have been forgiven – as her great love has shown. But whoever has been forgiven little, loves little.'

Then Jesus said to her, 'Your sins are forgiven.'

The other guests began to say among themselves, 'Who is this who even forgives sins?'

Jesus said to the woman, 'Your faith has saved you; go in peace.' (Luke 7: 47–50)

Jesus gives the same blessing to the woman of many sins as he does to the woman who touches his cloak as he walks towards the house of Jairus. The story calls attention to the importance of love and forgiveness, and implies that even the least of women has something to teach the disciples in this respect.

The link between faith, healing, and Jesus's friendship with women is clear for Luke. When Jesus begins his tour of the district, Luke notes that his entourage included women, including some whom he had cured.

> The twelve were with him, and also some women who had been healed of evil spirits and infirmities: Mary (called Magdalene) from whom seven demons had come out; Joanna, the wife of Chuza, the manager of Herod's household; Susanna; and many others. These women were helping to support them out of their means (*diēkonoun*). (Luke 8: 1–3)

These women become Jesus's most loyal supporters. Not only do they help their teacher, they provide for him and his other disciples from their own resources. The women from Galilee will remain central to Luke's story up to the time of Jesus's death.

Another story points up Luke's interest in the family. This is the story in which Mary and the siblings of Jesus try to visit him while he is preaching and are unable to reach him through the crowd that has gathered around him.

> Now Jesus' mother and his brothers came to see him, but they but they were not able to get near him because of the crowd. Someone told him, 'Your mother and brothers are standing outside, waiting to see you.'
>
> He replied, 'My mother and brothers are those who hear God's word and put it into practice.' (Luke 8: 19–21)

There is a twist in the way Luke tells this story. It is also told by Matthew and Mark, and in their version Jesus points to the disciples and says that they are now his mother and brothers (Matthew 12:

49 and Mark 3: 34). But Luke omits this saying, which may not have been original to Jesus. Read without reference to Matthew and Mark, Luke's version can be read not as rejecting Mary and her other children, but as using them to illustrate the kind of commitment that he expects from his disciples. For Luke, if there is a single individual other than Jesus himself who embodies the ability to 'hear God's word and put it into practice', it is Mary.[8]

In the theology of later centuries, this story will be seen as problematic for a different reason as well, because it reflects Luke's memory of Jesus as one of a tribe of siblings. In the late fourth century theologians such as St Jerome began to argue that Mary had preserved her virginity throughout her life. As the idea of virginity became ever more important, theologians began to suggest that the brothers referred to here were step-brothers, half-brothers, or cousins. But there is no early tradition that suggested that Mary had no further children, and while it is possible to explain the brothers of Jesus away, to do so is to miss Luke's point about Mary. For Luke, part of what made the mother of Jesus so remarkable was not the fact that she was unusual: it was the fact that she could have been anyone.

Luke's Story of the Resurrection

When Luke comes to tell the story of Jesus's death, he calls attention to the role played by the Galilean women and tries to see things through their eyes. Like the other evangelists, he is careful to mention that the women were witnesses to the Crucifixion: 'But all those who knew him, including the women who had followed him from Galilee, stood at a distance, watching these things' (Luke 23: 49). Like the other evangelists, he remembers the women as the first to discover, when they came to anoint his body in its tomb, that Jesus had been raised from the dead.

But in the Gospel of Luke, the women's discovery completes a pattern. Repeatedly he calls attention to their faithful devotion to Jesus, suggesting that they showed a greater readiness for commitment and loyalty than the male disciples were able to muster. Luke's recounting of the story of the empty tomb develops this theme.

Jesus was executed on a Friday afternoon, and shortly thereafter, as Luke tells the story, the Galilean women visited the tomb where his body was placed, in order to assess what they would need in terms of spices and ointments for anointing his body according to ancient custom. But by the time they reached their homes it was too late to return to the tomb the same evening, since the Sabbath begins on Friday at sundown. So the women remained at home to keep the Sabbath, and returned at dawn on Sunday morning to perform the anointing.

When they arrived, however, they saw that the tomb was empty. As they stood, perplexed, two men appeared, dressed in dazzling apparel. The women were frightened, and bowed their heads. Then the angels spoke to them:

'Why do you look for the living among the dead? He is not here; he has risen! Remember how he told you, while he was still with you in Galilee, "the Son of Man must be delivered over to the hands of sinners, be crucified and on the third day be raised again".' (Luke 24: 5–7)

When the women took this news to the disciples, however, they did not find a reception appropriate to the gravity of what they had to tell. Rather, the Apostles treated them with scorn: 'But they did not believe the women, because their words seemed to them like nonsense.' (Luke 24: 11)

Luke does not seem to be surprised by this reaction. In fact, he often underlines the readiness of the women to accept the Gospel message in contrast to the uncertainty of the supposedly superior men. But Luke turns away from the women here. They hear the news, they receive it with good grace, and then they move offstage, although they will reappear later. He has a different story of the Resurrection to tell from that of the other Gospel-writers, and he will return to describe the Galilean women's straightforward love and trust. But first he has a disturbing story to tell, about how the male disciples came to perceive the triumph of love over death.

Later that day, towards evening, two of the men had an experience which opened their hearts. As they were walking north-west from Jerusalem towards the village of Emmaus, they were trying to understand what had happened. Not only had they lost their teacher, a man whom they had loved and whom they had believed to be the son of God, but they had also been deprived of the consolation of a proper burial. This was crushing, and even worse, it was a loss that could not be soothed through the normal ways of caring for the beloved dead. It was a story without a proper ending; given what the women had told them, the men couldn't even be sure that Jesus was dead. At least, by talking about what had happened, they could perhaps attain some kind of equilibrium.

As they made their way, they became aware of a stranger walking alongside them, and he asked what they were talking about. They stopped to enquire whether he had heard what had happened – about the prophet Jesus of Nazareth, his execution and the mysterious fact of his empty tomb. They told him that the women in their group claimed to have seen two angels who said that Jesus was still alive. Now the stranger surprised them. It emerged that he was a rabbi of great learning, and he began to tell them about the ancient prophecies that had foretold the coming of the Messiah.

When the three reached Emmaus, the rabbi seemed intent on walking further. But the disciples called his attention to the fact that night would soon fall, and persuaded him to stay overnight with them at Emmaus. This act of hospitality was another way of remembering Jesus, for he had given his disciples to understand that every act of kindness to those in need was an act of love towards himself.

Later, during the evening meal, the stranger broke bread and gave thanks, just as Jesus had done on the night before his crucifixion.

Their beloved teacher had told them, whenever they should eat bread or drink wine, to do it in memory of him. Now, the disciples became aware that something miraculous had happened. They had understood that they should treat the stranger among them as if he were Jesus. But then they grasped that this stranger actually *was* Jesus. Their own teacher had returned to life, just as the women had told them he would. He had come to help them in their distress, and perhaps to test them. There was no way to be sure, for as soon as they recognized him, he disappeared.

> Then their eyes were opened and they recognized him, and he disappeared from their sight. They asked each other, 'Were not our hearts burning within us while he talked with us on the road and opened the Scriptures to us?' (Luke 24: 31–32)

In telling the Emmaus story, Luke seems to want to emphasize a number of points. The first, of course, is the spiritual fact of the living Jesus. Death is not powerful enough to quell his promise that he would remain with them always. What the angels had told the women was true. The men should take their simple willingness to trust what the angels had said as an example.

At the same time, Luke does not despise the men's need for a more dramatic sign. He understands how difficult it is to come to terms with a painful loss. And even if one is told that the loss isn't real, it is very difficult to believe it when there is nothing concrete to hold on to. This is why the resurrected Jesus seeks out his disciples at Emmaus. He wants to help them to make sense of what has happened. He also wants to show them how to make his presence real during the long years to come.

Luke's message here can be understood in a number of ways. On the one hand, he is trying to imagine the loss that the disciples felt at the death of Jesus. Now, years later, the pain has dulled, and he wants to make it real again, real for those who were not there, who never knew Jesus in the flesh. On the other hand, our writer is telling a story of consolation. The disciples have lost their beloved teacher and when he returns to console them, he reminds them that he has already given them, in the shared breaking of bread, a way to conjure his presence among them again and again. The appearance at Emmaus is a fleeting consolation, but the moment that they recognize him he is already gone again. His presence among them is difficult to capture, to fix. But it is his elusive presence that they must learn to watch for.

Luke is also saying something far more challenging about Jesus and the power of his love. He wants his audience to see that the Resurrection is the heart of what Jesus came into the world to do. It is not simply a miracle or a magic trick; it is something far greater than that and completely different – a manifestation of love. The story of the mysterious stranger is meant to convey the disarming reality of this love. Love is not bound by time in the normal way of mortal affairs. It has the power to upset the order of things. Whether in humility or in majesty, Jesus has conquered death, and he has done so by the power of his love. The disciples must not – cannot – forget the love Jesus has shown them. He will never leave them.

Luke knows how difficult it is to capture the attention of a reader or a listener. So he creates a space for his audience's distractedness with the distractedness of the disciples. In this way he shows that Jesus recognizes how easy it is to miss something that is so difficult to understand, difficult to believe, difficult even to hear. It is so easy to disregard the excited voice of a woman, so easy to miss the question in the eyes of a stranger. In telling the story of Emmaus, Luke wants to make vivid the fact that love is stronger than absence, it is stronger than death. It is stronger, even, than the disciples' own weakness.

The brief story of the supper at Emmaus carries within it a number of core principles of the Christian life as Luke understands it. First, the idea that one comes to know Christ through acts of generosity to other human beings. It is because of their kindness to a stranger that the disciples find the beloved teacher whom they had lost.

Second, there is the idea that they can conjure his presence in prayer and in communal acts such as the breaking of bread – by remembering his life, death, and resurrection – even in an undistinguished house in an anonymous village. The simple acts of generosity and community in daily life are the acts that make real the living presence of Jesus.

Finally, there is the importance of listening to the voices of those in the community who speak from a position of service. It was not to Simon Peter that the Resurrection was announced, but rather to the women who had shouldered the humble but essential task of caring for the lifeless body of their former teacher. From the courage of Mary, accepting the risk of bringing a fatherless child into the world, to the attentiveness of the Galilean women at Jesus's death and Resurrection, the Gospel of Luke framed the story of the ministry of Jesus as a reflection of the heroic reality behind the everyday life of families.

Women's Mission and Women's Preaching

We have seen by now that Luke doesn't think of women's authority as something unusual, or a problem to be solved – it is simply a part of the landscape. Yet there are traces of evidence to suggest that in the second century a battle was fought over the role of women. There is evidence that a number of traditions from the early period were 'edited out' as bishops began, around the end of the second century, to compile lists of sources which they understood to be authentic traditions handed down without alteration from the circle around Jesus. At this stage, a number of sources celebrating women disciples seem to have been excluded.

'Canon' is Greek for 'measuring stick', and the New Testament canon was a collection of texts that were understood to embody the measure against which the value of other texts could be assessed.

Some sources that were eventually accepted in the canon, such as the Book of Revelation, were hotly debated during the second century. Others were believed to be ancient and valuable, but left out of the canon because they contained ideas that not all could agree were those of the Apostles themselves. A third group were suspected of having been written dishonestly by later writers, who tried to put their own ideas into the mouths of Jesus and the early Apostles.

Perhaps the most contentious of the sources, which were eventually classed as non-canonical, are the gospels that claim to preserve the teaching of disciples other than Matthew, Mark, Luke, and John. The dates of many of these 'other gospels' are uncertain. Some preserve first-century traditions, while others seem to have been written afresh in the second or third century. Some are simply impossible to date.

One of the most important of these ancient narratives is the enigmatic Gospel of Mary, which tells how Jesus imparted some of his most precious teachings to a disciple named Mary – which Mary is uncertain – and how she struggled to convince the male Apostles to listen to what Jesus had told her. The Gospel of Mary was written in the first or second century and then forgotten for centuries, and only rediscovered at the end of the nineteenth century. The text as we know it today is incomplete, surviving in three overlapping fragments of different lengths.

An early third-century papyrus fragment, now in the John Rylands Library in Manchester, preserves an important segment of the narrative. In the Manchester fragment, Mary speaks to three of the male disciples, revealing what the Saviour has told her in private, and the men react with uncertainty to her revelation. The passage expands on a memory also preserved in Luke's Gospel, that after his Resurrection, Jesus spoke first to the women. Both Luke and the Gospel of Mary agree that when the women tried to tell the male disciples what had happened, they were met with disbelief, the only marked difference being that in the Gospel of Mary, Mary is not with the other women.

Peter and Andrew were disturbed by Mary's revelation that Jesus had entrusted her with a message for the disciples. Andrew believed that what she had to say must be false, because he and the other men would have recognized any genuine teaching of Jesus. He was sure that true teaching would strike them as familiar because they knew his way of thinking. Peter's objection was more personal. He did not like the fact that Jesus had spoken privately to Mary, when he could just as easily have addressed the gathered group. However, he does not directly accuse Mary of telling a falsehood. Instead, he takes the dismissive tactic of suggesting that, by definition, anything Jesus said in private to a woman could not be important. But the third man, Levi, defended the idea that Jesus could have chosen Mary to deliver a particular teaching.

> Levi says to Peter, 'Peter, thy angry temper is ever with thee and even now you question the woman as though you were her adversary. If the Saviour deemed her worthy, who are you to despise her? For He, who knew her well, truly loved her. So let us be ashamed, and, acting like proper men, let us do what has been commanded, to preach the Gospel without making rules or laying down laws other than the Saviour gave.' When he had spoken in this way, Levi left, and began to preach the Gospel according to Mary.[9]

Clearly, Levi represents the writer's own point of view here. The anonymous writer acts as Mary's champion and defends her teaching against Peter's hostility.

The argument between the four disciples seems to be our anonymous writer's way of exploring the different positions being taken by the men and women of his own day on the question of an alternative tradition being handed down by women. But he is also expressing his concern that the Church is changing, and not for the better. In his eyes, Peter seems to represent the voice of a faction in the community which wants to 'make rules or lay down laws other than the Saviour gave' – in other words, a group that wants to develop an institutional structure to replace the more fluid and informal movement of the early decades. This was clearly a topical warning after the death of the disciples who had known Jesus. Levi thinks that the new rules are a way of drawing the community away from fulfilling its task of preaching the gospel. The anonymous writer seems to be using Levi to suggest that too much emphasis on authority from the 'Peter faction' is stifling the Church.

The date of the Gospel of Mary is uncertain, but what is clear is that it was written at a time when the structures of authority in the churches were beginning to be more formal, or perhaps when a debate was emerging about whether the structures *ought* to become more formal. This offers a contrast to Luke, who sees roles in the community as fluid, including the position of women. He sometimes offers women as an example of morally attractive humility and single-minded devotion to Jesus; at other times he sees them as flawed in just the same way as men. So, for example, Mary of Bethany and the Prodigal Son both demonstrate a heightened devotion to Jesus despite their lack of standing within the family, while Martha and the Prodigal's older brother are asked to be generous from their own position of acknowledged leadership. All this means that the debate reflected in the Gospel of Mary was, among other things, a matter of growing pains. The movement had grown organically out of existing friendships and family networks, and at the end of the first century it began the long transition to a more institutional structure.

4

'THE GOD OF THECLA'

'Burn the lawless one! Burn her that is no bride in the midst of the theatre, that all the women who have been taught by this man may be afraid!'[1]

Among the mother–daughter arguments preserved in ancient literature, the most disturbing is the face-off between an early Christian saint, Thecla of Iconium, and her mother. In the passage here, the mother stands before Castellius, governor of the province of Galatia in Asia Minor (modern Turkey). Thecla has been called before the governor as an enemy of the gods of Rome; she is seen as subversive and dangerous because of her association with a Christian holy man. When Thecla's mother is called before the governor to vouch for her daughter, she refuses to do so. Instead, she condemns Thecla as a criminal.

Second-century writers remembered Thecla as one of the female companions of the Apostle Paul. No reference to her survives in Paul's own letters, and Luke, too, fails to mention her, so her story may well have been a pious creation of the second century. One of the principal characters in the story, Tryphaena, appears in Paul's list of greetings to the women of the community in Rome, but this does not help us to judge whether there is a kernel of truth in the story. It was not uncommon for second-century writers to take a figure from the earlier literature and imagine a story around them, rather like a modern historical novel. It has been suggested that the *Acts of Paul and Thecla* was based on stories that had been handed down orally by women, and this is certainly possible, though the version that survives would have been the product of literary reworking. Whatever the case, Thecla's story shows that ancient readers were hungry for detail about the lives of Paul's women. The story begins with Paul travelling in Galatia and preaching in the house of Onesiphorus, another figure who appears in Paul's letters as well as Luke's Book of Acts.

> While Paul was speaking in the gathering at the house of Onesiphorus, a certain virgin called Thecla, the daughter of Theocleia and the fiancée of a man called Thamyris, was sitting at a window close by, and listened night and day to his preaching . . . and never looked away from the window, but paid close attention to what she heard, and rejoiced greatly. She saw numerous women going into the house to be near Paul, and she, too, had an eager desire to be in the same room with him and to hear the word of Christ, for she had never laid eyes on Paul, but only heard his voice.[2]

This vignette of Thecla sitting at the window and listening to the words that will change her life begins a marvellous tale of adventure, which became one of the most popular stories of early Christian literature. According to the tale, Thecla left home to travel as a missionary for the new faith: first alongside Paul, and eventually alone, with the Apostle's blessing. It is not certain whether the story of Thecla's travels has any basis in fact, but it tells us a great deal about how Paul was remembered by later communities. The most important recollection is Paul's warning that because the end of the world is coming, a radical change of life is required. The young should give up the hope of a good marriage and remain virgins instead.

In the *Acts of Paul and Thecla*, the heroine decides to act on Paul's message as soon as she hears it. Thecla rushes to her mother to announce that she no longer intends to marry her fiancé. This leads to an argument between mother and daughter, and to a series of scenes in which the fiancé and the mother commiserate about how independent-minded Thecla has become, and try, unsuccessfully, to undermine her in her resolve. Like an angry modern adolescent, Thecla runs away from home when her mother refuses to listen to her. She intends to follow Paul as he travels from town to town. Later, she will strike out on her own, departing with Paul's blessing to preach and baptize in her own right.

Theocleia's harsh reaction to her daughter's conversion – 'Burn the lawless one!' – is more than simply the reaction of a parent who has been provoked beyond endurance by a difficult child. The story is designed to show how the new faith had turned the world upside down. Christian literature of the period is full of stories of families that had been torn apart by religion. Mothers had been set against daughters, and brothers against brothers. Parents felt it was their duty to steer their children towards piety for the old gods.

Judaism had successfully renewed its status as a legitimate minority religion despite the troubles in Judaea, but the Christians were still seen, in the second century, as enemies of the Roman order. As long as the Roman Empire lasted there would be adherents of the old state religion – the people for whom the Christians coined the name 'pagans' – who would argue that tolerance for Christianity could only undermine Rome's good standing in the eyes of her gods.

By the second century, Paul was remembered not only as predicting the end of the world, but also as preaching against marriage, one of the central institutions of the Roman social order. This wasn't quite Paul's point: he had suggested that since the world was about to end, people should not make plans for the future. Marrying and having children, divorcing and manumitting slaves all came under the category of actions which didn't make sense if the future wasn't going to happen. But by the second century, at least some Christians remembered him as preaching that by refusing to marry or have children Christians could prove their loyalty to God.

The story of Thecla fits this pattern perfectly. Our writer tells us that Thecla has reached a marriageable age – this meant the early teens in first- and second-century Asia Minor. The action begins when she sits at an open window and hears Paul preaching the message of virginity in the courtyard of a nearby house. We are invited to marvel at the intensity of her commitment when she decides to follow the new ideal. When her mother and fiancé realize what Thecla means to do, and express their disappointment, her response is to ignore them.

> And those who were in the house wept bitterly, Thamyris for the loss of a wife, Theocleia for that of a daughter, the maidservants for that of a mistress. So there was a great confusion of mourning in the house. And while all this was going on (all around her) Thecla did not turn away, but gave her whole attention to Paul's word.[3]

It is Thamyris who decides that Paul should be taken to the governor. Our writer tells us that Thamyris is a powerful man from an important family. In the normal way of things at this time, he would have been in his mid twenties, nearly twice his bride's age. In the story, the governor is willing to consider his charge against the girl, that her subversive views are a threat to public safety. But her accuser's motive is purely personal. He hides behind the idea that the Christians are dangerous, but the reality is that he sees Paul as a rival for Thecla's affections. No matter that Paul has made it clear that he doesn't want to marry her himself – he wants her not to marry at all.

In the logic of the story, Thamyris wants to destroy Thecla if he cannot have her himself. It is essentially an honour killing: the groom is an important man in the town and he feels that his honour will be ruined if he lets his prospective bride insult him in this way. More disturbingly, he expects – possibly correctly – that the Roman governor will take his word for it that the child is a menace to society. The story illustrates vividly the threatening environment that a young woman might face when she reached the threshold of adulthood in the Roman period.

It is harder to understand why Thecla's mother would take his side against her own child. Would a first-century mother really have reacted so violently to her daughter's religious conversion? It isn't impossible. The father is nowhere in sight in the narrative, so the mother, Theocleia, is probably an independent female head of household, perhaps a widow. Since they live in the Roman colony of Iconium, she may well be a citizen woman of the kind we know were part of Paul's circle.

But it is also possible that the parents were not married in the first place, since if the child was born in wedlock the governor would expect the father or the father's family to appear in court on the minor's behalf. Other sources show that widows often found themselves without close male kin on either side, and had to fend for themselves in the Roman legal system, so it is impossible to be sure. In either case, Theocleia would have been thrilled at the prospect of acquiring a powerful son-in-law.

It has to be said that the story of Thecla probably tells us more about its second-century writer than it does about the historical Paul and his followers. It is drawn from an important group of narratives that are well known to historians but almost completely unknown outside scholarly circles: the second- and third-century romances known as the *Apocryphal Acts of the Apostles*. They are called 'apocryphal' – which means 'hidden away' – because they were not included in the collection of holy texts that became established as the New Testament. Their writers would not have made this distinction, since the canon of the New Testament was not yet established in their day: it only began to take shape towards the end of the second century, and the list of books to be included did not begin to settle until over a century later, in the time of Constantine the Great.[4]

The *Apocryphal Acts* grew out from the canonical Acts of the Apostles written by the author of the Gospel of Luke. Acts solved a problem for the early Christians by explaining how the churches built by Paul traced their roots back to Jesus and his disciples, and the *Apocryphal Acts* built on this theme, each following a single disciple, such as Paul, Andrew, Peter, or Thomas. They are written in a style similar to modern magical fiction, and they seem to have been intended as something between popular history and pious entertainment. The historian cannot rely on them as trustworthy sources for the first-century events they describe. But they had an enthusiastic readership, and even the more fantastic tales were designed to see the world in a way the readers of antiquity would find compelling. This means that we can learn something from them about the second-century readers, if not the first-century characters.

One of the aims of the *Apocryphal Acts* was to explain, to the satisfaction of second-century readers, how the faith had spread so quickly. A single individual could travel hundreds of miles by ship along the ancient trade routes, but the individual carrying the message had to be outstandingly magnetic, and very good at persuading others to carry the message as well. This, of course, is exactly what we are told about Paul and his disciple Thecla.

The idea of Thecla sitting at an open window and listening to Paul preaching in a nearby house captured the imagination of both women and men in the second and third centuries. Her decision to turn away from her expected role as a wife and mother in order to follow the Apostle became a persistent point of reference for Christian women in the centuries to come. Like Mary, Thecla was remembered as a figure who captured the central ideal of the Christian community. To hear the word of God was an invitation to reconsider every aspect of one's life. Hearing the word meant giving up hopes and expectations that did not serve God's plan for humanity, and even refusing to fulfil obligations, however pious they might otherwise seem.

Put straightforwardly into practice, this kind of thinking could lead to a world in which daughters refused to obey their parents, and mothers declined to care for their children. So from the end of the first century, if not earlier, a complementary line of reasoning developed in Christian thought, to remind the faithful that the duties and obligations of family life had their own moral value. Many Christians believed that the faith community itself could – and perhaps should – offer the kind of safety and support that characterizes a good family.[5]

The Gospel of John recalled Jesus speaking from the Cross to his mother, who stood vigil alongside her sister and Mary Magdalene. He called out to her and pointed to the beloved disciple. 'He said to her [his mother], "Woman, here is your son," and to the disciple, "Here is your mother!" From that time on, this disciple took her into his home' (John 19: 26–27). The family of faith were expected to provide for Mary in her old age, even though she had a surviving adult son, whom Paul called 'James, the Lord's brother' (Galatians 1: 19).

Already in the middle of the first century, the Apostle Paul had wanted the Christian communities to assume responsibility for women – widows and fatherless daughters – who had no other protection. These female communities, which began as a form of organized charity, also constituted the earliest Christian monasteries. It was helpful if the moral standing of these women was irreproachable, so the female communities had stringent disciplinary norms, which were later reflected in the ideal of Christian virginity. A second-century writer suggested that the widows of each community should be enrolled on an official list (1 Timothy 5: 9–10). This was an attempt to keep track of who received financial support from the churches, but it was also an acknowledgement that the women enrolled as widows were perceived as representatives of the Christian community.

It should not surprise us that when second-century men and women mused about the earlier generations, the stories they chose to tell often turned on what Paul and the other Apostles had thought about marriage and family. Paul had told his followers to be constantly at the ready for the end to come without warning, putting it vividly to the Christians at Thessalonica: 'It will come like a thief in the night' (1 Thessalonians 5: 2). Marriage and family were a

way of making plans for the here and now, an unbecoming invest-
ment in a world that would pass away. But the early Christians were
part of a society that revolved around families and the ancient
commandment to be fruitful and multiply. How would they cope
with the idea that to marry and beget children was somehow to
betray the hope that God would gather His chosen people at the
end of time?

Paul had expected the end of the world to take place within his
own lifetime, and had thus discouraged his followers from making
plans for their private lives. In 1 Corinthians 7: 26–27, he says,
'Because of the present crisis I think it is good for a person to remain
as he is. Are you pledged to a woman? Do not seek to be released.
Are you free from such a commitment? Do not look for a wife. But
if you do marry, you have not sinned.' To embrace new responsibilities simply seemed an unnecessary risk that might aggravate the
distress of the coming end-time. Later generations built on this idea
and intensified it, remembering Paul as the founder of a cult of
virginity. But Paul's words meant one thing in the context of the
end to the world, and perhaps something very different to those
who had to wait, generation after generation, for an end that never
seemed to come.

The majority of early Christian households revolved around
feeding and clothing the young, and tending both young and old
when they became ill. Our sources do not give us much detail about
this 'silent majority'. It is almost as if the ancient Christian writers
took it for granted that the needs and interests of the average family
were well known, and thus concentrated their energies on recording
the exotic and the bizarre. Thus we hear a great deal in the second-
century sources about families whose offspring became ascetics and
martyrs, but rather less about Christian families who were conventional in their attitudes and got along well with their neighbours.
'Normal' families were not interesting enough to write about.

The story of a family torn apart by religion, by contrast, was one
in which anybody would be interested. Second- and third-century

writers repeatedly developed the theme of conflict within the household, exploring what would happen if a single family member, usually a child on the verge of maturity, were to convert to Christianity. The convert's biological family would throw up obstacles to the new faith, complaining that they could not see why it was necessary to make so many sacrifices for the sake of an unknown god.

'The God of Thecla'

After Thecla is brought before the governor of Galatia, her story takes an alarming turn. With Paul, she leaves Galatia and travels towards Antioch of Pisidia, with the intent that Paul will preach the word of God and that Thecla will accompany him as his disciple. But as soon as they arrive in Antioch, they encounter a seemingly insurmountable obstacle. A local dignitary, Alexander, falls in love with Thecla. She refuses his advances and insults him, and he reacts with humiliation and fury. Before long, she is facing another Roman governor, this time the governor of Pisidia.

At Antioch, Thecla is condemned to the beasts. It is a form of punishment which was not widely used in Thecla's own day, but it became widespread in the provinces just over a century later, around the time the *Acts of Paul and Thecla* were probably written.[6]

The story of Thecla and the beasts at Antioch is a marvellous fantasy of female solidarity. When she is condemned to the beasts, 'the women of the city were greatly amazed, and cried out to the governor's seat, "an evil judgement!", "an impious judgement!".' Thecla is placed under house arrest until the contest, but the individual who takes her into custody is 'a certain rich queen, Tryphaena, whose daughter had died'. The two become fast friends. On the day before the contest, Thecla is placed on the back of a lioness to be carried in the procession advertising the morrow's games, sporting a sign on which her accusation, 'guilty of sacrilege', is written.[7]

Thecla is returned to the custody of Tryphaena, to be held until the beginning of the games on the following day. But Tryphaena has seen her lost daughter, Falconilla, in a dream vision, and the child has asked that Thecla pray for her. So the pagan Tryphaena asks Thecla to pray to her own god for Falconilla, even as she fears for Thecla's own life. At dawn, the evil Alexander, the sponsor of the games, comes to take Thecla away. Tryphaena refuses to relinquish the girl, offering a prayer to 'the god of Thecla' that she not lose her second daughter – by this she means Thecla – while she is still mourning for the first.

When Thecla is delivered into the arena, again she finds friends among the crowd and among the beasts. A ferocious lioness running towards her lies down at her feet, submitting to Thecla as her mistress, while the women in the crowd cheer. Then the lioness tears apart the two male animals – a bear and a lion – that attack Thecla, although the lioness herself is killed in the second contest. As other beasts are released into the arena, Thecla simply stands still, stretches out her arms, and prays to her powerful God.

What happens next crosses the line into the fantastical. Thecla's eye falls on a tank filled with man-eating seals and, casting caution aside, she decides that the time has come to effect the baptism she has been waiting for. 'And she threw herself in, saying "In the name of Jesus Christ I baptize myself on the last day."' Now not only are the women in the crowd weeping, but the governor is too: the prospect of a beautiful child being devoured by the sea-creatures touches the hearts of all concerned. 'So then, she cast herself into the water in the name of Jesus Christ: and the seals, seeing the light of a flash of fire, floated dead on top of the water. And there a cloud of fire around her, so that the beasts did not touch her, nor could her naked body be seen.' This miracle leads to a truly bizarre scene in the arena. When a new array of beasts is released, the women in the crowd begin to shriek and throw sweet-smelling offerings into the arena – nard, cassia and balsam – 'so that there was a multitude of odours, and all the beasts that were thus struck were held as it were in sleep, and did not touch her'. Alexander then offers 'exceedingly fearful' bulls to the governor, who frowns but allows them, and Thecla is tied between the animals in order that they may pull her apart.[8]

Thecla is miraculously freed and Tryphaena, who has been waiting by the entrance to the arena, falls into a faint. Now the governor stops the games. Because Tryphaena is a relative of the emperor, everyone is afraid that there will be retribution against Antioch if she is harmed while she is staying there. Alexander falls at the governor's feet, and asks that Thecla be released. Whether for this reason or by coincidence, Tryphaena recovers and embraces Thecla, announcing that she has seen the truth of the Resurrection of the dead which Thecla has preached, and that she will now adopt Thecla as her child and heir to her worldly riches. The two return to Tryphaena's house. 'Thecla remained for eight days, teaching her the word of God, so that the greater part of the maidservants also believed, and there was great joy in the house.' There is a curious charm to the tableau of Thecla ensconced in yet another all-female household, holding forth learnedly on the word of God to an adoring audience.

There are certainly elements of fantasy in the story of Thecla's contest at Antioch. At the same time it reflects realities of the late second century. From the end of the first century, there is evidence of Christians being charged with sacrilege or disrespect to the gods – a capital crime – and by the late second century Christians were among the criminals condemned to the beasts. Around the same time as the *Acts of Paul and Thecla* were written, an open letter was circulated by the Christians at Lugdunum in Gaul (modern Lyons), describing a terrifying episode in which a number of Christians had been interrogated, tortured, and condemned to public execution in the arena.

It is difficult to know how often executions of this kind really took place. Numerous stories of martyrs survive from antiquity, but many of them were written a century or more after the fact, and may contain an element of wishful thinking. Later communities, in remembering the holy men and women of the past about whom little was known, would sometimes invent heroic stories to honour their memory. But the Lugdunum account is one of a small number of texts that most scholars believe to be authentic, and at least some second-century Christian writers definitely believed that Christians were being condemned to the beasts.

The Christian apologist Tertullian believed that these spectacular executions were being used to quell urban unrest that had nothing to do with Christianity at all. In a defence of the Christians addressed to the Roman governor of North Africa around 197, he put it thus: 'If the Tiber rises as high as the city walls, if the Nile does not send its waters up over the fields, if the heavens give no rain, if there is an earthquake, if there is famine or pestilence, straightway the cry is, "Away with the Christians to the lion!"'[9]

The letter from Lugdunum describes an uprising of mob violence against the Christians. The writer tells us that Christians were stoned and battered and dragged into the forum by an enraged mob for interrogation; they were then held in prison until the arrival of the governor, whose authority to offer a formal judgement against them the crowd was required to respect. The authorities were being called upon to appease the blood-lust of an angry crowd, rather than a more orderly judicial procedure. The Christians at Lugdunum were a despised minority and the unruly majority could enact hate crimes against them and expect the government to condone their action.

The Lugdunum martyrs included Christians of both sexes, different ages, and diverse walks of life. Among them were a slave, Blandina, and her earthly mistress. The mistress, whose name is not remembered, was terrified that she was too delicate to endure the treatment that awaited the group without seeming to fail in boldness. It is clear that the values of the group expected an equally fierce determination from the women as from the men. The slave Blandina was tortured repeatedly during the interrogation. This may reflect an ancient law that evidence given by a slave against his or her master must be given under torture. The law discouraged slaves from offering false testimony against their masters, but also protected slaves who revealed incriminating truths, since the slave was expected to fear the torture more than recrimination from the master. Blandina, however, 'was filled with such power that even those who were taking turns to torture her in every way from dawn to dusk were weary and exhausted. They themselves admitted that they were beaten, and that there was nothing further that they could do to her.'[10]

Our writer explains that a special day of gladiatorial games was arranged to dispense with the Christians in the arena at Lugdunum; here, too, Blandina was outstanding among the heroes of the faith. Her suffering in the arena was explicitly Christ-like:

> Blandina was hung on a post and exposed as bait for the wild animals that were let loose on her. She seemed to hang there in the form of a cross, and by her fervent prayer she aroused intense enthusiasm in those who were undergoing their own ordeal, for in their torment, with their physical eyes they saw in their sister Him who was crucified for them.[11]

Like Thecla, the animals refused to touch her, so she was taken down again, and taken back to prison to be held for a later contest. This was a stroke of good fortune for her companions: 'Tiny, weak, and insignificant as she was, she would give inspiration to her brothers, for she had put on Christ.' On the last day of the games, she was brought out with one of the younger Christians, Ponticus, whom she encouraged and supported until he was torn apart by the beasts. Only when the others had gone ahead did she join them in martyrdom:[12]

> The blessed Blandina was last of all: like a noble mother encouraging her children, she sent them before her in triumph to the King, and then, after duplicating in her own body all her children's sufferings, she hastened to rejoin them, rejoicing and glorying in her death as though she had been invited to a bridal banquet instead of being a victim of the beasts.[13]

Blandina's death is described as a progressive union with her Lord. She is tossed by an enraged bull, but 'she no longer perceived what was happening because of the hope and possession of all she believed in and because of her intimacy with Christ'. It is a fitting ending to her story: 'Thus she too was offered in sacrifice, while the pagans themselves admitted that no woman had ever suffered so much in their experience.' Our author never tells us what became of Blandina's mistress, but at least one Christian woman in Lugdunum was able to confound the pagans through a show of superhuman endurance.[14]

Blandina shows that there are different ways to be a heroine. Thecla's story is that of a child who attracts love and indignant protection from all the female creatures who encounter her. But Blandina plays a number of roles all at once: she is a servant, a bride, and a mother. While Thecla attracts the protection and encouragement of others, Blandina is the source of spiritual power for her community. The author of the Lugdunum account wanted to show that anyone, even a slave-woman, could put on Christ, and others could see Christ in her. A heroine like Blandina, able to turn in a towering performance despite being 'tiny, weak, and insignificant' in the eyes of the world, was everything a writer could hope for.

Through the trials and achievements of a beloved heroine like Thecla or Blandina, we can catch a glimpse of what ancient readers valued. Our writer is interested in how others – and in particular the pagans – will react to the Christian performance in the arena. If the Christians condemned to suffer are able to live up to their ideals, the public executions become opportunities to make the faith more broadly known and admired. But the emphasis on death in the narratives had another interest as well, especially for women.

Ordinary women in the ancient Mediterranean lived intimately with death. It was a daily presence in a way that is simply unfathomable in the modern world, at least in societies that have adequate access to modern medicine. Tending the illnesses of children and the aged was a staple of women's sphere of responsibility. Even a strong adult man could be snatched by fever within a matter of hours, and weaker members of a family were even more vulnerable. So the idea that Christians of both genders and all ages could accept death with heroic courage was an idea with real pastoral value.

'Go and Preach the Word of God'

We left Thecla in Antioch of Pisidia, safely ensconced in the house of Tryphaena after her ordeal in the arena, and teaching the word of God to the queen and her maidservants. But our heroine is soon restless and ready to move on to the next challenge. After a week, our author tells us, Thecla has begun to yearn for Paul, and she sends out messengers in every direction to try to find out where he has gone. Finally, she discovers that he is preaching at Myra, not far away, on the south coast. 'And she took young men and maids, and sewed her mantle into a cloak after the fashion of a man, and girded herself, and left for Myra.' What Thecla wants, it soon becomes clear, is not to follow Paul as his disciple, but rather to tell him what she herself has done. 'She said to him, "I have received the washing, O Paul"' – by this she means baptism – '"for He who worked together with you in the Gospel has worked with me also in the baptizing."' Paul receives her warmly, and brings her to the house of Hermias, the woman who is hosting him, and a group gathers there to hear Thecla's tale. When she has finished speaking, and the group have prayed for Tryphaena, Thecla rises to leave. Paul offers her his blessing, '"Go, and teach the word of God."'[15]

The story ends with Thecla's return to Iconium, to visit the house of Onesiphorus, where she first heard Paul speak, and to make her peace with her mother. Then she leaves again, for Seleucia on the south coast, where we are told that she 'enlightened many with the word of God'.

To a modern reader, it is quite surprising that the *Acts of Paul and Thecla* takes it for granted that Thecla wants to strike out on her own as an apostle, rather than playing sidekick to the great man. But in the ancient Christian environment, where female-run households seem to have been quite standard, Thecla's preference does not even seem to require comment. Our writer makes sure, however, to let us know that Paul was happy to give his blessing. Later generations would remember Thecla as the 'first apostle among women' – a designation which she holds in the Greek Orthodox Church to this day.

Yet there is evidence that in the late second century, at least some women embraced Thecla's example with such enthusiasm that it led to controversy. The North African writer Tertullian tells us of a group who allowed both women and men to perform sacred tasks such as baptism. Thecla's self-baptism, they claimed, was an example for other women, so the practice had Paul's authority. But Tertullian himself did not agree. He seems to have seen performing baptism as an activity reserved for men, and the general trend in the third and fourth centuries would follow his lead.[16]

The leaders of second-century Christian communities found them-selves in a curious position. Theirs was a community that had always thought of itself as a brotherhood of wandering prophets and apos-tles who were waiting for the end of the world. As a result, efforts to develop institutional rules and roles were originally frowned upon as a sign of uncertainty about whether the end was really coming.

But over time, communities naturally developed traditions and habits, even if they were only loosely organized. Both Jesus and Paul had spoken of the special importance of communal meals, but arrangements for community gatherings were still quite fluid. By the second century, however, it was becoming clear that the end was going to take longer to arrive than expected. As a result, commu-nities began to look for long-term solutions to the problem of how to organize themselves.

In the first and second centuries, travelling prophets and apostles were still in circulation. All agreed that many were bearers of the spirit of God who could bring messages to the faithful. Great defer-ence must be shown to them: prophets and apostles were shown the respect owed to the spirit of God. Yet as it became known that Christians would offer hospitality to strangers and shower them with gifts, swindlers sometimes tried to take advantage of this goodwill. So a trusted senior member of the community, a bishop (*episkopos*, literally 'supervisor' or 'overseer'), would interview each holy visitor to establish whether he or she was in good faith. By the second century, it seems to have been agreed that each community should have only one bishop, though there might well be more than one community in a given place.

At its best, this makeshift system meant that prophets and apostles could foster connections among the isolated communities of the small towns and villages. But there were sometimes tensions between the resident bishops and travelling prophets. A Christian manual of community life written towards the end of the first century, known as the *Didache* ('Teaching'), describes the difficult situation faced by Christian communities when a prophet or apostle came to call. The *Didache* warns that some visitors would even try to turn the community against its bishop, and offers advice for how the bishop could hold his own against a newcomer. The communities were edging, reluctantly, towards establishing an institutional hierarchy, and sometimes there were growing pains.[17]

Paul had mentioned in his First Letter to the Corinthians that Christians shared bread and wine in memory of the Last Supper of Jesus, but our first description of a Christian Eucharist, or meal of thanksgiving – *eucharisto* literally means 'I give thanks' – dates to the middle of the second century. The apologist Justin Martyr (d. 164) offers a description of a communal meal to which a newly baptized person was invited to join.

> We lead him . . . to those who are called the brethren, where they gather together to say prayers . . . we greet each other with a kiss when the prayers are finished. Then bread and a cup of water and wine are brought to the president of the brethren, and he having received them sends up praise and glory to the

> Father of all through the name of His Son and the Holy Ghost, and makes a long thanksgiving . . . when these prayers and thanksgivings are ended all the people present cry 'Amen!'[18]

After the prayers, the president gives thanks over the bread and wine; there is reason to think that Jesus's blessing over the wine, 'This is my body', is used here, in the same way as Paul had described.

> When the president has given thanks and all the people have answered, those whom we call supporters (*diakonoi*) give the bread and wine and water for which the thanksgiving has been made to be tasted by those who are present, and they carry them to those who are absent.[19]

One can see that the role of the 'deacon' here is not unlike the role that the Gospel of Luke remembered women like Martha and the mother of Simon Peter as having played.

The event described here took place in a domestic setting – probably the courtyard of a private home. In this very fluid and informal context, the best way to protect Christian communities was by making sure that their leaders were people who were widely respected and could bring authority to the role. But there were different ways of fulfilling this aim. If the *Acts of Paul and Thecla* remembered Paul as being in league with independent women, such as Thecla and Tryphaena, another second-century writer remembered him as proposing that the churches should rely on the protection of men who had established themselves as fathers.[20]

The First Stirrings of an Institution

The New Testament contains a group of letters called the Pastoral Epistles which address the growing pains of these communities. Some scholars believe that these texts were written by Paul himself, as they claim, but the view is not widely accepted. Most historians agree that they were written by a second-century church leader who felt inspired to imagine how the Apostle Paul would have responded to the new pressures faced by communities as they became more structured.[21]

The Pastorals reflect a distinctively second-century attitude towards the end of the world. It is no longer just around the corner, as it was for Paul. The writer's idea seems to have been to imagine how Paul would have reacted, if he had lived to understand how long it would take for the end of the world to come. The key is the need for communities to establish some kind of provisional order while they are waiting. In one of these texts, the First Letter to Timothy, our author explains that the ability to run a household is as good an indicator as any of the kind of personal authority that a community leader would need.

> Here is a trustworthy saying: whoever aspires to be an overseer (*episkopos*) desires a noble task. Now the overseer is to be above reproach, faithful to his wife, temperate, self-controlled, respectable, hospitable, able to teach, not given to drunkenness, not violent but gentle, not quarrelsome, not a lover of money. He must manage his own family well and see that his children obey him, and he must do so in a manner worthy of full respect. (If anyone does not know how to manage his own family, how can he take care of God's church?) (1 Timothy 3: 1–5)

One can see how far this writer is from the urgent sense of the end-time that we saw in Paul's own letters. This is most likely someone whose grandparents or great-grandparents would have been contemporaries of Paul, Chloe, and Prisca. Marriage is seen not only as a necessity, but even as a social good. A man should earn his standing in the community by governing his own household in a manner consonant with the group's ideals. If the children are inclined to be disobedient, it is a sign that the father has failed to educate them properly. It even raises the suspicion that he himself has failed to behave in a way that would command the respect of subordinates.

So far, we are in a thought-world entirely compatible with the idea of female leadership we have seen in Paul's letters. But directly preceding the passage above is another which makes it clear that the writer of 1 Timothy is agitated about where women fit into the picture. Here is the text:

> A woman should learn in quietness and full submission. I do not permit a woman to teach or to assume authority over a man; she must be quiet. For Adam was formed first, then Eve. And Adam was not the one deceived; it was the woman who was deceived and became a sinner. But women will be saved through childbearing . . . (1 Timothy 2: 11–14)

Obviously, this writer is worried by women teachers in the same way that Tertullian, above, was upset by women performing baptisms. In antiquity, as in the modern world, women's authority was a controversial issue, and this was particularly true of the transitional second-century church.

One scholar has suggested that the writer of the Pastorals was inspired by the *Acts of Paul and Thecla* – or by the oral traditions around Paul and Thecla on which the text was based. If this is true, it was an inspiration born of irritation. In a way, the idea makes perfect sense. On this reading, the writer knew that some communities remembered Paul as the mentor of women preachers and teachers, and wanted to correct what he perceived to be a misunderstanding of Paul's intentions. This is why he wrote in Paul's name: he felt he was defending the Apostle's memory and delivering the message that Paul would have wanted.

It was one thing, he may have thought, for Paul to accept the help of powerful women at a topsy-turvy time when everyone expected the world to end. Now that it was clear that the world was not going to end quite so quickly, the churches needed to support the idea of Christians marrying and begetting families. For this writer, this meant bolstering the authority of husbands and containing the exuberance of wives.

There is a link between this text and the passage on the silence of women which many scholars believe was added to Paul's first letter to the Corinthians in the second century. That passage used language very similar to that of 1 Timothy above. 'Women should remain silent in the churches . . . they must be in submission . . . if they want to inquire about something, they should ask their own husbands.'

If one tries to put the puzzle pieces together, it looks as if more than one writer in the second century became nervous about how the memory of Paul was being invoked, and decided to try to correct the record. This involved commenting on Paul's text at points where its meaning was open to question, and also adding a group of new letters to counteract the stories that were circulating about Paul. Now Paul could be remembered as a supporter of paternal authority, rather than as a mentor of women who defied their parents, left their husbands, and set off to travel the world as independent preachers.

The emphasis on children here is important: a bishop should be a father of obedient children, and 'women will be saved through child-bearing'. The writer of the Pastorals sees people who have raised children well as people who can be trusted. In suggesting that women are saved through child-bearing, he wants to link the value of raising children back to the story of Adam and Eve. In the Book of Genesis, when Adam and Eve ate of the fruit of the tree of knowledge, Eve's punishment was that all women would forever after suffer in childbirth. But now this curse has been redeemed: now women are *saved* by their painful work of giving birth to children and raising them.

Equally, our writer wants to warn his readers against the kind of people who think the best Christians do *not* have children. He seems to have in mind a rival faction who still believe the world is about to end, and who think, as Paul did a century earlier, that establishing a household and having children is beside the point.

In the long run, the pro-children faction within the Christian movement would prevail. When the expected end-time failed to arrive, placing value on raising families was an adaptation that suited the long future that followed. Yet the idea of living as if the world was about to end was not forgotten by later generations. To a modern understanding, it may seem curious that important debates about the shape of the community were channelled through telling stories about the Apostles. But our writers were wrestling over a legacy. Even if they also carried on more direct and obvious debates about the issues of their own day, they were acutely conscious of the need to measure themselves against the core principles of the heroic early days of the movement – the time of Jesus and Paul.

It was important to clarify how these founding figures would be remembered. Would their authority, and their memory, be invoked in order to justify independent women preachers or silent and submissive wives? Would Jesus be remembered as a teacher who sometimes had a message that he preferred to deliver through a woman, or did he reserve all his teaching to an established council of twelve men, and to Peter in particular? Already in the second century, as the living memory of teachers who had known Paul and Jesus personally was beginning to fade, Christians were beginning to differ in their ideas about how to answer these questions.

Matthidia's Wish

If there was a party forming around the memory of Peter in the second century, it could perhaps be characterized as the law-and-order party. Peter was remembered as the founder of the church in the city of Rome, and that church was on its way to becoming remarkably powerful. We might expect, then, that the 'Peter' party was not at all happy with the idea of women as preachers or missionaries. Indeed, we saw in the Gospel of Mary that Peter was remembered as rejecting the testimony of a female disciple. But like Paul, Peter was a figure whose memory different groups of Christians were willing to fight for, and so his name was borrowed to support diverse and sometimes conflicting ideas in the later centuries. The rival memories of Peter reflect a controversy about women, and also about marriage and sexuality.

On the one hand, there is a Peter who preaches virginity, and on the other, a Peter who is for marriage. On the virginity side of the equation, the memory of Peter looks very similar to the memory of Paul. The apocryphal *Acts of Peter* tell a story remarkably similar to the *Acts of Paul and Thecla*, with Peter playing a role very like Paul's, as a magnet for female disciples. Since Peter was remembered as the Apostle who brought Christianity to Rome, the scene has changed from the provinces to the capital, but the broad brushstrokes of the story – a charismatic apostle, love triangles, and the message of virginity – are entirely familiar.

But the Peter tradition preserves an unlikely witness for the pro-marriage side. One tale celebrating Peter's work as a missionary goes against the trend of portraying the new faith as a source of conflict in families. This is the early third-century *Recognitions*, which recounts the early years of Clement, the first bishop of Rome. The *Recognitions* is not a proper history but a historical novel, a pastiche of narrative elements similar to Shakespeare's *Pericles* or *Twelfth Night*. The *Recognitions* has it all: shipwreck, adultery, magicians, predatory evil relatives, and family members who disappear for years and, when the long-lost travellers return, go unrecognized until a dramatic denouement reunites them with their loved ones.

The main storyline of the *Recognitions* involves Matthidia, a married woman from a Roman senatorial family who converts to Christianity. Her conversion is the happy ending of a bittersweet family drama which turns on a painful secret. As the story begins, the family of the Roman senator Faustinianus are scattered along the eastern coast of the Mediterranean, penniless, and without means of communicating with one another.

How they came to be there is the first phase of the narrative. Some years ago, while Faustinianus was away from Rome, his wife Matthidia had found herself the object of an unpleasant sexual proposition from his brother. Instead of telling her husband what had happened, Matthidia had concocted a pretext and left Rome with her two elder sons. Now, as a result of a chain of narrative twists involving successive shipwrecks, all of the family members, including the husband, find themselves stranded. The task of the Apostle is to find and reunite the lost family members. As Peter travels, he encounters different members of the family and hears four diverging versions of the events that led to Matthidia's departure from Rome. When he pieces the four stories together, he recognizes that they are each versions of the same sequence of events, and reunites the troubled family.

Clement, the future bishop of Rome, is the youngest son, and he is the narrator of the tale. He begins by describing his trip east from Rome to the province of Palestine. There, he meets the charismatic holy man Peter, who converts him to Christianity. It is through Clement that Peter first hears the story of his family:

> Then said Peter, 'Is there no one of your family surviving?'
>
> I answered, 'There are indeed many powerful men, coming from the stock of Caesar; for Caesar himself gave a wife to my father, as being his relative, and educated along with him, and of a suitably noble family . . . Now, when I was barely five years old, my mother saw a vision – so I learned from my father – by which she was warned that, unless she speedily left the city with her twin sons, and was absent for ten years, she and her children should perish by a miserable fate.'[22]

Peter is separated from Clement directly after this conversation, and soon afterwards he encounters a beggar-woman, whom he berates for her unwillingness to work for a living.

Being born of noble parents, and having become the wife of a suitably powerful man, I had two twin sons, and after them one other. But my husband's brother was vehemently inflamed with unlawful love towards me; and as I valued chastity above all things, and would neither consent to so great wickedness, nor wished to disclose the business of his brother, I considered whether in any way I could escape unpolluted, and yet not set brother against brother, and so bring the whole race of a noble family to disgrace.[23]

As Matthidia speaks, the reader immediately grasps that she must be the long-lost mother of whom Clement had spoken. What happens next will come as no surprise. Not only does Peter bring Matthidia to the ship where Clement is waiting, and reunite the two, but into the bargain he discovers that two of his other disciples are in fact the twins whom she had lost sight of during her adventures.

But Peter warns the four that they cannot share a meal of celebration: now that the three young noblemen have accepted baptism, they are no longer able to eat at the table of the Gentiles. Matthidia counters this setback by urging that she be baptized as quickly as possible. The gods of the Romans have caused her only misery, but the God of the Hebrews has restored her lost sons to her.

Now, all that remains is for the father to be found. On the morning after Matthidia's baptism, Peter and the three brothers befriend an old workman, who engages them in a debate about fate and providence. The old workman argues that how his own life has turned out could have been foretold years ago by anyone who considered his astrological chart. It is a tragic story, he says, and he begins to tell how his wife left him alone with his young son many years ago.

'For she fell in love with her slave, and fearing at once danger and reproach, she fled with him, and going abroad, where she satisfied her love, she perished in the sea.'

Then I answered, 'How do you know that she cohabited with her slave abroad, and died in his society?'

Then the old man said, 'I know it with perfect certainty; not indeed that she was married to the slave, as indeed I had not even discovered that she loved him. But after she was gone, my brother gave me the whole story, telling me that first she had loved himself; but he, being honourable as a brother, would not pollute his brother's bed with the stain of incest.'[24]

Thus the tangled web of stories begins to unravel. The family was driven apart by the brother's lust and the deceptions meant to disguise it, but the evil brother has a positive counterpart in the Apostle Peter, whose dedication to truth restores the marriage of Faustinianus and Matthidia, and their family.

The biological family of parents and children and the new family of Christian fellow-feeling are reconciled in the tale of Faustianus and Matthidia. Our author wants his reader to understand that the 'family' of the Christian faith is not necessarily a danger to biological families. The invitation is open to everyone. Matthidia's craving to be baptized – simply because she has found her sons and her sons happen to have become Christian in her absence – reveals a spiritual truth that our author holds dear. Our true identity is not the name we were born with, but the spiritual self revealed in the moment of conversion. The truth which is then revealed is not about doctrines or creeds, it is about love.

Women Readers and their Heroines

Ancient writers thought carefully about how women would react to the heroines they read and heard about. So, for example, an early fourth-century pamphlet of advice for the parents of daughters imagines Thecla as a model for girls who first meet Paul when reading his letters in the New Testament. The young virgin was meant to think of Thecla's travels at Paul's side: like Thecla, the virgin should seek after Paul, and make every effort to follow in his footsteps. Bible study could thus be a way of participating in a feminine legacy. The breezy willingness of a Thecla or a Matthidia to accept the new faith and stake her life on it was an inspiration for ancient readers, and our writers aligned the details of each heroine's story in order to give emphasis to this central fact.[25]

Yet it may have been difficult to imagine them as flesh-and-blood women, who had encountered the same doubts and difficulties as ordinary women did in real life. Perhaps a heroine's virtue was not necessarily expected of ordinary women. Ancient Christian writers knew that the ordinary challenges of family life were daunting enough to keep all but the very few occupied. Female readers and listeners were not always beautiful or rich, but that did not mean that they could not identify with heroines. Similarly, ordinary women might not face shipwreck and martyrdom, but they could still draw inspiration from the example of legendary women from the first Christian century like Thecla and Matthidia.

The question of how real historical women tried to put into practice the ideas that they heard about in Christian literature is tricky. So often what we have to work with are figures like Thecla and Matthidia, whose historical status is uncertain: their second-century stories may have a root in first-century oral storytelling, or they may simply be inspiring literary heroines who speak to the concerns of their own day. Even Blandina comes to us in a source so strongly shaped by pastoral concerns that we cannot be sure where the historical woman ends and the martyr heroine begins.

Yet there is one and only one priceless text that breaks the pattern. The surviving records from the early third century preserve the voice of a single ordinary woman who found herself in circumstances in which the heroism of a Thecla or a Blandina was precisely what was needed. In the following chapter, we will encounter one of the most remarkable of the historically documented flesh-and-blood women of Christian antiquity. This is Perpetua, a young mother from a small provincial town of Roman Africa near Carthage, who kept a diary as she prepared to become a Christian martyr.

5

A MARTYR IN THE FAMILY

ometime in the winter or early spring of the year 203, a group of Christian catechumens – converts taking instruction in preparation for baptism – were arrested in the town of Thuburbo Minus, a Roman colony established in the fertile grain lands along the river Medjerda (the ancient Bagrada), around 45 kilometres to the west of the Roman governor's capital at Carthage. Once the Christian group had been apprehended – perhaps during a prayer meeting, although the possibility cannot be excluded that they were rounded up after having been identified by a hostile informer – they were arrested and taken to Carthage for questioning by the procurator, the emperor's personal representative in the province of Africa Proconsularis. Eventually, they would be executed as criminals, condemned to be attacked by wild animals during special gladiatorial games held in the military amphitheatre (*amphitheatrum castrensis*) at Carthage, to celebrate the fourteenth birthday of Geta, the younger son of the reigning emperor, Septimius Severus.

The story of the catechumens of Thuburbo is one of a thousand stories that could be told about individuals and families in the Roman provinces who fell foul of the imperial authorities. Whether they were Christian or not, these individuals and families depended on a network of friends and family to vouch for them if they came into contact with the judiciary system: public authority in the Roman Empire depended far more acutely on social relationships and personal loyalties than it does in the modern world. Families had to be wary in case some activity or characteristic singled them out as suspect in the eyes of their neighbours, who might pass on information to the authorities – 'information' which might be about something quite difficult to disprove, such as failing to show enough enthusiasm for the government and its policies. Sometimes there was real concern about subversive religious or political views, but in many cases the informer's motive was simple personal dislike, or – even worse – a wish to see a rival lose his or her grip on some status or benefit which the informer coveted.

In this atmosphere of intimidation, Christians were in a particularly dangerous position. It was widely known that their religion strongly disapproved of their taking oaths or making sacrifices of burnt incense to honour the emperor and the Roman gods. Such acts of loyalty were increasingly seen as indispensable by the authorities, and Christians who were unwilling to compromise their principles had to keep a very low profile indeed.

What marks out the group from Thuburbo from so many other cases is not that they were arrested, or even that their arrest led to a spectacular – and gruesome – execution (if we are to believe a later narrative which claims to be an eye-witness account). Rather, it is the curious fact that their story has come down to us in their own words. Two members of the group, a twenty-two-year-old mother named Perpetua and her spiritual brother Saturus, each kept diaries during their imprisonment. The diaries were preserved by the Christian community at Carthage, where they died, as a precious testimony of their commitment to the faith. Both narratives place a strong emphasis on the dreams and visions that the catechumens experienced during their time in custody. Perpetua and Saturus understood these dreams and visions as messages from heaven, through which they could seek to understand the true meaning of what they were about to endure.

Perpetua's prison diary offers a surprisingly intimate view of the weeks before her execution, and what she tells us about her prison experience seems almost unbearable to a modern sensibility. When she is taken away from her family, she is kept from her baby, who is young enough still to be nursing. At first she seems to be held in the household of a powerful resident of the city of Carthage, a standard practice in the Roman period. Then she is remanded to a dark and frightening prison, where her consolation is the company of the others who are also being held on suspicion of crimes against the state.

Yet in the act of writing her story Perpetua is conscious of giving a gift: her wish is that her readers take sustenance from the strength she has found during her ordeal. Like the diary of Anne Frank, Perpetua's narrative captures the moral courage of a young woman who knows that she has been called on to play a part in a story far larger than her own, and who refuses to feel sorry for herself. Rather, she explores her fears and experiences in a way that she hopes will have value to those who come after her.

Where Perpetua differs from Anne Frank is in the all-important fact that she is certain she will be remembered. What she suffers, she suffers as part of a group who stand alongside her. And she is sustained, too, by a vivid sense that the spirit of God is with her. She knows this from the dreams and visions that come to her during her days in prison, and from her own ability to act with unexpected courage.

So when we consider Perpetua's anxious weeks as a suspect and then as a condemned criminal, we do her an injustice if we fail to imagine her as equal to the challenge she faced. It is fairer to think of her as an ordinary person who discovered, under extraordinary circumstances, that she had access to a deep well of strength.

Perpetua's Baby

Perpetua had a baby, who was with her during part of her time in prison; she says that his welfare was her greatest cause for anxiety while she was in custody. Roman women of the upper classes tended to have wet-nurses for their babies, so the fact that Perpetua was suckling the child herself tells us something about her. It means one of two things. She may have come from an old-fashioned family who prized the old Roman custom of a simple and austere life, in which women worked at the loom and tended to their families personally, even if they were rich enough to have numerous servants. Or she may have come from a very modest background. The second possibility is more likely.

The presence of Perpetua's baby also raises a troubling question: where was her husband? In order to understand what may have taken place between Perpetua and the father of her son, we must first of all establish whether she was married. The question is not as scandalous as it may seem. Her diary implies strongly that she had no husband. A later editor, whose comment on the diary was handed down through the Middle Ages with the diary itself, suggested that Perpetua was married to the baby's father but, paradoxically, this should probably be taken as evidence that the editor could see that something did not look 'right'. The details of the custody arrangement which she makes for her baby make it clear that the child was born out of wedlock, since she arranges that her mother and her brother will take care of the baby after her death. If she were married, the baby would automatically belong to her husband's family, not her own.

The very essence of the institution of Roman marriage was as a treaty between families over who would have control over any children produced by the union. In a union between free unmarried partners, the maternal grandfather would have undisputed control over the child's upbringing, and undisputed custody in case the two parents ceased to live together. If a man wished his own father to have control – or if he were legally independent of his father and wished to have control over his child himself – then he had to contract an *iustum matrimonium*, a legal marriage, with the woman whom he wished to bear his children. In Roman law, the mother or her relatives could never against his will gain custody of a man's child born from marriage, and at the same time the father or his relatives could not gain custody against the mother's will if the child was born from an unmarried union, unless the mother was also the man's slave.

Surely, one may well object, it is impossible that a committed Christian like Perpetua should have had a child out of wedlock. After all, she was one of the great early heroines of the Christian faith. But this objection does not hold much weight, for two reasons. The first is theological. We have already seen in the case of Blandina that the God of the early Christians was no respecter of persons. The second reason is historical. Concubinage, the committed quasi-marital relationship between a woman of the lower classes and a man who had no need for heirs but nonetheless craved feminine companionship, was often the only reproductive relationship available to lower-class or non-citizen women. It was not looked down upon as a relationship of sexual promiscuity; if there was a stigma attached to it, it was one of class status rather than moral standing. From the point of view of the woman and her family, established concubinage was the hallmark of low-status respectability.

Our editor tells us that Perpetua was a catechumen. If this is true, it is possible that she had become estranged from her baby's father after she began her programme of Christian instruction. The second-century Christian philosopher Justin Martyr tells a story of just such a case from the time of the Emperor Antoninus Pius (d. 161). In Justin's story, a woman who was married to a dissolute husband initially shared his wild life, but when she fell in with the Christians and began to study their teachings, she decided she must distance herself. Eventually this led her to divorce him – in those days the churches had not developed the strong hostility to divorce that would emerge in later centuries.[1]

Justin says that the wife tried at first to stay on with her difficult husband, in the hope of having a good influence on him, but when it became clear that it was simply beyond her powers, she filed for divorce. At this point, the husband reported her to the authorities as a Christian, which is how the conflict came to Justin's attention.

Although she seems to have escaped punishment, the complaint against her led to the arrest of her teacher, Ptolemaeus, who was subsequently executed as a criminal. It is a curious story. Nothing else is known about the Christian woman, her husband, or her teacher, but the story illustrates the point that conversion to Christianity sometimes changed lives quite radically.

In Perpetua's case, it is possible that conversion led her to re-evaluate her relationship with her baby's father, and perhaps even to an open break. This would explain why there is no sign of him anywhere in her narrative, a point that would otherwise be difficult to explain. It may also explain how Perpetua came to the attention of the Roman authorities in the first place.

We will see below that Perpetua's most important relationship – after that with her baby – was with her own father. The fact that her father, mother, and brothers all feature in her narrative while her baby's father does not, may simply reflect the fact that these were the individuals to whom she was bound by Roman law, so when she came under suspicion, it was they who had responsibility for her. Whether she was married or not, Perpetua belonged to the family not of her husband but of her father. She could count on his protection and must in principle obey his authority. But there was no way to force obedience upon a daughter if she was willing to disobey even the Roman governor, and to face execution as a criminal.

I visited Tebourba, the town where Perpetua is believed to have lived, one summer a few years ago. It is now a dusty town of wide unpaved streets, lined with the walls of single-storey houses and courtyards. In this, it has not changed much from the Roman period. Today, Tebourba's olive oil and harissa are exported all over the world, and the remains of at least one ancient olive press have been found to confirm the long agricultural tradition. In antiquity, the town was prosperous enough to have a Roman amphitheatre, although it is now an overgrown and unrestored ruin. In antiquity, wheat and olives were the source of the region's prosperity. The town's position on a river means that water has always been plentiful, a rare stroke of good fortune in inland North Africa; in the eastern part of what is now Tunisia, summer temperatures routinely climb over fifty degrees centigrade.

Ancient Thuburbo was not much more than a long day's walk from Carthage, but one should not underestimate the psychological distance between a rural market town and a Roman governor's capital. Even today, when Tebourba is only a half-hour's taxi-ride from the business district and airport of Tunis, the feeling of disconnection to the wider world is remarkable. The local historical society has established a tiny museum in the Ottoman-period house and garden of one of the town's notable residents, and stepping into its courtyard one glimpses how easily the houses of the prosperous could create an oasis of shade and civility, shutting out the dust and poverty outside in the street.

As I was walking back from visiting the ruins of the Roman amphitheatre on the outskirts of town, along the last row of houses before the river, one of the many blue-painted doors opened and an elderly woman appeared and beckoned to me. She was a striking figure – a sort of ageing love-goddess from the 1960s dressed in a brightly coloured paisley kaftan. The pastel-coloured veil over her head set off dark eyes which had been outlined with kohl, and these made an intriguing contrast to her toothless smile. What I found mesmerizing, however, was her feet. She was wearing kitten-heeled leather flip-flops studded with fake jewels, and her toenails were painted beautifully in shocking pink.

This magnificent person was making enthusiastic hand movements in my direction, indicating that I should come over to the house and accept a cup of tea inside, but when I walked over to the door and greeted her in French, she smiled and shook her head vigorously, indicating that she could speak only Arabic. So I went back to the small group with whom I had been walking, a motley group of academics dressed in practical and unglamorous clothes, carrying an array of coloured umbrellas to shade us against the heat.

Since my prospective hostess was still gesturing, an Arabic-speaking friend returned to her door for a moment, and came back smiling. 'Don't worry,' she said, 'it's only a misunderstanding. She heard you speaking what she thought was French, so she thought you must be from the government. She was hoping you could put in a good word for her back at the capital about some land she wants to acquire.' Having seen the cosmopolitan chic of the female bureau-crats and office workers in Tunis, I was flattered but rather surprised. My friend explained that the country's status as a French protectorate until 1956 has cast a long shadow. In the 1990s the Tunisian govern-ment made it illegal for government departments to use French as a language of official business, but the French-speaking world is still one of privilege and power. The story has stayed in my memory as an example of how foreign and distant the Roman lords who controlled the region must have seemed in the days when Carthage was capital of Africa Proconsularis.

But this curious encounter is illuminating in another way. The woman at the door clearly saw the power of the state as something quite personal and circumstantial, and this is an attitude that would not have been out of place in Perpetua's day. The historian Dio Cassius, a contemporary of Perpetua's who became Proconsul of Africa, tells a story about the Emperor Hadrian (d. 138) which shows that face-to-face encounters with the powerful, if not a common occurrence, were at least on the horizon of possibility. Hadrian was known for making tours of inspection through the provinces of his empire. Once, the story goes, he was approached by a woman who wanted him to reconsider a case in which she thought the judgment by the lower authorities had been unfair, since it was known that any judgment by a Roman magistrate could in theory be overturned by the Emperor himself. The woman in Dio's story would have been delighted when she discovered that the Emperor would be travelling through her district, for getting a petition into his hands was an arduous busi-ness, involving expensive travel, tricky negotiations with successive gate-keepers, and long delays. So the opportunity to approach him

as he travelled was a god-send. At first, she was met by disappointment: Hadrian refused to stop to hear her petition, explaining that
he had no time. But she called after him, 'Cease, then, being Emperor!'
Dio tells us that on hearing her, Hadrian turned back, recognizing
that it was by responding to his people that he gave legitimacy to
his own position, and granted her a hearing on the spot.[2]

Awaiting Trial

Perpetua's prison diary shows that even a person of no importance
could face these Roman lords, if she was bold enough. We first meet
the martyr as she is being held for questioning. Initially she is held
in a private house rather than a prison, which was entirely normal.
In the Roman Empire, a suspect would often be taken into custody
by a trusted individual of standing in the community, who would
deliver him or her up to the authorities for questioning when the
time came. This mode of custody was partly a cost-cutting measure,
since it meant that the state could expend fewer resources on building
and staffing prisons. It was also a way of involving local landowners
in the maintenance of law and order, an enterprise that helped to
remind them of where their own loyalties ought to lie.

The house where Perpetua was held may have been an elegant
one. The friends of the governor in Carthage lived in imposing villas,
houses that can still be seen, with their magnificent mosaic floors,
in the ruins along the sea-front of the ancient city near the Antonine
Baths. Like all Roman residences on the grand scale, these elegant
houses had less conspicuous rooms where practical functions were
undertaken by slaves and other underlings. In these 'invisible' areas,
persons under suspicion could be held under a watchful eye without
causing offence to more distinguished guests.

Perpetua's father's visits may initially have been intended to
console, but if so they quickly turned sour. Perpetua may or may

not have anticipated how strongly her family would resist the prospect of her death. Perpetua wished them to accept it with equanimity, and to rejoice in the task of watching over her infant son after her death. But like so many other parents through history, Perpetua's mother and father found her steps towards independence far more distressing than she could imagine.

We have no way of knowing whether the family was pagan or Christian. Scholars have often assumed that they were pagan, both because of the later editor's suggestion that she was a catechumen and because her father was very firm in his wish that Perpetua should do what the imperial officials asked. If she and her fellows would cooperate with the authorities and make a burnt offering of incense, then the charges would be dropped.

Many Christians in Perpetua's day would have been unwilling, like her parents and like the majority of modern Christians, to see their children executed publicly as criminals for the sake of religious principles. This was not necessarily a matter of cowardice. Many Christians thought of themselves as law-abiding citizens, and felt a genuine repugnance at the idea that they should refuse to obey the governor's order to burn incense as a gesture of concern for the well-being of the Roman state. Perpetua paints a poignant scene of her father's attempt to get her to accept this offer:

> While we were still under arrest [she said] my father out of love for me was trying to persuade me and shake my resolution. 'Father,' said I, 'do you see this vase here, for example, or water-pot or whatever?'
>
> 'Yes, I do,' said he.
>
> And I told him: 'Could it be called by any other name than what it is?'
>
> And he said: 'No.'[3]

Perpetua understands that her father's intentions are good, and at the outset she has compassion for him. At the same time, she cannot

give in. She has already begun to steel her mind against her interrogation some days later. She knows that she will be asked 'Are you
a Christian?', and she will answer, 'Yes, I am'. Perpetua presents her
dilemma as both no more and no less than a problem of naming:
whether she should allow herself to be 'let off the hook' by allowing
her offensive religious views to be passed over in silence. Her next
words, however, are firm, and they make it clear that she intends
to hold her ground. She responds to her father:

'Well, so too I cannot be called anything other than what I am,
a Christian.' At this my father was so angered by the word
'Christian' that he moved towards me as though he would pluck
my eyes out. But he left it at that, and departed, vanquished
along with his diabolical arguments. For a few days afterwards
I gave thanks to the lord that I was separated from my father,
and I was comforted by his absence.[4]

This encounter seems gratuitously painful: a visit like this from her
father could only add to her distress instead of offering support or
consolation. At the same time, it is possible that the painful
encounter offered something like a catharsis for the tension she
felt in looking forward to her formal interrogation. Focusing her
attention on the familiar figure of her father may have helped her
to keep her courage up.

Why did Perpetua feel empowered, one wonders, to talk back to
her father so boldly? It was certainly not the behaviour expected of
a Roman daughter. Her father's furious reaction shows that he found
it galling. We saw in the last chapter that there was some concern
among both pagans and Christians that disobedient wives and daughters were being encouraged to think for themselves. This was seen
as dangerous by a society that placed importance on paternal authority.

But there is logic to Perpetua's own position. If she meant to
stand for the faith as a martyr, she would have to stand firm in the
face of men far more powerful than her father, men who were

accustomed to intimidating persons far more important than herself. In all likelihood, Perpetua was practising on her father. He was the person of authority most familiar to her, and she was preparing to defend herself not only against the emperor's legal representative, but against the very gods of Rome. If she could hold her ground against her father, she might have a fighting chance of doing the same when it came to the formal interrogation. We will see below that in the event she was indeed able to hold her ground. The Christian community in Carthage would later remember her as a martyr of extraordinary courage.

Afterwards, she tells us, she was moved to a prison. Here we find another clue that Perpetua did not come from an imposing background: the accommodation was by no means appropriate to a person of rank.

A few days later we were moved to the prison, and I was terrified. I had never before been anywhere so dark. What a difficult time it was! With the crowd the heat was stifling . . . and to crown it all, I was tortured with worry for my baby.[5]

The sense of community meant everything to the would-be martyrs, who were faced with the prospect of isolation and intimidation. Under the difficult conditions of the prison, an ascetic discipline allowed them to prepare for physical pain. Equally important was the lore handed down through the community, which helped them to find meaning in the challenges they faced, when their own families were often unable to understand.

A few days later there was a rumour that we were going to be given a hearing. My father also arrived from the city, worn with worry, and he came to see me with the idea of persuading me. 'Daughter,' he said, 'have pity on my grey head – have pity on me your father, if I deserve to be called your father, if I have favoured you above all your brothers, if I have raised you to reach this prime of your life. Do not abandon me to be the reproach of men. Think of your brothers, think of your mother and your aunt, think of your child, who will not be able to live once you are gone. Give up your pride! You will destroy all of us! None of us will ever be able to speak freely again if anything happens to you!'[6]

Perpetua tells us that she comforted him, but that he went away unable to understand why she felt she had to sacrifice herself, even to the extent of putting the rest of the family at risk as sympathizers of an illegal and potentially dangerous religious cult.

Here we need to stop and try to understand why Perpetua's allowing herself to be condemned and publicly executed was so dangerous to the rest of the family. To be a victim was not to be voiceless in the Roman Empire. Rather, it was to risk notoriety, not only for oneself but also for one's associates, in a context where there was safety in obscurity. In allowing herself to be executed for a crime that carried connotations of political treason, Perpetua knew she would place her surviving family at risk in the game of the patronage and mutual surveillance governing Roman civic life. This willingness to sacrifice the safety of others to serve one's own sense of religious duty was painful to all parties, and frightening to those left behind.

Recent scholarly attention has tended to focus on the hierarchical reversal implied by this scene. A Roman paterfamilias is reduced to begging, rather than ordering, his daughter to conform to accepted social norms. It is not impossible, then, to feel some sympathy for Perpetua's father, even though our sympathy is limited by his frightening behaviour.

The Interrogation

Now we come to what is in many ways the crucial moment of Perpetua's ordeal. 'One day while we were eating breakfast we were suddenly hurried off for a hearing. We arrived at the forum, and straight away the story went about the neighbourhood near the forum and a huge crowd gathered.' The crowd was not part of the official protocol, but its presence, with its restless energy and the eyes of the curious – and probably hostile – spectators, will have added considerably to the intimidation felt by anyone who was not already a hardened criminal. A crowd of this kind might prove sympathetic, but it could also be very dangerous.[7]

The Forum of Carthage, where Perpetua tells us she was interrogated by the Roman procurator Hilarianus, is now a ruin, and the terrace on which it is built is the site of the Carthage Museum. The size and majesty of the ancient public buildings are still discernible, however, reflecting the grandeur of the Roman colonial power. The Acropolis of Carthage, where the Forum stood, is a plateau at the summit of the Byrsa Hill, overlooking what is now the Bay of Tunis, one of the most stunning city sites in the Mediterranean. It offers sweeping views out over the bay to the low blue line of Cap Bon across the water, and off to the left a dazzling blue sea that stretches all the way to Sicily, 150 miles to the north-east.

Even in antiquity this was a site redolent with stories, most notably of the Phoenician queen Dido, great-niece of the biblical Jezebel. Legend held that it was from the cliff at Byrsa that Dido had thrown herself to her death, when her lover Aeneas left her to continue his journey on to Italy, where Virgil tells us he founded the city of Rome. A friend with whom I visited the site remarked that no one who had been to Carthage would ever want to return to Rome, and even though history argues against it, looking out over the water I felt that it was not a ridiculous thing to say. Hilarianus, we agreed, must have counted himself fortunate to land such a posting.

Where exactly Perpetua's hearing took place is uncertain. It is likely that it was in the Roman law courts, along the eastern end of the Forum, facing over the sea. Another early martyr text from North Africa, the Acts of the Scillitan Martyrs, refers to a hearing before the governor as taking place *in secretario*; the *secretarium* was probably a council chamber in the law courts, though it is a term that can describe a closed chamber in both public and private buildings.

What is more certain is the effect such majestic public buildings would have had on a young woman from the rural districts as she was brought in for questioning. The whole setting was designed to underline the power of the Roman presence in Africa, and no expense was spared in pursuing this aim. Especially to one who had never seen them before, the law courts would have been awe-inspiring. On entering, one had to cross an immense vaulted hall whose roof was supported by dozens of columns so massive that to an untrained eye they seemed to have been set in place by giants. Even the lawyers whose work brought them there daily would not have been immune to the effect of this kind of Roman public architecture. It was calculated to remind all those who entered of the power of Rome.

Perpetua makes it clear in her diary that what was at stake in her trial was her unwillingness to burn incense as a sacrifice for the welfare of the emperors. As she approached her interrogation, she had to face stone-and-mortar proof of the greatness of the power against which she had set her one small life. At the same time, she had to wrestle with her own doubts about just what she was doing there. It was still possible to declare that she had made a mistake, offer the sacrifice, and return safely home.

Perpetua mentions that when she was summoned, the governor Minucius Timinianus had recently died, and in his place, the procurator Hilarianus, the senior tax-collector in the province, was officiating. As the person responsible for ensuring that the agricultural wealth of Africa was safely collected and shipped to Rome to feed the urban population, Hilarianus was acutely conscious of Rome's need for peace and prosperity in Africa. What we know of him from other sources suggests that he was a severe judge, acutely concerned to stamp out any resistance against the imperial authority.

Like most Roman officials, Hilarianus saw the Christians – when he thought about them at all – as a subversive sect who might well intend to overthrow the government. It was his job to stop them before they got started: the Romans had not fought for the fertile grain-fields of Africa in order to hand them over to a rag-tag collection of prophets from the market towns. It was Perpetua's refusal to 'offer sacrifice for the welfare of the emperors' that formed his motive for condemning her and her companions to the beasts.

As she recounts it, Perpetua's interrogation with Hilarianus was short and sharp. She tells us that her interview consisted of only two questions, and this is entirely possible. The procurator's secretaries would have collected evidence and briefed him thoroughly, since he would normally have dozens or even hundreds of cases to hear in a single day. Even her own cohort of catechumens needed to be processed individually. 'We walked up to the prisoner's dock. All the others when questioned admitted their guilt.' Her own case was complicated by her father's appearance. He was still beside himself in his distress: 'Then, when it came my turn, my father appeared with my son, dragged me from the step, and said, "Perform the sacrifice – have pity on your baby!"' We have no way of knowing whether Perpetua's father's actions were a sign of his unbalanced mental state or a performance calculated to signal to the Roman authorities that he had done everything in his power to stop Perpetua. He may have believed that, in this way, he could protect his surviving family from the displeasure of the authorities.[8]

Now, finally, we come to Perpetua's own moment with the procurator. Despite her father's effort to dissuade her, he cannot control how she will respond to the procurator's questions. It is worth citing Perpetua's account of the key exchange in full:

Hilarianus the procurator, who had taken up judicial powers in place of the deceased governor Minucius Timinianus, said, 'Have pity on your father's grey head; have pity on your infant son. Offer to sacrifice for the welfare of the emperors.'

'I will not,' I responded.

'Are you a Christian?' said Hilarianus.

And I said, 'Yes, I am.'[9]

After this brief exchange, Perpetua's father breaks in, trying to undo the damage created by his daughter's refusal to acknowledge the authority of Rome. The reader is not quite prepared for what happens next: 'When my father insisted on trying to dissuade me, Hilarianus ordered him to be thrown to the ground and beaten with a rod.' Perpetua's reaction to this affront, the beginning of the brutal treatment that she and her family will experience as a result of her act of defiance, shows that she is not entirely without feeling. 'I felt sorry for my father, just as if I myself had been beaten. I felt sorry for his miserable old age.' She will have known that his future was bleak as a result of her actions.[10]

Still, she closes the scene with another surprise. 'Then Hilarianus passed sentence on all of us: we were condemned to the beasts (*ad bestias*), and we returned to the prison in high spirits.' For Perpetua and her companions, it was a relief that they had passed the first hurdle of their contest. They had stood before the most fearsome figure the Roman authority in North Africa could produce, and they had not been found wanting in the service of their cause. Now, they must prepare themselves to win glory in the arena on behalf of their God.[11]

Perpetua tells us that instead of being beheaded as most criminals were, she was condemned to fight the beasts as part of the birthday games honouring Geta, the son of the Emperor Septimius Severus. These games were sponsored by prosperous regionally based landowners of the kind who held magistracies and priesthoods, and membership in the city council. Generally, games were sponsored by magistrates as part of the attempt to leave a memorable impression of their period in office, but the cult of the imperial family offered an occasion for other families of high standing to make competitive displays of loyalty.

A chilling aspect of Perpetua's interrogation was the fact that the procurator Hilarianus was permitted to sell condemned criminals to these landowners in order to set them to fight with the beasts during their games. In 176 (or early 177) the Emperor Marcus Aurelius

(161–180) and the Senate had cooperated in a measure designed to relieve the richer landowners of the provinces of some of the expenses of gladiatorial games, by allowing them to acquire condemned criminals from the imperial procurators at the cost of six *aurei* per head, or one-tenth of the price of hiring a fifth-class gladiator, and of course the savings were even higher if the criminal could replace a gladiator from the higher grades. The measure served a dual purpose. It added the *frisson* of public execution to the games, since the criminals would be killed, either dying during the fight or executed on the spot at the end of the contest. At the same time it dramatically lowered the cost of sponsoring games, so the development was popular with the aristocracy. [12]

The games have been seen as a ceremonial display of the power of empire, and this is certainly true. All parties knew that in order to maintain his dignity and the public order, the governor or his representative must be seen to crush those who refused to bow to Rome's authority. So the sale of criminals was a stroke of genius. It was a way of encouraging the collaboration of the civic elites, while at the same time sending a message to the public assembled in the amphitheatre.

By executing the miscreants in a way that was both brutal and humiliating, it was possible both to entertain the crowd and to discourage it from sympathizing with their cause. And the games were also an assertion by the richest families of their own right to stand with Rome against their inferiors, a point symbolized by the lesser mortals whom they bought from the procurator in order to display them as objects of destruction. It reflects the genius of Roman government that it was able so efficiently to harness the competitive self-interest of its subjects, and so effectively to activate their potential for mutual cruelty.

The Carthage amphitheatre today is a romantic site, overgrown with pines and eroded away so that only a few rows of its tiered seating remain. It was once the largest in North Africa, with a capacity of 35,000, two thirds of that of the Roman Colosseum.

Filled to capacity, it must have been alarmingly loud. Yet it is surprisingly intimate: when you stand in the centre of the arena looking towards the remaining first tiers of seating, you can see the faces of the people sitting there. The editor of Perpetua's prison diary passes down the tradition that as she stood in the arena, Perpetua fixed the crowd with an unsettling, luminous gaze.

Perpetua's Dreams

After her interrogation, Perpetua's diary takes on an almost hallucinatory quality. From this point forward it becomes a record of the dreams and visions that came to her in the days before she faced the beasts. Perpetua clearly believed that these dreams contained signs sent from heaven in order to guide her and to help her to understand what she was being asked to do, and the later Christians who preserved her prison diary seem to have accepted this.

The first of her dreams is in many ways the most painful and evocative, for it concerns one of the children in her family – her own brother – who had died a terrible death, aged seven, of a cancerous growth on his face. 'Some days later when we were all at prayer, suddenly while praying I spoke out and uttered the name Dinocrates . . . at once I realized I was privileged to pray for him. I began to pray and sigh deeply for him before the Lord.' Now she has passed the point of no return, Perpetua begins to gain a new understanding of herself, as someone to whom the Holy Spirit has given a rare and precious gift.[13]

While she has had to turn away from her living family, including her infant son, another child comes forward to claim her attention: this is the suffering boy Dinocrates, who had died not only in pain but also, it becomes clear, without the consolation of baptism. 'That very night I had the following vision. I saw Dinocrates coming out of a dark hole, where there were many others with him, very hot and thirsty, pale and dirty. On his face was the wound he had when he died.' Perpetua's vision expresses and explores her sense of helplessness with respect to the child's suffering, for she tells us that 'there was a great abyss between us: neither could approach the other'. And yet she sees that the thirsty child is in need of assistance: 'where Dinocrates stood, there was a pool full of water, and its rim was higher than his height . . . I was sorry that, though the pool had water in it, Dinocrates could not drink because of the height of the rim. Then I woke up, realizing that my brother was suffering.'[14]

Perpetua's reaction to this dream is to begin to work on her brother's behalf. 'I was confident that I could help him in his trouble, and I prayed for him every day until we were transferred to the military prison.' Subsequently she tells us of her consignment to the next stage of imprisonment, at the same time as her brother is freed through her prayers:[15]

> On the day we were put in chains, I had this vision shown to me. I saw the same spot that I had seen before, but there was Dinocrates all clean, well dressed, and refreshed. I saw a scar where the wound had been, and the pool that I had seen before had had its rim lowered . . . and Dinocrates kept drinking water from it. And when he had drunk enough of the water, he began to play as children do.[16]

Even though her own boy has not reached the same age, this is a writer who knows children: one somehow recognizes a mother's eye in this detail of the boy beginning to play once he feels well again. 'Then I awoke, and I realized that he had been delivered from his suffering.' In her imagination, healing her brother's cancer is bound up with the urgent need to protect him from the suffering that the unbaptized were believed to encounter in the afterlife.[17]

A number of lines flow together in Perpetua's thinking in this passage. On the one hand, the water is linked in her imagination to baptism. Dinocrates is cleansed and refreshed; he is made whole and spared from suffering. There is a pardox here: as she moves forward towards her own ordeal, and the net of her fate closes around her, Perpetua grows in power to bring her loved ones to safety.

The vision is also, one imagines, a way of coping with the loss of her son. Immediately before the vision of Dinocrates, she has told us that after her confession of faith before the procurator, her father refused to send the baby to her in prison. A door has closed between herself and her family, who must now be seen to reject her entirely in order to protect themselves, although at least one family member is kind enough to send a message that the baby has accepted weaning without too much difficulty. Perpetua tells us that, despite her distress, she is grateful to discover that she does not feel the expected pain in her breasts. It is as if God is helping her to accept that giving up the baby is the right thing to do.

But it is no coincidence that she turns from thinking about the baby to telling us about a little boy who became ill, suffered, and died – and about her own sensation of helplessness in watching his suffering. She knows that there is every chance that her own baby will suffer a similar fate. Given a child mortality rate higher than that of the most deprived areas of the modern world, there was a less-than-even chance that Perpetua's boy would reach adulthood.

So the abyss between herself and Dinocrates in the vision offers her a way of thinking about how death will separate her from her baby. She has to face the fact that whatever befalls him, she will not be there with him: he will have no mother to heal and comfort him. And yet, the vision of her small brother reassures her that somehow, through her prayers, she has the power to intercede on his behalf.

Perpetua turns from her vision of Dinocrates to tell us that the power within her and her companions has been recognized from an unexpected quarter. Pudens, the prison governor, has been inspired by their courage and begins to help them, allowing visitors to come to the prison to honour the martyrs. But as the day of her contest in the arena approaches, Perpetua must contend with one last visit from her father. Again, his conduct is not really what we expect from a Roman paterfamilias; his attempts to steer his daughter's will are far wilder and more desperate than one might anticipate.

> Now the day of the contest was approaching, and my father came to see me overwhelmed with sorrow. He started tearing the hairs from his beard and threw them on the ground; he then threw *himself* on the ground and began to curse his old age and to say such words as would move all creation. I felt sorry for his unhappy old age.[18]

Merely by withholding the proper obedience expected of a Roman daughter, Perpetua has reduced him to something very like hysteria. What she tells us next suggests that she is aware, at least at an unconscious level, that she has undergone a profound transformation, and has acquired the power to prevail over not only her own father, but even the most frightening of men.

Perpetua and the Egyptian

Perpetua's next vision shows that for all her bravura, the fact has not escaped her that the punishment for her act of defiance against the procurator will be a cruel death. She knows that in order to maintain his dignity and the public order, the emperor must crush those who brazenly refuse to bow to his authority. Of course, the point is to put a stop to the challenge posed by their disobedience, but it is also an act of communication to the civic body assembled in the amphitheatre. By executing the miscreants in a way that is both brutal and humiliating, the crowd are both entertained and discouraged from sympathizing with their cause.

The Christian apologist Tertullian, who was living in Carthage at the time of Perpetua's execution, argued that this policy of humiliating the Christians as criminals in the arena could only backfire. Men and women who knew their God would sustain them had nothing to fear, he suggested, and so they could not be humiliated. In his *Apology* (written *c.* 197–8), Tertullian warned an earlier Roman governor that 'whenever we are mown down by you, the blood of Christians is seed for the Church'. This ideal was inspiring, but at the same time it raised the bar for those who intended to face the beasts themselves. Perpetua's diary shows that as the time of the contest approached, even her unconscious mind was working to prepare her to face her ordeal with valour.[19]

The day before we were to fight with the beasts I saw the following vision. Pomponius the deacon came to the prison gates and began to knock violently . . . And he said to me, 'Perpetua, come; we are waiting for you.' Then he took my hand and we began to walk through rough and broken country. At last we came to the amphitheatre out of breath, and he led me into the centre of the arena. Then he told me, 'Do not be afraid. I am here, struggling with you.' Then he left.[20]

The idea here that she would be sustained by a powerful presence was one which reached back to the Apostle Paul's idea that 'I have been crucified with Christ and I no longer live, but Christ lives within me.' (Galatians 2: 20)

Next Perpetua turns to face what awaits her in the arena. 'I looked at the enormous crowd who watched in astonishment. I was surprised that no beasts were let loose on me; for I knew that I was condemned to die by the beasts.' There is a surprise: 'Then out came an Egyptian to fight against me, together with his seconds. Some handsome young men came along, too, to be my seconds and assistants. My clothes were stripped off, and suddenly I was a man.'[21]

This is a wholly unexpected development in Perpetua's narrative. What can we make of her statement that she became a man? At one level, we can see it as the logical development of a theme that has been present throughout: this is a woman who is fearless and refuses to accept the subordinate role that might be expected of a Roman daughter. At another level, however, her self-transformation is a marker of the surreal visionary landscape she has entered. In the logic of this thought-world, she must prevail because she is fighting for God; her perception of herself as a man is a sign of her growing confidence. Now she is ready to take on the Egyptian:

> We drew close together and began to let our fists fly. My opponent tried to get a hold of my feet, but I kept striking him in the face with the heels of my feet. Then I was raised up into the air and I began to pummel him without as it were touching the ground.[22]

There are a number of important things to notice here. The first is Perpetua's intense involvement in the vision. It has clearly come to her in vivid detail, and one can almost feel her thrashing as she tries to shake her feet free in order to use them against her opponent. The second is that Perpetua herself has clearly been a spectator at many such contests. She knows what men do when they wrestle, and there is none of the uncertainty about the goings-on in the arena that one might expect from a young woman who had lived most of her life indoors. Thuburbo was in fact a large enough town to have its own Roman amphitheatre, so she may well have gone along to watch wrestling matches there during her childhood, even if her own contest would be held in the more prepossessing amphitheatre at Carthage. Certainly, this was not a woman who was afraid of the world of men.

As Perpetua looks ahead to her day in the arena, she knows that those who have raised their voices against Rome will be destroyed, and the civic order will be re-established. It has not escaped her that the fatal games of the amphitheatre are a perfectly suited vehicle for the message of asserting the Emperor's authority, because the amphitheatre itself is one of the great monuments of Roman power in North Africa. At every step along the way, Perpetua's story has been intertwined with that of Roman power in Africa.

Even the most intimate details of her story, such as the painful relationship with her family, is somehow bound up with the presence in the land of a colonial power – that of Rome – that has changed life immeasurably for both the urban and rural populations. Even the reassuring vision of the little brother finally able to slake his thirst is a mark of the Roman power in the land. The great works of civil engineering, which meant that aqueducts fed baths and fountains in virtually every town across the land, were a ubiquitous sign of Roman occupation – and the element that makes us understand why so many Africans were happy to accept the yoke of Rome. The basin from which the child Dinocrates was able to drink, in Perpetua's vision, was as much a sign of Roman occupation as was the amphitheatre in which Perpetua would meet her death.

Perpetua's diary ends with the vision of her struggle with the Egyptian, on the eve of her appointed day in the arena. The story of her death the next day, alongside her companions, will be told afterwards by an anonymous editor, who claims to be an eyewitness to her brave conduct when thrown to the beasts. It is possible that the editor was working centuries later on the basis of legend or oral tradition – the date has never been satisfactorily established. The Latin text of the prison diary survives in nine manuscripts copied in medieval monasteries, with a single tenth-century manuscript surviving in Greek. All of the manuscripts add the editor's frame-story, which takes pains to emphasize Perpetua's feminine modesty as well as her bravery. It is almost as if on reading Perpetua's own account the editor has been alarmed by the martyr's vision of herself as a naked male wrestler in a wrestling match.

It is the immediacy and alarming frankness of the prison diary that lies at the root of Perpetua's peculiar magnetism. While other martyrs' stories are told in the idealizing tones of those who remember them, Perpetua's narrative gives us access to the bold and unapologetic voice of the martyr herself.

Her boldness reveals itself, too, in the honest way in which she handles the problem of how she will be remembered after her death.

She knows that her story has already spun beyond her own control. Her voice will endure into the future, but in a form chosen by others, to serve the needs of later communities unknown to her and beyond her imagining. If her willingness to die for her faith shows extraordinary physical and moral courage, her last words are brave in a different way: 'This is what happened up to the day before the contest. As for what is to happen at the contest itself, let him write of it who will.'[23]

6

THE EMPEROR'S MOTHER

She . . . consecrated to the God whom she adored two shrines, one by the cave of his birth, the other on the mountain of the ascension. For the God with us allowed himself to suffer even birth for our sake, and the place of his birth in the flesh was announced among the Hebrews by the name of Bethlehem. Thus then the most devout Empress beautified . . . the sacred cave there. The Emperor himself shortly afterwards honoured this too with imperial dedications, supplementing his mother's works of art with treasures of silver and gold and embroidered curtains.[1]

Around the year 327, the bishop of Caesarea, the capital of the Roman province of Palestine, had a remarkable visitor in his city: the Empress Helena, mother of the first Christian emperor, Constantine. Her son had recently acquired the eastern provinces of the Empire as the victor of a civil war, and Helena was making a goodwill tour of the eastern provinces on his behalf.

Helena began life as an innkeeper's daughter in Drepanum, a modest seaport in Bithynia, Asia Minor, on the Black Sea. She became a soldier's wife or, more probably, concubine – in any case, she seems to have met her son's father Constantius Chlorus in the 260s or early 270s while he was an obscure soldier. In 272 or 273, she gave birth to Constantine, her only child as far as we know. When the boy had come of age, his father Constantius was proclaimed Caesar, then the title accorded to the Roman Emperor's deputy. As a gesture of goodwill towards his patron, the Emperor Maximian Herculius, Constantius was invited to marry Theodora, the Emperor's daughter. So Helena, the mother of his only son, was cast aside. Her loss of status would be redeemed handsomely when her son became Emperor.

A number of ancient sources suggest that it was Helena who converted her son to Christianity. On the face of it, the suggestion makes sense. We know that across the long years of the third century, Christianity had been growing steadily, and there is no reason it could not have reached an innkeeper's family in Bithynia. The neighbouring Black Sea region of Pontus was home to Christian families who went into hiding during times of persecution. So it is entirely possible that the tide of female networking reached the imperial family through the person of Helena. But the conversion of the Emperor Constantine to Christianity was an event so significant that a variety of theories emerged in antiquity to account for how and why it happened.

At the turn of the fourth century, there was no reason to expect that Christianity would be singled out for imperial favour, and certainly not that the reversal of fortune would happen so quickly. By February of 313, the Emperor Constantine would begin issuing laws to secure the position of the Christian Church, now recognized for the first time as an empire-wide institution, though this ideal was never satisfactorily translated into a single institution on the ground. But ten years earlier, in 303, things had looked very different. At that time, the joint emperors Diocletian and Maximian pursued an aggressive policy against groups who refused to honour the gods of Rome. From 303 to 311, they aimed a general persecution against the Christians – the Great Persecution. It is likely that this nine-year period produced more Christian martyrs than the first three centuries combined.

The seeds of change were planted in 305, when Diocletian and Maximian retired. In the eastern part of the Empire, Diocletian's deputy Galerius succeeded him without too much difficulty, but in the west, the early death of Constantius, Maximian's appointed heir as Emperor, gave rise to bloody civil wars. Out of these wars a new attitude to Christianity arose. The victor was the son of Helena and

Constantius – known to history as the Emperor Constantine. It was he who made the decision to adopt Christianity as a religion for the Empire.

All of our ancient sources agree on this much, but there was far less agreement about why. Constantine himself told a story that was more dramatic, though somehow more ambivalent, than the later story that he was converted by his mother. He remembered that on the eve of an important battle, he had had a vision of protection offered by a powerful war-god.

Constantine did not come to the purple easily. On Maximian's retirement, Constantine's father Constantius had received the rank of *augustus*, co-emperor with responsibility for the western provinces, and appointed Flavius Severus as his deputy. At Constantius' death in July of 306, his son, who was at the death-bed and already had a brilliant military career behind him, was a natural candidate to succeed him. The soldiers at York duly proclaimed Constantine Emperor. But the Senate and the Praetorian Guard in Rome had other ideas. On hearing of Constantius' death they initially elected Flavius Severus. But Severus was abandoned when Maxentius, Constantine's uncle by marriage and the son of Constantius' predecessor Maximian, approached Rome with a substantial army.

So Constantine's first task was to secure his own position. From 306 to 312 he fought his way towards Rome. It was not until the Battle of the Milvian Bridge in October of 312 that he was able to capture the capital from Maxentius. In the aftermath, he established a treaty with Licinius, the Emperor of the East who had also fought against Maxentius, and a marriage between Licinius and Constantine's sister Constantia sealed the agreement for an amicable sharing of power. But soon war erupted again between the two men, and it would take over a decade, until September 324, for Constantine to unify the Empire under his command. Years later, the Emperor told the story of how a vision had appeared to him on the afternoon before the Battle of the Milvian Bridge, showing a cross-shaped trophy of the type to be carried into battle. That night, Jesus himself appeared to him in a dream, and ordered him to have one like it made for his army, and on waking he obeyed. As a result, the battle was his.[2]

This divine intervention convinced Constantine that the god of the Christians must take the place of Victoria, the winged victory goddess of the ancient traditional religion. If the new god could bring an end to civil war, there was every reason to believe he had the power to protect the Empire in other ways. If this story is true, it was probably only later – not directly after the victory had been won and the dust had settled, but months or even years later – that Constantine began to understand who this God really was, and what He expected of those under His protection.

The spring after the battle of the Milvian Bridge, Constantine began publishing laws that erased the long-standing legal discrimination against the Church. To Christian *sacerdotes* (scholars disagree as to whether this means bishops or all members of the clergy), the victorious Emperor now offered the same protections traditionally accorded to the ministers of legitimate religion. Over the next decade, the incremental changes to the status of the churches would put Christianity in the position of one among many state-sponsored cults.[3]

If Constantine had discovered a special intimacy with the God of the Christians through his victory, the fact that the new god came with a human entourage may have been a surprise. The Christian bishops quickly made themselves known to Constantine, and they had ideas of their own. The Emperor had certainly received the blessing of their god – the critical military victory at the Milvian Bridge was recognized by all concerned as an undisputed sign of divine favour – but the Christian Churches had not endured nearly three hundred years of persecution in order to hand over control of their movement at the first sign of an emperor's goodwill.

A source from the fifth or sixth century, the *Passion of Agnes*, shows the attempt of a later writer to 'personalize' the Emperor's conversion by linking it a healing miracle involving his daughter Constantia. (The princess shared the name of her aunt who had married the

Emperor Licinius, a point that has caused considerable confusion to both ancient writers and modern scholars.) According to this source, the princess suffered from a terrible skin disease, and her inability to find relief from pagan doctors led her to seek healing at a martyr's shrine.

> Now, Constantia was herself a Princess, and a very wise Virgin, but she was so beset by sores that from her head right down to her feet there was no part of her body unaffected by them. Having taken advice, and in the hope of recovering her health, she went at night to the tomb of the Martyrs; and, pagan though she was, it was with a believing heart that she poured out her prayers full of faith.[4]

It was not unusual for individuals to bring their ailments for cure at a religious sanctuary. Interestingly, it was not unusual to visit the shrine of a god whom one had not previously worshipped. Most famous among healing shrines was the campus of the great god Asklepios at Epidaurus, where 160 guestrooms accommodated male and female pilgrims. After sacrifices to the god and rituals of purification, each would spend a night in the sanctuary, and in the morning a priest-doctor would interpret any dreams, which were understood to contain clues for treatment sent by the god himself.

It makes sense that Christian saints had become involved in the healing business. Even pagans knew that the Christian martyrs had triumphed over death, and why should they not be equally powerful in the face of disease? In its description of Constantia at the tomb of Agnes, the *Passion of Agnes* evokes the standard protocols. When she had said her prayer,

> She was swiftly overcome by a sweet sleep, and in a vision she saw the most blessed Agnes, offering her the following advice, 'Act with determination, Constantia, and put your trust in the Lord Jesus Christ as your Saviour, through whom you will now

obtain recovery from all the sores from which you have suffered in your body.' After this message, Constantia awoke cured to such an extent that not the least sign of any scar still remained.[5]

There is a difference here, however: our source claims that Agnes could offer more than advice. Unlike the priests and priestesses at the great pagan healing shrines, she actually had the power to effect a cure. A miraculous cure in the imperial family was the best possible publicity for the god who bestowed this power on Agnes.

So then, returning to the palace in the best of health, she gave [great] joy to her father the *Augustus* and to her brothers the Emperors. The whole city was wreathed about and there was rejoicing among the military, among private citizens and among everyone who heard about it. The wrong faith of the pagans was in destroyed, the faith of the Lord [could] rejoice.[6]

To an ancient reader, it would seem entirely plausible to suggest that the Emperor Constantine had decided to stop persecuting the Christians because a Christian saint had healed his daughter.

This version of events shares an important element with the story of Constantine's Dream. Both stories reflect a belief that only the favour of the gods could bring *salus* – peace and health – to an individual human being or an entire empire. The Latin concept of *salus* is often translated into English as 'salvation' – but the bland piety of that word misses the force of the Latin. *Salus* encompasses safety and protection from harm by natural or supernatural forces, and at the same time an idea of well-being, wholeness, or healing.

Eusebius, Constantine's biographer, remembers yet another variation on the conversion theme. Although he records the Emperor's story that the decisive moment took place on the eve of the Battle of the Milvian Bridge, he also touches on the theme of conversion that runs through families. Speaking of Constantine's relationship to his mother Helena, he celebrates their shared Christian piety.

And his character may well be described as blessed, for his filial piety as well as on other grounds. Through Constantine's influence Helena became so devout a worshipper of God (though she had not previously been such) that she seemed to have been instructed from the first by the Saviour of mankind.[7]

Instead of remembering Helena as the mother of imperial Christianity, as some other writers did, Eusebius suggests that it was the Empress who was converted by her son.

Family Values

Christians certainly welcomed the end of the Great Persecution under Diocletian and Galerius, but there remained a suspicion among some of them that the Emperor's favour had not been an unmixed blessing for the Church. A hundred years later, the historian Sozomen told a story that captures the atmosphere of suspicion surrounding the Emperor, shedding a grim light on his personal involvement in the religion of his new allies.

It is reported by the pagans that Constantine, after slaying some of his nearest relations, and particularly after assenting to the murder of his own son Crispus, repented of his evil deeds, and inquired of Sopater, the philosopher, who was then master of the school of Plotinus, concerning the means of purification from guilt. The philosopher – so the story goes – replied that such moral defilement could admit of no purification. The Emperor was grieved at this repulse, but happening to meet with some bishops who told him that he would be cleansed from sin, on repentance and on submitting to baptism, he was delighted with their representations, and admired their doctrines, and became a Christian, and led his subjects to the same faith. It appears to me that this story was the invention of persons who desired to vilify the Christian religion.[8]

Sozomen argued that the story was groundless, but he still had to grapple with the fact that Constantine was remembered not only as a general who had been responsible for the deaths of thousands in battle, but also as the instigator of other deaths that could not be explained away.

The deaths of the Emperor's second wife and eldest son in 326 were the most important of these. Like his father, Constantine had put away Minervina, the mother of his first son Crispus, when he was proclaimed Emperor. In her place, he married Fausta, a daughter of his father's patron Maximian. Some sources suggest that in 326 Fausta had brought Constantine a warning that her stepson meant to usurp his father's position. When, after having his son put to death, the Emperor grasped that there had been no conspiracy and Fausta had merely wanted Crispus dead to make way for her own sons, his anger now resulted in a second death. On Constantine's orders, the treacherous Fausta was trapped in an over-heated bath by a corrupt attendant.

Another version of events circulated in antiquity, however. In this version, the Emperor discovered an illicit liaison between his son – now in his early twenties – and Fausta who, if her marriage to Constantine in 307 was her first, could have been just over thirty at the time of her death.

What both of these stories have in common is the idea that the Emperor's family was characterized by treachery. The Emperor himself was not the only culprit: in neither version of events does Fausta come out well. In one version she is an adulteress, while in the other she is a wicked stepmother who destroys her stepchild to serve the ambition of her own offspring. Neither version of the story can be said to be trustworthy. Both owe something to a fairy-tale insistence, on the part of the ancient historical writers, that second wives and stepmothers must always be wicked.

Nevertheless the stories call attention to something important. The imperial court had always been a dangerous place, and Christian ethics seem to have made little difference to the atmosphere there. The Emperor's own creed was not a Christianity of faith, hope and charity. Rather, it was a cult honouring the warrior god who had brought Constantine victory against his rivals for the imperial purple.

Not long after the death of Fausta, in or around 327, the Emperor's mother Helena made her journey to the Holy Land. She travelled to Jerusalem to find the remains of the True Cross, the death-scaffold on which Jesus was believed to have been nailed and left to die. Some scholars argue that this was a public-relations tour to the East after her son had acquired the eastern half of the Empire in his civil war with Licinius, since there was a rumour that the Christians of the East had done their best to work for Constantine's side in the civil war.[9]

Later tradition remembered her as working to expand Christianity's new role as a religion of empire. During her visit to the Holy Land, Helena built a shrine to the Nativity in Bethlehem. We saw above that the church historian Eusebius – who was bishop of Caesarea in Palestine at the time of Helena's visit – records that at the place where Mary had given birth to Jesus, Helena built a shrine to the Virgin as *Theotokos*, or Mother of God (literally 'God-bearer'). At face value, this was a bland enough gesture of piety, but it also carried a message about the imperial family. The point was to build up an idea of Jesus as part of a heavenly family, whose supernatural power would reflect and enhance the power of the imperial family on earth. Helena could thus remind her subjects that just as her own son, the Emperor, was the chosen representative on earth of the Son of God, so she herself had a counterpart in the Mother of God, who was becoming ever more popular as a figure to whom Christians could address their most intimate prayers and petitions. Loyalty to the imperial family and piety for Mary and her Son went hand in hand.

A Woman's Bible:
The *Cento* of the Poetess Proba

The new climate of state-sponsored Christianity brought an institutional 'hardening' of the faith. The Christian churches were losing their old improvised quality, and this was a development whose importance cannot be stressed enough. Christian communities moved their meetings out of the courtyards of members' households and into elegant new purpose-built basilicas with marble columns. In many cases, the new basilicas were paid for by the Emperor himself – indeed, the original meaning of the term 'basilica' is an audience-chamber for a king (*basileus*).

Before 313, the Christian communities included only those who had joined the movement through personal ties or because they were attracted to its philosophy. There was certainly no earthly advantage to be had from joining the Church. But after 313, the character of the Christian communities began to change. Christian bishops were now people of distinction. As the role of Christian leaders in the cities became more important, access to positions of authority in the Christian communities began to be structured more formally.

Now that Christianity was established as a legitimate and even a powerful organization within Roman society, this had consequences for women. To begin with, a wider mix of women found themselves drawn under its canopy. Of course, some of the Christian women of the fourth century came from families that had adhered to the faith from its earliest days, but far more numerous were those to whom the stories and doctrines of the Christians were something of a novelty. From the mid-fourth century, we begin to find women of the highly literate upper classes bringing Christianity into the cultural mainstream.

Many historians believe that in the families of the Roman Senate, it was the women who converted to Christianity first, while their husbands and sons continued to fulfil the inherited pagan religious obligations of their illustrious forebears. Contemporary sources often paint a picture of a kind of triangle, in which noble women became indispensable social mentors to a Christian clergy who tended to come from rather more modest backgrounds, while the women's husbands tried to maintain the old ways. In other elite families, however, both the husband and the wife became involved as patrons of the Christian churches. It is just after mid-century that we begin to see members of these elite families working to put Christianity at the heart of a new flowering of Roman culture.

One such family were the gens Anicia, one of the senatorial dynasties known for cultivating a close relationship with the imperial family. Their involvement in the Roman church of the fourth century was equally enthusiastic, and they are attested as having made numerous gifts of buildings, sculpture, and mosaic to the churches of the capital during the age of beautification inaugurated by Constantine. Among their benefactions was a baptistery for the fourth-century cathedral of St Peter in Rome, known as 'old St Peter's' to historians since it was destroyed and replaced by the masterpiece of Michelangelo in the sixteenth century. Some contemporaries suspected, however, that their highly visible role as patrons of Roman Christianity was a matter of social climbing. As in any age, the cultural patrons of fourth-century culture may have had mixed motives, even if what they created was of enduring value.

Most interesting among the fourth-century members of this family as a contributor to the new Christian culture is the poetess Proba, who was remembered throughout the Middle Ages as having produced a much-beloved summary of the Old and New Testaments in Latin verse. Curious from our perspective is the fact that the poem is a patchwork of lines stitched together from Virgil, the greatest of Roman poets. This was a kind of poetry that was very much in vogue in the fourth century, and of course it took quite a bit of skill to make sensible Christian narrative out of pagan epic poetry without violating the metre of the ancient half-lines thus stitched together.

Though eccentric from a modern viewpoint, the formula was dazzlingly apt as a way of exploring the contrast between the inherited literary tradition and the new Christian patrimony.

Proba's is a curious kind of poem. It is a cento, a form beloved of late classical poets, composed entirely from the lines (and sometimes half-lines) of an earlier, longer poem or sequence of poems. A cento is a showpiece, capturing perfectly the love of the past that is the distinguishing feature of Roman culture. It can only be written by a person of considerable learning, because knitting together the lines and phrases of the original without losing their sense or their music requires a great confidence with poetic metre, and a deep understanding of the earlier poet's work.

Only one of Proba's poems survives, and it is ambitious enough to be mind-boggling. The poet she chose to draw from should come as no surprise if one considers her Roman education – he is Virgil, author of the *Aeneid*, the founding myth of the city of Rome. Pieced together entirely from borrowed lines and phrases from Virgil's *Aeneid*, *Eclogues* and *Georgics*, the 694 lines of Proba's poem offer a flying summary of biblical history from the Creation to the post-Resurrection appearance of Jesus to his disciples. (According to an ancient source, Proba was also fluent in classical Greek, and wrote a second cento in Greek from the works of Homer.)

Proba's project of reclothing biblical epic in the harmonious and familiar dialect of cultural prestige seems strange to us, but it would have appealed to a group of readers who found the rough diction of the Gospels distasteful. Whether in the original Greek or in the old Latin translation, the *Vetus Latina*, the versions of the New Testament circulating in Proba's day were couched in provincial dialect that sounded harsh and barbaric to the metropolitan ear. For Proba's readers, the high-flying language of Virgil was just right for a story of divine intervention in history. The contrast between the heroic age of Israel and that of Rome – or between the home-spun fishermen's stories of the New Testament and the elevated language of the greatest of the golden Latin poets – was exhilarating.

142

At the same time, we have to remember that many of the Roman literati of the fourth century actually knew very little about Christianity. Who was this Jesus? Why was he associated with fish and fishermen? What – where? – were Nazareth and Galilee? What kind of barbarian tribe were the *Iudaioi*, the Judaeans? These were questions that not every Roman hostess could answer. And, of course, such questions *needed* to be answered, because if people who counted were following the imperial family and becoming Christian, it was important – not only for the converts but for everyone else – to have some idea of what was involved. This was especially true since there was a legacy of hostility between Roman culture and the upstart faith of Nazareth. Could an educated person adopt the new faith without deeply compromising her commitment to Roman culture?

To answer this question the poetess puts forward a deliciously counter-intuitive suggestion. What if Virgil were somehow a fore-runner of Jesus, preparing the way in the arena of high culture just as John the Baptist had done in the Judaean wilderness? Indeed, in his fourth *Eclogue* Virgil had spoken of a child whose birth would bring the dawn of a golden age. It was not lost on fourth-century Christians that Virgil (d. 19 BC) had been writing shortly before the birth of Christ. Perhaps Virgil, like Isaiah and John, was one of the prophets whom God had sent to announce the coming of the Messiah? To the daughter of a Roman senator, it would have seemed natural that the court of the Emperor Augustus was among the chosen destinations for such an important message.

Proba's intimate knowledge of both Virgil and the Bible allowed her to play freely with the familiar phrases and stories, and to make the stories her own. There is an intimacy to her way of handling her material. To retell sacred history in language borrowed from Rome's most beloved poet required fluency in both the Roman and biblical traditions, and it is clear that Proba was equally at ease with each of them. Her poem made the Bible come alive to the ear of a fourth-century reader.

Proba's is very much a version of the Bible from the woman's point of view. The attentive reader can see that she repeatedly recasts the narrative ever so slightly to focus on husband–wife and parent–child relationships. So, for example, when Proba tells the story of the Nativity, the emphasis is on Mary's passionate devotion to her child. This can be seen most clearly in her heroic efforts to protect her baby from King Herod during the Massacre of the Innocents. Painting a picture of a town seized by terror, Proba singles out Mary as a heroine of bravery and intelligence, one whom a Roman materfamilias would naturally wish to imitate. Hers was a version of the Nativity designed to capture the imagination of women and girls.

If we turn to the religious ideas and values within the poem, we will see that Proba wants to find the connection between Virgil's values and those of Jesus. Her version of the story of the rich young man is a case in point. In the Gospel of Matthew, Jesus tells a young man who asks for advice to 'go, sell all you have, and give it to the poor'. (Matthew 19: 21) In Proba's version, the young man is told to keep a modest household and live a Spartan lifestyle. Her Jesus seems to be recommending the old values of the Roman republic, the ethos of a frugal warrior aristocracy.

The poem's translators Elizabeth Clark and Diane Hatch have shown that in her choice of passages from Virgil, Proba drew particularly on scenes of filial piety and conjugal devotion – for example those involving Aeneas and his father Anchises, his first wife Creusa, or the Trojan hero Hector's wife Andromache. In many instances, she has 'borrowed across' the ideas of harmonious family life from the original setting of her texts into her narrative about Jesus.[10]

Proba seems unaware of the idea that Mary had miraculously remained a virgin after giving birth. It was an idea that would become popular in the last quarter of the fourth century, but it may not yet have been in wide circulation at the time she wrote. For Proba, the relationships between Mary, Jesus, and Joseph are those of a normal family. Proba is aware that the child's father is not Joseph, but this fact is taken as an occasion to emphasize the brilliant *nomen* of the child's true father rather than the sexual history of the mother.

Some scholars believe that Proba had a more anxious reason for writing her *Cento*. In 361 Julian, the nephew of Constantine, came to the throne, and one of his first acts was to reveal that he had secretly turned against Christianity and returned to the traditional religion. His apostasy sent shockwaves through the newly converted Christian elite, many of whom had come to think of the Church as a route to imperial preferment. Especially distressing was Julian's announcement, in 362, of his view that Christian teachers could not in good conscience serve as teachers in the state-sponsored schools in the municipalities. A system of examination was put into place by which magistrates could approve the candidates who wished to serve as teachers in each district. There is reason to believe that the aim of the scheme was religious discrimination, for the Emperor argued publicly that for a Christian to teach the works of Plato, Homer, and Virgil was an act of hypocrisy, since the great philosophers and poets had all believed in the old gods.[11]

Proba's *Cento* may have been designed as a pragmatic response to the Emperor's initiatives, an introduction to Christian ideas for schoolchildren couched in the terms of a classical education. The logic here seems to be that Christian parents who wanted their children to benefit from both exposure to the Bible and the shared pagan literary culture of their peers would have wanted to supplement the teaching available in the schools. The dedication of Proba's poem supports this reading. In the closing lines of the poem, Proba speaks to her husband: 'This observance do you keep, sweet husband, and if we win merit through our piety, then – pure in heart – may our children's children keep the faith.' If Proba is not thinking of a readership of children, she is at the very least thinking of a legacy of Christian teaching to be preserved within families.

It was a bold act, and at the same time a delicate intervention. Her affectionate self-confidence where sacred history was concerned was matched by a confident respect for the Word of God. Proba's poem stands clear of any attempt to tamper with the biblical text, inviting her reader to see the tradition through new eyes while leaving the text itself safely undisturbed.

Yet it would be a mistake to think of Proba as bound by her sex to avoid the more theologically ambitious aspects of biblical interpretation or textual criticism. Women were at the forefront of biblical scholarship in fourth-century Rome. Much of their effort was aimed at understanding the sacred text in its original Hebrew and Greek. In fact, the greatest monument of medieval biblical scholarship, the Vulgate translation of the Old and New Testaments, had its origin in the wider circle of Proba's acquaintance. Aristocratic women were to play an important role in supporting the project.

A Bishop, a Widow, and an Empress

We turn now to Olympias, heiress of one of the most powerful Christian families of her generation. She was a figure of equal standing to Proba, but her way of embracing Christianity was very different. While Proba was a Christian version of the old Roman materfamilias, and advocate of fertility and family values, Olympias was an advocate for the cult of virginity.

Born around 368, Olympias spent her childhood as an orphan in the household of an aristocratic widow in Constantinople. Her grandfather Ablabius had been one of Emperor Constantine's favourites a half-century earlier, at the time of the city's founding. Constantine's new capital, named after himself and built upon the site of the ancient city of Byzantium, had given the Emperor a valuable base from which he and his ministers could have ready access to the eastern Mediterranean. Established in 330 as a royal city second only to Rome, Constantinople became the favourite eastern residence of the imperial family and it would retain this honour for over a thousand years.[12]

Constantinople in the early fourth century was a magnet for fortune-seekers. The Emperor's choice to re-found the city as a capital gave an unparalleled opportunity to the families who had helped to establish it as a new centre of prestige. The atmosphere of the new capital was not unlike that of a nineteenth-century frontier town, in that those who arrived early could, within a few years, be seen as the great and the good.

The rise of Ablabius and his family also illustrates the importance of religion to the careers of fourth-century men. When the Emperor established a second Senate for his new capital in the 330s, he chose many Christians, often distinguished by their piety or good fortune rather than their birth. The pagan orator Libanius later complained that the new Christian senators tended to come from undistinguished backgrounds, having been bath attendants and sausage-makers before they were singled out by imperial favour.

This seems to have been the case where the grandfather of Olympias was concerned. Ablabius rose from humble beginnings, first as an office clerk in the service of the governor of Crete, to fill the highest offices of the Empire. From 327 to 329 he was Praetorian Prefect and, in 331, Consul. Power of this kind could go as easily as it came, and indeed, after Constantine's death in 337, Ablabius fell from grace.

But by this time Ablabius was already rich, and he used the money wisely. He bought extensive estates in the Black Sea region. After his death, one of his daughters married the king of Armenia, a friendly client kingdom at the north-eastern corner of the Empire, a comfortable sail from Constantinople along the Black Sea. Olympias was the new queen's niece, and she would make good use, late in her life, of her connection to the Armenian royal family. A son of Ablabius, Seleucus, became one of the Emperor's counts, and around 368 he produced Olympias by a wife whose name is not recorded. They did not live to raise their daughter. Seleucus, the father, seems to have died in the early 370s, though we do not know the date of the mother's death.[13]

When Olympias was orphaned, she came into the care of Theodosia, the cousin of Gregory of Nazianzus, who became bishop of the city in 379. It has been suggested that Theodosia was the wife of one of his sons, a second Ablabius, an older brother of Olympias. We know that the family of Olympias was one of the wealthiest of the eastern capital, and Theodosia herself seems to have had virtually unlimited resources at her disposal. She was almost certainly widowed before the return of her cousin Gregory to the capital as its bishop in 379.[14]

Olympias came from a wealthy and influential Christian family, but her good fortune went further than this. The first great theological Council held at Nicaea in 325 produced a creed that would later be established as a pillar of Christian orthodoxy, but in the 330s the imperial family abandoned the Nicene faith and took up the faith of the losing party at Nicaea, known to history as the Arian heresy. It happened that the family of Olympias had adhered to the Nicene Creed across the long years, from the mid-330s to 378, when that creed was out of favour with the imperial family. This single fact made a decisive difference to the family's fortunes at least twice in its history. Nicene Orthodoxy had played its part in the fall of Ablabius, and it would play its part in the rise of Olympias.

The Arian controversy turned on the question of whether Jesus had existed since the beginning of time as the Word of God. The Gospel of John had emphasized the power of the Word – *logos* in Greek – in its opening lines: 'In the beginning was the Word, and the Word was with God, and the Word was God.' The bishops who signed the Nicene Creed held that the Word of God was eternal. It had existed since God first spoke, to say 'Let there be Light' in the Book of Genesis. The dissenters took as their rallying cry a saying of Arius, a priest of Alexandria: 'There was a time when He was not.' As far as they were concerned, Jesus had not existed before he became incarnate by the Virgin Mary. Although the Nicene party won the battle at the Council of Nicaea, by the mid-330s they seemed to have lost the war, and this situation continued for decades. In the 370s, to say that the Word was eternal, as the Nicene party did, had acquired a significance that was political as well as theological. To disagree with the theological position of the imperial family had become a way of announcing that one was willing to defy the Emperor's judgement.

But everything changed in August of 378 when Olympias was around ten. The Emperor Valens was killed in battle at Hadrianople, roughly 200 kilometres west of Constantinople, and a new dynasty was established. The new emperor was the Spanish general Theodosius, and his family were notoriously loyal to Niçaea. When he arrived for his coronation in November of 380, Theodosius brought with him as his consort the Spanish noblewoman Aelia Flavia Flaccilla, along with their two small children, a daughter, Pulcheria, and a son, Arcadius. A host of other Spanish relatives accompanied them, and we will see below that the Spanish court played an important role in the politics of the capital. Even before the arrival of the new emperor, the prospect of a Nicene invasion changed the social landscape of the imperial capital virtually overnight.

Nowhere was the significance of the reversal felt more acutely than in the household of Theodosia, which was noted for the outstanding Nicene piety of its inhabitants. Soon after the death of the Emperor in August of 378, Theodosia seems to have grasped that the death of the Arian emperor would open up new possibilities for the Nicene faction, although it is not clear whether the residents of the capital were yet aware of the identity of the new emperor, who was proclaimed far away in Milan. Acting on behalf of the embattled Nicene community in the city, Theodosia sent for her cousin Gregory of Nazianzus, who was already known for his fierce Nicene faith and his brilliance as a preacher.

At the time, Gregory was living in retirement as a monk, hundreds of miles away at the shrine of St Thecla in Seleucia, on the south coast of Asia Minor. He came as soon as he could, and in 379 he arrived in the capital. According to his own memoir, he came 'That I might revive souls parched but still producing green growth, and that if the lamp were fed with oil, the light might shine.' Theodosia made a house available to Gregory, which he promptly renovated as a church dedicated to the Resurrection. From there he worked to build up the Nicene community in the city. By 380, when the new Emperor Theodosius arrived in the capital, he had emerged as the leader of the Nicene community.[15]

The new emperor's arrival set off a chain of events that were decisive for the Nicene community. This was nowhere more true than for the circle around Gregory and Theodosia. One of the first acts of Theodosius was to expel the Arian bishop, Demophilos, and enthrone Gregory in his stead. Theodosius then summoned a general council, the First Council of Constantinople, in order to reassert the Nicene faith. Gregory was to play a prominent role as bishop of Constantinople. At the same time, his preaching in the city laid an indispensable intellectual foundation for Nicene theology.[16]

Gregory's idea was of God as Being, itself mysterious and unknowable, and yet understandable. What mortal humans could understand of this mystery was captured in three Persons: the Father, Son, and Holy Spirit. Each of these three reaches out to humanity in a loving relationship. In one sense, they are artificial: God's own Being remains unknowable except in mysticism, but the Persons are his way of giving humanity a glimpse of Himself. Theodosius's council gave Gregory's theological brilliance the stage it deserved. But the political stresses involved in a gathering of 150 bishops from across the eastern half of the Empire proved too much for Gregory, and during the council he offered his resignation as bishop.

Gregory left the capital shortly thereafter, but Theodosia continued to play an important role in the now dominant Nicene community. It is even recorded that Theodosia's protegée Olympias, who was thirteen at the time of the Council, became a trusted adviser to the new bishop, Nectarius. We know from other sources that bishops of the day did indeed rely on the pious women of the aristocracy, both to help them understand the feuds and alliances of the political families and also as an important source of financial patronage.

Olympias herself entered an important alliance sometime between 384 and 386, when she was in her late teens. She married one of the outstanding men of the Theodosian court, the widower Nebridius, whose first wife had been the sister of Flaccilla, the wife of the Emperor. Nebridius was clearly still in favour at court at the time of his second marriage, since he was granted two of the Empire's highest offices around that time. He became *comes sacrarum largitionum* – the imperial minister of finance – from 383 to 384, and Urban Prefect of Constantinople in 386. Theodosia's cousin Gregory, now retired to his native Cappadocia, was invited to the wedding, but sent his apologies, along with a poem to celebrate the marriage. Nebridius died not long afterwards, leaving Olympias a widow before the age of twenty.

Olympias was immediately put under pressure to marry again. All parties seem to have agreed that a fortune as vast as hers should be put to the use of some great man. Even if a husband could not directly control his wife's property, it was very useful to have influence over how it was used. At the same time, the bonds of marriage were indispensable in solidifying the relationships among political families. The Emperor probably saw an amiable bride from one of the great court families as a handsome gift to bestow on an up-and-coming man in his entourage. Theodosius tried to marry Olympias to 'a certain Elpidius, a Spaniard, one of his own relatives' not long after the death of Nebridius. But the young widow would have none of it. 'The pious Olympias, however, explained her position to the Emperor Theodosius: "If my King, the Lord Jesus Christ, wanted me to be joined with a man, he would not have taken away my first husband immediately. Since he knew that I was unsuited for the conjugal life and was not able to please a man, he freed him, Nebridius, from the bond and delivered me of this very burdensome yoke and servitude to a husband, having placed upon my mind the happy yoke of continence."' It is perhaps an indicator of her power, and certainly of her self-composure, that Olympias was able to make her views stick.[17]

In Bishop Nectarius, Olympias had a valuable ally. If she was able to help him with her wealth and connections, his standing and moral authority certainly put him in a position to be able to assist her in protecting her interests. It may be in this connection that he ordained her as Deaconess of the Church of Constantinople. Olympias followed up her ordination with a move to broadcast her commitment to the Church in such a way that no man, other than the bishop, could aspire to guide her, and none could control her fortune.

> Then by the divine will she was ordained deacon (*diakonos*) of this holy cathedral of God and she built a monastery at an angle south of it. She owned all the houses lying near the holy church and all the shops which were at the southern angle mentioned. She constructed a path from the monastery up to the narthex of the holy church, and in the first quarter she enclosed her own chambermaids, numbering fifty, all of whom lived in purity and virginity.[18]

In the fourth century, a monastery such as that of Olympias would not have come under direct control of the bishop. It would have remained a private property under control of its legal owner, but one can see how, to Nectarius, it would have been a great asset to see the cathedral precinct reach into the surrounding city in this way.

At the same time, for Olympias, part of the charm of her foundation must have been that it attracted a crowd of women from similarly powerful families:

> Olympias, the niece of the aforesaid holy Olympias, with many other women of senatorial families, chose the kingdom of heaven and disdained these lowly things below which drag us down, in accordance with the grace and good favour of God who wishes all to be saved and who fosters the divine love in them. They entered also with all the rest, so that all those who gathered together according to the grace of God in that holy fold of Christ

numbered two hundred and fifty, all adorned with the crown of virginity and practising the most exalted life which befits the saints.[19]

It is a curious fact that at the same time as the Christian bishops of the late fourth century were preaching against the vices of the rich, they were acquiring a dedicated following amongst the daughters of the richest families. If the bishop could count on the moral support of these women, he could also look to them for political and financial patronage. As long as he was able to accept their help without compromising his principles, the alliance between bishops and aristocratic women meant that the bishops found themselves increasingly able to take an independent stand against the abuses of the rich and powerful. We will see below that in the imperial cities, the bishops were often in a strong enough position that they felt they could challenge the Emperor himself, although this sometimes had disastrous consequences.

If the alliance between bishops and aristocratic women was valuable to the bishops, it was also extremely useful to the women themselves. The instinctive attraction of the daughters of high society to noble ideals was probably reinforced by an idea that, in dedicating themselves to the Church, they could escape the sometimes grim realities of marriage. It was not only the problem of volatile husbands raised in a society that prized aggressive masculinity and constant pregnancy; there was also the painful fact that only a few of the numerous babies would survive to adulthood. Against these harsh realities, the new monastic communities offered an appealing alternative, a rigid but somehow delicious atmosphere similar to that of a girls' boarding school. To a virgin, this must have seemed attractive, and to a teenage Roman widow weighing the dangers of a second marriage, it must have seemed positively utopian. And, of course, there was the chance to do good works. We should not underestimate the delight that these women found in being able to pool their resources in trying to better the lot of the city's poor.

When Nectarius died in 398, a new bishop was appointed who seemed to be perfectly suited to guiding the enthusiasm of the city's aristocratic virgins and widows. On 26 February 398 John, a priest of Antioch, was enthroned as bishop. He was by all accounts a worthy successor and it was understood that he would be an asset to the imperial family in their work of promoting the Nicene cause. One writer of the time suggests that the Emperor hoped that his 'learning and eloquence' would strengthen the people's 'attachment to the dynastic faith'. Indeed, John would be remembered as Chrysostom, 'Golden-mouth', for the brilliance of his sermons.[20]

In Antioch, John had waged a ferocious moral battle against the rich, and even against the good intentions of rich Christians who wanted to adorn the altars of the Church with gold and candles while the city's poor went hungry. An example from one of his sermons preached in Antioch brings home how uncomfortable his words must have sounded to the kind of rich Christians who were happy to soothe their consciences by making extravagant gifts to the clergy.

> Do you wish to honour the body of Christ? Do not ignore him when he is naked. Do not pay him homage in the temple clad in silk, only then to neglect him outside where he is cold and ill-clad. He who said: 'This is my body' is the same who said: 'You saw me hungry and you gave me no food', and 'Whatever you did to the least of my brothers you did also to me' . . . What good is it if the Eucharistic table is overloaded with golden chalices when your brother is dying of hunger? Start by satisfying his hunger and then with what is left you may adorn the altar as well.[21]

Olympias proved an indispensable ally for the new bishop. Her advice and contacts must have been invaluable, and her wealth meant that he could draw on virtually unlimited resources for charitable projects. The two seem to have fallen into a happy collaboration almost immediately. The *Life of Olympias* characterized their relationship as like that of Jesus with the women of Galilee, although the Great Church of the imperial city was a far cry from the humble surroundings of Luke's Gospel.[22]

> For no one from the outside, neither man nor woman, was permitted to come upon them [the virgins and widows who lived in Olympias's house], the only exception being the most holy patriarch John, who visited continuously and sustained them with his most wise teachings. Thus fortified each day by his divinely inspired instruction, they kindled in themselves the divine love so that their great and holy love streamed forth to him. The pious and blessed Olympias (who in these matters too imitated the women disciples of Christ who served him from their possessions [Luke 8: 1–3]) prepared for the holy John his daily provisions and sent them to the bishop, for there was not much separation between the episcopal residence and the monastery; only a wall.[23]

The Young Empress

If John had found his guardian angel in Olympias, another of the pious women of the capital would prove his nemesis. This was the star of the imperial court: the young empress. On 27 April 395, three months after the death of Emperor Theodosius, his son Arcadius, the heir to the Eastern throne, had married Eudoxia, the daughter of a Frankish general, Bauto, *magister militum* in the Western Empire in the 380s and Consul in 385, who had died in 388.

Like Olympias, Eudoxia was an orphan. We first hear of her as a ward in the household of Promotus, the *magister militum* in the East from 386 to 391. After the death of Promotus in 392, she seems to have come under the care of Promotus's widow Marsa and one of his sons. We know that attention was paid to her education, since her tutor, Pansophius, was made Bishop of Nicomedia after her marriage.[24]

We do not know how old Eudoxia was at the time of her marriage, or what her young husband's motives were for marrying so soon after his father's death. He was not older than eighteen at the time of the marriage, so he was unusually young. It is likely, given the habits of the age, that she was even younger. Nonetheless, Eudoxia assumed the role of empress with composure and panache, displaying all the innate authority and presence of the daughter of an outstanding military commander.

Her first task was to establish her ability to produce an heir, and this she did swiftly, producing seven children in the nine years of her marriage, although only the fourth, Theodosius II, born in April 401, was a healthy boy. (Three of his sisters, Pulcheria, Arcadia, and Marina, would also survive to adulthood, and would play an important role in the fifth-century Church.)

Eudoxia was known for her intense dedication to the Nicene faith. After nearly two decades of Nicene dominance, the Arians no longer controlled churches within the city walls of Constantinople, but from their suburban churches they engineered dawn processions into the city on a regular basis. The fifth-century historians, Socrates of Constantinople and Sozomen, record that Eudoxia played an important role in organizing the Nicene counter-processions. These processions were important symbolically but also as an exercise in education of the faithful: they were built around the singing of hymns, whose words, made memorable in verse, served as a crucial vehicle for the leadership on either side to educate their followers about the doctrines they were expected to support. Eudoxia offered the services of one of the imperial eunuchs to organize the singing.[25]

Similarly, the Empress played a leading role in the festivals of the saints. On one occasion, probably in 400 or 401, Bishop John Chrysostom himself celebrated her piety, when she played a leading role in a nocturnal procession by torchlight from Constantinople to Dryphia, 15 kilometres from the city, to carry the bones of unnamed martyrs to be placed in the chapel of St Thomas. In a sermon afterwards, John noted that the Empress had carried the bones herself the entire way:

> She who wears the diadem and purple would not abide the slightest separation from the relics through the whole distance but attended the saints like a handmaid, clinging to the relic box and to the linen that covered it? . . . Through the whole distance, they saw her, holding tightly to the bones, not flagging or giving in to weakness.[26]

An Empress who could win God's favour was sorely needed during the troubled years of the end of the century, when the Empire's borders were notoriously unstable. In 395, the year of Eudoxia's marriage, the Huns broke through the Caucasus frontier and ravaged the eastern provinces. In late 399, the Goths threatened to invade Constantinople; they had already come dangerously close to the city in 378, killing Emperor Valens, who rode out to repel them at Hadrianople.

On 9 January 400, Eudoxia, who was pregnant with her third child, was elevated to the rank of *Augusta*, in a coronation ceremony that lifted her above the status of Emperor's consort and conferred on her a God-given authority in her own right. Coins were minted showing the right hand of God reaching down from heaven to crown her head with a wreath symbolizing the divine favour. The coronation, with its religious overtones and the publicity that surrounded it, was designed to bolster support for the imperial family. It was also meant to enhance Eudoxia's ability to rouse the people of Constantinople against the Goths and their Arian heresy. The strategy seems to have worked: indeed, it was a popular uprising that led to the expulsion of the Goths in June of the same year.

On the face of it, Eudoxia and the new bishop, John Chrysostom, should have been allies. He was famous for his ability to work with women, and she was famous for her fierce support of the Nicene faith. But somehow the relationship soured. As late as January of 402, when John presided at the christening of Theodosius II, the infant heir to the throne, the relationship was solid enough that he was asked to officiate, but by late 403 there was an open rift.

All of the early sources agree that the trigger was a sermon preached by John against the vices of women, which the Empress interpreted as a veiled attack against herself and, by extension, against the imperial family. This has the ring of a historian's attempt to fabricate a plausible motive for the rift on the basis of received wisdom about the imperiousness of the Empress and the fieriness of the Bishop's preaching. But there may be a grain of truth, nonetheless.[27]

In late 403, the Urban Prefect Simplicius had erected a silver statue of the Empress on a porphyry column in front of the Senate House, in the city's imperial forum just to the south of the Great Church. This was, in itself, a non-controversial gesture: the erection of public statues was an important way of rallying civic support around public figures and the installation of such a statue offered an opportunity for a public festival. Usually, it was the individual or group who had paid for the statue who would sponsor the festivities, and the more lavish the provision of music and dancing-girls, the greater the honour to both the statue's subject and to its donor. Here, too, the early historians found a point of conflict between John and Eudoxia: the bishop was understandably hostile, as they saw it, to such worldly goings-on taking place so close to his church. Again, he complained in a sermon, comparing Eudoxia to Herodias, who had set her daughter to dance for King Herod and told the girl to ask for the head of John the Baptist on a plate.[28]

In this case, the inventiveness of the ecclesiastical historians has the ring of truth. John had already been in trouble at that point. In the summer of 403, the Synod of the Oak had deposed him over a theological matter, but it had in fact been the Empress who restored him to his post. Nonetheless, John is known to have felt strongly that Christians should not participate in the kind of festivals that involved dancing-girls. Rather, he wished to channel the city's energies into the kind of processions and festivals that developed around theological controversies and the cult of the saints.

It is possible that the tension between the Bishop and the Empress reflected a larger struggle over who should take responsibility to ensure that the Roman people were found pleasing in the sight of God. Traditionally, this had been the task of the Roman emperor, and we saw in the case of Constantine that the ability to attract the divine favour was one of the characteristics that the people and army looked for in a potential emperor. But in the late fourth century, the power of the Church was becoming considerable, and Christian bishops no longer felt it necessary to defer to the emperor's judgement in matters of religion. John Chrysostom, who could hold a crowd of thousands with the rapturous quality of his preaching, seems to have felt that the sound and fury of imperial ritual was a distraction from the Gospel message in its rough simplicity.

In the end, whatever caused the conflict between John and Eudoxia, it would not last long. John was sent into exile in June of 404, and the Empress would die later the same year, in childbirth.

This fact adds a poignant nuance to the support that Chrysostom drew, once he had fallen out of favour, from the community of widows and virgins gathered around his cathedral. Olympias and her circle were steadfast in their support of John, whose fall was if anything accelerated by the Empress's death. 'And she did this not only before the plots against him, but also after he was banished; up to the end of his life she provided for all his expenses as well as for those who were with him in exile.'[29] John's earliest biographer paints a vivid scene of the bishop's departure.

> But he went into the baptistery, and called Olympias . . . and Pentadia, and Procle, the deaconesses, and Silvina, the widow of the blessed Nevridius, who adorned her widowhood by a beautiful life, and said to them, 'Come here, my daughters, and listen to me. I see that the things concerning me have an end; I have finished my course and perhaps you will see my face no more. What I want to ask you is this: let no one dissever you from the good-will you have always borne to the Church; and

whoever succeeds me, if he be brought forward for ordination not by his own wish, and without place-hunting, with the approval of all, bow your heads to him, as you have done to John. The Church cannot exist without a bishop. And so may you find mercy. Remember me in your prayers.'[30]

The same night, Palladius tells us, the church erupted in flames.

A flame appeared from the middle of the throne in which John usually sat, like a heart set in the midst of a body, to expound to the other organs the oracles of the Lord; and sought for the interpreter of the Word. Not finding him, it devoured the chamber used for the Church vessels. Then it spread like a tree, and crept through the rafters to the roof . . . It seemed as though God was paying the reward of iniquity appointed as its penalty.[31]

With this send-off, John departed from his city.

Olympias and her companions were accused of starting the fire, and she was brought before the Urban Prefect Optatus.

'Great fortitude was evinced in the midst of these calamities by Olympias, the deaconess. Being dragged for this reason before the tribunal, and interrogated by the prefect as to her motives in setting fire to the church, she replied, 'My past life ought to avert all suspicion from me, for I have devoted my large property to the restoration of the temples of God.'[32]

Afterwards, Olympias was exiled to the former capital, Nicomedia, in large part to protect the position of the new bishop, Arsacius. The community of like-minded women she had gathered was too powerful not to be a danger to a successor to John who had failed to gain their respect. Olympias died in Nicomedia, of a long illness, in 408.

Her beloved John would live on in exile for three years in Armenia. The aunt and namesake of Olympias had been queen there, and it is possible that Olympias was able to influence the destination of his exile, and to smooth his way once he arrived. She was still, after all, a kinswoman of the emperor. Ancient writers report that John was able to continue in his ministry while in exile, doing good works and consoling the troubled with kind words, and continuing to preach memorable sermons. He also kept close touch, by letter, with his friends in Constantinople and further afield. Pope Innocent attempted from Rome to intercede with the emperor on his behalf, but this only backfired, and led to his being sent to a more remote location in 407. The fifth-century historian Sozomen reports that he died on the journey: 'It is said that during this journey, Basiliscus, the martyr, appeared to him at Comani, in Armenia, and apprised him of the day of his death. Being attacked with pain in the head, and being unable to bear the heat of the sun, he could not prosecute his journey, but closed his life in that town.'[33]

But both John and Olympias lived longer and in many ways fuller lives than Empress Eudoxia, who died in childbirth a year after her silver statue was erected, on 6 October 404. Even if we do not know her birth date, we can be certain that she died before the age of thirty, victim to a punishing regime of continuous child-bearing. Even a Roman empress was not immune to the dangers of motherhood.[34]

Still, thanks to her children, Eudoxia's legacy was secure. Her oldest daughter, Pulcheria, would survive her to become a powerful force over the next half-century, and the little boy, Theodosius, would grow up to be emperor, enjoying a reign of more than forty years. We will return to Pulcheria and Theodosius in a later chapter, to discover what they had gleaned from their mother's memory. In countless ways their empire was stronger for what they had learned.

7

'THE LIFE OF ANGELS'

When the due time came for her baby to be delivered she fell asleep and seemed to be carrying in her hands [the baby] which was still in her womb. And someone in form and raiment more splendid than a human being appeared and addressed the child she was carrying by the name of Thecla – that Thecla, I mean, who is so famous among the virgins. After doing this and testifying to it three times, he departed from her sight and gave her an easy delivery, so that at that moment she awoke from sleep and saw her dream realized.[1]

Writing in the last years of the fourth-century, a Christian bishop remembered a story about his mother. Just before the birth of her first child, she had received a visit from an angel, who indicated that her baby would be a girl and would follow in the footsteps of Thecla, the virgin who had been the travelling companion of the Apostle Paul. The meaning of the dream was clear to Gregory. By the fourth century, the virgin of Iconium was celebrated throughout the Greek-speaking East for her willingness to give up marriage and dedicate herself to Paul's preaching. The vision of her daughter as a second Thecla told her that the girl would grow up to be a leader of virgins.

The bishop's mother was one of the engineers of a revolution in the Christian way of thinking about human relationships – with other people and with God. It was a revolution that would change the way people thought and lived for the next thousand years.

As we have already begun to discover, the flesh-and-blood women about whom we know most in antiquity were the female relatives of famous men. A case in point is St Macrina of Annesi (d. 379), the subject of the first biography written about a woman in antiquity. It almost goes without saying that Macrina's story was recorded by a famous younger brother, Gregory, Bishop of Nyssa, who survived her. But Gregory's *Life of Macrina* is more than a biography: it is the story of a Christian dynasty, and of how an ideal of Christian commitment was handed down through the women of a family across three generations.

Gregory and Macrina's older brother, Basil the Great, is remembered as the intellectual architect of coenobitic monasticism. This form of Christian ascetic life, in which individuals cultivate openness of heart by living together in communities rather than by withdrawing into solitary contemplation, became the basis for monasteries from Egypt to Ireland throughout the Middle Ages, and Basil is justly celebrated as one of the founding fathers.

Yet his younger brother argued that Basil's monastic ideal was actually the fruit of a larger family project centred on the 'family monastery' which his mother Emmelia and his older sister Macrina founded in their own home. Gregory's aim in writing a life of his sister was certainly to muse on the lives of beloved family members who had died. But it is also clear that he wanted to set the record straight about how the achievements of the men in the family had their roots in the quieter achievements of the women.

The enthusiastic participation of women was one of the driving forces of the ascetic revolution of the fourth century. In the early centuries, Christian literature had certainly offered ideas that could change women's lives. But in the fourth century, the ideals of ascetic renunciation and virginal purity had come to the foreground. The shift in emphasis offered surprising opportunities for women, even for the grandmothers who were by no means virgins themselves.

From the beginning of classical antiquity, the virgin had held a special place as a symbol of vulnerability and moral purity. Chastity was a virtue that could be shared in principle by all women, but virginity was something set apart. It was an image of all that was immaculate and untouched. Chastity, the refusal to give undue attention to men other than a legitimate husband, was seen as a social necessity. It was the foundation of an orderly society in which children could have a clear idea of who their father was. Virginity, on the other hand, was an impractical and conspicuous virtue, one that captured the imagination.[2]

The virgin of marriageable age was the poster-child for the ascetic movement, and many young women embraced a vow of virginity with real fervour. The qualities of innocence and inexperience made young women so evocative as icons of purity, but they also meant that the young women's understanding of the part they were playing in the larger social drama was not always clear. So the younger virgins often ended up serving the interests of adult 'handlers', whether their own parents or leaders of local communities. Older virgins, or younger virgins with trusting relationships to older sponsors, were in a much stronger position.

Women who had been married but whose husbands had died were particularly well placed to benefit from the opportunities for independence that came with the new value accorded to sexual renunciation. The women of previous generations had faced a dilemma when their husbands died. Women married young and normally to older husbands, so a woman could easily expect to be widowed in her teens or twenties. The Christian ideal of marriage as a lifelong bond did not sit well with economic realities that gave a strong incentive to remarriage. For centuries, the marriage laws of Augustus, aimed among other things at supporting the birth-rate, had provided a further motivation, but in the fourth century the Emperor Constantine had repealed the laws, and women who could afford to remain widows found that their position was viewed with increasing honour, as a 'second virginity'. The women who practised this 'second virginity' began to find that their moral authority was respected by men and women alike.[3]

What all this adds up to is that a mother–daughter pair – one a virgin in her early teens and the other a still-young widow – were in a position, in the late fourth century, to experiment quite liberally with organizing their lives in pursuit of Christian perfection. If they were fortunate, they had material resources to work with, but the real luck was in the like-minded companionship of female relatives with the spirit and curiosity to embark on a new life.

Gregory's Story of Emmelia and the Two Macrinas

In Gregory's *Life of Macrina*, the life of the mother Emmelia is sketched out briefly as the prelude to the achievements of her daughter Macrina, the bishop's sister, but the bond between mother and daughter is the luminous axis around which the story turns. Their close relationship was in all likelihood entirely natural and instinctive. In thousands of other households around the Mediterranean, a similar story may have been lived out quietly, without ever reaching the historical record.

It was Emmelia's good fortune to enter widowhood in an era when a proposal to keep a beloved daughter in the parental home could be seen as a sign of virtue rather than of failure. An eldest daughter tended to be born while her mother was still in her teens, so there was a potential for quite an equal partnership between the two over time. The female-centred household of Emmelia and Macrina was the product of the chances available to women in the new fourth-century climate.

If Emmelia was blessed with good fortune in her adulthood, she had earned it during a very difficult youth. Gregory tells his readers in an almost offhand fashion of his mother's very dramatic early life. She spent her childhood in the region of Pontus, near the eastern frontier of the Empire, during the years of the Great Persecution of 303–11, and her father had died as a Christian martyr during those years. Her mother seems to have died around the same time of natural causes – in any case, Gregory makes no mention of her martyrdom. In the 320s Emmelia married Basil, a master of rhetoric who worked both as a teacher and as a lawyer in the courts of the provincial capital at Neocaesarea. Gregory recalls that Emmelia had wished to live as a virgin, but as an orphan she was in an unprotected position.

> She loved the pure and unstained mode of life so much that she was unwilling to be married. But since she had lost both her parents, and was in the very flower of her youthful beauty, and the fame of her good looks was attracting many suitors, there was a danger that, if she did not marry someone willingly, she might suffer some unwished for violent fate seeing that some men, inflamed by her beauty, were ready to abduct her.[4]

Gregory's story has something of a frontier-town atmosphere to it, and this may reflect the realities of the Black Sea region in the early fourth century.

Emmelia inherited considerable property from her parents, and the phrase 'the very flower of her youthful beauty' suggests that she was still in her teens. Her concern to find a protector was not unreasonable. Marriage by abduction was not unheard of in the Roman provinces, and a very young woman with a considerable inheritance was a classic target. It seems that she did not have trusted relatives to protect her. It is possible that her closest relatives had died along with her parents, and that she was dependent on more distant relations who might turn a blind eye if a friend of the family took advantage of her position. We cannot rule out another, darker possibility that her mother had lived long enough to remarry, and that Emmelia had to contend with a stepfather who would have been happy to see one of his own relations benefit from her fortune.

Under the circumstances, Emmelia seems to have reasoned that the best protection against an unwanted marriage was one she herself had chosen. 'She chose for her husband a man who was known and approved for the gravity of his conduct and so gained a protector of her life.' In the event, she chose well.

Basil's family were Christians. His own mother, Macrina the Elder, had begun life as a pagan in Pontus. As a young woman she was converted to Christianity through her friendship with Gregory the Wonder-worker, one of the outstanding theologians of the late third century, who had sat at the feet of the great Origen. (We will see that thanks to the esteem in which the Wonder-Worker was held, there were a confusing number of Gregorys in Emmelia's world.) At the turn of the fourth century, the sporadic persecution of Christians gave way to the Great Persecution of 303–11, and during their early married years, Basil's parents spent seven years in hiding during the height of the persecution, living in the forest along the coast of the Black Sea. When the persecution ended, Macrina and her husband returned to their home near Neocaesarea. They had two sons: one, another Gregory, became a bishop in the region, while the other, Basil, became a *rhetor*, a master of rhetoric, serving both as a teacher and an advocate in the courts. Basil went on to marry Emmelia.[5]

The couple had nine children, and the first, Macrina, was named after Basil's mother, Macrina the Elder. They then had a son, who was named Basil, after his own father and his paternal grandfather. We know the names of the other three sons: Gregory – named after the Wonder-worker; Naucratius came next; and Peter seems to have been the baby of the family. Then there were five more sisters, whose names have not been recorded.

It was to her eldest daughter Macrina that Emmelia entrusted her own love of virginity. Gregory presents his mother's dream as a foreboding of his sister's virtue; it may have been Emmelia's own wish that the child follow in the footsteps of Thecla. Because of her difficult circumstances, she had had to give up her own wish for virginity and she hoped – correctly as it turned out – to give her daughter a safe home within which to flourish.

If we read between the lines, there is also the possibility that

Emmelia had told the story of her vision as a way of letting it be remembered that she had wanted to name her daughter Thecla.

> . . . this name was used only in secret. But it seems to me that the apparition spoke not so much to guide the mother to a right choice of name as to forecast the life of the young child and to indicate by the name that she would follow her namesake's mode of life.[6]

Local custom tended towards a first daughter being named after her paternal grandmother, and since this is what happened, handing down the story about the name given by the angel may have been a way of keeping it alive in the family memory. But it is also possible that the story had the flavour of a family joke, since Thecla was famous for having refused to obey her own mother's wishes.

Emmelia was devoted to the idea that her daughter would imbibe the tradition of spiritual literature from an early age. In this, Thecla of Iconium, the principal literary heroine of the age of the Apostles, was the ideal patron saint for the child.

> The education of the child was her mother's task. She did not, however, employ the usual worldly method of education, which makes a practice of using poetry as a means of training the early years of the child. For she considered it disgraceful and quite unsuitable, that a tender and plastic nature should be taught either those tragic passions of womanhood which afforded poets their suggestions and plots, or the indecencies of comedy to be, so to speak, defiled with unseemly tales of 'the harem'. But such parts of inspired Scripture as you would think were incomprehensible to young children were the subject of the girl's studies; in particular the Wisdom of Solomon, and those parts of it especially which have an ethical bearing. Nor was she ignorant of any part of the Psalter but at stated times she recited every part of it.[7]

Gregory takes it as a given that in fourth-century Pontus a lawyer's daughter would be educated in the classics, memorizing Homer as both a model of Greek expression and as a source of the heroic history of the Fall of Troy, so Emmelia's choice was eccentric.

Gregory and Macrina's brother Basil would write an influential treatise arguing that Christian children should not be required to master the pagan classics, so it is of interest that the children had grown up with a debate on just this topic in the household. Emmelia was not only their mother but also the daughter of a Christian martyr, so her views on spiritual matters would have had a larger-than-life quality for her children, and it is not surprising to see her views echoed, a half-century later, in Basil's treatise *On Education*. Gregory remembers Macrina as playing an important role in the upbringing of the younger siblings. It is difficult to disentangle the influence of Emmelia from that of Macrina in the narrative. In all likelihood, Gregory himself had difficulty disentangling it.

Three of Macrina's brothers – Basil, Gregory, and Peter – would go on to become bishops, and thus the public face of the family. Basil and Gregory were both distinguished writers. Gregory was the family historian and an important theologian in his own right, while Basil is remembered as the outstanding bishop-theologian of his generation and as the father of Eastern monasticism. (Indeed, Basil is known to history as Basil the Great.)

Yet both men emphasize repeatedly that they drew on the wisdom of the women of the family, and both commemorate the teaching of their grandmother, mother, and oldest sister. One of Gregory's treatises, the *Dialogue on the Soul and Resurrection*, takes the form of a Platonic dialogue and casts his older sister in the role of the philosopher-teacher. From her deathbed, she consoles her younger brother with an explanation of the immortality of the soul, just as Socrates had consoled his disciples in the *Phaedo*.

Both Macrina and Basil died in 379, and the *Dialogue* and the *Life of Macrina* were written shortly afterwards. They represent Gregory's effort to preserve the tradition handed down by the women of his family. He also wrote the *Life of Gregory the Wonder-worker* around 380, which was based on his grandmother Macrina the Elder's recollections of her youthful acquaintance with the saint. This cluster of writings are the product, in all likelihood, of Gregory's sense that as his generation died off, the family stories would be lost if he did not commit them to writing.

We owe the survival of *The Life of Macrina* more to the fame of Macrina's brothers than to her own incontestable brilliance, and we cannot be sure that her younger brother represents her own views accurately. It is very likely that Gregory idealized his sister in his grief. But his memoir is priceless nonetheless: it is the earliest biography of a woman to survive from antiquity, and it situates Macrina in a female tradition reaching back to her grandmother.

Despite her mother's dream suggesting that Macrina would be a second Thecla, when Macrina was a girl the family planned for her to marry in the traditional way, as her mother and grandmothers had done before her. At twelve, 'when the flower of youth begins to flourish in particular splendour of beauty', she was betrothed to a suitable young man chosen by her father. Her fiancé had just completed his studies, so he would have been in his mid-twenties.[8]

But Envy cut off these bright hopes by snatching away the poor lad from life. Now Macrina was not ignorant of her father's schemes. But when the plan formed for her was shattered by the young man's death, she said her father's intention was equivalent to a marriage, and resolved to remain single henceforward, just as if the intention had become accomplished fact.[9]

Macrina's situation was far more secure than had been that of Emmelia before her. Her parents were both living, and she was surrounded by numerous younger siblings who could easily take up the task of cementing the ties to other local families through marriage, if their parents chose. So there was no reason, really, why she should not hold firm in her idea of declaring herself a Christian widow.

And indeed her determination was more steadfast than could have been expected from her age. For when her parents brought proposals of marriage to her, as often happened owing to the number of suitors that came attracted by the fame of her beauty, she would say that it was absurd and unlawful not to be faithful to the marriage that had been arranged for her by her father, but to be compelled to consider another; since in the nature of things there was but one marriage, as there is one birth and one death.[10]

Gregory remembers their mother Emmelia as having been in favour of the idea that Macrina should marry. But this seems somehow out of character, given what Gregory tells us about her desire as a young woman to live the life of a Christian virgin. Why had she not supported her daughter's wish for the same thing? One wonders if Gregory is reporting his mother's own views accurately. He wrote the *Life of Macrina* nearly forty years after the events in question, after his sister's death in 379, so his memory may well have been uncertain. Was he simply remembering his mother's dreams for her daughter as overshadowed by those of her husband? Or was he trying to bring out the force of Macrina's own character, by claiming that her wish had met resistance from both parents?

There is another possibility, however. Gregory does not give the date of his father's death, which might be important for understanding how he represents his mother's view of Macrina's future. Basil seems to have died shortly after the birth of the youngest son, Peter, around 343, when Macrina would have been in her teens. If Basil had died shortly after Macrina's fiancé, Emmelia may have changed her position on the marriage in light of her own widowhood. She may have allowed her daughter to persuade her, after Basil's death, that their position together was secure enough to dispense with the need for a male protector. Alternately, she may have supported her husband's wishes – perhaps reluctantly – while he was alive, and quietly changed course on his death.

In any event, it was by blurring the boundary between widow-hood and virginity that Macrina was able to prevail.

> She maintained that the man who had been joined to her by her parents' arrangement was not dead, but that she considered him to be only absent, not dead, because he was alive in God, thanks to the hope of the resurrection. So it was wrong not to keep faith with the bridegroom who was away.[11]

By declaring herself a widow, Macrina, still in her teens, could claim to be her mother's peer. This allowed their relationship to continue on a new basis.

When her husband died in the early 340s, Emmelia was in her early thirties, and for nearly twenty years she had run a large establishment in the provincial capital while producing nine children, the youngest of whom was still a baby. Gregory presents Emmelia as a serene and passive figure, though in reality she must have had a very strong constitution. Even so, it was a great gift that her eldest daughter did not leave home when she came of age.

Macrina's vow and her father's death changed her position in the household. On Basil's death, Macrina came into an inheritance, for Roman law did not observe community of property between husband and wife. A share was reserved by law for each of his children, and custom suggested that the estate should be divided equally among them, sons and daughters alike, alongside any other bequests. Emmelia was in fact a woman of substantial property in her own right and Macrina's wealth is not likely to have rivalled her mother's, since Macrina was one of nine children. But now, although she was very much the grande dame, Emmelia would have begun to see her daughter as an equal.[12]

Running the household was no small matter. Where a woman of Emmelia's wealth was concerned, this involved running a substantial business.

She helped her mother to bear the burden of her responsibilities. For Emmelia had four sons and five daughters, and paid taxes to three different governors, since her property was scattered in as many districts. In consequence her mother was distracted with various anxieties, for her father had by this time departed this life. In all these matters Macrina shared her mother's toils, dividing her cares with her, and lightening her heavy load of sorrows. At one and the same time, thanks to her mother's guardianship, she was keeping her own life blameless, so that her mother's eye both directed and witnessed all she did; and also by her own life she instructed her mother greatly, leading her to the same mark, that of philosophy I mean, and gradually drawing her on to the immaterial and more perfect life.[13]

Around the time of her husband's death, Emmelia decided to retire to one of the family estates, in Annesi around 50 kilometres to the west of Neocaesarea. Once there was no need to be close to Basil's legal practice in Neocaesarea, there was no reason to stay there. Gregory paints the motivation for the move as arising from an aristocrat's preference for the life of his or her country estate.[14]

But there may also have been more compelling reasons to leave. Probably around 344, a severe earthquake struck Neocaesarea, and the city was devastated. Gregory's *Life of Gregory the Wonder-worker* tells us that only the Wonder-worker's church was preserved 'unshattered and unshaken'. If the earthquake struck close to the time of Basil the Elder's death, as modern scholarship suggests, it could well have triggered Emmelia's moving the household to the country. We don't know whether there was damage to the family's property in the capital. It is possible that the move was originally a practical measure, undertaken initially on a temporary basis.[15]

Gregory describes Macrina as having taken a principal role in organizing life at Annesi. She and Emmelia were accompanied there by the two younger sons, Peter, born in the same year as his father's death, and Naucratius, and an unspecified number of girls. As the boys passed from childhood into young manhood they seem to have established independent living quarters on the estate, so that the main household acquired the atmosphere of a female monastery. In the 340s Gregory seems to have commuted between Annesi and his education in Caesarea in Cappadocia, where Emmelia's brother was bishop. Basil travelled even further for his studies, first to Caesarea and then to Constantinople and Athens.[16]

Gregory tells us less about the fate of his other sisters. If they had joined Macrina in remaining as virgins at Annesi, Gregory would almost certainly have celebrated the fact, so it is likely that they married, probably in the 340s and 350s. In the 360s, Basil sent a treatise of *Advice to Adolescents* to his nephews, and these may well have been the sons of a sister or sisters, though there is some evidence to suggest that Gregory himself was married, in which case the boys could have been his.[17]

As Gregory describes the new household established by his mother and older sister at Annesi, he wants his reader to notice how Macrina's love of asceticism led the whole family to be transformed. Gregory credits her with working to persuade their mother to give up the luxuries of an upper-class matron and to live alongside the household slaves as an act of Christian humility. Annesi was the perfect place for a Christian experiment of this kind.

Years later, the oldest brother Basil recalled that as a child he had visited his grandmother Macrina the Elder in Annesi and had received the foundation of his Christian training from the stories of her youthful acquaintance with Gregory the Wonder-worker. The region held evocative memories, as well, of the same grandmother's years in hiding during the Great Persecution.

The fact that Macrina the Elder had lived at Annesi raises the possibility that it was Macrina, and not Emmelia, who was the owner of the estate there. It was after Basil's death, when Macrina came into her inheritance that she and her mother took up residence at Annesi. Emmelia's family came from Caesarea in Cappadocia, 300 kilometres south of Neocaesarea in Pontus. Still, it is not impossible that she owned an estate in Pontus, since she had land in a number of areas and had been in Pontus in her youth. It is also conceivable that there were two estates at Annesi, and Emmelia had married the son of the neighbouring landowner.

But it is likely that at least one estate at Annesi had belonged to Basil's family, since his mother Macrina had lived there. If so, he would have left it directly to one or more of his and Emmelia's children rather than to his already rich wife. Sadly, Gregory does not make clear whether Emmelia or Macrina was the owner of their shared home. He is far more interested, in this narrative, in emotional relationships and Christian virtues than in undignified matters like money and property.

At one level it did not make much difference. Children did not reach majority until the age of twenty-five in the fourth century. If their father died before they reached maturity, a guardian would be appointed to administer their property, and it was not unheard of, in the late fourth century, for a mother to act as guardian. Since Macrina was in her teens when her father died around 343, she could easily have held title to the estate under her mother's guardianship, feeling somehow that it still belonged to the older generation even though she was the legal owner. As far as Gregory is concerned, the important thing is Macrina's progressive efforts to turn the household into a monastery and her mother, siblings, slaves, and other dependants into monks and nuns.

But it is a shame that a clearer picture of these practical details cannot be established, since they affected the shifting balance of power. One would dearly like to know whether the older sister's authority in the household rested entirely on her charm and personal virtue, or whether it was also buttressed by an ability to pay the bills.

Macrina's greatest ally in the ascetic revolution at Annesi was her younger brother Naucratius, whom Gregory presents as the star of the family. Naucratius 'excelled the rest in natural endowments and physical beauty, in strength, speed and ability to turn his hand to anything'. At twenty, Naucratius decided, after tasting the glory of giving a brilliant public speech, that such worldly successes held no real charm. He decided to live a life of solitude in the wilderness and found a solitary place on the estate by the banks of the River Iris. 'He took nothing with him but himself, save that one of the slaves called Chrysapius followed him, because of the affection he had towards his master and the intention he had formed to lead the same life.' If his choice was inspired by the years that his grandparents had spent in hiding in the forest during the Great Persecution, Gregory does not mention it.[18]

The idyll lasted five years. During this time Naucratius and Chrysapius earned a reputation for holiness in their rustic life. Their aim was to live a life somewhere between traditional philosophy and Christian asceticism, and this meant living simply and doing good for those around them.

> . . . with his own hands he looked after some old people who were living in poverty and feebleness, considering it appropriate to his mode of life to make such a work his care. So the generous youth would go on fishing expeditions, and since he was expert in every form of sport, he provided food to his grateful clients by this means. And at the same time by such exercises he was taming his own manhood.[19]

If his austere life was inspiring to his siblings, his failure to leave Annesi to establish a household of his own was a source of great joy to his mother.

> . . . he also gladly obeyed his mother's wishes whenever she issued a command . . . In this manner he completed the fifth year of his life as a philosopher, by which he made his mother happy, both by the way in which he adorned his own life by continence, and by the devotion of all his powers to do the will of her that bore him.[20]

To keep a second grown child close to home was another stroke of good fortune. But in the mid-350s, while Emmelia was away from the estate, the bodies of Chrysapius and Naucratius were found – the victims, Gregory explains in one of his poems, of a fishing accident. In *The Life of Macrina*, Gregory's emphasis is not on the details of the accident but rather on how it affected the rest of the family.

> His mother was far away, three days distant from the scene of the tragedy. Someone came to her telling the bad news . . . she collapsed, and in a moment lost both breath and speech, since her reason failed her under the disaster, and she was thrown to the ground by the assault of the evil tidings, like some noble athlete hit by an unexpected blow.[21]

It was Macrina who found a way to pick up the pieces. 'Facing the disaster in a rational spirit, she both preserved herself from collapse, and becoming the prop of her mother's weakness, raised her up from the abyss of grief. By her own steadfastness and imperturbability she taught her mother's soul to be brave.' This, Gregory tells us, was the turning-point for Emmelia. After this crisis, she was happy to let Macrina lead the household more firmly towards a life of ascetic renunciation.[22]

Elsewhere, Gregory tells us that by deft management Emmelia managed to leave each of her children an estate as large as that which she and her husband had enjoyed together. He wants to strike a fine balance, calling attention to her careful husbandry, but also to her lack of worldly interest in her wealth. Once she had settled her daughters and seen to the education of her sons, she divided most of her property among her children.

But from Gregory's other writings, we know that Emmelia was also using her wealth for philanthropic projects of the kind that were customary for the local gentry. In the 350s, she was the patron of a major building project, a shrine at Ibora, the village not far from Annesi where she had buried her husband Basil in the family mausoleum. The shrine housed the ashes of the forty soldiers martyred at Sebaste in nearby Armenia, and the project was a source of great pride for the family.[23]

In a sermon given on the feast day of the martyrs years later, in 379, Gregory remembered that as a young man, while on leave from his studies, he had accompanied his mother to the festival at which the shrine was dedicated. He confessed that he had fallen asleep during the service and the martyrs themselves – appearing in a dream – had taken him to task for failing to support his mother's venture. The dream is a wonderful illustration of how a Christian family could blend seamlessly with the Church and its saints: in Gregory's dream, the saints take on the role of older relatives, admonishing the child on behalf of an absent parent.[24]

But as he remembered his mother's life with Macrina, Gregory's focus was not on Emmelia's standing as a personage in the district, or her abilities as an organizer. It was on her life as a Christian ascetic, and her willingness to obey her daughter's wishes.

> Weaning her from all accustomed luxuries, Macrina drew her on to adopt her own standard of humility. She induced her to live on a footing of equality with the female slaves, so as to share with them in the same food, the same kind of bed, and in all the necessaries of life, without any regard to differences of rank . . . For just as souls freed from the body by death are saved from the cares of this life, so was their life far removed from all earthly follies and ordered with a view of imitating the angelic life.[25]

For Gregory, it almost went without saying that their lives were transformed by this refusal of all the little luxuries that rich women were accustomed to, such as soft bedding, elegant clothing, and rich food. Rather than feeling downcast, their spirits were uplifted: 'For no anger or jealousy, no hatred or pride, was observed in their midst, nor anything else of this nature, since they had cast away all vain desires for honour and glory, all vanity, arrogance and the like.' It seemed as if their virtue had a magical power to transform their reality. 'Continence was their luxury, and obscurity their glory.'[26]

For a writer like Gregory who had studied philosophy, it was obvious that giving up luxuries and social ambition ought to lead to happiness. Philosophers since the time of Plato have argued that social ills have their root in the greed and ambition that set individuals against one another as rivals for an object of desire. The way to happiness, Gregory knew, was in the ability to step back from trying to fulfil the cravings that turned friends into competitors.

The Christian ascetic ideal was rooted in a similar philosophy, though Gregory's version was at the mystical end of the spectrum. There was something exalted in the way Gregory remembered his mother and older sister during this period of their lives, 'living in the body and yet after the likeness of the immaterial beings, they were not bowed down by the weight of the body, but their life was exalted to the skies and they walked on high in company with the powers of heaven'. By the time Gregory was writing, both his mother and Macrina had died, so there is a poignant quality to his meditation on their yearning to reach the heavenly kingdom.[27]

It is while he is discussing the angelic lives of his mother and sister that Gregory turns to address a prickly challenge faced by the household. This was the return, a year or so before Naucratius' death around 356 or 357, of the eldest brother Basil, who had been away for his studies, first in Caesarea, then later Constantinople and Athens, where he was a fellow student with the future Emperor Julian. Basil was part of an elite group among the sons of the provincial aristocracy who spent years together as students in their youth, and then returned to their native regions equipped with invaluable connections to the great and the good across the Empire.

Within a few years, Basil would become one of the great lights of fourth-century literature, a bishop, a theologian, and a monastic writer of extraordinary importance in the history of the Church. If he was arrogant, he may have had good cause, though arrogance itself was no virtue.

But in the 350s, his achievements were all in the future. He was in his twenties, and returned from more than a decade in the urbane and almost entirely masculine atmosphere of the rhetorical and philosophical schools to join a household in which his new-found polish carried little weight. It is entirely likely that his arrival in the little world at Annesi was a shock. His mother and younger brothers were happily fitting in with the home-spun inclinations of his older sister. The domestic atmosphere at Annesi was very different to the urban establishment that his mother had managed, in earlier years, for his distinguished father.

Gregory pulls no punches about the impression Basil made on his arrival in Pontus. 'He was puffed up beyond measure with the pride of oratory and looked down on the local dignitaries, excelling in his own estimation all the men of standing and position.' There are reasons to think that the relationship between Macrina and Basil was never especially easy, and it is not unlikely that she and her mother bore the brunt of Basil's immature arrogance. Over the years, Gregory's friends and male relatives would complain openly and sometimes bitterly about Basil's bossiness. They might admire his ability to coerce everyone within his reach into surprisingly effective coalitions when there was a job to be done, but they did not find him easy to live with.[28]

It is hard to know whether Macrina was quite as decisive in dealing with Basil as Gregory wants us to think. He clearly takes pleasure in the idea that his older sister was not at all impressed by his older brother. By no means unsettled by an upstart younger sibling, she decided to do what she could to set Basil on a better path.

Macrina took him in hand, and with such speed did she draw him also towards the mark of philosophy that he forsook the glories of this world and despised fame gained by speaking, and deserted it for this busy life where one toils with one's hands. His renunciation of property was complete, lest anything should impede the life of virtue.[29]

In the end, of course, Basil was a more than worthy pupil. 'Indeed, to tell of his life and the subsequent acts, by which he became renowned throughout the world and put into the shade all those who have won renown for their virtue, would need a long description and much time.'[30]

Basil would remain in Annesi for three or four years. Following the example of his brother Naucratius, he established his own hermitage in the woods on the estate. In 360 he returned to Cappadocia, to take up a more public role in the theological disputes that were convulsing the churches. He became Bishop of Caesarea a decade later in 370, and remained there until his death in 379.

In his handling of Basil, Gregory raises an issue that still puzzles scholars. Basil is remembered as the first of the great Christian thinkers to develop a pastoral theology for the monastic life, and he is viewed as the founding thinker of monasticism as a communal way of life. Yet Gregory suggests that the credit for his fame as a thinker about the communal life should be laid at his sister's door. On Basil's arrival in Pontus, Macrina had been practising asceticism for over a decade, and had progressively turned the family estate into a monastery. What that meant, in those days, was still to be discovered, and Macrina and her mother were among the pioneers. It was as a result of Macrina's guidance, Gregory suggests, that Basil joined the ascetic movement. It was somehow ironic that Basil became one of the most celebrated monastic thinkers, while Macrina remained unknown, an imbalance that Gregory may have wanted to correct. There is something here of the younger brother rooting for the older sister, when he sees that the older brother has developed a habit of taking all the credit.

One also wants to account for why Basil himself did not leave traces of his debt to his sister in his writings. If there was a frisson of tension between Basil and Macrina, it may account for another aspect of the *Life of Macrina*: its tendency to minimize the leadership of Emmelia. Gregory acknowledges that it was Emmelia who had kindled the ascetic flame in her daughter's imagination, but he paints her as a serene and passive figure. This may, of course, reflect her character. But it may also reflect the benefit of hindsight: by the time Gregory was writing, Macrina had survived her mother for a decade, during which time she was the sole head of household. Yet it is also possible that in foregrounding the contributions of Macrina, Gregory wanted to build up a figure who could hold her own in the imagination by comparison to his celebrated brother. Though he had no need to exaggerate his sister's merits, he may have had a motive for gently downplaying her dependence on their sympathetic mother.

Things seem to have settled into a stable pattern on the estate during the years from Basil's departure in 360 to Emmelia's death in 371. Peter had now reached manhood, but chose to stay at Annesi with his mother and sister. The other sisters seem all to have been settled with husbands, while Basil and Gregory were established in Caesarea. Macrina had meanwhile collected a community of dependants living around her on the estate.

In many ways, this was not unusual for a rich landowner. Whether she was herself the owner of the estate at this time, or acting on behalf of her mother, her actions were well within the norm of a landowner who could offer shelter to dependants and long-term guests, and in exchange set certain standards for their behaviour. The difference was that the standards in question were those of an intensely pious ascetic Christianity, and the guests she took in were women who were willing to live as Christian widows or virgins – as Christian 'sisters'.

All in all, it was Macrina's charity that provided the organizing principle for the household during these years. The household's population increased, since her readiness to provide a home to the destitute brought in new members. Years later, after her death, some of those who mourned her most bitterly were sisters to whom she offered refuge when she found them 'wandering along the roads in time of famine'.

It was not only to the destitute that Macrina offered a home. There were women of all ages and stations in the district who were grateful for the opportunity to live among sympathetic female company.

> Among these was a lady of gentle birth, who had been famous in youth for wealth, good family, physical beauty and every other distinction. She had married a man of high rank and lived with him a short time. Then, with her body still young, she was released from marriage, and chose the great Macrina as protector and guardian of her widowhood, and spent her time mostly with the virgins, learning from them the life of virtue.[31]

Around 371 Emmelia died, with her eldest and youngest children, Macrina and Peter, at her side. It is not certain how long Peter stayed with Macrina after their mother's death, but there is no reason to think that he did not stay on in Annesi initially. In 380 or 381, not long after the deaths of Macrina and their brother Basil in 379, he was ordained Bishop of Sebaste, the town where his family's beloved martyrs had died.

Gregory lived in Caesarea from the 350s until some time after 370, when he became bishop of the nearby city of Nyssa in Cappadocia at the urging of his brother Basil. (During his years as Bishop of Caesarea from 370 to 379, Basil persuaded many of his friends and relatives to become bishops of the minor cities in his region.) When Basil died in 379, followed shortly afterwards by Macrina, Gregory lost the two most significant mentors of his early years.

Gregory does not give very much detail about Emmelia and Macrina's community in the stable years from 360 to his mother's death in 371, or the years afterwards, before his sister's final illness. We are given to understand that both men and women joined the community. The two sexes thought of themselves as separate units and on the whole the women kept away from the men for the sake of modesty. There was a little church on the estate, and a sequence of hours through the day was marked by ritual and prayer, such as the lighting of the lamps in the evening. It appears to have been a community in which every possible aspect of life was given a spiritual flavour. If there was little to report, this was understood to be a good thing.

Where Gregory's narrative shows greatest interest is in the turning points of his sister's life. Gregory is perhaps thinking, as he writes, of his readers: the most useful thing for a reader to know about his mother and sister was the courage with which they faced the difficulties they encountered. He may also have had specific readers in mind. By the time he wrote his memoir, Gregory was a widely published writer. We know little about his intentions for the memoir, whether he meant it to be copied and read widely or only by his family and friends. It is possible that the text was addressed primarily to the surviving members of Macrina's community at Annesi, to help them remember their beloved host and teacher. If this is the case, it would explain why he did not describe their communal life in great detail, since it would have been well known to his readers.

The Death of Macrina

The narrative of Macrina's death is the culmination of Gregory's memoir. One almost feels as if the long years of life have been only a period of training to allow his heroine to meet death with serenity. This emphasis on serenity in the face of death would become a commonplace in the lives of the saints, but at the time Gregory was writing there was not yet an established way of talking about such things. His narrative draws heavily on his studies in philosophy. Later, he would write a philosophical dialogue based on his last conversation with his sister, to explore further the spiritual insight that had shone forth as she spoke with him during her final hours.

Gregory tells us that in late 379, some months after their brother Basil's death in January of that year, he felt a strong craving to return to Annesi to visit his sister. It was because he acted on the urge that he was able to be present at her death-bed.

The journey from Cappadocia was difficult. If Gregory began at Nyssa he would have had to travel roughly 400 kilometres on horseback, a journey of perhaps ten days. He sent word ahead that he was coming: we know this because when he arrived, a family servant told him that his younger brother Peter had gone by another road to meet him, and had missed him. Peter seems to have returned only after his sister's death.

Already on the journey Gregory had an intimation of what was to come. 'Now when I had accomplished most of the journey and was one day's journey distant, a vision appeared to me in a dream and filled me with anxious anticipations of the future.' The vision did not directly involve death, but it did so indirectly, by showing the radiance of the bones of a long-dead martyr. 'I seemed to be carrying martyrs' relics in my hands. A light came from them, such as comes from a clear mirror when it is put facing the sun, so that my eyes were blinded by the brilliance of the rays. The same vision recurred three times that night.'[32]

The three repetitions are, of course, an echo of Emmelia's vision during her pregnancy with Macrina, when the angel addressed her three times. Its meaning was not immediately apparent to Gregory, but he knew that something was amiss. 'I could not clearly understand the riddle of the dream, but I saw trouble for my soul, and I watched carefully so as to judge the vision by events.'[33]

As he arrived at the estate, he was greeted by a delegation made up of all the men of the community, who had dropped what they were doing as soon as they heard the sound of his arrival. But the women hung back: 'the band of virgins on the women's side modestly waited in the church for us to arrive'. The men joined them there for a liturgy of prayers and blessings. When the service was over, the women disappeared again quickly and Gregory guessed that they did not want to remain long in the company of the men if their leader Macrina was not there to supervise.[34]

Then Gregory was admitted to see his sister. Even in her illness Macrina practised extreme self-renunciation. 'She was lying not on a bed or couch, but on the floor; a sack had been spread on a board, and another board propped up her head, so contrived as to act as a pillow, supporting the sinews of the neck in slanting fashion.' She was in a weakened state from fever, but tried to raise herself to greet him. Then, as well as she could from where she was lying, she made a bow. It was customary to do this in the presence of a bishop, and her gesture showed her pride in her younger brother's standing. Gregory was moved, if somewhat alarmed. 'I ran to her and embraced her prostrate form, and raising her, again restored her to her usual position.'[35]

Gregory speaks with great warmth about their last conversations. To an untrained ear, the account he gives makes his sister sound almost irritatingly detached from the cares of mere mortals. But of course both were conscious that this would be their last chance to muse together about the great questions of life and death, whose sharp reality they now faced. Each – Gregory in his loss and Macrina in her passage to the next life – would need strength and understanding to face what lay ahead.

Gregory had not seen her since the death of their brother, but when he tried to express his grief she refused to hear it. Instead, she took the fact of his death as an opportunity to talk about the immortality of the soul. '. . . she discussed the future life, as if inspired by the Holy Spirit, so that it almost seemed as if my soul were lifted by the help of her words away from mortal nature and placed within the heavenly sanctuary.' This seems to have been the conversation that Gregory would later cast as his dialogue *On the Soul and the Resurrection*, and he clearly found not only comfort but inspiration in her words.[36]

We are led to understand that it is on the basis of this last conversation that Gregory had come away with such a clear idea of her story: 'she began to recall her past life, beginning with childhood, and describing it all in order as in a history'. This was not only for the pleasure of reminiscing together, however: ever the elder sister, Macrina wanted to draw a moral from the fortunate life of their family. 'But her aim throughout was gratitude towards God, for she described our parents, life not so much from the point of view of the reputation they enjoyed in the eyes of contemporaries on account of their riches, as an example of the divine blessing.'

Macrina's final hours are described as the beginning of a welcome journey, at whose end she would be united with Christ. 'Her eagerness did not diminish. As she approached her end, it was as if she discerned the beauty of the Bridegroom more clearly, and she hastened towards the Beloved with the greater eagerness.' Soon she turned away from those keeping watch at her death-bed, '. . . ceasing to converse with us, she spoke henceforward to God in prayer . . . whispering with a low voice, so that we could just hear what was said'.

Gregory then describes Macrina's final prayer, which took place as part of the familiar daily ritual of the household, with the virgins gathered around their mistress.

> Meanwhile evening had come and a lamp was brought in. All at once she opened her eyes and looked towards the light, clearly wanting to repeat the thanksgiving sung at the Lighting of the Lamps. But her voice failed. She fulfilled her intention in the heart and by moving her hands, while her lips stirred in sympathy with her inward desire.[37]

In a moment of perfect alignment between heaven and earth, Macrina left them just as the liturgy ended. 'When she had finished the thanksgiving, and her hand brought to her face to make the sign had signified the end of the prayer, she drew a great deep breath and closed her life and her prayer together.'[38]

Now Gregory turns with surprise to describe the reaction of the gathered virgins to her departure. While she had remained alive, they had contained their feelings about losing her, since they had no wish to disturb her or to cause her distress. But once she was gone, they suddenly gave expression to all the anguish that they had fought against. 'Grief like some inward fire was smouldering in their hearts. All at once a bitter and irrepressible cry broke out.' Even more surprisingly, Gregory found himself joining them: 'my reason no longer remained calm, but a flood of emotion, like a watercourse, swept it away . . . I gave myself up to lamentation.'[39]

The memoir closes with a description of Macrina's burial, alongside her parents in the family mausoleum at the shrine of the Forty Martyrs in Ibora. Gregory tells us that Macrina and her mother had been particularly attached to the idea of being together even in death. Gregory describes the funeral as something of a carnival. On the appointed day, the party from Annesi set out on foot from the estate in the morning, accompanied by Macrina's body in a cart. They found themselves stopped repeatedly by well-wishers from the district, who wanted to pay their respects to the holy virgin. In the end, it took them the best part of the day to make their way to Ibora, a journey of not more 7 or 8 stadia he tells us, less than 2 kilometres. Once they arrived, Gregory joined with the local bishop in saying the prayers and placing the body in the tomb.

Gregory presents the honour paid to his sister in life and death as the result of her holiness, yet we should not be misled into thinking that there was no element of reverence for fortune involved. As a landowner of distinguished parentage, Macrina was not an inconsequential person in worldly terms. When Gregory tries to persuade his reader of her humility, what he intends to evoke is not genuine insignificance but generosity of spirit. He wants us to see in Macrina a distinguished figure who has chosen not to exact from others the deference that all acknowledge is owed her.

Emmelia and Macrina's story is important for modern readers because it reveals the sense of possibility that the rise of the virginal ideal brought to fourth-century women. It is difficult to know how unusual their experience was. There is no way of knowing how many women transformed their households along similar lines in the fourth century. By their very nature, the heroines of the domestic revolution of the fourth century went unnoticed by those outside their closest family circle. It was only the accident of Emmelia and Macrina's having such an illustrious circle of male relatives that brought the little world at Annesi into the stream of historical evidence. Of course, on Gregory's reading, the fact that the men-folk of such spiritually powerful women turned out themselves to be unusually gifted was not a coincidence.

Gregory's memoir is firm evidence that the Christian atmosphere of the fourth century encouraged women to experiment with organizing their lives in a way that would reflect their spiritual values. And it is equally evident that instead of standing in their way, the men of their families were at least sometimes happy to cheer them on. The new ideal of virginity and widowhood opened up a new era of sympathetic collaboration between men and women, and for male–female friendship. By establishing a category of women who were understood to be off-limits with respect to romantic entanglements, writers like Gregory were able to support and even celebrate a feminine version of Christianity without being afraid to seem as if they had fallen under the influence of feminine charms.

Whether Macrina's story had any direct effect on the development of women's monasteries elsewhere is a question that our sources do not allow us to answer. To begin with, the experiment at Annesi may have been virtually unknown. Eventually, Macrina and Emmelia would both gain lasting fame, joining their beloved Thecla as saints of the Orthodox Churches. If the holy household at Annesi was only a step away from the domestic establishment of a Lydia or a Chloe in the first century, it was the first step towards the monastery as an institution, of the kind that would endure into the Middle Ages and beyond.

8

A WORLD APART

Often when a daughter yearns to strive after higher things, the mother – concerned for her children, or misled by their imagined temporal beauty, or perhaps consumed by jealousy – tries to make her daughter a child of this age instead of a bride of God. As many wicked things as one can imagine set their traps, my child, but do not flinch in fear! Lift your eyes upward to where your Beloved is; follow in the footsteps of that famous one, Thecla, who has gone before you . . . let nothing extinguish your love.[1]

These words, from an anonymous fourth-century Greek sermon, capture the fervent atmosphere that the virginal ideal could arouse. The sermon points to a 'youth culture' element: the young woman being addressed is encouraged to assess whether her mother shows signs of being committed to the wrong values. But at the same time, there is an element of antiquity in the mix: the benchmark against which she is to measure her own values is the legendary companion of the Apostle Paul. The sermon goes on to explain that the way to ask 'What would Thecla do?' is in fact to study the Scriptures: if she reads Paul's Letters with as much dedication as Thecla showed in following Paul in his travels, she will find in them a powerful resource.

The intensity with which fourth-century women took up the study of the Bible is one of the most intriguing aspects of the Christian culture of the period. From the unlettered who memorized stories and sayings to the educated aristocrats who made scholarly investigations of the Old and New Testaments in the original Greek and

Hebrew, women were deeply involved in the study of the Bible, and surprisingly influential in the scholarly world.

The Ladies of the Aventine

To begin, we will return to the city of Rome, where Proba wrote her poems in the middle of the fourth century. Like the pious daughters of nineteenth-century British manufacturers who funded theological colleges and visited the Holy Land by camel in search of precious manuscripts, the well-born women of the ancient capital enjoyed a scope to pursue such interests, which most women could only dream about. Their fathers and brothers were men of ambition, who forged careers in the imperial administration, and it was to their advantage if the women in their families were accomplished and culturally literate. Meeting with one another to study Christian literature offered these women a parallel sphere in which their own concerns and interests could take centre-stage.

To acquaint ourselves with the circle of women who took up biblical scholarship in the late fourth century, we have to rely on the letters of a controversial male writer, the monk who would later be remembered as St Jerome. Jerome was a man of immense charm and many enemies. Brilliant and difficult in equal measure, the future Christian saint was a lively correspondent. His letters are full of gossip alongside discussions of more serious theological and biblical themes, and they offer a window onto the splendid and troubled world of the later Roman aristocracy during the years when he began to revise the ancient Latin translations of the Bible. It was Jerome who produced the new version that would endure, through the Middle Ages, as the Vulgate, and his friendships with Roman women were a source of inspiration, advice, and material support.

When he arrived as an unknown in Rome in 382, Jerome moved swiftly to gain an invitation to the literary *salons* of the Aventine Hill, which was then, as now, an exclusive residential district just south of the Emperor's palace and the Circus Maximus. The new networks of Christian patronage and friendship had destabilized an older Roman aristocracy based on the military glory and the worship of the old gods, and there was an opening in influential circles for a gifted man of letters from the provinces; the same would hold true for Saint Augustine, who arrived in the following year. Through Jerome's letters, we gain an insight into a disarmingly modern world of clever, opinionated women debating with each other about books, and especially about the Bible. We learn, from his not always generous descriptions, about his friends and enemies among the Roman literary elite. These included the poetess Proba – to whom Jerome, for some reason, took an intense dislike – and the austere Marcella, the leader of a group of women living as virgins and widows in the airy villas of the Aventine. Particularly interesting among the letters are a number of memoirs of friends from Marcella's circle who died before him. Jerome was a hot-headed star on the rise when he lived in Rome, but he lived to be an old man. In his old age he wrote fondly about those whom he had known during his stay in the capital.

Nearly thirty years later, in 410 or 411, when he had lived for a long while at the other end of the Mediterranean in Judaea, Jerome heard that the city of Rome had been sacked by Gothic soldiers. His old friend Marcella, he learned, had died as a result of wounds suffered during the looting of the city. A group of virgins had gathered in her house for protection and when the soldiers arrived she stood up to them. Jerome's memoir of Marcella, written to Principia, one of the virgins who had taken shelter with her, stands as a memorial to a generation of women who lived through Rome's last days as a capital city.

Jerome would stay in Rome for just over two years, from the autumn of 382 to the spring of 385, and by the time he arrived, Marcella was already long established as a Christian widow in the city. She was the leader of a group of aristocratic virgins and widows who had dedicated themselves to a life of prayer and Bible study.

The heiress of a long line of consuls, Marcella had been widowed very early, probably while still in her teens. Her mother Albina had encouraged a second marriage proposal from a man at the pinnacle of Roman politics, the ex-consul Cerealis, who was smitten by Marcella's great beauty. He even offered to treat her as a daughter, exchanging the pleasure of her company for the fortune of a man whom she could expect to die far ahead of her.

But Marcella would have none of it. She had heard that some men and women in Egypt were living the life of angels – refusing to marry and sharing a communal life of asceticism and self-denial – and she wanted to imitate them. If she could not go to Egypt, she could bring the desert to Rome, by living a life of simplicity and self-denial in her own Roman establishment.

During her youth, Marcella had known the venerable Athanasius, Bishop of Alexandria, and he had planted a seed in her imagination that would flourish in her adulthood. The great champion of the Nicene Creed had lived in Rome from 339 to 346, when the Arian Emperor Constantius, son of Constantine, had exiled him from his see. During his Roman stay, Athanasius had cultivated support for the Nicene cause, which did not return to favour with the imperial family until a generation later, under Theodosius (379–95).

Athanasius was a spellbinding storyteller, and he brought news of the heroic life being lived in the desert, which captured the imagination of the young Marcella. Jerome made sure to mention Marcella's connection to the great bishop.

It was from some priests of Alexandria, and from Father Athanasius . . . that Marcella heard of the life of the blessed Antony, then still alive, and of the monasteries in the Thebaid founded by Pachomius, and of the discipline laid down for virgins and for widows.[2]

In the 340s, the stories of the desert fathers and mothers were only known to those who learned of them by word of mouth, but after

Antony's death in 356, Athanasius would commit the *Life of St Antony* to writing, the first great saint's life of desert Christianity. The story of Antony has fascinated Christians for centuries, and Marcella was one of those who heard it first-hand, from the bishop who became his biographer. We can gain an idea of the stories Athanasius would have told in the 340s from the *Life*.

As Athanasius tells it, Antony's story is more than anything a story about how the Bible can change a person's life. He begins in the late third century, the time when Christians were still a persecuted minority and Macrina the Elder had sat at the feet of Gregory the Wonder-worker. In his youth, the future saint Antony had found himself unexpectedly head of a prosperous household.

> After the death of his father and mother he was left alone with one little sister: his age was about eighteen or twenty and on him the care both of home and sister rested. Six months after the death of his parents and going, according to custom, into the Lord's House, Antony communed with himself and reflected as he walked how the Apostles (Matt. 4: 20) left all and followed the Saviour; and how they in the Acts (Acts 4: 35) sold their possessions and laid them at the Apostles' feet for distribution to the needy, and what and how great a hope was laid up for them in heaven.[3]

As the *Life* tells his story, Antony offered a model for each Christian to follow, to allow the Gospel to reach into his or her life:

> Pondering over these things he entered the church, and it happened the Gospel was being read, and he heard the Lord saying to the rich man (Matt. 19: 21), 'If you want to be perfect, go, sell your possessions and give to the poor, and you will have treasure in heaven.'[4]

Antony's response to this saying of Jesus – one which he would have heard dozens of time before, but which he was ready, at this particular moment, to be changed by – was to hear the advice of Jesus as if it were addressed directly to himself. He had inherited his family's three hundred *arourai*, around eight tenths of a square kilometre, and he made these over to the village elders to use as they saw fit. He then sent his sister 'to live with the virgins' so he could himself strike out into the desert to live the life of a hermit.[5]

Our author does not record whether Antony's sister felt any craving for the ascetic life. It may not be out of place to feel some sympathy for a younger sister whose future was settled not by the considered judgement of wise parents but by impulse of a somewhat impetuous older brother. Her new life with the virgins could have been the fulfilment of her own dreams, but it could also have been nothing more than a respectable kind of imprisonment. There is no way of knowing. Up to the time of Antony's sister, in the late third century, there is evidence of Christian virgins living together, but the establishments within which they did so were understood as charitable establishments – an effort by wealthier members of the churches to provide for respectable unmarried women – rather than something more aspirational.

But thanks to Athanasius, virginity was an ideal for Marcella and her generation, and the story of Antony was an inspiration. And it was something more than that: Antony's example gave Marcella a solid reason to refuse an unwelcome marriage much desired by her adored mother. Her mother, Jerome tells us elsewhere, was someone whom Marcella found she could never easily refuse.

For Jerome, too, Antony and the desert Christians had been an inspiration. Jerome had travelled, in his own youth, to the deserts of the East, and he had come to Rome as a monk vowed to celibacy. One of his friends made a translation of the *Life of Antony* into Latin. It was this fact of his own sexual renunciation that allowed him, he believed, to cultivate spiritual friendships with women that were unusually free and intimate by comparison with the norms of their society. Both sides could seek out the 'inner man' in one another, aiming to set aside the attraction between men and women to aim at a more tranquil bond of friendship.

In his memoir of Marcella, Jerome tells Principia that in her youth, Marcella was known not only for her beauty but also for her seriousness. In her widowhood, she was constantly reading the Bible, and frequently at prayer. It was this that brought them together in the first place: Jerome says that when he came to Rome she sought him out, having heard of his reputation as a scholar. He found in her a worthy discussion partner:

> I in my modesty was for avoiding the eyes of high-born ladies, yet she pleaded so earnestly, both in season and out of season as the apostle says, that at last her perseverance overcame my reluctance. And, as in those days my name was held in some renown as that of a student of the scriptures, she never came to see me that she did not ask me some question concerning them, nor would she at once acquiesce in my explanations but on the contrary would dispute them; not, however, for argument's sake but to learn the answers to those objections which might, as she saw, be made to my statements.[6]

Yet though she would disagree with him in private, he remembers with pleasure that she often found a way to flatter him and others unnecessarily in public, attributing her own ideas to someone else if she thought they would bring credit.

It was through Marcella that Jerome made the acquaintance of the other women of the Roman aristocracy who had followed her into the life of Christian asceticism. Many became his friends and confidantes. His status as a monk gave him the opportunity to get to know the women on their own terms, in a way that Roman society normally denied to men. Jerome was by no means the only monk to take advantage of this privilege, but the self-revealing warmth of his letters makes it clear that he did so with relish. As a result, he often offers a privileged insight into the lives of the women he befriended.

Among the women whom Jerome came to know during his brief time in Rome was Paula, who would become his closest companion for over twenty years, until her death in 404. After her death, Jerome would write lyrically to her daughter describing the depth of his feeling for this beloved friend:

> If all the members of my body were to be converted into tongues, and if each of my limbs were to be gifted with a human voice, I could still do no justice to the virtues of the holy and venerable Paula . . . We do not grieve that we have lost this perfect woman; rather we thank God that we have had her, nay that we have her still.[7]

Yet for all his sense that their friendship was grounded in the shared pursuit of Christian ideals, Jerome could not fail to be dazzled by her position. Paula was the daughter of one of Rome's illustrious senatorial families.

> Noble in family, she was nobler still in holiness; rich formerly in this world's goods, she is now more distinguished by the poverty that she has embraced for Christ. Of the stock of the Gracchi and descended from the Scipios, the heir and representative of that Paulus whose name she bore, the true and legitimate daughter of that Martia Papyria who was mother to Africanus, she yet preferred Bethlehem to Rome, and left her palace glittering with gold to dwell in a mud cabin . . . Others may go back a long way even to Paula's cradle and, if I may say so, to her swaddling-clothes, and may speak of her mother Blæsilla and her father Rogatus. Of these the former was a descendant of the Scipios and the Gracchi; while the latter came of a line distinguished in Greece down to the present day. He was said, indeed, to have in his veins the blood of Agamemnon who destroyed Troy after a ten years' siege.[8]

Paula became a source of help and inspiration to Jerome over the years. Yet it does not seem too ungenerous to suggest that in their friendship Jerome cherished, among other things, a connection to the man who had led an army to recapture Helen of Troy.

Jerome's close friendship with Paula led him to claim the privilege of an uncle, almost a stepfather, with her children. There were five of them and they seem to have ranged in age from the early to late teens at the time he came to know their mother. Toxotius, the only boy and the youngest, may not yet have been ten. It is ironic, given the Roman aristocracy's ideas of the importance of bloodlines, that we know as much as we do about Paula's children not because they came from an important and ancient family – which they did – but rather because in her widowhood their mother adopted a wandering scholar as her protégé. Jerome, as it turned out, was a man with a future, but at the time he was a dark horse.

Paula's girls, Blaesilla, Paulina, Eustochium, and Rufina, were at a delicate age – the age of marriage. Some of their mother's friends thought that an unmarried man in his forties around the house – especially one who as a monk had no intention of marrying any of them – might queer the pitch for the search for suitable husbands, and this he almost certainly did. Three of the four girls seem to have married well, but Jerome made every effort to dissuade at least one of the younger sisters, Eustochium, from marrying at all.

It was through his brilliance as a Bible scholar, not his charms as a man, that Jerome was able to wield influence over Paula's daughter Eustochium, although there may have been a bit of both. The child was a native in the atmosphere of biblical immersion that her mother had adopted in widowhood. Jerome himself was on the threshold of discovering his real brilliance as a biblical scholar during his Roman stay. He was taken on as a secretary by Damasus, the Roman bishop, and from the older man he received encouragement for a most ambitious project, that of translating the Bible afresh into Latin from the original Greek and Hebrew. Jerome seems to have completed translations of the four Gospels while in Rome, but this was only the beginning of a project that would eventually reach back to include translations of the books of the Old Testament from their original

Hebrew, and would form the basis for the Vulgate Latin Bible, which has survived in use up to the present in the Roman Church.

Jerome's letters to friends, including Paula and her family, are crammed with references to biblical texts – questions for discussion, points of interpretation – and one can see how his work as a translator grew out of the lively discussions with members of his circle. He sometimes addressed letters to Paula and her daughters even when they were all in Rome, as a way marking his thoughts on a particular topic.

The best known of all Jerome's letters is one he wrote to Paula's daughter Eustochium as a present for her thirteenth birthday, the charming and provocative *Letter to Eustochium concerning Virginity*. It was to become one of the monuments of early Christian literature, and one of the patristic writings most often cited and copied by medieval readers. It is easy to see why. The letter offers an imaginative vision of how a woman can 'read herself into' the Bible, a freewheeling and sometimes alarming meditation on the figure of the Bride in the Song of Songs.

This extraordinary text encourages the girl to imagine herself as the Bride of Christ in a way that is far more intimate and concrete than one would expect. The child is encouraged to take the love poetry of the Song of Songs as her guide to what this marriage might involve. In all likelihood the resulting exercise in imaginative exegesis surprised and disconcerted her: it certainly captured her attention.

> Do you pray? You speak to the Bridegroom. Do you read? He speaks to you. When sleep overtakes you He will come . . . and your heart shall be moved for Him; and you will awake and rise up and say: 'I am sick with love'.
>
> Then He will reply: 'A garden enclosed is my sister, my spouse; a spring shut up, a fountain sealed . . .'[9]

The modern reader may be nearly as disturbed as were some of the Roman matrons of the day by this way of addressing a widow's adolescent daughter. At the same time, Jerome's letter carries the atmosphere of a heady moment in the history of biblical interpretation. A generation of women who hailed from the ancient pagan families of the Roman senate found themselves asking, as they read the stirring poetry of ancient Israel, both what it meant to be Christian and even what it meant to be women.

One of Paula's daughters, Blaesilla, had already made a good marriage and her second, Paulina, would marry the brilliant young senator Pammachius in 385. So, all eyes were on Eustochium in 383 and 384, as the next of the sisters to make her debut in Roman society. We have no way of knowing whether she had already begun to model herself on the widows and virgins of her mother's company before Jerome's arrival in Rome. The friendship with Marcella suggests that this was entirely possible.

In his letter to Eustochium, Jerome was clearly aware – and worried – that his was not the only influence in the child's life. 'Do not court the company of married ladies', he says, 'or visit the houses of the high-born. Do not look too often on the life which you despised to become a virgin.' We shouldn't necessarily think that the social traffic of senatorial married ladies was terribly attractive to Eustochium: after all, she may have found the company of grown-ups more enervating than alluring.[10]

Jerome knows only too well that the real problem is not Eustochium's interest in the older women, but theirs in her, of which she seems to be blissfully unaware. She is at an age to capture the imagination of the ladies of the court and senate, and her own relatives will want to put her charm to work in an advantageous marriage alliance. And then, there are the ladies of other families, almost all of whom have a son or other male protégé whom they are hoping to steer towards a chaste, respectable and innocent bride. Jerome shows awareness and distaste, in other letters, for a married aunt, Praetextata, who has been trying to adopt Eustochium as her protégée. (This Praetextata may have been the sister of Vettius Agorius Praetextatus, the leader of the pagan party in the Roman senate, which would help to explain Jerome's hostility.) Jerome knows all too well that the radiant virginal piety of a girl like Eustochium is the ideal credential for a daughter-in-law.

So he adopts a characteristically brilliant tactic. He distracts the girl from his real concern and plays on her sense of loyalty. 'Women of the world, you know, plume themselves because their husbands are on the bench or in other high positions. And the wife of the emperor always has an eager throng of visitors at her door.' Holding herself aloof from these people is a matter of defending the position of Jesus in the sharply articulated hierarchy of Roman senatorial culture. Jerome is deft enough here to flatter Eustochium's emerging ability to hold her ground when faced with pompous grown-ups. 'Why do you, then, wrong your husband? Why do you, God's bride, hasten to visit the wife of a mere man? Learn in this respect a holy pride; know that you are better than they.'[11]

Now he reveals a flash of his malicious sense of humour. It is the pomp of the widows of the capital that is his best target. 'To see them in their capacious litters, with red cloaks and plump bodies, a row of eunuchs walking in front of them, you would fancy them not to have lost husbands but to be seeking them.' Jerome and his protégée can share, here, a comfortable sense that whatever its other virtues, Christian austerity is far less ridiculous than the self-important posturing of the Roman senatorial classes.[12]

He steers next towards a more dangerous topic. If the senatorial women are known to parade their wealth in the streets, the culture of display is if anything more magnificent in their splendid mansions on the Esquiline and Aventine Hills of Rome. Even the pious Christian ladies are not immune to the accusation:

Their houses are filled with flatterers and with guests. The very clergy, who ought to inspire them with respect by their teaching and authority, kiss these ladies on the forehead, and putting forth their hands (so that, if you knew no better, you might suppose them in the act of blessing), take wages for their visits.[13]

There is something charmingly brazen about Jerome's criticism. He is well aware that he himself has been censored for paying court to rich ladies – indeed, his relationship with Paula and her daughters is the most conspicuous evidence against him in this respect.

But Jerome does not intend to criticize Eustochium's own mother Paula. He is almost certainly thinking of other women among their acquaintance whose company he finds less spiritually uplifting. His own position as a dependant of the wealthy Paula adds a certain acuity to his criticism of the wealthy ladies who act as patronesses of the Roman Church. 'They, meanwhile, seeing that priests cannot do without them, are lifted up into pride; and as, having had experience of both, they prefer the license of widowhood to the restraints of marriage, they call themselves chaste livers and nuns.'[14]

In Jerome's day, the city of Rome was host to vast Christian building projects, many of them paid for by aristocratic women, so the Church's dependence on the wealth and patronage of these eminent laywomen was a live issue. Thanks to their generosity – and perhaps also to their craving for display – the pagan character of the built environment of the city had begun to be supplemented by visible signs of the Christian presence. Most noticeably in the cemeteries that clustered near the city gates along the principal roads leading out of Rome, vast basilicas decorated with dazzling mosaics and coloured marble commemorated the piety of these women and their families. In the eyes of a child on the verge of womanhood, such as Eustochium, the Christian heiresses who played such an important role in this transformation must have seemed glamorous and powerful.

Yet Jerome wants to capture her imagination with a different kind of glamour. He wants her to understand that a Christian virgin is a person whose spiritual pedigree reaches back to the beginning of history. This means that she needs to gird herself with study. Even as he encourages her to stay at home, he offers her an open horizon: the thrilling and often bizarre landscape of the Bible and its ancient commentaries. For this landscape, of course, there was no more competent guide than Jerome. 'Read often,' he tells her, 'learn all that you can. Let sleep overcome you, the volume still in your hands; when your head falls, let it be on the sacred page.'[15]

So much of this sacred history, he tells her, is directly relevant to her own enterprise as a Christian virgin. In the beginning, Adam and Eve brought a curse upon humanity by eating the fruit of the tree of knowledge. 'But now that a virgin has conceived [Isaiah 7:14] . . . now the chain of the curse is broken. Death came through Eve, but life has come through Mary.' Mary's act of acceptance has changed the course of history.[16]

Jerome wants to make a connection between Mary's virginity and that of the women of his own day. 'And thus the gift of virginity has been bestowed most richly upon women, seeing that it has had its beginning from a woman.' Here Jerome moves off at a tangent which tells us something about how he sees the little world of the Aventine that he has wandered into. Having celebrated the birth of Jesus, he turns to talk of his unusual way of life: 'As soon as the Son of God set foot upon the earth, He formed for Himself a new household there; that, as He was adored by angels in heaven, angels might serve Him also on earth.' He seems to want to make the connection between the story of Jesus and Mary in Bethlehem and the fact that the ascetic women of his own day have begun to build a different kind of life for themselves. He wants, too, to give richness to the virgin's sense of herself as playing a privileged role in the Christian story. 'Read the gospel and see how Mary sitting at the feet of the Lord is set before the zealous Martha.' He reprises Luke's story of the two sisters:[17]

In her anxiety to be hospitable Martha was preparing a meal for the Lord and His disciples; yet Jesus said to her: 'Martha, Martha, you are worried and upset about many things, but few things are needed – or only one. And Mary has chosen what is good, and it will not be taken away from her.' (Luke 10: 41–2)[18]

Jerome is quite dismissive of Martha's standing as the host in Luke's story, but his reason is clear: he wants Eustochium to focus on the second sister. 'Be then like Mary; prefer the food of the soul to that of the body. Leave it to your sisters to run to and fro and to seek how they may fitly welcome Christ.' Eustochium's own older sisters Blaesilla and Paulina had made brilliant marriages. Both sisters were to die young – as did so many women who followed the gruelling regimen of constant pregnancy – but at the time, the fuss made over them must have been great. Jerome may well suspect that Eustochium has set an envious eye on their new status.[19]

So Jerome throws his imagination into a higher gear. If Blaesilla and Paulina have chosen the glittering world of the senatorial *matrona*, he, Jerome, can offer something more glamorous still, if one looks at it in the right light. The ace up his sleeve is his intimate knowledge of the great biblical scholar Origen of Caesarea, whose brilliant writings on virginity, written in Greek in the third century, were only available in the Latin-speaking West through men like Jerome, who had travelled in the East and immersed themselves in Greek intellectual culture.

Origen had spun a marvellous web of biblical commentary around the idea that the bodily purity of Christian virgins was both a metaphor for and a path to the spiritual purity of the soul. He had found a way to bring even the esoteric books of the Old and New Testaments into focus as repositories of spiritual insight, but his towering achievement was in his reading of the ancient Hebrew love-poetry of the Song of Songs. It is a text whose charm rests in large part on its evocative – and sexually suggestive – nuptial imagery. Origen proposed that it could be read as an allegory of the soul's love for God, which made it possible to reconcile its imagery to the austere sensibilities of Christian asceticism.

Jerome knows that he is in a unique position of strength to bring this kind of edgy biblical imagery into play, and he takes advantage of his position to push Origen's thinking one step further. The Bride of the Song of Songs is still an allegory of the soul, but for Eustochium Jerome wants to make her into something more specific, vivid, and relevant. She is his model for the Bride of Christ.

So Jerome directs Eustochium's eye away from the uncomfortable Martha. He wants the child to think of herself not only as Martha's sister Mary, the one who chooses to sit at the feet of Jesus, but also, at the same time, as the Bride of the Song of Songs. 'But do you, having once for all cast away the burden of the world, sit at the Lord's feet and say: "I have found the one my heart loves. I will hold him and will not let him go."' (Song of Songs 3: 4)[20]

Now the reader is in a kind of exegetical echo-chamber. She is asked to imagine herself as Mary of Bethany, who in turn re-enacts a voice from the Hebrew Bible, the Bride, in an act of Christian prayer. Eustochium will recognize instantly that the words are not Mary's but the Bride's, and she will love Jerome's audacity in making the switch. 'And He will answer: "My dove, my perfect one is unique, the only daughter of her mother, the favourite of the one who bore her."' (Song of Songs 6: 9) Now the Bride has an answer from her Bridegroom. At the same time, the element of sibling rivalry has found its fulfilment: the troublesome sister has vanished, and the Bride stands alone, ready to be adored single-mindedly by her Bridegroom, and as 'the only daughter of her mother'.[21]

Does Eustochium recognize, too, that if she is Mary, then Jerome – her teacher – is dangerously close to being Jesus? And what does her mother think of the way her daughter is being encouraged to think about herself? We have no way of knowing. No reply to the letter is recorded. And we have no way, even, of knowing whether Jerome is entirely conscious of where he stands in his own echo-chamber. Possibly not, for he steers next into territory that, to a modern sensibility, is even more disturbingly sensuous.

Now the idea of the virgin as bride of Christ takes on a rapturous aspect. The language is so lush that one almost forgets that Jerome is encouraging her to do something entirely harmless. Essentially, he is asking her to stay at home rather than going out, and to spend her time in Bible study when she is at home. It is *how* he asks her that is somewhat disturbing.

> Ever let the privacy of your chamber guard you; ever let the Bridegroom sport with you within. Do you pray? You speak to the Bridegroom. Do you read? He speaks to you. When sleep overtakes you He will come behind and put His hand through the hole of the door, and your heart shall be moved for Him; and you will awake and rise up and say: 'I am faint with love.' (Song of Songs 2: 5) Then He will reply: 'You are a garden locked up, my sister, my bride; a spring enclosed, a sealed fountain.' (Song of Songs 4: 12)[22]

The modern reader may be nearly as disturbed as were some of the Roman matrons of the day by this way of addressing a widow's nubile daughter. At the same time, Jerome's letter captures a heady moment in the history of biblical interpretation. A generation of women who hailed from the ancient pagan families of the Roman senate found themselves asking, as they read the stirring poetry of ancient Israel, what it meant to be Christian and even what it meant to be women.

The letter breathes humour and charm, and Eustochium may well have been too innocent to be shocked by the strong erotic undercurrent in the language. But it is also possible that she simply did not find it shocking. It is difficult to judge what it meant, in the late fourth century, for a man of Jerome's age – in his early forties if he was born in 340 as scholars believe – to write in this way to a chaste virgin of marriageable age.

It's natural to assume that it meant something very different then. Neither Paula nor her daughter was heir, as readers in later centuries would be, to a vision of sexuality coloured by centuries of ascetic imagining. Even in Christian ascetic circles, a certain Roman bawdiness may still have held sway. Ultimately one can only guess how much Eustochium was expected to know about what went on in the bedroom, and whether it was considered appropriate for her elders to let on that they knew what she knew.

And Jerome himself may have felt that by encouraging Eustochium to bind herself to her Bridegroom with bonds of erotic intensity, he could instil in her a fierce protectiveness about her vocation as a virgin of the Church. This would stand her in good stead should senior relatives try to marry her off. He knew that as a titled heiress, Eustochium's right to withhold herself from the marriage market was dependent on the good intentions of a single person, her mother Paula. And Paula, like any of her contemporaries, was always only a fever away from death. Should Paula die unexpectedly, Eustochium would have to fight tooth and nail to protect her choice.

The Church could protect the vocation of enrolled virgins, but church tradition frowned upon the idea of women taking a vow of virginity before the age of forty, past the peak of fertility. Bishops were well aware that the Christian communities needed to produce children and grandchildren in order to survive. So Jerome threw the considerable force of his own charisma into his own attempt to bolster Eustochium and any other young women who might read his letter.

The closing passage of the letter strikes a more sombre note. After the lyrical intensity and playful humour of the letter itself, its final lines offer a moving evocation of how Eustochium can expect to be released from the bonds of the flesh at her death. The passage from this life to the next now figures as a luminous threshold, a moment when biblical history and the heavenly future will be revealed to be one and the same.

Emerge, I pray you, for a while from your prison-house, and paint before your eyes the reward of your present toil, a reward which 'no eye has seen, what no ear has heard, and what no human mind has conceived'. (1 Cor. 2: 9) What will be the glory of that day when Mary, the mother of the Lord, shall come to meet you, accompanied by her virgin choirs! When, the Red Sea past and

Pharaoh drowned with his host, Miriam, Aaron's sister, her timbrel in her hand, shall chant to the answering women: 'Sing to the Lord, for he is highly exalted; Both the horse and driver he has hurled into the sea.' (Exodus 15: 21) Then shall Thecla fly with joy to embrace you. Then shall your Spouse himself come forward and say: 'Arise, my darling, my beautiful one, come with me. See! The winter is past, and the rains are over and gone.' (Song of Songs 2: 10–11) Then shall the angels say with wonder: 'Who is this that appears like the dawn, fair as the moon, bright as the sun?' (Song of Songs 6: 10)[23]

What Eustochium must try to understand is that the stories of biblical women are not stories of the past: they are windows that can offer her a glimpse into the parallel kingdom in which she can hope to join them. Her careful study of the Bible is a means to that end. In striving towards the angelic life and studying the scripture, she is preparing herself to return to her spiritual homeland. The Bible, both Old and New Testaments, is an invitation to this country, and the women of scripture are her fellow countrywomen. At a time when the canon of the New Testament had not been firmly established, the idea of scripture was broader than our own would be, so Jerome, the most distinguished biblical scholar of the age, did not hesitate to number Thecla along with Mary and Miriam among the heroines of the Bible.

Jerome is reaching here to describe and develop an idea – the communion of saints – that would take a central place in the pastoral thought of the medieval Church. It is a powerful idea, both reassuring and inspiring, invaluable in a world where the hovering presence of death was never far from view. Jerome's letter survives in hundreds of medieval manuscripts from monasteries and convents all across Europe, and the final passage of the letter was repeatedly imitated by other writers, so there is evidence that both monks and nuns found the letter uplifting.

Eustochium herself would have to reason to test the pastoral value of these ideas almost immediately. In the same year, her twenty-year-old sister Blaesilla was widowed, and fell ill not long afterwards with a fever from which she never properly recovered. After the first brush with illness, she changed dramatically. From a frothy young socialite, she became a pale and fragile ascetic. She could hardly bear to eat or sleep. For those around her, it was difficult to distinguish between illness and otherworldliness as factors in her altered state. She immersed herself deeply in a programme of meditation on the Psalms, and began to prepare in earnest for the journey to the heavenly country. Within weeks of her husband's death, Blaesilla too had died – of starvation, some suspected – and was buried alongside her husband.

Jerome now found himself in a dangerous position. He wrote a very moving letter of consolation to Paula, but it was difficult to avoid the suspicion that he had played a part in her daughter's declining health by encouraging her to feel that it was unnecessary to care for the body.

The controversy over Blaesilla's death raised anxious questions about what the adults around her could or should have done differently, questions not entirely unlike those that arise in a modern case of life-threatening anorexia. Never a man for pointed self-introspection, Jerome was confident that he had been in the right. In any event, he was confident that if Roman opinion turned against him he could count on the protection of a man who, more than any other, was the final arbiter in matters of Christian pastoral care, since his mentor was none other than Damasus, Bishop of Rome. Yet many members of Paula's circle turned against Jerome, suggesting that his encouragement of the girl's fasting had been at best unwise and at worst criminal.

Towards the end of the year, however, everything changed. In late November of 384, Pope Damasus developed a fever and by early December he too was dead. Jerome must have seen that his situation would quickly become intolerable, so he began to plan his escape. Soon afterwards he sailed east to the Holy Land, maintaining that now Damasus no longer needed him, he could concentrate his energies more fully on his great project of translation. In the long run, it turned out to be an inspired decision. Jerome's Latin Bible would benefit enormously from his ability to consult with the rabbis of Palestine when he encountered difficulties with the Hebrew text of the Old Testament. In the short run, it put him beyond the reach of his critics.

Sometime later, in the spring of 386, Paula and Eustochium followed him eastwards. Once they arrived in the Holy Land, mother and daughter used their inheritance to establish a hospital and monasteries at Bethlehem, the birthplace of Jesus. The Church of the Nativity there had been known since the time of the Empress Helena as a shrine to the Virgin Mary *Theotokos*, the God-bearer, so it is possible that their choice of Bethlehem as a home reflected their own exalted idea of Christian virginity. Paula, Eustochium, and Jerome would spend the rest of their lives in the Holy Land.

We can be grateful for their self-imposed exile, because Jerome's letter-book records not only the new life of the three pilgrims in the Holy Land, but also passages about the other members of their circle left behind in Rome. One of the most interesting letters is from Paula and Eustochium – not Jerome himself – and it was written around 386 to Marcella, who had remained in Rome, inviting her to visit them in Bethlehem. The letter mentions, one by one, the places of sacred history that await her, and where they fit in the puzzle of biblical narrative. Then the two writers turn to evoke the thrill of reunion:

> Will the time never come when a breathless messenger shall bring the news that our dear Marcella has reached the shores of Palestine, and when every band of monks and every troop of virgins shall unite in a song of welcome? In our excitement we are already hurrying to meet you: without waiting for a vehicle, we hasten off at once on foot. We shall clasp you by the hand, we shall look upon your face; and when, after long waiting, we

at last embrace you, we shall find it hard to tear ourselves away. Will the day never come when we shall together enter the Saviour's cave, and together weep in the sepulchre of the Lord with His sister and with His mother?

Again we see the theme of longing and reunion, but this time Paula and Eustochium will be on the other side, joining the chorus who welcome their beloved friend Marcella. We will see below that a steady stream of women from the Latin West did indeed make the journey to Jerusalem, but there is no record that Marcella herself was among them.

In the end, Paula would spend nearly twenty years in the Holy Land, and Eustochium over thirty. After her mother's death in Bethlehem in 404, Eustochium became an independent woman of impressive means – she financed four monasteries from her inheritance. At thirty-four, she was forced to stand free of her long partnership with Paula, and she had both the opportunity and the burden of choosing her own way. The obvious choice might have been to return to Rome. It would not have been impossible to free herself from commitments that, in all likelihood, her mother had chosen for her. Instead, she chose to stay close to her mother's memory, and to remain in the Holy Land with Jerome.

But she did think of Rome: she invited her fourteen-year-old niece – also named Paula – who had grown up there, to come from Rome to Bethlehem and to take up the position as beloved protégée, which Eustochium herself had held for so many years. Jerome remained with the two of them there, until Eustochium's death in 419 or 420, aged around forty, roughly the age Jerome had been when he arrived in Rome so many years earlier. Jerome himself died in 420, one of the most important scholars of antiquity despite his many enemies, and the legacy of their life together echoes in the Latin Bible as it was handed down to the medieval Church.

The Blessings of Pilgrimage

As Paula and Eustochium discovered, the most evocative way of engaging with the stories of scripture was to make a physical journey to the places where they had taken place. The impulse to visit holy places was a power to conjure with for those women who had the means and the occasion to travel. Both the stories of the Bible and the more recent stories of the desert exerted their pull. From the fourth century, we begin to find evidence of women who withdrew from family life for an extended period in order to undertake a pilgrimage to the places where the heroes and heroines of the faith had lived and died. This is one of the most surprising and intriguing practices of the ancient Church.

Christian communities all across the Empire were encouraging the faithful to visit the shrines of their local heroes, and to crave the special blessing that came from the places where a martyr of the faith had lived or died. Places where no saint had set foot could become sites of veneration too, if the bones of the saint were brought there to be buried. Even a small fragment of a long-dead saint's desiccated bones could serve as a highly charged token of the saint's power to intercede with God on behalf of the faithful.

Yet among these sites, it was the Holy Land above all that captured the imagination. As early as the second century, Christians had begun to travel to the provinces of Egypt and Palestine in order to visit the famous sites of biblical history. By the end of the fourth century, this trickle of visitors to the Holy Land had swelled to a substantial current. Christian communities were flourishing in the Holy Land, especially the monasteries of the Egyptian desert, and they began to attract numerous visitors in their own right. Some visitors would progress systematically around the principal sites as swiftly as ancient methods of travel would allow, while others would remain for a year or two to immerse themselves in the wisdom of the desert.

Egeria, who made a pilgrimage to the Holy Land in the late fourth century, offers an interesting case in point. No other contemporary source refers to her, so we have to learn as much as we can about her from a single remarkable source, the travel diary which she wrote for her 'sisters' who were unable to come with her on her journey. The source survives in only one incomplete manuscript, so we are lucky to know what we do about her.

Whether the women to whom Egeria wrote were her biological sisters or simply sisters in Christ is uncertain. 'Sister' was often used as an affectionate term of address, for example by husbands writing to their wives. Some scholars have argued that Egeria was a nun, but if she was, she fails to mention it, and in some ways it seems unlikely. She is more interested in touring the holy sites of the biblical lands than in learning about the communities of virgins that had gathered there, and when she encounters these communities she shows curiosity rather than familiarity with the habits and special vocabulary of their way of life.[24]

Many scholars believe that Egeria's 'sisters' must have been in the Rhône Valley, perhaps in the great port of Arles at the mouth of the Rhône, because her way of describing the River Jordan offers the Rhône as a point of comparison.

> After having travelled fifteen miles from Hierapolis, in the Name of God, I arrived at the river Euphrates, which Scripture very well described as *the great river Euphrates* (Genesis 15: 18). It is large and rather frightening, for it flows down with as swift a current as the river Rhône, except that the Euphrates is much larger.[25]

This single mention is perhaps slim evidence, but it is at least compatible with the only other evidence for her geographical origin. She mentions that when she met the Bishop of Edessa, he expressed amazement that she had come from the end of the world all the way to his city, and this is certainly compatible with her having come from Gaul.

It has been suggested that Egeria, like Lydia the purple-seller, came from a merchant family, and this makes a great deal of sense. Certainly her background was prosperous; otherwise she could not have afforded a journey that lasted for three years and that seems to have involved frequent last-minute changes of itinerary. A mercantile background fits well with her easy approach to travel. If she drew on a network of family business contacts across the Mediterranean, it would have made it easier to organize not only sea passages, but also the tents, camels, mules, and local guides required for desert travel in the Roman period.[26]

It is even possible that her journey had a practical aim. The beginning of Egeria's narrative is lost, so we don't know whether she recorded her reason for travelling. She does not by any means account for every day of the long journey, and there is no reason she could not have been visiting business contacts in the region and making her stops at the places of Christian interest as she went.

During the fourth and fifth centuries, it became increasingly popular for both men and women of means to make a journey to the Holy Land in order to bring the stories of the New Testament to life by seeing where they had taken place. At the same time, Egeria's is one of the very first surviving accounts of this kind, so there was no established pattern to follow.

Although Egeria was no stylist, and her Latin has none of the embellishments of the literary writers of her day, her narrative reveals an eye for detail and a very fresh and direct way of looking at things. Here is Egeria describing her first sight of Mount Sinai, at the beginning of the surviving narrative.

We came to a certain place where the mountains through which we were travelling, opened out to form an immense valley, vast, quite flat, and extremely beautiful, and across the valley there appeared Mount Sinai, God's holy mountain . . . When one reaches this place, 'it is customary', said the holy men who were guiding us and so advised, 'for those who are coming to say a prayer . . . And that is what we did.[27]

One of the points to which Egeria consistently attends, in describing her adventures, is an account of all the small actions and rituals that she and her companions performed in order to drive home the importance of what they were seeing. Here is her account of her stop at the plains of Moab, along the eastern shore of the Dead Sea, in what is now Jordan.

> Here Moses, the holy man of God, blessed the children of Israel, each in his turn, before his death. On arriving in this plain, we proceeded to this very place; there we said a prayer and read a certain passage from Deuteronomy, as well as the canticle and the benediction which Moses had said over the children of Israel.[28]

This was the song which Moses taught to the Israelites in Deuteronomy 32, as a legacy that they could carry with them across the Jordan into Canaan, while he, Moses, would be left behind. He would die having seen – but not entered – the Promised Land.

> We said a second prayer after the reading from Scripture, and, having given thanks to God, we moved along. Whenever we were empowered to reach our destination, it was always our custom first to say a prayer, then to read a passage from the Bible, sing a Psalm fitting the occasion, and finally say a second prayer.[29]

Every effort was made to cultivate an extraordinary resonance, in the journey, between the excitement of 'being there' and the sense of going deeper into already familiar stories from the Bible. In her narrative, Egeria invites her readers to imagine the connection, even as she delivers the moment of insight back into the world of words.

It was not only stories from the Old and New Testaments that attracted this kind of effort to bring the past to life. Certain places had a special importance to women because of the non-canonical traditions that had been handed down from the age of the apostles and martyrs. Among these was the shrine where St Thecla was said to have died after her long years as an itinerant preacher and apostle, at Seleucia of Isauria on the south coast of Asia Minor.

Egeria's account of her visit to the great shrine of Thecla at Seleucia illustrates how women sought to make the story of Thecla come alive. When Egeria arrived at Thecla's shrine, she found that a community of nuns was established there. To her surprise and delight the abbess of the community was a sympathetic deaconess whom she had met at an earlier stage of her journey, when she was in Jerusalem.

> At the holy church there is nothing but countless monastic cells for men and of women. I met there a very dear friend of mine, and a person to whose way of life everyone in the East bears witness, the holy deaconess Marthana, whom I had met in Jerusalem, where she had come to pray. She governs these cells of *apotactitae,* or virgins. Would I ever be able to describe how great was her joy and mine when she saw me?[30]

It is no surprise that it was at Thecla's shrine that the two women found each other, since she was a figure of such vivid interest to women, a point of unparalleled identification within the biblical landscape.

One of the forms of hospitality offered by the resident nuns was an invitation to the visiting pilgrims to worship in Thecla's church, and to read the *Acts of Thecla* out loud together. Of course, the pilgrims already knew the story, but reading it together allowed them to engage with it more vividly, inspired by the landscape where the last part of Thecla's story was understood to have taken place.

> There are many cells all over the hill and in the middle there is a large wall which encloses the church where the shrine is. It is a very beautiful shrine . . . Having arrived there in the name of God, prayer was said at the shrine, and the complete Acts of St Thecla was read.[31]

A Christian network was emerging, of women and men whose lives, for a time at least, were oriented around meditating on the heroic days of the early Church. As one travelled throughout the Mediterranean, Christian history served as a guide to the places one might want to visit. At the same time, it was at those places that one could find others who shared an interest in a deepened understanding of Christianity.

The Dangers of Pilgrimage

The impulse to leave home and discover the sacred in a distant land could disrupt established relationships, routines, and hierarchies. For some, this was part of its value, but for others the craving for disruption was the sign of a disturbed mind. For every fourth-century writer who rhapsodizes about the inspiration to be gained from making sacred history come alive, another is worried that curiosity about the wider world will simply distract the travellers from making themselves useful within their home community. When women were involved, anxieties of this kind seem to have been particularly pointed.

We turn now to consider a very different view of pilgrimage, that of Gregory of Nyssa, the late fourth-century bishop whom we encountered earlier as the son of Emmelia and the younger brother of Macrina. Gregory was the author of one of the most influential tracts celebrating Christian virginity. In this treatise, the idea of female sanctity involves women being modest and retiring, in a way that should not surprise us coming from the author of the *Life of Macrina*. So it is understandable that Gregory was ambivalent about the new popularity among Christian women of travelling to visit the historical sites of the Holy Land.

Modesty, he argues, is one of the core principles of Christian virtue – he takes it as a given that serious Christians will want to avoid an unnecessary mixing of the sexes. Yet such scruples become inconvenient, if not impossible, in the context of long-distance travel.

> The necessities of a journey are continually apt to reduce this scrupulousness to a very indifferent observance of such rules. For instance, it is impossible for a woman to accomplish so long a journey without a conductor. On account of her natural weakness she has to be put upon her horse and to be lifted down again; again, she has to be supported in difficult situations.[32]

Gregory goes on to make it clear that whether she brings along her own servant to do this job, or relies on the help of strangers along the way, her modesty will be compromised. He also wants to warn that prospective pilgrims seem to have an unrealistic idea of the spiritual uplift they will encounter in the Holy Land. The traveller will encounter pitfalls there, all the more so if she or he arrives with naïve expectations.

> If the Divine grace was more abundant about Jerusalem than elsewhere, sin would not be so much the fashion amongst those that live there; but as it is, there is no form of uncleanness that is not perpetrated amongst them; rascality, adultery, theft, idolatry, poisoning, quarrelling, murder, are rife . . . Well, in a place where such things go on, what proof, I ask, have you of the abundance of Divine grace?[33]

Gregory himself had travelled to Jerusalem on ecclesiastical business after the Council of Constantinople, so he was writing from experience. He came away unconvinced of the necessity of such journeys: 'We derived only this profit from our journey, that we came to know by being able to compare them, that our own places are far holier than those abroad.'[34]

Athanasius of Alexandria, the ring-leader of the virginity movement, had also emphasized the importance of making sure that those who did undertake pious journeys knew that the mere fact of having travelled could not be brandished as a trophy. Each point along a journey should be directed at discovering a site of sacred history, and every effort must be made to draw the spiritual lesson. In his 'Letter to Virgins who Went to Pray in Jerusalem and Have Returned', Athanasius explained how this would work.

> You have seen the place of the Nativity: he has given birth to your souls anew. You have seen the place of the Crucifixion: let the world be crucified to you, and you to the world [Gal. 6: 14]. You have seen the place of the Ascension: your minds are raised up. Let your bodies be on earth, but your minds in heaven. Your dwelling place is your father's house, but your way of life is with the Heavenly Father.[35]

By this way of reckoning, the physical pilgrimage was only a starting-point; the more important journey was the journey of the imagination.

Gregory of Nyssa had a similar outlook. His mother and sister had made their home into a spiritual power-house, and Emmelia had built a church near Ibora, not far from her estate at Annesi, to house relics of the Forty Martyrs of Sebaste. She had buried Gregory's father there, and afterwards she herself and Gregory's sister Macrina were buried there in turn. 'I laid the bodies of my parents next to the relics of the soldiers so that at the time of the Resurrection they will arise together with the saints and with their intercession.' To a family that had devoted such energy to cultivating spiritual power in their own village, travel to the Holy Land was less an inspiration than a distraction.[36]

It has been argued that Gregory of Nyssa's reason for trying to contain the vogue for pilgrimage to Jerusalem had, as much as anything, to do with a suspicion that the Bishop of Jerusalem was trying to profit from the waves of visitors travelling to his city from all around the Empire. Gregory did not see why Jerusalem should receive a disproportionate amount of attention from the faithful.

Surely God meant for his blessings to extend to Christians every-where?[37]

One of the most interesting figures to weigh in on the debate over pilgrimage was the desert father remembered as Evagrius of Pontus. Evagrius had grown up in Ibora near Emmelia's Church of the Forty Martyrs, and he seems to have been discovered by Gregory and his brother Basil. Evagrius climbed the ladder of ecclesiastical patronage first by serving as lector at Caesarea when Basil was bishop there, and then, after Basil's death, as deacon under Basil's friend Gregory Nazianzen at Constantinople. His mastery of the classics and his rhetorical gifts brought him a marvellous success in the capital, and he was able to remain in his position even when Nazianzen suddenly retired. But it was a bitter victory. An infatuation with a married woman unsettled him, and he fled the capital. He later claimed that he had been visited by a vision of the governor's soldiers arriving, at the behest of the woman's husband, to throw him in prison.

In 383, Evagrius came to Jerusalem, where he joined the monas-tery founded on the Mount of Olives by the Spanish heiress Melania the Elder and her spiritual partner Rufinus. A contemporary of Paula and Jerome, Melania was born in Spain, but had lived in Rome in her early years, where her future husband Valerius Maximus was Urban Prefect from 361 to 362. Around 372, at the age of twenty-two, she found herself a widow when her husband and two of her three sons died suddenly. She took the opportunity to make a dramatic break with her past. Leaving her surviving son with a guardian, she embarked for Egypt, where she lived for some time with the desert fathers in the mountain of Nitria, around 70 kilo-metres south-east of Alexandria. In 373 or thereabouts, she travelled to Palestine to assist a group of Nicene fathers from Nitria, who were sent into exile by the Arian Emperor Valens after the death in May 373 of the great Nicene champion, Bishop Athanasius of Alexandria. By 375 she and Rufinus had settled in Jerusalem.

Her biographer Palladius says that it was Melania who persuaded Evagrius to dedicate himself to the ascetic life. Initially, he lived with the community on the Mount of Olives, but his struggles with temptation continued and he fell gravely ill. It was only upon resolving to move again, to the Nitrian desert, that he was able to recover both his health and his spiritual composure. He spent the remaining years of his life in Egypt, from 383 to his death in 399.

Once he was established in Egypt, Evagrius wrote back to Melania and Rufinus in Jerusalem to offer advice regarding a mutual friend, Severa, who lived with them and was considering undertaking a pilgrimage on foot through the Holy Land.

> As regards the chaste deaconess Severa, I praise her intentions but I do not approve of her undertaking. I do not see what she will gain from such a long walk over such a laborious route; whereas, with the help of the Lord, I could easily demonstrate the damage she and those with her will suffer.[38]

In another letter, addressed to Melania, Evagrius warns that both women and men should think carefully before undertaking such a journey:

> teach your sisters and your sons not to take a long journey or to travel through deserted lands without examining the matter seriously. For this is misguided and unbecoming to every soul that has retreated from the world.[39]

The danger, he suggests, is especially insidious for women. In another text sent to his friends in Jerusalem, a collection of instructions for the virgins in Melania's ascetic community addressed to the same deaconess Severa, Evagrius warns them against listening to 'wandering old women'.

Melania's biographer Palladius was a disciple of Evagrius, and he too put emphasis on the point that travel should not be an end in itself. It should only be a way of coming into contact with deeper truths by meeting men and women who had dedicated themselves to those truths. 'In the words of Palladius, "the object of our inquiry is not the place [*topos*] where they have settled but the fashion [*tropos*] of their plan of life".'[40]

Part of the problem with the vogue for pilgrimage to holy places was that the pilgrims were often restless and volatile. They were not clearly accountable to any structure of authority, and they could disturb the equilibrium of more settled Christians. A traveller who returned from a journey with wonderful stories could strike envy into the hearts of others bound to a comparatively dull routine. But the enviable stories sometimes came at a high price.

The Christian heiress Poemenia was criticized for travelling through the Holy Land with a large entourage – including her own bishop – and for presuming to ignore the advice of the holy men she met along the way. Palladius tells the story of how her scorn for the advice of one of the desert fathers, John of Lycopolis, led to trouble.

When Poemenia the servant of God came to interview him, he did not meet her, but he had a number of secret matters told to her. And he enjoined her, when she went down from the Thebaid not to turn aside to Alexandria, 'for you will fall into temptation'. But she, thinking differently, or forgetting, turned aside to Alexandria to see the city. But on the way she moored her boats near Niciopolis to rest. So her servants went on shore and after some disorderly behaviour had a fight with the people of the place who were desperate characters. They cut off the finger of one eunuch and murdered another, and even threw Dionysius the most holy bishop into the river, not recognizing him, and after wounding all the other servants, loaded the lady herself with insults and threats.[41]

If travel could expose the Christian to new truths, it could also offer hard lessons to those who failed to listen to sound advice.

Interestingly, it was around this time that Rufinus of Aquileia, the friend of Evagrius, Melania, and Severa, made a translation into Latin of the *Recognitions*, the romance of the shipwrecked family of the first-century Pope Clement which we encountered in an earlier chapter. Although it was a historical romance rather than an account of contemporary events, the story of the *Recognitions* revolved around the mishaps that could befall travellers in the Holy Land. Its heroine Matthidia, the mother of Clement, had begun her journey as an heiress of the Roman senate and had ended as a beggarwoman in Roman Palestine, a fate very similar to that of Melania, though at the same time wonderfully different. In Matthidia's case, the misadventures were an instrument of God's purpose, serving to bring her to the Christian faith. This is an idea that Rufinus and Melania would have been delighted with – even if not all of their friends agreed.

9

THE DESERT MOTHERS

We also visited Oxyrhyncus, a city in the Thebaid, whose wonders beggar description. So full it is of monasteries inside that the monks themselves make the walls redound, and it is surrounded outside by other monasteries, so that there is another city outside the city . . . who could state the number of monks and virgins, which was innumerable? From the holy Bishop we had precise information: ten thousand monks under him, and twenty thousand virgins. As for their hospitality and charity, I cannot express it: our cloaks were torn apart as each group pulled us to their side.[1]

A half-century after the death of Constantine, a visitor to Oxyrhyncus, a royal city of the pharaohs that had become a regional capital of Egypt in the Roman period, bears witness to how swiftly the new imperial Christianity had changed the landscape of cities and towns. What would most have surprised a time-traveller from the pagan years would not, however, have been the city's religious zeal – or even the fact that it was so zealously Christian. Egypt had long offered fertile soil for larger-than-life religious developments. It was here that the Red Sea had been made to part, here that the Emperor Hadrian's favourite Antinnoös had drowned in the Nile and been proclaimed a god. That the Christian god had turned out to be more powerful than Isis and Osiris had perhaps come as a surprise to the people of Oxyrhyncus, but surprises of this kind were not unusual.

But no one could have predicted that Constantine's dream would result, in a few short decades, in the presence of ten thousand monks and twenty thousand virgins in Oxyrhyncus. If modern estimates of the city's population are accurate, this means that roughly a quarter of the city's population had taken a vow to remain unmarried, and among these, women outnumbered men two to one. What could account for so many young women choosing to give up marriage and motherhood, and for so many of their parents failing to insist on grandchildren?

We have already seen that the Egyptian desert and the Holy Land exerted a great attraction on women's imagination in the fourth century. It is remarkable that so many women chose to reorganize their lives around this interest. Most, to be sure, were already living in that region, while others came as pilgrims from the other end of the Empire, and stayed. Their way of life was diverse. A heroic few chose to strike out on their own in the desert as solitaries, while the majority joined organized communities numbering in the thousands.

Why did the Christianity of the desert become so important in the fourth century? And why did women play such an important role in bringing the ideal to reality? The ideals of sexual renunciation and retreat from pursuing the pleasures and hopes of this world were not new in the fourth century. Already in the first generation after the death of Jesus, the Apostle Paul had argued that by giving up the dream of a future here on earth that naturally accompanied the raising of children, people of faith could show how ardently they hoped for the end of time, and the coming of the kingdom of heaven. But at the same time, most of the New Testament writers had assumed that marriage and child-rearing would be the norm for the majority of Christians, as for anyone else, and this tradition had continued across the first three centuries.

Constantine's conversion had changed all this. For the first three centuries, affiliation with the Christian movement had been against the law, even if the authorities were often prepared to turn a blind eye. Yet adversity can sometimes bring out the best in people. During this period, the Christian leaders had been comparatively humble individuals, who knew it was not in their interest to attract unnecessary attention, but who could be counted on to exhibit fortitude in the face of trials.

Paradoxically, the success represented by Constantine's conversion presented the most insidious challenge the churches had yet faced. What were Christians to make of a situation in which their bishops were now the Emperor's favourites? The end of the persecutions was, paradoxically, a source of disappointment for many Christians. In the new climate of imperial favour, bishops were increasingly at war with their congregations and with one another, arguing about matters ranging from the mundane to the mystical. Money was often at the root of the problem, and this was distressing. If bishops were quarrelling over money, it is not surprising that many of the faithful wanted no part of it.

After the peace of Constantine, ascetic renunciation allowed the Christian communities to raise up new heroes of the faith at just the time when inspiration was most sorely needed. Even if three centuries of outsider status and intermittent persecution had tested the endurance of individuals and communities, coping with the patronage of a newly Christian emperor posed a challenge. The challenge was all the more threatening for its moral complexity. Was it right for the churches to accept the Emperor's favour, knowing full well that if they did so, they also tacitly accepted his right, so evident in all other aspects of life in the Roman Empire, to call the shots?

To be fair, there was never really a choice. When Constantine perceived that the god of the Christians could help him to gain and govern the Empire, the earthly representatives of that god were in a position not very different from that of a slave who catches the eye of his or her master, with the resulting benefits and dangers. Very quickly, Christians discovered that a bishop or other leader who stood against the will of the Emperor would quickly be replaced.

So the new interest in asceticism came at a time when many Christians were reassessing their relationship to the institutional Church. Whether by becoming an ascetic or by showing support for the ascetic movement, ordinary Christians could take a stand against the greed and corruption that threatened to erode the values of the Church in its new, privileged, circumstances. And the monks and virgins of the fourth century did not disappoint. They were women and men whose willingness to sacrifice themselves for the kingdom of heaven was just as fierce as that of the martyrs before them.

The Passion of Eugenia

A historical romance set in the age of persecution, but written later, sometime between the late fourth and sixth century, illustrates the point. The *Passion of Eugenia* borrows and reinvents the story of Thecla, and it shows a self-conscious pleasure in the literary tradition that has evolved around the heroine who leaves her parents to strike off on her own. It takes special delight in the suggestion that in order to follow the Apostle Paul, Thecla had disguised herself as a boy. Eugenia takes up the same disguise, a choice that leads to repeated and often humorous plot complications.

Like the Clementine romance, the *Passion of Eugenia* is a fanciful narrative involving a young member of a Roman senatorial family on the cusp of adulthood. We saw with Clement that the problem of religious conversion was explored by means of a Shakespearian comedy of mistaken identity, and the same is true with Eugenia. Yet in Eugenia's case, the Roman virgin's need to set aside the trappings of feminine identity in order to follow Christ becomes one of the driving forces both of the story and of its comedy of mistaken identity.

The story opens as Eugenia, the daughter of the Roman Prefect of Egypt, sits musing with her father about a marriage proposal. The candidate is a man of outstanding rank, the son of the consul Aquilinus, but they have yet to discover anything about his character. When Eugenia's father asks her view of the match, she responds with a philosophical flourish that would have pleased Plutarch, the great (pagan) philosopher of marriage. 'A husband ought to be chosen for his character more than his birth; indeed, he should be accepted by us because of his behaviour, not his public honours.' So far, the text follows the formula of the ancient romance, an archetypal tale that normally leads to a happy ending, with the marriage of hero and heroine.

What happens next, however, alerts us to the fact that the *Passion of Eugenia* is no ordinary romance:

> Then, while she struggled with these and other entreaties, with a chaste heart, the letters of the Apostle Paul [and the history of the virgin Thecla] fell into her hands. Reading them secretly she wept every day, and although she lived under the most pagan of parents, in her heart she began to be a Christian.[2]

With her father's permission, Eugenia takes a carriage and two eunuch chaperones and leaves Alexandria for one of the family estates, where she intends to reflect on the proposal.

This is where the interest in how reading could change women's lives becomes almost exaggerated. In the carriage, Eugenia reads the second-century Christian romance the *Acts of Paul and Thecla*, and decides to embrace Christianity. The narrative is very clear about the role that the example of Thecla plays in her conversion: 'Reading in her litter during the journey, she turned the experiences of the virgin Thecla over in her heart.'

Eugenia's encounter with the story of Thecla leads to a surprising decision: in imitation of Thecla, she decides to refuse her marriage proposal and abandon her position as the daughter of a powerful family, taking to the road and disappearing among the mass of peasant humanity in her father's province. In order to do so, she cuts her hair and disguises herself as the brother of her eunuch attendants, Protus and Hyacinthus.

Our writer here makes a number of suggestions that are of interest. First, we are led to understand that young women could choose their reading material without parental approval – an intellectual freedom that accords well with the fact that Eugenia has at least some philosophical education in the narrative. This shatters some of our preconceptions about the cloistering of women in an honour-based society. Our writer implies, as well, that he (or she) knows that women readers can be expected to pay special attention to aspects of the text that relate to their own experience. When Eugenia turns the experiences of Thecla over in her heart, we know she is thinking about how Thecla's experience measures against her own. And of course our writer is reaching out to his or her own reader here: just as Eugenia was changed by Thecla's story, so the reader's own life should be somehow changed by Eugenia's.

The episode clearly bears an echo of the second-century *Acts of Paul and Thecla*. The scene in the carriage evokes the famous episode where the young Thecla refuses to marry her fiancé Thamyris, refusing for three days to move from an open window through which she can hear the preaching of the Apostle Paul in the house of a Christian neighbour. (And it is of course in imitation of Thecla that Eugenia cuts her hair and disguises herself as a boy.) But there is an important difference here – rather than being reached by the sound of a voice from across a narrow alley, Eugenia is reached by a book. Our writer has a very different kind of woman on his or her mind than did the writer of the *Acts of Paul and Thecla*. Like Jerome, our writer is thinking about the kind of woman who sits quietly with a book.

Reading had come to mean something new to the women of the fourth and later centuries. In the imagination, it is deeply linked to travel: both were methods by which an individual could explore the world. Equally, both were a way to nudge a person out of an unquestioning view of the world. Writers knew that readers were tightly bound within the network of relationships and obligations which governed their position in the Roman world, and one of the goals of literature was to persuade readers to adopt a more thoughtful approach to these commitments and relationships.

What happens next in the story picks up in a playful way on this theme of cutting ties. Eugenia and her two companions come to a monastery, the paradigmatic place for withdrawing from earthly ties. Almost immediately the three – two eunuchs and a teenage virgin – decide that they like the look of things in the monastery and make their profession as monks. Soon, the other monks begin to revere Eugenia for her intelligence and wisdom, and not long afterwards she is elected abbot.

This is only the beginning of the game of confusing appearances. After some time, a rich woman, Melantia, comes to the monastery, seeking a cure for a malarial fever, and the holy abbot Eugenios cures her. Melantia falls in love with her healer, and here the story takes a turn that again plays on its parallel in the *Acts of Paul and Thecla*. Just as Alexander had brought Thecla to the governor as a criminal when she refused to marry him, so, when Eugenios refuses Melantia's advances, the scorned heiress brings the abbot to the authorities in Alexandria. The accusation this time is one of seduction.

The prefect before whom the abbot Eugenius is brought is of course none other than Philip, Eugenia's father. It falls to him as governor of the province to arrange for games at which the abbot and his companions will be executed. But the abbot, when he is led before the prefect, bears his breast and reveals himself to be Eugenia, Philip's lost daughter. The intended execution gives way to rejoicing, and the charge is forgotten. In a development that calls to mind Matthidia and her sons, all of Eugenia's family convert to Christianity and are baptized as a result of the reunion, and Philip is made Bishop of Alexandria.

In the final act of the narrative, persecution comes to Alexandria. Philip is martyred and Eugenia sees to his burial. Then she returns to Rome, where she converts Basilla, a granddaughter of the Emperor, to Christianity and to virginity. This leads to yet another encounter with the law when Basilla's abandoned fiancé accuses both women as Christians before the Emperor. The two virgins are martyred, and afterwards Eugenia appears in a dream to her mother to promise a swift reunion in death. During the Eucharist the following Sunday, the mother dies and is buried alongside her daughter.

At times, the *Passion of Eugenia* reads like a compilation of highlights from the literature of virginity. Each element of the story would have been familiar to an ancient reader: the abandonment of the fiancé, the near-martyrdom, the disguise of the virgin as a beardless youth or eunuch, the Egyptian desert, the scenes of family reconciliation and recognition, the persecution by abandoned lovers. The collection has a magpie quality that repeatedly spills over into comedy.

Yet something momentous is happening in this text. We have already seen that it shows a new self-consciousness about the role of books, and especially the Bible and the stories of the Apostles, in women's lives. It also reveals, perhaps less self-consciously, a change in the relationship between Christian daughters and their parents. The concord between Eugenia and her parents is a far cry from the tense relationship of the mother and daughter in the *Acts of Paul and Thecla*. It is a relationship that is characterized by warmth and at the same time by parental acknowledgement of the daughter's independence. In the writer's eyes, the virgin Eugenia's moral independence from her earthly family becomes the foundation for an idealized kind of family harmony, in which the parents follow the lead of their pious daughter.

Eugenia's relationship with her father reflects this change, and one sees it particularly clearly at the point where she refuses to marry. In accordance with Roman law, the father solicits the girl's consent when a marriage alliance is offered to the son of the consul Aquilinus. The bride's consent was required by law for a marriage to be valid, but there is reason to suspect that some families, in their haste to use their daughters for strategic marriage alliances, saw this as a mere formality – the hostile reaction of Thecla's mother to her announcement is a case in point. Our author sees it as perfectly normal that a young woman should call her father to account – and that the father should defer – when he offers a match that is motivated more by dynastic plans than philosophical values. Eugenia does not have to run away to the desert in order to escape her marriage. When she decides to withdraw from the world, she has no difficulty obtaining permission from her *paterfamilias* to make an extended journey to another family estate, accompanied only by her own attendants. Although she has barely reached the age of marriage, she is a person of some independence and financial means, and this fact is taken for granted by the writer of her story. It is by no means an accident that it is to a monastery that Eugenia retreats, for the ascetic way of life had captured the imagination of the women of the Roman Empire.

Economic Pressures and the Lives of Village Women

But if the wealthy daughters of senators were fascinated by the desert, women from more humble backgrounds may have been interested in the monastic communities for more practical reasons. From the late first century, Christian communities had offered economic support and an institutional structure of some kind for economically vulnerable unmarried women and widows. But it is in the third century that we begin to find evidence that both men and women were living in organized ascetic communities.

In the mid-third century, the Empire had passed through a period of civil wars, and our first substantial evidence for Christians of both sexes living in organized ascetic communities comes from this period. Some scholars have argued that this communalism was a form of organized Christian response to the threat of famine. On this reading, the monasteries may have had their roots in charitable foundations or village cooperatives developed during the third-century crisis. Stability was restored after 284, under the Emperor Diocletian, who reorganized the structure of the Roman provinces to establish clearer lines of accountability and to stabilize the economy, policies developed further under Constantine.

In Egypt, the unusually dry climate allowed a far greater survival of everyday documents than in other parts of the Empire. We can see in the surviving papyrus documents that at least some ascetic communities were organized in a way that allowed them to undertake charitable functions. By the early fourth century, they were called on to serve as orphanages where this was practical, which filled a glaring gap in Roman charitable provision. Even where one or both parents were living, impoverished families were often grateful to place their children with the monks or virgins so that what little they had could be distributed among a smaller number. There is also evidence that more prosperous families began to send their children to monks or nuns for the sake of education.

Papyri also allow us a window into the harsh realities faced by unmarried women, which help us to understand why women would have been attracted to an organized communal life. A petition addressed to the Prefect of Egypt in the late third century by a widow allows us to see how easily neighbours could take advantage of women's position if they were without a male protector.

Aurelia Artemis lived in a village near Arsinoe, the ancient city of the crocodile god Sobek, in the Fayum in central Egypt, 300 kilometres up the Nile from the province's capital at Alexandria. In order to seek justice when a village administrator took advantage of her husband's death, it was necessary for her to take the matter all the way to the Prefect of Egypt, the Emperor's personal representative – the role played by Eugenia's father in the *Passion of Eugenia*.

Perceiving your love of equity, my lord praefect, and your care for all, especially women and widows, I approach you praying to obtain your aid. The matter is as follows. Having become *decaprotus* [a member of the municipal finance committee] of the village, Syrion persuaded my husband Ganis to allow him to pasture his flock, and removed my husband's goats and sheep, 60 in number, into his own keeping. So long as my husband lived each derived the profit of his own flock, my husband from the one, and the individual aforesaid from the other. But when my husband went the way of men, Syrion rushed in, wishing by the use of his local influence to tear the property of my young children from the very bed of my husband where his body was lying.[3]

The petition goes on to request that the prefect send a representative to the village to discipline Syrion and restore the disputed flock to the widow and her children.

In closing her petition, Aurelia Artemis expresses her reliance on the prefect's benevolence. 'By your direction, Lord and kindly benefactor of all, I hope to recover my property, and be able to live with my children in my own home and ever to avow my gratitude to your fortune.' But the prefect had far more pressing matters to attend to than sixty sheep and goats of dubious ownership in a provincial village, and we do not know whether his representative ever took the matter up. It is unlikely that Aurelia Artemis was a Christian, though the fact she was named after Artemis, the Greek goddess of the hunt, does not exclude the possibility. In all likelihood, the most hopeful course for a non-Christian was to remarry, if she was able. A husband could help her to hold her ground against the neighbours, though a point of anxiety was whether he would treat her children unkindly. A Christian in similar circumstances would in all likelihood have welcomed the opportunity to join a community of virgins and widows, who could act collectively to support one another in the face of injustice, and could call on the bishop and other elders within the Christian community for additional support.

Life in the communities of virgins and widows clearly offered advantages beyond simple protection. We should not underestimate the value of a chance to live with other like-minded women, and a degree of autonomy from the judgements of fathers, brothers, and husbands may have been equally welcome. In addition, for many women a main attraction of the life of sexual renunciation was an honourable release from the virtually constant pregnancies married women were expected to endure, all in the knowledge that childbirth was perilous for both mother and child.

Those who did not join ascetic communities would have respected the choice of those who did. Nuns and monks were viewed as having made a worthy and admirable choice to live with their eyes fixed on the world to come. The presence of such individuals in a community, it was believed, was of value even to those who did not participate directly. Indeed, many felt that families could not afford to be left out. An anonymous rule-book for monks and virgins written in Egypt between 350 and 450 argued that each of the children in every household should be educated in the love of virginity, with careful attention to discover 'which among [the] daughters is worthy of holiness'. It was a moral requirement for every Christian family to participate in the search for the ascetic movement's next generation of stars.[4] The author of *On virginity* puts it this way: 'In every house of Christians it is needful that there be a virgin, for the salvation of the whole house is this one virgin.'

It was expected that the difficulty of the ascetic life would exclude many, so early training was recommended in order to enhance the chance of success. Clearly, the view was that parents were in the best position to instil a love of virginity in their children; at the same time, they could observe each child's progress and assess whether such aspirations were realistic. It is by no means certain that all Christian parents were happy to see this as their responsibility, but at least some bishops wished that they would.

In the third century, this would have been a very provocative statement, and its author might well have been suspected of heresy. By the end of the fourth century, however, the tables had turned. The virginal ideal gained wide enough currency that those who disagreed with it had to defend themselves. Towards the end of the fourth century, Jovinian, a monk from northern Mesopotamia, argued that marriage and virginity were equally worthy vocations in the sight of God, and synods in both Rome and Milan swiftly condemned his views as heretical. Eminent married Christians defended Jovinian, since his views represented the more traditional strand of Christian thought – one of the most vocal was the Roman senator Pammachius, the friend of Jerome and husband of Eustochium's sister Paulina. But these traditionalists were met by the ancient equivalent of a media blitz. Jerome himself wrote a vituperative tract *Against Jovinian*, a passionate argument for the merits of virginity spiced by character assassination against his opponent. *Against Jovinian* became an enduring bestseller, second only to the Bible as a staple for the libraries of medieval convents and monasteries.

We saw above that Jerome warned his protégée Eustochium to avoid the company of married women, even Christian married women. 'Learn of me a holy arrogance,' he told her. His memorable phrase called attention to the gap that at least some writers were beginning to perceive between the simple Christian laity – even those of exalted rank – and the 'athletes of Christ' who had been set apart by a vow of continence or virginity.

'A Virtue Which Is Known, Vanishes': The Desert Mothers

Women pursued a splendid variety of paths under the aegis of asceticism, but they were conscious that something connected them. The senatorial daughters at Rome and Constantinople who simply never married, and quietly transformed their households into living temples of virginity were inspired by, and did what they could to support, the wanderers and cave-dwellers of the Egyptian desert.

In Egypt, like other parts of the Empire, many virgins lived the life of renunciation in an informal household setting. But Egypt was also the heartland of the austere tradition of the desert, which invited both women and men to leave their families behind and to begin a new life, whether as solitaries or in the monasteries that sprang up all across Egypt and the Holy Land in the third and fourth centuries. The women of the desert sought a life of poverty and displacement, a living death to the life they had previously known.

The desert was an appropriate place for this life not only because it was empty, but also because it was harsh. The unbearable heat in the summer was balanced out by bitter cold on winter nights: even the piercing sound of the desert winds could be chilling. The fathers and mothers of the desert courted these extremes. Thirst, hunger, and sleeplessness were the most important challenges, but there were also the human deprivations, of family, and the constant struggle to give up one's pride. It was a life that only made sense if one had chosen it for a reason. Yet for those who chose it, its hardships offered an incomparable opportunity to test and cultivate the power of the human spirit.

Though most of the women of the desert were illiterate, many stories and sayings about them were preserved in written form. During the fourth and fifth centuries, a number of collections were made of the teachings of the desert by the disciples who gathered to learn from them and others by the travellers who came to discover what lay behind their fame. The sayings of a number of women are preserved in the collections. Monks and virgins might visit teachers of either sex, so it makes sense that a single tradition of wisdom was shared by women and men alike. The male teachers by far outnumbered the women, but the more committed disciples would seek to apprentice themselves to a teacher of their own gender, so the mothers of the desert had an important role to play.

For the most part, the mothers of the desert are remembered only in short passages and single sayings, but there are three – Amma Sarah, Amma Theodora, and Amma Syncletica – who stand out as figures for whom a quantity of stories and sayings have survived. Syncletica and Theodora became known as teachers of a wisdom that had little to do with the fact of their femininity, while Sarah turned her wit and wisdom to the special problems that faced women.

An important strand in Amma Syncletica's thought was her emphasis on humility, a concern that occurs again and again in the sayings of the desert elders. Ascetic communities were often beset by an inverted form of conspicuous consumption, in which each member of the group tried to outshine the others in some mode of self-denial. If one nun was able to refrain from eating more than once a day, there was another who only ate every other day; if one nun was able to sleep on a hard board without a pillow, there was another who was able to sleep standing up. This friendly competition was not without its usefulness. But there was always the danger that the rivals would start to think of the feats of renunciation as an end in themselves. Amma Syncletica reminded the sisters that they were only means to an end. A nun who made progress in the spiritual life would slowly wear away her tendency even to notice such things.[5]

One of Syncletica's sayings makes it clear that spiritual advancement could only be fostered by such austerities if they were undertaken in the right spirit. With its solitude and its harsh climate, she suggested, the desert was nothing more or less than a grand, interactive metaphor for the pursuit of wisdom.

Amma Syncletica said, 'There are many who live in the mountains and behave as if they were in the town, and they are wasting their time. It is possible to be a solitary in one's mind while living in a crowd, and it is possible for one who is a solitary to live in the crowd of his (her) own thoughts.'[6]

The spiritual danger attributed to the presence of others was not in fact caused by their presence – it came from within. The desire to see oneself reflected in the eyes of others, and to garner their praise, was only vanity, and it was the Devil's most effective snare. Syncletica warned that the ascetic could not afford to give vanity even a toehold:

She also said, 'Just as a treasure that is exposed loses its value, so a virtue which is known vanishes; just as wax melts when it is near fire, so the soul is destroyed by praise and loses all the results of its labour.'[7]

This is why humility was so important. It was the soul's way of short-circuiting damage that could be done by the constant need to know where one stood with respect to others.

The point of humility was not to think ill of oneself but to protect oneself from this craving for status. This, in turn, would free the spirit to see life in a new way. Amma Syncletica drew on the metaphor of Moses on Mount Horeb drawing water from a stone: 'She also said, Choose the meekness of Moses and you will find your heart is a rock changed into a spring of water.'[8]

Another of the desert mothers, Amma Theodora, reminded her disciples that their conduct must serve two aims at the same time. It was their duty, within reason, to correct others, but this had to be done while avoiding the snare of vanity. She told the following story: 'A devout man happened to be insulted by someone, and he said to him, "I could say as much to you, but the commandment of God keeps my mouth shut."'[9]

Guiding others in the spiritual life was a dangerous business, because it required a rare ability to strike this balance:

> The same Amma said that a teacher ought to be a stranger to the desire for domination, vainglory, and pride; one should not be able to fool him by flattery, nor blind him by gifts, nor conquer him by the stomach, nor dominate him by anger; but he should be patient, gentle and humble as far as possible; he must be tested and without partisanship, full of concern and a lover of souls . . .[10]

The desert air was thick with demons, who could feed on any vice that an ascetic had not yet managed to eradicate. But Amma

Theodora warned that the demon was not interested in mere feats of physical renunciation – it was the power of the spirit that must be cultivated and this could only be done through humility.

She also said that neither asceticism, nor vigils nor any kind of suffering are able to save, only true humility can do that. There was an anchorite who was able to banish the demons; and he asked them, 'What makes you go away? Is it fasting?'
They replied, 'We do not eat or drink.'
'Is it vigils?'
They replied, 'We do not sleep.'
'Is it separation from the world?'
'We live in the deserts.'
'What power sends you away, then?'
They said, 'Nothing can overcome us, but only humility.'[11]

Within the desert setting, women faced an additional challenge because they had to manage not only their own spiritual progress but also the constant tension caused by men's reactions to them. A story about an anonymous leader of virgins demonstrates the need to deal gracefully with men who often treated them as a source of temptation rather than as fellow seekers. When some monks made a detour to avoid encountering her and her sisters, she commented, 'If you were a perfect monk, you would not have seen us as women.' The same approach was taken by one of the most intriguing of the desert mothers, Amma Sarah of Pelusium, at the eastern edge of the Nile Delta. Sarah was known for dispensing pithy rejoinders to the 'male egos' of the desert scene, and she was pointedly critical of the monks who made a show of avoiding women. But she was able to turn the same critical eye on her own temptation to be proud:[12]

Once the . . . spirit of fornication attacked her rather intently, reminding her of the vanities of the world. But she gave herself up to the fear of God and to asceticism and went up onto her little terrace to pray. Then the spirit of fornication appeared corporally to her and said, 'Sarah, you have overcome me.' But she said, 'It is not I who have overcome you, but my master, Christ.'[13]

Here there is an echo of Paul's letter to the Galatians – 'I have been crucified with Christ and I no longer live, but Christ lives in me.' (Gal. 2: 20). The desert mothers aspired to discover the real meaning of this saying. Amma Sarah knew that her spiritual power was infinite, if she could truly forget herself and allow Christ to work through her.

More enigmatic is Sarah's rejoinder to two visitors, themselves experienced solitaries, who offered her a word of not particularly gentle advice.

Another time, two old men, great anchorites, came to the district of Pelusium to visit her. When they arrived one said to the other, 'Let us humiliate this old woman.'

So they said to her, 'Be careful not to become conceited thinking of yourself: "Look how anchorites are coming to see me, a mere woman."'

But Amma Sarah said to them, 'According to nature I am a woman, but not according to my thoughts.'[14]

For Sarah, it was necessary to make every effort to move beyond the concerns of sex and gender, even if they threw up obstacles to some.

On another occasion, she put it as a bald paradox: 'She also said to the brothers, "It is I who am a man, you who are women."' Whether she meant the monks to see her 'manliness' as a sign of a woman's capacity for spiritual progress, or simply to give up thinking in earthly terms about physical bodies, is deliberately left ambiguous.[15]

Sarah's sayings on the issue of gender were a commentary on both the gender tensions of the desert and a wider spiritual truth.

Amma Sarah said, 'If I prayed God that all men should approve of my conduct, I should find myself a penitent at the door of each one, but I shall rather pray that my heart may be pure towards all!'[16]

In their more lucid moments, the monks were well aware of their own failings where the women were concerned. They knew that many women offered an example of steadfastness from which they would do well to benefit. At the same time, women hovered in their minds as a symbol of temptation, so they were fascinated by the idea that members of the opposite sex could actually be pursuing the ascetic goals that they cherished, and even outstripping their own progress. When men told stories about female virtue, it was usually in a way designed to shame one another.

A number of stories play with the idea that any monk one admired might turn out to be a woman in disguise. A story told of Abba Bessarion by his disciple Doulas sheds light on how the idea of the virtuous woman in disguise, quietly pursuing the common goal of ascetic perfection, could serve as a tool to shame the brothers. Bessarion and Doulas were travelling on foot to visit another desert father. As Doulas later told the story, during their journey they entered a cave where an old man was making rope by plaiting together palm leaves, the subsistence work practised by many of the solitaries. Since the old man did not acknowledge them, the abba and his disciple decided not to disturb him. However, on their return, they saw that the man had died. Bessarion suggested that they should bury him.

'The old man said to me, "Come, brother, let us take the body; it is for this reason God has sent us here." When we took the body to bury it, we perceived it to be a woman. Filled with astonishment, the old man said: "See how the women triumph over Satan, while we still behave badly in the towns."'[17]

A number of longer stories develop the idea further. We saw in the *Passion of Eugenia* that the young woman who dressed as a man was a figure who touched the imagination of readers. Both monks and virgins found this kind of heroine interesting, though for different reasons. For virgins, the idea that one of their own might be among the monks served as a metaphor for their particularly demanding position in the world of the desert. For monks, by contrast, the idea that a woman could be hidden within the monastery represented a reminder that even the advanced monk was often guilty of the sin of pride.

Within the desert setting, women faced an additional challenge. They had to manage not only their own spiritual progress but also the constant tension caused by men's anxiety about their presence. Sexual temptation does not figure nearly so strongly in the women's sayings as it does in the men's. Given the balance of power in ancient society, this makes a certain amount of sense. Women were accustomed to making substantial efforts to please men, while men spent comparatively little of theirs trying to please women. The reports women received from their mothers and married older sisters about intimacy with men probably suggested that it was not all sweetness and light. Living with men required something of the caution needed for handling wild animals. Even for women who were skilled at managing them, there was always an element of danger because of their power and unpredictability. So it would not be at all surprising if women were less troubled by distracting thoughts of the opposite sex.

For the men, by contrast, even chaste affection among family members could pose an obstacle to spiritual progress – not only sex but the innocent company of a mother or a sister was the source of a craving so powerful that it was difficult to suppress. A story is told of one of the most revered abbots of fourth-century Egypt, Pachomius the Great, who refused to see his sister Maria when she came to visit him. The explanation was his own urgent need to avoid someone who might entangle him in the bonds of family feeling, and he was even praised for his self-control in being able to forgo the pleasure of her visit. It is not surprising that women sometimes found the self-involvement of male ascetics irritating.

A story is told of Abba Arsenius, a Roman senator who retreated to the desert towards the end of the fourth century, which captures the agitation of the monks as they wrestled with their anxieties about the opposite sex. We have already seen that women travelled from all over the Empire to visit the Holy Land. Visits to monasteries had become part of the circuit along which like-minded men and women could explore biblical history and the ideals of the faith.

One Roman visitor received a shock when she paid a visit to Arsenius in Canopus, in the Nile Delta.

At one time when Abba Arsenius was living in Canopus, there came from Rome in hope to see him a lady, a virgin, of great wealth, and one that feared God. Theophilus the archbishop [of Alexandria] received her. And she prayed him to use his good offices with the old man, that she might see him. And the archbishop came to his and asked him, saying, 'A certain lady hath come from Rome, and would see thee.' But the old man would not consent to have her come to him. So when this was told the lady, she commanded her beasts to be saddled, saying, 'I trust in God, that I shall see him. For in my own city there are men to spare, but I am come to see the prophets.' And when she came to the old man's cell, by the ordering of God it chanced that he was found outside his cell. And when the lady saw him, she cast herself at his feet.[18]

The abba's reaction is surprisingly hostile. Rather than treating his visitor as a fellow-seeker, he treats her as an unwelcome reminder of the world he has fled.

But with indignation did he raise her up, and, gazing upon her, said, 'If thou dost desire to look upon my face, here I am: look.' But she for shame did not lift her eyes to his face. And the old man said to her, 'Hast thou not heard what I do? To see the work is enough. How didst thou dare to take upon thee so great a voyage? Dost thou not know that thou art a woman, and ought not to go anywhere? And wilt thou now go to Rome and say to the other women, "I have seen Arsenius, and turn the sea into a high road of women coming to visit me?"'

But she said, 'If God will that I return to Rome, I shall let no woman come hither: but pray for me, and always remember me.'

He answered and said, 'I pray to God that He will wipe the memory of thee from my heart.'[19]

The abba seems far more interested in the effect her presence will have on him than in the effect his teaching may have on her.

And hearing this, she went away troubled. And it was told the archbishop that she was sick; and he came to comfort her, and asked her what ailed her. And she said to him, 'Would that I had not come hither! For I said to the old man, "Remember me," And he said to me, "I pray God that He will wipe the memory of thee from my heart", and behold I am dying of that sorrow.' And the archbishop said to her, 'Knowest thou not that thou art a woman, and through women doth the Enemy lay siege to holy men? For this reason did the old man say it, but he doth ever pray for thy soul.' And so her mind was healed, and she departed with joy to her own place.[20]

The story offers a vivid illustration of the double-bind women found themselves in. Sometimes, in their dealings with ascetic men, they would find an honest spiritual companionship with people who had learned to see beyond the accidents of birth and flesh. But they could never be sure when they might be treated as an instrument of temptation. Even men who were trying to rise above seeing women in a sexual light were not always successful.

Melania the Younger

One of the most effective ways for women to diffuse the unpredictable reactions they encountered in their travels was to bring a man along. Paula and Melania the Elder had each found a like-minded partnership, with Jerome of Stridon and Rufinus of Aquileia respectively, and the choice had both practical and spiritual merits. A more unusual strategy was that of Melania's granddaughter herself, known as Melania the Younger, who cultivated an ascetic partnership with her own husband.

Melania the Younger seems to have been her grandmother's principal heir when the elder woman died in 410, and soon afterwards she and her husband arrived in the Holy Land, where they would remain for the rest of their lives. The fifth-century *Life of Melania the Younger* seems to have been written by a monk from the ascetic entourage that gathered around her and it is the most vivid and animated biography of a woman to have survived from antiquity.[21]

The *Lausiac History* written by Palladius includes a biography of Melania the Elder, along with a shorter account of Melania the Younger. Writing in *c.* 420, not long after Melania the Younger's arrival in Palestine around 414, Palladius paints the younger woman as the heir who would take up her grandmother's work. Palladius saw Melania the Elder as establishing a family tradition, even though it had skipped a generation. The younger Melania's father, Valerius Publicola, was the son who had been left behind when Melania the Elder left for Alexandria in the 370s. He had been raised by a guardian while his mother was in the Holy Land, and on maturity he had married Caeonia Albina, the daughter of an Urban Prefect, and established a traditional senatorial household.

Palladius stresses continuity between the generations, but Melania the Younger's biographer writes her saintly grandmother out of the picture altogether. Certainly he would have known of Melania the Elder's fame as a biblical scholar and as the founder of communities on the Mount of Olives in Jerusalem, along with Rufinus. Melania died there in 410 and Rufinus in 411. Jerome and Rufinus had fallen out with one another during their years in the Holy Land, and this seems to have been the root of the problem. When Melania the Younger arrived in Palestine after her grandmother's death, she and her husband struck up a friendship with Jerome, Eustochium, and the younger Paula (Paula the Elder had died already in 404). This friendship may have coloured the amount of credit her biographer wanted to accord to the grandmother.

At fourteen, Melania was married off to Pinian – a youth not much older than she and the son of a Roman consul, with blood equally blue to her own and heir to a similarly vast fortune. In 397, around the time of the marriage, the grandmother, Melania the Elder, returned to Rome, remaining until the death of Publicola in 408, and Palladius tells us that her main aim in returning to Rome was to guide the younger generation.

Her biographer presents Melania the Younger as resisting the attempt of the older generation to steer and guide her. The enormous wealth of the family meant that there was an unsavoury level of interest in the question of what she should do with herself and her money. In the end, the necessity to manage the overbearing supervision of parents, relations, and servants while still a child would serve her well. By the time she reached adulthood, neither civic magistrates nor Christian bishops were any match for her persistence and skills of persuasion.

Melania resisted the marriage, but soon came to value the companionship of a partner who had had, from earliest childhood, to cope with similar handling from the older generation. According to her biographer, it was in the end a happy match: in Pinian she had found someone who would cheer her on in her schemes and ambitions.

This blessed Melania, then, was foremost among the Romans of senatorial rank. Wounded by the divine love, she had from her earliest youth yearned for Christ, had longed for bodily purity *(tou somatos hagneian)*. Her parents, because they were illustrious members of the Roman Senate and expected that through her they would have a succession of the family line, very forcibly united her in marriage with her blessed husband Pinianus, who was from a consular family, when she was fourteen years old and her spouse was about seventeen.[22]

As her biographer tells the story, Melania tried to persuade Pinian on their wedding night that the two should live as brother and sister, but he prevailed, arguing that their families needed them to produce heirs.

The couple did produce two children, but both died in infancy and after the death of the second Melania was able to persuade her husband that it was God's will that they should remain childless. Her biographer argues that she became mother not to biological children but to the children in Christ – both sons and daughters – who lived within the religious communities she founded.

Melania's biographer allows that after her father's death, her mother Albina made considerable efforts, financial and otherwise, to support the ascetic ambition of her daughter. Indeed, until the death of Albina in 431 or 432, Melania seems to have spent most of the year with her mother when she was not travelling. After Albina's death she adopted the Mount of Olives – the site of her mother's burial – as her own principal residence and established a community for virgins there. When Pinian died in 432, he was buried alongside Albina, and a community for men was established in 435 or 436. The death of Melania's mother and husband seems to have triggered a final round of founding ascetic communities, although Melania herself died less than a decade later, in 439. In this way the process begun by the death of her own children had come full circle.

The fact that Melania was not legally or economically dependent on her husband influences our understanding of her decisions. We saw in an earlier chapter that a woman of property in Roman law was not dependent on her husband in the way that she would have been in England in the nineteenth century. Her legal dependence was focused on her father, to whose *familia* she belonged whatever her marital status. (In cases where the paternal grandfather was still living, legal dependence could in fact focus on the grandfather rather than the father, but this was rare.)

Her father was thus the most important figure for Melania. This explains why it was so important that Melania fulfil her parents' wishes. In order to become an ascetic, she had to defy her father's wishes by refusing to produce children, and this very nearly put a stop to her whole project. Filial piety was not only a virtue, it was enforceable by law. Another factor may have been economic dependence, in both the short-term sense of cash flow and the long-term sense of inheritance. In the Roman system, the legal, economic, and moral factors were intertwined. Primogeniture was unknown to the Romans, and Roman law required that each daughter must inherit her share if there was property in the family. Each child had a right by law to the 'share of piety', as it was called, which represented at minimum a quarter of what would be due if the parent had died without leaving a will and the estate had been divided equally among legitimate offspring.[23]

Melania had only one brother, so piety would have assigned her a substantial fraction of the estate of each of her parents, and Palladius tells us she was her grandmother's heir as well. The estate in question would have been vast. In an agricultural empire whose economy was structured in a pyramid of senatorial landholding, the greatest landowners had an economic reach comparable to the assets of a substantial modern corporation through their estates, which were widely dispersed across the Mediterranean.[24]

The reciprocal obligations of parents and children were based in the ideology of *pietas*. Every effort was made to ensure that neither parents nor children failed in this virtue. From the mid-fourth century, gifts from parents to children could be recovered 'if it could be proved that the children had not shown proper *pietas* towards them'. Thus, while children could take action to retrieve the inheritance that piety required their parents assign to them, children who themselves failed in piety could be cut off, even retrospectively.

Melania knew that she could not claim even the 'share of piety' from her parents' estates if a rival heir could prove that her conduct towards her parents had been impious. She also knew that under Roman law, refusal to marry or to bear children, unless she had her parents' permission, was considered a form of impiety.

So in order to protect her good name and claim her inheritance, Melania needed to demonstrate that she had made every effort to fulfil her parents' wishes with respect to grandchildren. When her biographer emphasizes her craving for poverty, he is trying to persuade readers that it was honour and not money that motivated Melania. In fact, Melania did not want her parents to disinherit her, even if her intent was then to channel the inheritance to the Church.

Even after her marriage, Melania's father had power. It is possible that she had been emancipated – a process similar to the freeing of slaves that allowed a child to become *sui iuris*, independent in the eyes of the law. But she was a minor until after her father's death – the age of majority for women in the late fourth century was twenty-five – so she would have had a guardian even if she was *sui iuris*.

While she was a minor, if it was felt that she was mismanaging her affairs, her parents, or her guardian if the parents were dead, would have had recourse to the *praefectus urbi,* the magistrate responsible for the city of Rome. The Urban Prefect acted as judge for disputes involving the guardianship of minors of the senatorial class. Indeed, the *Life* remembers that Melania had been 'persecuted' by the Urban Prefect around the time of her father's death, and the likelihood is that rival claimants to Melania's fortune had tried to bring a charge against her.

This provides the context for the *Life*'s emphasis on the blessing that Melania's father Publicola gave her just before his death. When Melania received his blessing,

They heard these words with much joy. Right away they felt free from fear; they left the great city of Rome and went to her suburban property where they devoted themselves to training in the practice of the virtues. They clearly recognized that it was impossible for them to offer pure worship to God unless they made themselves enemies to the confusions of secular life, just as it is written, 'Hear, daughter, and see; turn your ear and forget your people and your father's house, and the king will desire your beauty.'[25]

His blessing meant that his death brought Melania not only accession to a sizeable inheritance and the scope to act as a patroness in her own right, but also, perhaps more importantly, the security that a charge of impiety could not be brought on his behalf.

Melania, it seems, could never fully extricate herself from property ownership, although in the years from 408 to her death in 439 she was constantly giving money away. More than once she is portrayed as 'giving away all her property' or 'assigning authority to another' so that she can be divested of responsibility and power, only to reappear in the next chapter of the *Life* with a full purse and full authority.

The likelihood is that the long journey from Rome to Sicily, Africa, and finally the Holy Land, which Melania and Pinian undertook between 408 and 414, was motivated in part by the need personally to supervise the liquidation of their estates. Selling one's goods and giving the proceeds to the poor can be an astoundingly complicated business, if one's goods include agribusinesses scattered across the Mediterranean.

Even at the very end of their journey, new sources of funds appear. At one point, her biographer mentions with pride the Melania was enrolled in the Church's register of the poor, yet not long afterwards she was embarking on new building programmes, including the establishment of the biographer's own monastery. She seems to have reorganized a number of her estates as monasteries, but this did not alter her role as materfamilias, the property owner responsible for the estate.

Monasteries were not yet recognized as legally independent institutions, so re-establishing a country estate as a monastery could have little or no impact on the structure of responsibility or authority within the estate; it was simply a matter of choosing how the life of the estate's inhabitants was organized. In many cases, it consisted in a new layer of obligations imposed on the dependants living there. The hope was that it would foster a new spirit of community to the benefit of all concerned. But Melania's dependants numbered in the thousands. The *Life* reports that she owned estates in eight provinces, while Palladius tells us that she offered freedom to her slaves and 8,000 accepted her offer. The rest – a substantial number – preferred to be sold to her brother-in-law Severus, believing they were safer under the protection of an owner than as free labourers.[26]

If Melania intended to found an institution that would survive the end of antiquity, she failed. The *Life of Melania* was written at the request of the senior monk who took charge of her Jerusalem community after she had died, and this suggests that an effort was made to keep the community alive. But there is no evidence that it lasted very long. Still, a monument to Melania's efforts does survive, in the form of the *Life* itself. Her biographer succeeded in capturing for posterity a crucial moment of experimentation in the history of what would become Christian monasticism, a moment at which very little had been resolved definitively, and a great deal was at stake for the future.

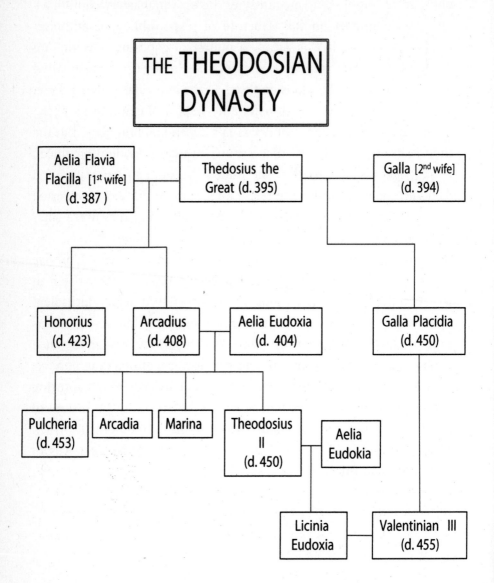

THE **THEODOSIAN**
DYNASTY

Aelia Flavia Flacilla [1st wife] (d. 387) — Thedosius the Great (d. 395) — Galla [2nd wife] (d. 394)

Honorius (d. 423)

Arcadius (d. 408) — Aelia Eudoxia (d. 404)

Galla Placidia (d. 450)

Pulcheria (d. 453)

Arcadia

Marina

Theodosius II (d. 450) — Aelia Eudokia

Licinia Eudoxia — Valentinian III (d. 455)

10

———

THE QUEEN OF HEAVEN

Stretching out her hands, she prayed thus to the Lord, 'Lord God, you who healed me of leprosy by the prayers of your martyr Agnes and graciously showed me the path of your love, and moreover preserved the marriage-bed of the Virgin your mother, where you the Son have shown yourself to be a Bridegroom, you born of Mary and you true progenitor of Mary, you having suckled at her breast and you in turn feeding the whole world . . . I ask, Lord, that you win over these daughters of Gallicanus . . . that they may seek to attain entry to your celestial bed-chamber.'[1]

A sixth-century hagiographical romance, the *Passion of Gallicanus*, records the prayer of Constantia, daughter of Constantine the Great, remembering her as a virgin of the Church. Beseeching Jesus, son of Mary, to move the daughters of the Roman general Gallicanus to dedicate themselves as virgins of the Church, Constantia illustrates the firm belief of Christians in later antiquity that human relationships echoed or reflected the mysterious workings of the heavenly realm. According to this view, the Virgin Mary stood as an intercessor before God for the interests of women, and among women virgins enjoyed a special, though not exclusive, claim to her protection.[2]

Constantia's prayer captures a number of themes that are important in understanding Christianity at the end of antiquity. First, in the Roman imagination, the heavenly sphere was punctuated, like the earthly empire, by relationships of patronage and intercession. The women of the imperial family were seen to play a role as intercessors on behalf of the weak, very similar to that which

Mary and other female saints – such as the virgin martyr Agnes – were understood to play in heaven. The spiritual power of Mary and her cohort of heavenly women reached across the divide between the heavenly and earthly spheres, and became a source for the spiritual power on which their earthly counterparts, Christian holy women of both low and high rank, could draw.

We turn now to one of the most remarkable women of the ancient world, the Empress Pulcheria, eldest daughter of John Chrysostom's nemesis Eudoxia. Pulcheria did more than any other member of the imperial family to make the connection between the powers of heaven and the authority of the *augusti* on earth. She has often been wrongly vilified because, like her mother before her, she was not afraid to stand up to any bishop who seemed to her to neglect the concerns of her family or of her wider constituency – the women and men who were devoted to the cult of the Virgin Mary. Pulcheria's story offers a pointed reminder of the critical role played by women of the imperial family in crafting a church that would outlast the Roman Empire.

Born at the end of the fourth century, in 399, Pulcheria lived through the extraordinarily turbulent years of the fall of the Roman Empire in the West from the comparative safety of the Eastern capital at Constantinople. In 395, on the death of Theodosius the Great, the Empire had been divided between his two sons, Arcadius and Honorius. The two parts would meet alarmingly divergent fates. The Western Empire centred on Rome, and subsequently Ravenna would fall into barbarian hands by the end of the fifth century, while the Eastern Empire, governed from Constantinople, would weather the waves of barbarian invasion relatively unscathed. It is not an exaggeration to say that the success of the Eastern Empire owed a great deal to the Empress Pulcheria and to the sense of safety and prosperity that she was able to confer on her capital city. In this, contemporaries believed, she was aided by an otherworldly counterpart, the Virgin Mary. It is during Pulcheria's lifetime that the cult of Mary became a central institution of the Christian tradition.

We meet Pulcheria first at the death of her father, the Eastern Emperor Arcadius, in 408. The nine-year-old princess was left in an extraordinary situation on her father's death. She was the eldest of four surviving siblings. Her sisters Arcadia and Marina had been born in April of 400 and February of 403 respectively. The third youngest, and only boy, named Theodosius after his grandfather, was seven.

. All eyes were on the boy, since by his father's death he became Emperor, and most parties seem to have expected that he would be killed by a general or civil official who wanted to try his own luck as emperor. Later, stories circulated that one usurper, the *magister militum* Lucius, had penetrated the imperial palace as far as Theodosius' bedroom only to discover that his sword would not dislodge from its scabbard. Indeed, the contemporary historian Sozomen expressed astonishment that the boy survived to adulthood. The children seem to have been lucky in the eunuch Antiochus, the official appointed by their parents as *praepositus sacri cubiculi* or head of the imperial household, who seems to have shown unshakeable loyalty. The eunuch's later influence shows that the children were grateful. Nonetheless, for the first few years they were in danger, and their danger was shared by the Empire itself.[3]

As heir to the throne, Theodosius had been a political pawn all his life. It was at his christening, on the feast of Epiphany in 402, that Bishop Porphyry of Gaza had brought the petition asking that the Temple of Zeus in his city be destroyed. With the permission of his mother, the Empress Eudoxia, he had been made, by the courtier who carried him in procession, to nod assent to the wishes of the holy bishop. On his father's death in May of 408, the boy had just passed his seventh birthday.

His sister Pulcheria was only two years older, but she seems to have risen to the occasion nonetheless. The enlightenment historian Edward Gibbon, no champion of the influence of Christianity on the Roman Empire, put it this way: 'she alone, among all the descendants of the great Theodosius [the children's grandfather], appears to have inherited any share of his manly spirit and abilities.' Anyone who has had a nine-year-old daughter knows that they can be both heart-stoppingly charming and astoundingly fierce in defending what they hold dear.

The only way to understand what happened across the next decade in this remarkable family is to imagine that the nine-year-old Pulcheria, who by all accounts was one of the larger-than-life personalities of the fifth century, was able to mobilize a coalition of grown-ups to protect herself and her sisters and to keep her brother on the throne.

The orphaned princess managed, somehow, to play the grown men in her coalition off against one another. The ancient historians complain that she controlled access to her brother, and that courtiers who defied her will were promptly sidelined. Indeed, we will see below that even Antiochus, the chief eunuch who had protected the children in the immediate aftermath of their father's death, was unable to hold his own when Pulcheria came into her full powers. Behind Pulcheria's successes there may have been a network of fiercely loyal women: like her mother before her, she may have had the help of older friends who had contacts and experience at court. The widow Marsa, who had been her mother's mentor before her marriage, was probably still alive, since women were often widowed at a very young age and it was not much more than a decade since Eudoxia had married Arcadius. Whatever the case, ancient sources refer to Pulcheria's ladies of the bedchamber, the *cubiculariae*. It is perhaps to these women that we should look to account for the princess's improbable achievements.

The fact remains that, however she did it, Pulcheria prevailed. She would remain in power for forty-nine years, first as the Emperor's gate-keeper, and then, at her brother's death, as the consort of a successor of her own choosing. The reign of Theodosius II (408–50) was the longest since Augustus and the most stable the Empire had ever known. This was a remarkable achievement under any circumstances.

Part of Pulcheria's success can be put down to the lessons she had taken from her mother's short life. Unlike her younger siblings, Pulcheria was old enough to remember her extraordinary mother Eudoxia, who had died in childbirth in October of 404 when the princess was nearly six. So she may have had an idea of the role her mother had played.

The first lesson had to do with the Empress's own position. Like Pulcheria, Eudoxia had been an orphan – and yet, with the help of family friends, she had not only survived but made a brilliant marriage. This must have been what was expected for her daughter. But Pulcheria had seen the thankless – and dangerous – fate that awaited her if she followed her mother into the expected role of marrying and producing children. Her mother had died in her twenties, during the last of seven pregnancies. In light of this fact, there was a logic to her choice of sidestepping the marriage offers, when they came. Pulcheria would look for support not to a husband, but to the Church.

For a bride like Eudoxia, marriage had been the route into the imperial family. But for her daughter, who was born to the purple, any marriage would not only bring the physical danger of repeated pregnancy but it would also compromise her relationship with her brother. She might bring him a valuable ally as a brother-in-law, but, once married, her own position at court would be ambiguous. She would now be viewed as the representative of a man who had his own noble family to protect and whose ambitions might conflict with the best interest of the Emperor. We will see below that Pulcheria repeatedly made brilliant use of her position as the Emperor's most trusted relative, and it was this uncompromised position that would allow her, years later, to avert a civil war when her brother died without leaving an heir.

The second lesson Pulcheria learned from her mother had to do with what kind of man one could trust. Fundamentally, any outstanding man at court who had sons of his own – or hope of having them – was a potential usurper. This is why eunuchs played such an important role in the imperial palace. But Christian priests

259

and bishops constituted another class of men who – even if they did have children – had sworn themselves to a vocation in the Church. This meant that however much trouble they stirred up, they could not threaten the Emperor's person. Still, they had to be managed expertly. Eudoxia had discovered that bishops could be valuable allies and formidable enemies, and Pulcheria took this lesson to heart.

Ancient writers offered two competing theories about how Theodosius and Pulcheria were able to survive the difficult first years after their father's death. The first view lays their success at the feet of the Praetorian Prefect Anthemius, who had been appointed under Arcadius in 405 and remained in office until 414. Anthemius was a brilliant politician and the great champion of civilian government at a time when barbarian war-lords and roman generals alike threatened a military takeover. His outstanding achievement in office was to build a great new wall to fortify Constantinople, a wall that would not be breached until the city fell to Ottoman armies in 1453. It is uncertain whether it was meant to protect the city from the Huns, who had threatened the city in 408, or from a military coup whose origin was closer to home. But the wall was both a fitting symbol for the safety of the Emperor whose palace it guarded and a monument to the man who intended both to protect and control him.

The second theory held that it was the Christian piety of the Emperor and his sisters that protected them from harm: more than one ancient writer explained that the Hun Uldin had been turned back when he crossed the Danube in 408 because the children's piety had won them protection from God. Whatever the contribution of Anthemius, it is certain that as the children grew in independence from the adult protectors they inherited from their father, they would turn openly to the Church as a source of support. Not only the monks and clergy but the warm support of the simple faithful would be crucial to their position as beloved leaders of the Roman people.

The first crisis of the children's independence came in 412 when Pulcheria was thirteen and her brother eleven. The eunuch Antiochus seems to have fallen out of favour and Theodosius dismissed him as head of the imperial household and installed Pulcheria in his place. Under her rule, the palace became something like a monastery. The princesses gave up the finery of the aristocracy and began to follow a programme of fasting, study, and homely occupations such as spinning and weaving. Pulcheria also began to do good works in the city, founding churches and monasteries, as well as hostels for beggars and the homeless. If she and her siblings were trying to court God's protection by acts of piety and charity, they were certainly making a go of it.

The modern historian Kenneth Holum has suggested, however, that there was another reason behind the ejection of Antiochus and the adoption of a monastic style of life within the palace. Antiochus, despite himself being a eunuch, seems to have decided to ally himself with a potential husband for Pulcheria. Since the princess was now thirteen, there is no reason this should not have been the case. But a husband was the last thing Pulcheria wanted. Such a person would likely be older – husbands tended to be in their mid-twenties – so he would be a threat not only to Pulcheria's authority but to that of her brother.

There is reason to think that the husband proposed by Antiochus was the son of the Urban Prefect of Constantinople, and the grandson of the Praetorian Prefect Anthemius. This was a dynasty to contend with and the senior Anthemius had enjoyed imperial favour since well before Theodosius became Emperor. The fact that he had managed to install his son as prefect of the city showed that he was building a formidable power base. At around the same time his daughter married a distinguished soldier who claimed descent from Constantine the Great. So if the eunuch Antiochus was working to help her brother gain the hand of the Emperor's eldest sister, it was not wrong to suspect that his loyalty had been compromised and that the groom in question had aspirations to be emperor himself. At any rate, Antiochus lost his post in 412, and by 414 Anthemius, too, had been sidelined. Pulcheria, it seems, was unstoppable.

Sometime before her fourteenth birthday, Pulcheria took another step that would have decisive repercussions for the stability of the dynasty. In a splendid ceremony held in the Great Church of Constantinople, she professed her vocation as a Christian virgin. As a gift to commemorate the occasion, she commissioned a new altar, decorated with gold and precious stones, and inscribed with a dedication 'on behalf of her own virginity and her brother's rule'.

With this bold public act, the princess made a number of points at once. First, she consolidated her position at the centre of her brother's world and cut off any pretender's hope of using her to displace him. Second, she indicated her intention to work closely with the Church to bring prosperity to the Empire and stability to her brother's reign. And finally, Pulcheria sent the message that her sense of duty to her people was intimately connected to her faith as a Christian. By this last act, although she did not know it at the time, she planted the seed for a controversy that would remain unresolved for decades.

Pulcheria was certainly the most powerful woman of her century and among the most important people, even measured by the standards of men. In this, she took full advantage of aspects of the Roman civilization which would last, in Byzantium, for a further thousand years. The establishment of a civilian society based in cities, a culture where intelligence and cultural accomplishment were valued as highly as military valour, a sense of the rule of law in which the rights of women and children could hope to be protected – all of these essentially Roman values weighed in Pulcheria's favour.

If one compares Pulcheria with a very different fifth-century figure, Hereka, Princess of the Huns and consort of their most famous warlord Attila, the differences are not quite what one would expect. Hereka, too, had her own property and her own household – indeed, a Greek envoy travelling to negotiate with Attila around 450 remarked on the power she was able to exert. But in the world of the Huns there was no place for a Pulcheria: the value of women was very closely linked to their ability to give birth to future warriors.

Pulcheria, by contrast, could find power in a formal dedication of her virginity to God.

In this, Pulcheria showed how much she had learned from the women of her mother's generation. Like her mother she had a gift for the use of Christian ritual to cement the relationship between the palace and the Christian faithful, while at the same time she had the freedom of an Olympias to cultivate her moral authority as one of the Church's own virgins. Pulcheria found herself, in the first decade of her brother's reign, in a position where she had to draw on her gift for alliance-building, and it was through the Church that she found invaluable support. Her great ally in the early years seems to have been Atticus, Bishop of Constantinople from 406 to 425. A number of his sermons survive, and in them we can see that he shared many of Pulcheria's enthusiasms.

Pulcheria's most brilliant stroke was to cultivate a powerful symbol to convey her affection for the people of her brother's empire. This was none other than the Virgin Mary, now known as the mother of God and remembered as the first of the virgins of the Church. Pulcheria was by no means the first Christian virgin to claim a special relationship to Mary. But she was in a unique position and she had unique gifts. In the first years of her brother's reign, she also seems to have had a mentor in the person of Bishop Atticus, himself a great promoter of Mary's cult.

One of Atticus' Christmas sermons celebrates the Virgin in terms which show that not only professed virgins, but all women, could find a point of identification in Mary's story:

Through Mary all women are blessed. The female can no longer be held accursed, for the rank of this sex surpasses even the angels in glory. Now Eve is healed, the Egyptian woman passed over in silence. Delilah is sealed in a tomb, Jezebel given to oblivion. Even Herodias herself is no longer mentioned. Now behold the catalogue of admirable women: all praise Sarah, the fertile field of the people. Rebekah is honoured, a capable provider of benedictions, and Leah too they admire as mother of the ancestor in the flesh. Deborah wins praise because she led in battle despite her sex. Elizabeth also they call happy, for she carried the precursor in her body, and he leapt in delight at the approach of grace.

And you also, women, you who have been renewed in Christ, who have cast off every stain of sin and have partaken of blessing in the most-holy Mary: you also may receive him in the womb of faith, the one who is born today of the Virgin. For even the blessed Virgin Mary first opened herself through faith, and not until she had made her body worthy of the kingdom did she receive the King of the universe in her womb.[4]

Atticus implies that *all* women can partake in the blessing of the *Theotokos*. But the subsequent specification of women who 'have cast off every stain of sin and have partaken of blessing in the most holy Mary' is open to interpretation. This may simply be a reference to the baptism in which all women participated, but it may also refer to a particular blessing conferred on women as they renew their faith in the Advent season.

A Christmas sermon delivered after Atticus' death by his secretary Proclus, one of Pulcheria's circle, reveals that, by this date, the church at Constantinople celebrated an annual festival, known as the Virginity Festival, on 26 December to exalt Mary because she had erased the sin of Eve. From ancient liturgical calendars, it seems that in at least some cities, the Sundays leading up to Christmas were dedicated to meditation on Mary: in Antioch, the Sundays of Advent included meditations first on the Annunciation, then on the Visitation of Mary and Elizabeth, and later, on Mary's announcement of her pregnancy to Joseph, and her meditation on the meaning of her Son's impending birth.

Pulcheria's patronage formed part of what Leslie Brubaker has called the 'matronage' tradition of late antiquity. The aristocratic and imperial women of Constantinople built up a distinctive tradition of patronage, in which women of later generations commemorated the achievements – and indeed the patronage – of their female forebears. The iconic figure whom female patrons invoked again and again in memory was the Empress Helena, the mother of Constantine the Great, and her iconic act was the founding of a shrine to the Nativity in Bethlehem, at 'the place where the *Theotokos* gave birth'. The imperial mother and the Mother of God were bound in a reciprocal relationship of patronage, and this was something that later imperial women could not afford to forget.[5]

Socrates of Constantinople argued that this tradition had been important already in Constantine's day. To illustrate his point he gives a citation from Eusebius' *Life of Constantine*: 'And in fact Emmanuel submitted to be born for our sake, and the place of his nativity in the flesh is by the Hebrews called Bethlehem. Wherefore the devout Empress Helena adorned the place where the *Theotokos* gave birth with the most splendid monuments.' It is likely that Pulcheria was conscious of the resonance between her role as patroness to the Virgin's cult and that of her illustrious predecessor Helena.[6]

The special name *Theotokos* would later become a point of controversy. Literally 'god-bearer', the title *Theotokos* celebrated the paradox of Mary's maternal virginity and it became a central element of the cult of the Virgin. A strong popular following was attached to the cult of Mary, through which an empress could mobilize a following of women from all social classes, and in turn be perceived as speaking on behalf of a constituency. As a patroness with special responsibility for women from the different levels of society, Pulcheria may have acted as an intercessor on behalf of less fortunate women in much the way that the Virgin herself was understood to do.[7]

In the century that separated Helena and Pulcheria, the special relationship of virgins to the Virgin had become a staple of the ideology of virginity. Pulcheria seems to have been a gifted impresario who could cultivate popular support by finding the connection between her own piety and that of the people, while Nestorius defied the people's love for the Virgin to his own ruin. The sixth-century

Syriac writer Barhadbeshabba Arbaia, who was not at all fond of Pulcheria, remembered her as having given one of her own cloaks to act as an altar-cloth in the Great Church of Constantinople where she had professed her virginity. In doing so, she was deliberately blurring her own persona with that of the Virgin, in a way that gave greater power to the image of both. The writer reported with some distaste that Pulcheria had wrapped the clergy of the Great Church around her finger, and was in the habit of officiating with them in the sanctuary there. There is no way of knowing whether the accusation was true but it captures how the Empress's virginity combined with her well-developed personal relationships to create a powerful mood of piety and awe among her supporters.

To understand the circumstances within which Pulcheria was having to manoeuvre, it is instructive to compare her to another outstanding woman of the Theodosian dynasty, her aunt Galla Placidia, the half-sister of her father Arcadius and her uncle Honorius, the Western Emperor. Placidia, who was perhaps ten years older than Pulcheria, was living in the household of her cousin Serena in the city of Rome while it was under siege by the Gothic army of Alaric from 408 to 410. Serena was accused of conspiring with Alaric and was put to death at the order of the Roman Senate, but somehow, before the city fell to Alaric, Placidia herself was captured and taken hostage. She seems to have lived in the Gothic camps while they besieged Rome, and when Goths left Italy and moved west to Gaul, Placidia went with them. After Alaric's death, the Goths were ruled by Athaulf, and in 413 he contracted an alliance with Honorius, and asked to marry Placidia to cement the alliance. But when Athaulf was murdered in 415, Placidia was returned to her brother, who promptly married her to his *magister militum* or master of soldiers, Constantius. Two children were born to the union, and in 421 Honorius proclaimed his brother-in-law co-emperor. Constantius died shortly afterwards, but the succession had now settled on the couple's son Valentinian III. At this point, the ancient sources suggest that Honorius made incestuous advances to his sister; whether this was the cause or not, she left Italy for Constantinople, where she would spend a number of years in the company of Theodosius and Pulcheria.

Their help would prove invaluable at the death of Honorius, since it was the armies of Theodosius who asserted Valentinian's claim to the throne. On 23 October 425, the five-year-old Valentinian was proclaimed Augustus of the Western Roman Empire by the Roman Senate. Placidia then served as regent of the Empire until her son reached the age of eighteen in July of 437, the year of his marriage to Licinia Eudoxia. It was a remarkable reversal of fortune for a princess who had left Italy as a prisoner of war in 412.

Two Empresses

But if Pulcheria's position was far less exposed than that of her aunt, she still had a number of challenges to face before she could be secure in her good fortune. Her status as the principal virgin of the imperial Church would stand her in good stead when she and her siblings came to their second crisis, that of Theodosius' emergence into manhood. Pulcheria, Marina, and Arcadia were safely established as virgins, but when he reached twenty, their brother needed a wife. He would never be the kind of emperor who led his armies into battle, but there was a firm expectation that on reaching manhood Theodosius would marry and produce an heir.

Pulcheria knew that this new member of the family could destabilize the oasis of safety she and her siblings had managed to establish in the palace. The noble families were grooming their daughters in the knowledge that the father and brothers of the Emperor's chosen bride would experience a dramatic change of fortune, and this was not necessarily a good thing for the Emperor and his sisters.

On 7 June 421, Theodosius married Athenais, daughter of the Athenian sophist Leontius. The wedding was celebrated with chariot races in the hippodrome. It was a surprising choice of bride, not least because the girl was a pagan. She was an accomplished poet, and deeply interested in Hellenic cultural tradition. Later writers remembered Pulcheria as having chosen her brother's bride for her wide eyes, golden curls, and humble demeanour. But it is more likely that the noble families who had clustered around Anthemius had sought a voice in the palace who would stand for their more traditional interests, and found it in the lovely young Empress. On this theory, even once she had been baptized as a Christian, the former pagan Athenais would act as a counter-weight to Pulcheria's attempt to turn the palace into a monastery. Beauty would win out over austerity, and the birth of imperial children would give her ever greater power even as her beauty faded.

In fact, this is not how things turned out. To be sure, men of learning began to play a more visible role at court, and the new Empress, who took the name Eudokia at her christening, was able to secure important posts for her brothers and uncle. But Pulcheria's coalition of the Christian faithful and their clergy had allowed her influence to reach far beyond the palace. In her seeming unwillingness to be displaced in the popular imagination by her brother's legitimate consort Eudokia, Pulcheria put forward an idiosyncratic vision of imperial Christianity, but in her own way she reinforced the miraculous connection between fertility and divine power, which Christian empresses since Helena had sought to establish.

During the 420s, the two princesses seem to have led parallel lives in the palace, with Eudoxia producing two daughters and a noticeable absence of sons. Licinia Eudoxia was born in 422. She would herself grow up to be an imperial bride – in 437 she was sent to Italy to marry her slightly older cousin Valentinian III, who had become Emperor of the West. A younger sister, Flacilla, died in 431, and this may have been a turning point for the imperial couple. Although in all likelihood the Empress Eudokia was still in her twenties at the time of the child's death, either a medical crisis or a decision not to risk further pregnancies ended her career as a mother of future emperors before it had begun. Later writers ascribed the change to a religious vow: on this view Theodosius had decided to return to a life of prayer and asceticism as his best chance to win the favour of God for his Empire. But whatever the case, from the late 420s there were no more imperial pregnancies.

During this period, Pulcheria had problems of her own. Having steered gracefully through difficulties in the palace, she now found herself beset by problems in the Church. The trouble began in October 425 with the death of Atticus, the Bishop of Constantinople who had stood with her as she negotiated her role as the Church's principal virgin and the impresario of the Cult of Mary *Theotokos*. Many favoured his secretary, the priest Proclus, as a successor – and Proclus would in fact become bishop years later, in 434. But a consensus could not be reached, and in the end a compromise candidate was put forward, the blameless and very elderly Sissinius, who could be trusted to hold the see uneventfully until the next election. When Sissinius died, however, in December of 427, it was clearly time to appoint a younger man.

This time, the consensus candidate was an outsider, the learned Nestorius from Antioch, a preacher so gifted that his reputation had reached the capital. It is a profile that curiously mirrors that of the gifted Antiochene preacher John Chrysostom a quarter-century earlier, and in fact Nestorius would clash with the Empress Pulcheria just as John Chrysostom had done with her mother. Perhaps memories were not long in Constantinople. Or perhaps Pulcheria's enemies had a hand in the election. It is difficult to tell, at this distance.

If the bishop and the palace had heretofore worked closely together, one might have expected that there could be trouble when the see changed hands. A new man would naturally want to find space for his own ideas and his own trusted colleagues and contacts and this was always going to create ripples. The surprise, here, is not so much the fact that Nestorius clashed with the palace, as how he did so. He seems to have chosen, almost by accident, to take aim at one of the great successes of the Constantinopolitan church, a figure whose fame was as widespread as her character was known to be blameless. This was none other than the Virgin Mary.

The contemporary historian Socrates of Constantinople accounted for the spark of conflict between Bishop and Empress in the following way.

> Nestorius had an associate whom he had brought from Antioch, a presbyter named Anastasius; for this man he had high esteem, and consulted him in the management of his most important affairs. This Anastasius, preaching one day in church, said, 'Let no one call Mary *Theotokos*; for Mary was a human being, and it is impossible that God should be born of a human being.' These words caused a great sensation, and troubled both the clergy and the laity, they having been heretofore taught to acknowledge Christ as God, and by no means to separate his humanity from his divinity on account of the economy of incarnation . . .[8]

According to Socrates, Nestorius then found himself forced to defend his associate. 'While great offence was taken in the church, as we have said, at what was thus propounded, Nestorius, eager to establish Anastasius' proposition – for he did not want to have the man who was esteemed by himself found guilty of blasphemy. . . assumed a controversial attitude, and totally rejected the term *Theotokos*.'[9]

But it was a dangerous business, for the question of Mary's divine power lay close to thorny problems in the theology of the Trinity. In 381 the Council of Constantinople had established that God could be known in three Persons: the Father, Son, and Holy Spirit. The tensions between Nestorius and Pulcheria would trigger a further theological crisis, whose central question was whether the Son was fully human or fully divine. As we shall see, this theological argument would lead to the fall of Nestorius. He would be deposed as Bishop of Constantinople and condemned at the Council of Ephesus in 431.

The Council of Ephesus is one of the most significant landmarks in the development of patristic theology, and it is a well-known fact that its core Christological problem can be reduced to the simple question, whether the Virgin Mary gave birth to a man or to a god. The title *Theotokos* seems to have had broad popular roots in the Marian piety of early fifth-century Constantinople, carrying with it a surge of devotional feeling along with a somewhat variable Christological content. But the problem of how to understand the Incarnation, with its implications for the relationship between Christ's humanity and his divinity – the so-called Two Natures – was never definitively resolved. Over a thousand years later, the Eastern Churches are in schism over it still.

In the early fifth century, Christian theology was, in many respects, still in its infancy. Questions as basic as whether the Son of God referred by the Bible was in fact the historical Jesus, born from the line of David, were still not fully resolved. Also in its infancy was the problem of how to accommodate the divine feminine, which the traditional religions of the Roman Empire so often emphasized. At the Council of Ephesus Nestorius was deposed from his position as Bishop of Constantinople for having made statements such as the following: 'Has God a mother? If so we may excuse paganism for giving mothers to its deities . . . No, Mary was not *Theotokos*. For that which is born of flesh is flesh. A creature did not bring forth him who is uncreated; the Father did not beget by the Virgin a new God.' For Nestorius, the real theological problem was not about Mary but about Jesus as Logos, the divine Word of God.[10]

According to the first chapter of the Gospel of John, the Word already existed in the beginning when God created the world, 'In the beginning was the Word, and the Word was with God, and the Word was God.' (John 1: 1) According to Nestorius' reasoning, the name *Theotokos*, 'God-bearer', for Mary implied that the Logos, having been born, also suffered the crucifixion. This was simply unacceptable. The divine Logos and the human Christ might be the same person, but they were distinct.

Cyril of Alexandria, who emerged as Nestorius' principal opponent, would take the view that with his Birth, the Logos had undergone a profound metamorphosis, accepting a new condition of existence. Here is how the modern theologian Frances Young summarizes Cyril's position: 'It was the Logos who was incarnate, and there is only one Lord and Christ and Son. He admits that two Natures are involved, but their union, he says, is hypostatic' – this means that the two natures are fused within the person of the Logos. This idea drew on a tradition reaching back at least as early as the early second-century martyr-bishop Ignatius of Antioch, who had talked about 'the suffering of my God' and of 'God . . . [who] was conceived of Mary'. What bothered people like Nestorius about people like Cyril was that the Alexandrian idea of the Son as 'Word-Flesh' seemed to be a way of saying that He was really the Word and not the Flesh: in other words, the critics of the Alexandrian Jesus suspected that he did not *really* live and die the way other human beings do.[11]

During the 420s and afterwards, a number of prominent churchmen began to compose hymns and sermons on the Virgin Mary, defending her honour against Nestorius and praising her in terms that were often drawn quite brazenly from the formal speeches of praise composed in honour of the Emperor and his family. The most influential of the orators was Proclus, who served as secretary to Bishop Atticus until 425, and later as bishop himself, first of Cyzicus and later, from 434, of Constantinople.

The theological controversy seems to have reached its first peak on the Sunday before Christmas of 428. Proclus, now Bishop of Cyzicus, preached a sermon full of praise for Mary in the Great Church of Constantinople.

The virgin's festival, my brethren, summons us today to words of praise, and the present feast has benefits to bestow on those who assemble to keep it. And surely this is right, for its subject is purity (*hagneia*). What we celebrate is the pride of women and the glory of the female, thanks to the one who was at once both mother and virgin. Lovely is the gathering! See how both the earth and the sea serve as the Virgin's escorts: the one spreading forth her waves calmly beneath the ships, the other conducting the steps of travellers on their way unhindered. Let nature leap for joy, and let women be honoured! Let all humanity dance, and let virgins be glorified![12]

The sermon went on to break into a hymn of praise for Mary:

She who called us here today is the Holy Mary:
The untarnished vessel of virginity;
The spiritual paradise of the second Adam;
The bridal chamber in which the Word took the flesh in
    marriage . . .
Handmaid and mother, virgin and heaven, the only bridge for
    God to mankind;
The awesome loom of the divine economy upon which the robe
    of union was ineffably woven.[13]

At the end of the sermon, Nestorius, who as bishop was present, stood up to congratulate the preacher, but then he offered a polite critique of what he had heard. The claim that Mary had given birth to God, he argued, would bring Christianity into disrepute with the pagans, who would refuse to see anything good in 'a god who was born, died, and was buried'.

Another hymn of Proclus made it clear that all men and women were implicated in the Virgin's great blessings.

Let women come running, for a woman . . . has given birth to
    the fruit of life.

Let virgins also come running, for a virgin has given birth . . .

For the child came forth without ruffling the bed-chambers of
    the womb . . .

> Let mothers come running, for through the Tree of Life a virgin
> mother has set aright the tree of disobedience.[14]

The allegiance between virgin Empress and Virgin Mother was the
fruition of a long inheritance of divine and human female power in
the cities of Asia Minor, stretching back through the cults of Tyche,
Isis, Artemis, and Cybele. These goddesses were a potent source of
protection. The pagan historian Zosimus attributed the safety of
another city, Athens, from invading Huns in 396 to such divine protection: 'But this ancient city won some divine protection for itself despite
the impiety of the age [by this, he means Christianity] . . . When
Alaric and his whole army came to the city, he saw the tutelary goddess
Athena walking about the wall, looking just like her statue, armed
and ready to resist attack.' Thus, the war-lord left the city unscathed.
Constantinople could only hope to find so powerful and loyal a protec-
tress.[15]

That the House of Theodosius drew on this inheritance with good
sense and enthusiasm was a sign to contemporary eyes that their
brand of Christian rulership was firmly rooted in the traditions of
the imperial city. At the same time, it was an appropriation of the
Virgin's power. If Constantinople belonged to the Virgin, the Virgin
belonged to Theodosius and his sisters.

Another hymn of Proclus develops the Angel's greeting to Mary
from the Gospel of Luke, 'Hail, full of grace!', into a pattern of repeated
acclamation that evokes the acclamations with which the people of
Constantinople saluted the Emperor on formal occasions:

> Hail, full of grace! The joy from you, Holy Virgin, is infinite,
> Hail, full of grace! You are adorned with many virtues, you are
>   the torch-bearing light,
> And the inextinguishable light brighter than the sun.[16]

One can see how assimilating the Virgin to the imperial family in
this way might be cause for alarm to someone who felt that the

Church should be independent of the palace. According to the *Letter to Cosmas* written by supporters of Nestorius as early as the mid 430s, theological ideas were not really the root of the problem between Nestorius and Pulcheria. Rather, what was causing the trouble was Pulcheria's self-importance, and her insistence, as a laywoman, on claiming privileges that ought to be reserved only to priests.

'Let me enter according to my custom!'

But he said to her: 'This place should only be entered by priests.'

She said to him: 'But I have given birth to God!'

He said to her, 'You have given birth to Satan,' and chased her from the entrance to the Holy of Holies. She departed in a state of rage, and went to find the Emperor, recounting the episode to him. 'On your life, my sister, and by the crown that is on your head, I will not stop before I have taken vengeance on him.'[17]

A later writer, Barhadbeshabba Arbaia, was clearly on the side of Nestorius as well, but his view was that it was all really a power-play: Nestorius' main opponents, John of Antioch and Cyril of Alexandria, had each taken an alternate route to attempt to divert the Emperor's favour from Nestorius. It was Cyril who chose the vehicle of the Empress: 'He [Cyril] worked on the sister of the Emperor, Pulcheria, who helped to ensnare the whole East in the flatteries of the Egyptian.' In Pulcheria, on this reading, Cyril clearly found someone who had her own reasons for wanting to bring the new bishop down to size.[18]

We saw above that the Letter to Cosmas, which was written within a few years of the events it describes, accuses Pulcheria of having claimed to 'have given birth to God'. The writer clearly thinks that she used her virginity and her special devotion to the Virgin as a way of building up her own power, and that the Cult of Mary was somehow rigged to the Empress's advantage. If Pulcheria were able to pose as the human embodiment of the *Theotokos*, in so doing she would be blurring the line between Christianity and the rituals of imperial cult, which had existed since pagan times.

This would also raise the disturbing question, whether it was the bishop or the imperial family who had the right to define the nature of Christian piety and liturgical practice. A law of Theodosius II promulgated in 425, for example, reassures those who fail to participate in some public ceremony related to civic cult in order to attend a church service, because 'due reverence is paid to the emperor when God is worshipped'. This law reveals that Christian liturgy had now taken precedence over the old civic cult, but it also shows a blurring between the person of the emperor and the person of Christ. One can see why a bishop of Constantinople might have resisted this. Nestorius may have suspected that Theodosius was using Pulcheria to draw the Church even more tightly under the control of the imperial family.

Years later, Nestorius would complain that Pulcheria had avoided his authority by cultivating a clerical retinue of her own. Here is how he characterizes the situation in his polemical treatise, the *Bazaar of Heraclides*, prepared before the Council of Chalcedon in 451:

> You have . . . with you against me a contentious woman, a princess . . . a virgin, who fought against me because I was not willing to be persuaded by her demand that I compare a woman corrupted of men to the bride of Christ. This I have done because I had pity on her soul and that I might not be the chief celebrant of the sacrifice among those whom she had unrighteously chosen.[19]

Barhadbeshabba makes a similar point in somewhat more sensationalist language.

> She resented Nestorius because he had called public attention to her corruption. She had vowed herself to virginity and had

gathered other virgins around her. Here is why she hated him: She asked that he place her image above the altar [of the great Church] and that her [own] garment serve as an altar-cloth. He did not want to do it . . .

Barhadbeshabba does not explain why Nestorius would have rejected such a gesture of imperial piety. But we begin to see the political implications that Pulcheria's claim to have given birth to Christ would have had, if indeed she made such a claim.[20]

It seems fairly certain, in any event, that the coalition between Pulcheria and Cyril was a marriage of convenience. In 430, Cyril addressed two treatises to the imperial family, one *To the most pious Emperor Theodosius on the Correct Faith* and another, *To the most pious princesses*. Cyril's main interest seems to have been in the relationship between Christ's human and divine natures, while Pulcheria's was in Mary herself. He may only have attained the support of the Empress insofar as his theological commitments overlapped with her desire to promote the cult of the Virgin Mary as a form of imperial civic religion.

In 431, the Emperor called an ecumenical council to resolve the theological dispute between Cyril and Nestorius. The choice of Ephesus as a venue for the council was evocative: on the one hand, it was a practical choice, since it was close to the western coast of Asia Minor (modern Turkey) and easy to reach both by land and by sea. But on the other hand, Ephesus was a city dedicated to virginity: it boasted the ancient shrine to the virgin goddess Artemis. It was also the city where, according to legend, the Virgin Mary had gone to live with the disciple John, the author of the fourth Gospel, after the death of Jesus.

The Council itself seems to have been something of a circus, with the assembled bishops often on the point of violence, and constant disruption due to one or the other side's unwillingness to conduct an orderly examination of the issues. In July, Cyril was able to obtain a pronouncement against Nestorius, but it was not accepted by all, and the Council lasted all summer as a result. Finally, in early autumn Nestorius wrote to the Emperor, who had remained in Constantinople, to ask permission to abdicate his position as bishop and return to Antioch to live as a monk. Many saw this as a sign that the Virgin Mary herself had intervened to see Cyril vindicated and Nestorius proclaimed a heretic. When Cyril's decree against Nestorius was read out in the Great Church of Constantinople in July, the crowd is remembered as having cheered, 'Many years to Pulcheria! She it is who has strengthened the faith!'[21]

The Council of Ephesus was a victory for Pulcheria, and the new bishops of Constantinople seem to have been more cooperative. Meanwhile, relations with her sister-in-law Eudokia seem never to have settled into a real collaboration. Eudokia came into her own for a brief phase when her daughter Licinia Eudokia came of age and was married, as had always been planned, to her first cousin once removed, the Western Emperor Valentinian III, in October 437. But then Eudokia surprised the court. During the festivities surrounding the royal wedding, the pagan senator Volusianus had been in the capital and his niece, the famous Christian ascetic Melania the Younger, had travelled from Palestine to join him. But Volusianus had died during his visit and Melania had stayed on to complete the forty-day period of mourning. During this time, she evidently frequented the palace and asked the Emperor to allow her to bring Eudokia back with her to the Holy Land. Eudokia was eventually to settle permanently in Bethlehem, close to the church founded by the Empress Helena over a century earlier. She gathered around her a society of literate men and women.

But she left a legacy in her daughter's marriage, which held out hope that the Roman Empire, which had been divided since the death of Theodosius I in 395, might again be united under a single crown. During the 440s, Licinia Eudoxia's new mother-in-law, the Dowager Empress Galla Placidia, corresponded with Pulcheria, attempting from her position in Italy to strengthen an alliance between Pulcheria and Pope Leo the Great, in the still unresolved debates about the *Theotokos* and Christ's two natures. These negotiations would result in a further ecumenical council at the ancient port of Chalcedon, not far from Constantinople on the Sea of Marmara, in 451.

As it happened, it was left to Pulcheria to bring these matters to a conclusion. In July 450, her brother Theodosius II died in a hunting accident, at the age of forty-nine. Pulcheria's close relationship to the Church and to her cousins in the Western Empire made her indispensable in the crisis. She maintained order in the city in the weeks directly following her brother's death, and during this time selected one of his most sensible generals, Marcian, as a consort, extracting a vow that he would respect her virginity if she married him. The vow having been obtained, a royal wedding followed, and the groom was immediately acclaimed as Emperor.

Marcian proved a worthy choice. Not only was he happy to co-operate with Pulcheria in religious matters, but he was good at the business of government. The pair were able to steer the Eastern Empire safely through a phase of sustained barbarian invasions that would prove the undoing of the West. Where religion was concerned, the new Emperor and the more experienced Empress worked together to host the Council at Chalcedon in October 451. The Council had originally been intended to take place at Nicaea, where the great council under Constantine had taken place in 325. However, because Marcian had been with his armies fighting against the Huns through the summer and into early autumn, he advised the bishops that the Council should be held closer to the capital.

The Council of Chalcedon remains as a landmark in the theological reflection of the early Church. Its main accomplishment was to reconcile the imperial family's intense commitment to the cult of Mary as *Theotokos* with the idea, championed by Pulcheria's enemy Nestorius a quarter-century earlier, that Christ must be fully human even if he was also fully divine. The Formula of Chalcedon makes a brilliant compromise: it allows that Mary gave birth to God while at the same time it asserts that Jesus is fully human. It reads thus: 'born from the Virgin Mary, the *Theotokos,* as touching the manhood . . . to be acknowledged in two natures, without confusion, without change, without division, without separation; the distinction of natures being in no way abolished because of the union'.[22]

The acts of the Council record that at its close, the gathered bishops addressed the Emperor and Empress with a series of acclamations, praising their piety and their success in bringing peace among the bishops. Fittingly, the praise for Pulcheria remembered the first empress to contribute her resources to the cult of Mary *Theotokos*: 'Marcian is the new Constantine, Pulcheria the new Helena! You have shown the faith of Helena! You have shown the zeal of Helena! Your life is the security of all! Your faith is the glory of the churches!'[23]

The legacy of Pulcheria and Marcian endured beyond their own lifetimes. After their deaths – Pulcheria's in 453 and Marcian's in 457 – Marcian's successor Leo I would write a biography of Pulcheria to keep her memory alive. Leo is also known to have continued Pulcheria's policy of showing special reverence to the Virgin Mary *Theotokos*. Annexed to the Church of the Blachernai in Constantinople, which Pulcheria had built and dedicated to the Virgin, Leo and his own Empress Verina dedicated a chapel. It contained an altar surrounded by a mosaic of gold and precious stones and within the altar they deposited a casket holding a garment believed to be Mary's own shroud. On the casket, the Emperor and Empress ordered the following dedication to be inscribed: 'By showing reverence here to the *Theotokos*, they secured their reign (*basileia*).' The *Theotokos* would prove an invaluable ally for the emperors and their city.[24]

That Pulcheria and Marcian had achieved stability in Constantinople at the death of Theodosius was no small achievement given the instability of the Mediterranean during the barbarian invasions of the fifth century. To appreciate their achievement, we can consider the devastating sequence of events that unfolded in Italy five years afterwards in 455, on the death of Valentinian III, the Emperor of the West, Pulcheria's blood cousin and nephew by marriage.

Valentinian was murdered by two of his own soldiers, and some weeks later, his successor, Petronius Maximus – who some believed had colluded with Valentinian's murderers – was himself murdered in turn. This laid Rome open to invasion: only days after the death of Maximus, King Geiseric of the Vandals sacked the city, remaining for two weeks and carrying away a group of royal hostages including Valentinian's widow, Licinia Eudoxia – now also the widow of Maximus because of a forced marriage at her first husband's death – and her two daughters by Valentinian, Placidia, and Eudokia, named after their two grandmothers. Ancient sources speculated that the Empress had in fact invited the Vandal king to Rome, as an act of revenge against Maximus. Whatever the cause, with Geiseric's sack the city of Rome, and the Western Empire itself, entered a period of instability from which they would never recover. Twenty years later, in 476, the last Roman Emperor of the West, the child-emperor Romulus Augustuus, was deposed by the barbarian general Odoacre. The Eastern Roman Empire, by contrast, would endure for another thousand years.

So, paradoxically, Rome's Empire survived long after the decline of Rome herself. The city around which the Empire revolved was now Constantinople, the city of Constantine, also known by its ancient name, Byzantium. Modern historians tend to refer to the Eastern Roman Empire as Byzantine, on the view that even if the Empire's law and culture were Roman, its breathing heart was now Byzantium. But after the fall of the Western Empire, the emperors of the East continued to think of their Empire as what remained of the Roman Empire – as indeed it was.

Byzantium's remarkable staying power as an imperial capital had much to do with its strategic and naturally defensible site. Sited on the high promontory overlooking the Golden Horn, the city enjoyed a sheltered harbour on the Bosporus and a location close to the centre of the Mediterranean. There was genius in the city's position along the straits that link the Mediterranean to the Black Sea, and at the ferry-point of the principal land route linking Europe to Asia. The city's good fortune was also helped by the massive land walls which had been built, after 408, by Anthemius, to protect the child-emperor Theodosius from barbarians and usurpers alike.

But Byzantine theologians believed there was another reason. The city, they would repeatedly remind the faithful, had the incalculable advantage of relying not only on these man-made defences, but on incomparable supernatural protection. The city was protected by the peculiarly conscientious love of Mary *Theotokos*. Her position as the Queen of Heaven and the saint most closely bound up with God's love for humanity meant that her intercession on the city's behalf was outstandingly effective.

One of the great hymns of the Byzantine Church, the *Akathistos* hymn, captures the city's reliance on the Virgin's protection. The *Akathistos* was written in Constantinople during or shortly after the reign of Pulcheria. Its language still lives on in the liturgy of the Eastern Orthodox Churches today as the oldest of the Marian hymns that has been used continuously from antiquity. The *Akathistos* is the culmination of the tradition of Marian praise which Pulcheria had encouraged in such gifted preachers and hymnographers as Atticus and Proclus.

In the eyes of the hymnographer, when the angel had visited her centuries earlier, Mary had joined heaven and earth by her radical willingness to enact God's will. Her bold act of faith had been a source of strength to other women, and to men, who found them-selves in equally unpromising circumstances across the centuries. This current of spiritual power – not the offices and institutions that had sprouted like weeds in the fertile soil of fellowship – was her lasting legacy.

By her willingness to rely on Him, the Virgin of Nazareth had established a bond of trust with God that would have consequences for all humanity. This bond of trust allowed her not only to bring God's Son into the world, but – now that her Son had fulfilled his own mission – it allowed her to intercede with God on behalf of those she loved on earth. Mary's openness to God's word had made her love into an impenetrable shield for those who depended on her for protection.

Of course, she was not the city's only protector. Two centuries later, the poet George of Pisidia wrote that when the Emperor Heraclius rode out to defend the city against the Persians, he was accompanied by a war-band of angels, led by the Archangel Michael. But Byzantium was above all the Virgin's city and, until the city fell to the Ottoman armies a thousand years after the death of Pulcheria, in 1453, the Christian faithful of Byzantium could rely on the simple, remarkable fact of Mary's protection. A passage from the hymn captures the grateful praise of a city and an empire that trusted for a millennium on a heavenly protector who had shared, during her years on Earth, the life of the Empire's humblest inhabitants.

Hail! O unshakeable tower of the Church.
Hail! O impregnable wall of the kingdom.
Hail! To you, through whom trophies of victory are assured.
Hail! To you, through whom enemies are vanquished.
Hail! To you, who are the healing of my body.
Hail! To you, who are the salvation of my soul.[25]

Epilogue

It is October 451, and nearly four hundred bishops from around the Mediterranean have gathered at the basilica of the virgin martyr Euphemia in Chalcedon, just across the Sea of Marmara from the Emperor's city of Constantinople. Their task is to hammer out a formula to reconcile warring theologians, men of learning who have been arguing about whether the humanity of Jesus was fused with his divinity or whether his two natures remained separate and distinct throughout the course of his birth and life, death, and resurrection. They also must settle the question, once and for all, whether it is correct to refer to his mother as *Theotokos*, or Mother of God. The atmosphere, though pious, is that of a travelling circus. Each bishop has his own entourage of runners, advisers and hangers-on, so the crowd is enormous. Those who speak must struggle to be heard, and those who listen must struggle to hear.

Imagine, now, a young woman on the fringes of the crowd – a time-traveller from the first century. She has made a long journey from a distant province, and she slips among the jostling men and begins to listen. She is a shepherd's daughter, barely of marriageable age but already expecting a baby, and she has never seen so large a crowd of dignitaries gathered in one place. Our traveller's native tongue is Aramaic, not Greek, but we can imagine, for the sake of the thought-experiment, that she is able to follow the speeches. Such a listener would make very little of the high-level talk about divine and human natures, and she would know nothing about bishops and their councils. Their talk about the Son of God reminds her of the Hebrew Scriptures. Would she recognize that when these men in embroidered tunics speak about the Mother of God, are speaking about a shepherdess like herself?

It goes without saying that our visitor does not entirely understand who these men are. They seem not to be proper Jews, and yet they make repeated reference to the Hebrew Scriptures. They seem to be part of an empire-wide organization, one of a type not known in the first century. There are two representatives from Rome who are playing a very active role in the discussion.

Imagine further that our visitor has a gift for hearing the unspoken anxieties behind what is actually said. She has no ear for the philosophical issues, but she can hear the emotions. She can hear that a number of the bishops do not want to return to face the ladies in their congregations without having fought to honour this Mother, who seems to be a beloved figure and the one to whom they direct their prayers for protection. Others are conscious that the Emperor – and the Empire – are in need of a new guarantee of safety, since the pagan goddess Fortune, who had long patrolled the walls of the Emperor's city, has now been banished. The Emperor himself has recently taken a stand against Attila the Hun, but the barbarians are not likely to lose interest in the fertile lands of the Empire any time soon. These men seem to have responsibility for the safety of the cities, and they are clearly troubled.

Our visitor asks herself, can she do something to help them? She has recently come through a difficult period. If she has a weakness, it is probably a tendency to be a bit rash. She made a promise to an angel and the promise led to all kinds of confusion and difficulty with her parents and with her husband. Now, as a result, she has dangers and difficulties of her own to face. No one, certainly not these friends of the Emperor, would be likely to look for help from an awkward creature like herself.

And yet, she does have something she would like to tell them. When the angel spoke to her, her spirit rejoiced, and she knew that if she placed her trust in God, there was nothing she could not accomplish. Sometimes, she thinks that even her own small life will amount to something, though she is not sure exactly how. She is unsure about so much of what lies ahead, but she will try not to worry. For the moment, the main thing is to try to take care of herself, for the sake of the baby.

A Note On Translation

For biblical quotations throughout I have used the New International Version (British Text), checking them against the Greek and occasionally calling attention to the Greek phrasing where the English does not reflect its meaning completely. For other translations, I have cited the best or failing that the most easily available English translation where one existed; in the notes I have indicated the translator's surname, and publication details can be found in the bibliography. In the case of sources not yet wholly translated into English, I have where possible cited a translation of the passage in a published scholarly discussion, indicating the basis in the Greek or Latin if I have varied the English phrasing.

Notes

Chapter 1: Looking for Chloe

This chapter looks at Paul's women from the perspective of an ancient historian rather than a theologian, and for the most part reflects my own historian's eye view of 1 Corinthians rather than current debates among biblical scholars, which often address issues that had little currency in the 'parallel universe' of women. As a result, the suggestions for further reading made below are eclectic, citing scholars from both liberal and conservative traditions, based on their ability to shed light on the texts under discussion (and, where possible, on readability). Here, as elsewhere, I have tried to acknowledge the work of writers who contradict my own views; where that is the case I would encourage readers to consider the evidence and form an independent judgement.

1. **Phoebe as *prostatēs*:** Murphy O'Connor, *St Paul's Corinth*, 82–84 offers a full discussion of the Junia Theodora inscription, and Sampley, *Paul in the Greco-Roman World*, 122–26, offers a useful discussion of Phoebe in light of Junia Theodora and other female patrons. On female patrons generally, three older articles are still especially valuable: Nicols, '*Patrona civitatis*'; Taliaferro Boatwright, 'Plancia Magna of Perge'; and Van Bremen, 'Women and Wealth'.

2. Phoebe as **diakonos** (or *diakonon*): In Madigan and Osiek, *Ordained Women in the Early Church*, the authors have collected extensive documentation on the use of the term *diakonos* in early Christian texts and inscriptions; see especially Chapter 2 ('New Testament Texts and their Patristic Commentators').

3. **Junia 'outstanding among the apostles':** For discussion, see Hammer, 'Wealthy Widows and Female Apostles'; Lampe, 'The Roman Christians of Romans 16'; Bauckham, *Gospel Women*, 109–202; and Epp, *Junia: The First Woman Apostle*.

4. **a mechanism similar to compounding interest:** On women as agents of conversion, see MacDonald, 'Was Celsus Right? The Role of Women in the Expansion of Early Christianity'. On applying a modern social network approach to early Christian conversion, see Stark, *The Rise of Christianity*, 5–11. Biblical scholars have cautiously accepted Stark's application of modern social-science methods to the study of

early Christianity; see Klutz, 'The Rhetoric of Science in the Rise of Christianity', and Castelli, 'Gender, Theory and the Rise of Christianity'.

5. **Linen tents and awnings**: Chapter 18 ('Aquila and Prisca') of Lampe, *From Paul to Valentinus*, offers an insightful and lively overview of how the scholarly debate on first-century tent-making can shed light on Paul and his Corinthian friends.

6. **Ancient Judaism was based on a family partnership**: Jewish family under the Roman Empire is a growing area of scholarship; see, for example, Guijarro, Santiago, 'The Family in First-Century Galilee', and Peskowitz, *Spinning Fantasies*. A number of the essays in Hezser, *The Oxford Handbook of Jewish Daily Life in Roman Palestine* are helpful here, especially Hezser, 'Graeco-Roman Daily Life', and Ilan, 'Gender Issues and Daily Life'. This said, it should be remembered that the lives of Greek-speaking Jews in the cities of the Aegean may not have been identical to those of Aramaic-speaking Jews in the villages of Galilee and Judaea.

7. **Lydia . . . traded the rare purple dye**: Spencer, 'Women of "the Cloth" in Acts', 147–49 offers an overview of the scholarly debate about the social status of a purple-seller such as Lydia.

8. **The wife . . . remained part of her father's family**: See Chapter 2, 'Marriage in Roman Law and Society', in Evans Grubbs, *Women and the Law in the Roman Empire*.

Chapter 2: The Gospel of Love

Again, this chapter offers an ancient historian's reading of Paul, rather than a biblical exegete's contribution to the ongoing scholarly conversation in the field of Pauline studies. With this in mind, I have given only limited references to the secondary literature, but it is worth calling attention to a group of studies that may offer a starting-point for further reading. Worth singling out is the work of Margaret Y. MacDonald, whose *Early Christian Women and Pagan Opinion*, *The Pauline Churches*, and 'Reading Real Women through the Undisputed Letters of Paul' are invaluable. Wire, *The Corinthian Women Prophets*, and Martin, *The Corinthian Body*, are illuminating on the disputes involving women at Corinth, while Boyarin, *Paul: A Radical Jew*, and Lieu, *Neither Jew Nor Greek?*, offer a wider view of Paul as a figure formed by both Greek and Jewish cultural traditions.

1. **meat sacrificed to idols**: See Kraemer, 'Food, Eating, and Meals', and Willis, *Idol Meat in Corinth*.

2. **the irritated comment of an early reader**: In the Western manuscripts of 1 Corinthians, verses 34 and 35 appear after verse 40 (instead of after verse 33). This suggests that they may have originated as a gloss made in the margin of the text, and the fact that verse 36 makes better sense following directly after verse 33 than after verse 35

supports the hypothesis. There is also a problem in that the two verses seem to contradict Paul's readiness to acknowledge female prophets in 1 Corinthians 11. See Haines-Eitzen, *The Gendered Palimpsest*, 92, for further discussion.

Chapter 3: The Galilean Women

The suggestions for further reading below focus on understanding where the biblical narrative fits into the world of first-century Roman Galilee and Judaea. Other useful starting-points can be found in the essays collected in Levine, *A Feminist Companion to Luke*, especially Arlandson, 'Lifestyles of the Rich and Christian'; Hezser, *The Oxford Handbook of Jewish Daily Life in Roman Palestine*; and Horsley, *Galilee: History, Politics, People*, especially Chapter 8 ('Village and Family').

1. **the story takes place in her [Martha's] own house**: On the archaeological evidence for households in first-century Palestine, see Meyers, 'The Problems of Gendered Space in Syro-Palestinian Domestic Architecture', and Galor, 'Domestic Architecture'.

2. **the personal papers of an early second-century Jewish heiress**: On the Babatha archive, see Ilan, 'Women's Archives in the Judaean Desert'. On her family relationships, see Kraemer, 'Typical and Atypical Family Dynamics: The Cases of Babatha and Berenice', with H. M. Cotton, 'The Guardianship of Jesus Son of Babatha' on the legal complexity of Babatha's situation. Schwartz, 'Ancient Jewish Social Relations' offers historical context for the unique position of the Jews within the Roman social order. Kehoe, 'Law and Social Formation in the Roman Empire' explores how families often interacted with more than one legal system simultaneously.

3. **'These are the labours that a wife does for her husband'**: Mishnah Ketubot 5. 5, cited in Peskowitz, *Spinning Fantasies*, 97–98.

4. **a doctor called Luke**: A number of New Testament texts refer to Luke. Among the seven undisputed letters of Paul (which include Romans, 1 and 2 Corinthians, Galatians, Philippians, 1 Thessalonians, and Philemon), only Philemon mentions Luke, in a list of 'fellow workers' whose greetings Paul offers in Philemon 1: 21. The Letter to the Colossians, which may be by a later author, offers greetings to 'Luke the beloved doctor' at 4: 14.

5. **As many as 30 per cent of babies were born alive**: Chapter 4 ('Death in Rome') of Hopkins, *Death and Renewal*, discusses how Romans coped with the harsh realities of a high death rate. The study of a fifth-century infant cemetery in Soren, *A Roman Villa*, sheds light on the archaeological sources for infant mortality, with extended discussion of relevant primary and secondary literature at 482–86.

6. **Luke knows that in Galilee . . . economically vulnerable position**: On provision for widows, see Ilan, *Jewish Women in Greco-Roman Palestine*, 149–51.

7. **It is also told by Matthew and Mark:** In Matthew 12: 46–50 and Mark 3: 31–35, Jesus responds to the interruption by saying 'Who are my mother and my brothers?' and then pointed to the disciples.

8. **The Gospel of Mary**: The Manchester Gospel of Mary fragment (Rylands Greek Papyrus 463) is published in Roberts, *Catalogue of Greek and Latin Papyri*, 18–23; the papyrus dates to the early third century, though the text itself may have been written much earlier. I have here used Roberts's somewhat flowery translation. For contrasting views of the date and significance of the Gospel of Mary, and the relationship of the Greek fragment to the longer version preserved in Coptic, see Tuckett, *The Gospel of Mary*, and King, *The Gospel of Mary of Magdala*.

Chapter 4: 'The God of Thecla'

A marvellous study of the second-century battle for Paul's legacy, MacDonald, *The Legend and the Apostle*, offers a good starting-point for those interested in further reading on this topic. MacDonald argues that when the Christian communities began to develop an institutional approach to authority in the second century, they started for the first time to question the older tradition of oral storytelling, dismissing female storytellers as the purveyors of 'old wives' tales'.

This idea has proved controversial. MacDonald, *Early Christian Women and Pagan Opinion*, offers a good introduction to the issues, and Kraemer, *Unreliable Witnesses*, a useful introduction to the scholarly debate. My own view (Cooper, *The Virgin and the Bride*, 56) has been that if these stories do reach back to an early oral tradition, the surviving versions reflect a later process of shaping and pruning by the people who put them into writing. This means that our access to the voice of earlier storytellers is compromised by the layering of other later voices in the text. Some scholars (including the otherwise valuable Kraemer, *Unreliable Witnesses*, 127–33) have taken this to mean that I do not believe that the female storytellers existed, but this is a misunderstanding. The evidence for early storytellers is inconclusive, but listening for their voices is a worthy exercise of the historian's craft. Still, it is important to remember that the aims of the later writers who reinvented their traditions may have differed – sometimes dramatically – from those of the earlier storytellers, and the meanings which their readers and listeners 'read into' the narratives may have been different yet again. For further discussion of this last point, see Cooper, 'The Bride of Christ, the Male Woman, and the Female Reader'.

1. **'Burn the lawless one!'**: *Acts of Paul and Thecla*, 20. Here and below I have given my own translations, adapted from those of R. McL. Wilson, in Hennecke and Schneemelcher, *New Testament Apocrypha*.

2. **'While Paul was speaking in . . . the house of Onesiphorus'**: *Acts of Paul and Thecla*, 7.

3. **'And those who were in the house wept bitterly'**: *Acts of Paul and Thecla*, 7.

4. **second- and third-century romances known as the Apocryphal Acts of the Apostles**: An introduction to this genre, which might be described as the Christian historical novels of the second and third centuries, can be found in Klauck, *The Apocryphal Acts of the Apostles*. See also Cooper, *The Virgin and the Bride*, Chapter 2 ('The Ancient Novel') and Chapter 3 ('"The Bride that is no Bride"'); Konstan, 'Acts of Love', and Calef, 'Thecla Tried and True' on the relationship of the Apocryphal Acts to the pagan novels of antiquity.

5. **a world in which daughters refused to obey their parents**: Osiek, 'The Family in Early Christianity' offers a useful overview of attitudes to the family in the first centuries.

6. **Thecla is condemned to the beasts**: *Acts of Paul and Thecla*, 27; on changing legislation about criminal executions, see Chapter 5, note 11 below.

7. **'The women of the city were greatly amazed'**: *Acts of Paul and Thecla*, 27; 'a certain rich queen, Tryphaena': *Acts of Paul and Thecla*, 27; **a sign on which her accusation, 'guilty of sacrilege', is written**: *Acts of Paul and Thecla*, 28.

8. **'I baptize myself on the last day'**: *Acts of Paul and Thecla*, 34.

9. **'Away with the Christians to the lion!'**: Tertullian of Carthage, *Apology* 40 (tr. Thelwall).

10. **Blandina, however, 'was filled with such power'**: Anonymous, *The Martyrs of Lyons*, 18. Here and below I have cited the translation in Musurillo, *Acts of the Christian Martyrs*.

11. **'Blandina was hung on a post'**: *The Martyrs of Lyon*, 41.

12. **'Tiny, weak, and insignificant as she was'**: *The Martyrs of Lyons*, 42.

13. **'The blessed Blandina was last of all'**: *The Martyrs of Lyons*, 55.

14. **'she no longer perceived what was happening . . . because of her intimacy with Christ'**: *The Martyrs of Lyons*, 56; 'Thus she too was offered in sacrifice': *The Martyrs of Lyons*, 56.

15. **'And she . . . sewed her mantle into a cloak after the fashion of a man'**: *Acts of Paul and Thecla*, 40; **'I have received the washing'**: *Acts of Paul and Thecla*, 40. **'Go, and teach the word of God'**: *Acts of Paul and Thecla*, 41.

16. **Thecla's self-baptism, they claimed, was an example for other women**: Tertullian, *On Baptism*, 17.

17. **The *Didache***: This late first- or early second-century text gives instructions for how local leaders can test visiting prophets to tell whether they are in good faith. An English translation can be found in Staniforth's *Early Christian Writings*.

18. **'We lead him . . . where they gather together to say prayers'**: Justin Martyr, *First Apology*, 65.

19. **'When the president has given thanks'**: Justin Martyr, *First Apology*, 65.

20. **The event described here took place in a domestic setting**: See Burrus and Torjesen, 'Household Management and Women's Authority'; Osiek, MacDonald, and Tulloch, *A Woman's Place*; and Lampe, 'The Language of Equality in Early Christian House Churches'. MacMullen, *The Second Church*; Snyder, *Ante Pacem*; and White, *Building God's House*, offer valuable overviews of the evolution of early Christian meeting spaces.

21. **The New Testament contains a group of letters called the Pastoral Epistles**: See MacDonald, *The Pauline Churches*, Part 3 ('The Pastoral Epistles'). Meeks, *The Writings of St Paul* offers clarification of the status of the different writings attributed to Paul in antiquity.

22. **'Then said Peter, "Is there no one of your family surviving?"'**: Pseudo-Clement, *Recognitions*, 7. 8. On the date and context of the *Recognitions*, see Edwards, 'The Clementina'. My discussion of the *Recognitions* here is based on an earlier scholarly article, Cooper, 'Matthidia's Wish'. Here and below I have cited the translation of Thomas Smith, *The Recognitions of Clement*.

23. **'Being born of noble parents . . .'**: Pseudo-Clement, *Recognitions*, 7.15.

24. **'For she fell in love with her slave . . .'**: Pseudo-Clement, *Recognitions*, 9. 32.

25. **like Thecla, the virgin should seek after Paul**: Anonymous, 'Homily: On virginity' (tr. Shaw), 99–101.

Chapter 5: A Martyr in the Family

The standard English translation of the diary can be found in Musurillo, *Acts of the Christian Martyrs*. (I have used Musurillo's translation below, and have indicated where I have made minor adaptations.) More recently, Bremmer, *The Passions of Perpetua* and Heffernan, *The Passion of Perpetua and Felicity*, have offered their own versions, with useful commentary.

For contrasting views of how the different texts connected with Perpetua's martyrdom relate to each other, see Halporn, 'Literary History and Generic Expectation', and Kraemer and Lander, 'Perpetua and Felicitas' (who argue that the text is not in fact by Perpetua herself). For further discussion of the text and its context, see Shaw, 'The Passion of Perpetua', Salisbury, *Perpetua's Passion*, and Cobb, *Dying to be Men*. My own views, with scholarly documentation, can be found in Cooper, 'The Voice of the Victim', and Cooper, 'A Father, a Daughter, and a Procurator', from which the present chapter has been adapted. On the procurator Hilarianus, see Rives, 'The Piety of a Persecutor'.

1. **a woman who was married to a dissolute husband**: The story is told in Justin Martyr's *Second Apology*, 2, 1–20. Useful discussion of the passage can be found in MacDonald, *Early Christian Women and Pagan Opinion*, 205–13, and Buck, 'The Pagan Husband'.

2. **'Cease, then, being Emperor!'**: The story is told by the early third-century Greek historian Dio Cassius (*Histories*, 69.6.3).

3. **'While we were still under arrest . . .'**: *Passion of the Holy Perpetua and Felicitas*, 3.

4. **'Well, so too I cannot be called anything rather than what I am'**: *Passion of the Holy Perpetua and Felicitas*, 3.

5. **'A few days later we were moved to the prison'**: *Passion of the Holy Perpetua and Felicitas*, 3.

6. **'A few days later there was a rumour that we were going to be given a hearing'**: *Passion of the Holy Perpetua and Felicitas*, 5.

7. **'One day while we were eating breakfast'**: *Passion of the Holy Perpetua and Felicitas*, 6.

8. **'We walked up to the prisoner's dock'**: *Passion of the Holy Perpetua and Felicitas*, 6; **'Then, when it came my turn, my father appeared'**: *Passion of the Holy Perpetua and Felicitas*, 6.

9. **'Hilarianus the procurator'**: *Passion of the Holy Perpetua and Felicitas*, 6 (tr. Musurillo, with minor adaptations).

10. **'When my father insisted on trying to dissuade me'**: *Passion of the Holy Perpetua and Felicitas*, 6 (tr. Musurillo, with minor adaptations); **'I felt sorry for my father, just as if I myself had been beaten'**: *Passion of the Holy Perpetua and Felicitas*, 6 (tr. Musurillo, with minor adaptations).

11. **'Then Hilarianus passed sentence on all of us'**: *Passion of the Holy Perpetua and Felicitas*, 6.

12. **A chilling aspect . . . Hilarianus was permitted to sell condemned criminals to these landowners**: The *Senatusconsultum* of AD 176 or 177 survives only as an inscription (*Corpus Inscriptionum Latinarum* ii. 6278 = Dessau, *Inscriptiones Latinae Selectae* 5163); it is discussed in Frend, *Martyrdom and Persecution in the Early Church*, 5.

13. **'Some days later . . . I realized I was privileged to pray for him'**: *Passion of the Holy Perpetua and Felicitas*, 7.

14. **'That very night I had the following vision'**: *Passion of the Holy Perpetua and Felicitas*, 7; **'there was a great abyss between us'**: *Passion of the Holy Perpetua and Felicitas*, 7; **'where Dinocrates stood, there was a pool full of water'**: *Passion of the Holy Perpetua and Felicitas*, 7.

15. **'I was confident that I could help him in his trouble'**: *Passion of the Holy Perpetua and Felicitas*, 7.

16. **'On the day we were put in chains'**: *Passion of the Holy Perpetua and Felicitas*, 8 (tr. Musurillo, with minor adaptations).

17. **'Then I awoke'**: *Passion of the Holy Perpetua and Felicitas*, 8.

18. **'Now the day of the contest was approaching'**: *Passion of the Holy Perpetua and Felicitas*, 9.

19. **'whenever we are mown down by you, the blood of the Christians is seed'**: Tertullian, *Apology*, 50 (tr. Thelwall).
20. **'The day before we were to fight with the beasts, I saw the following vision'**: *Passion of the Holy Perpetua and Felicitas*, 10.
21. **'I looked at the enormous crowd'**: *Passion of the Holy Perpetua and Felicitas*, 10; **'Then out came an Egyptian to fight against me'**: *Passion of the Holy Perpetua and Felicitas*, 10.
22. **'We drew close together and began to let our fists fly'**: *Passion of the Holy Perpetua and Felicitas*, 10.
23. **'This is what happened up to the day before the contest'**: *Passion of the Holy Perpetua and Felicitas*, 10 (tr. Musurillo, with minor adaptations).

Chapter 6: The Emperor's Mother

Early fourth-century women have not been well served, either by the sources or by modern historians. Valuable exceptions are Drijvers, *Helena Augusta*, and Harries, 'The Empresses' Tale', but from mid-century aristocratic women such as Olympias and Proba begin to come into view, and after that there is a landslide. Kenneth G. Holum, *Theodosian Empresses*, is invaluable on women at court in the latter part of the century, while Brown, 'The Christianization of the Roman Aristocracy', discusses the role of women in the Christianization of the senatorial classes.

1. **'She . . . consecrated to the God whom she adored two shrines'**: Eusebius, Bishop of Caesarea, *Life of Constantine*, 3.43 (tr. Cameron and Hall).
2. **Years later, the Emperor told the story of how a vision had appeared to him**: Eusebius, *Life of Constantine*, 1. 28.
3. **To Christian *sacerdotes* . . . the same protections traditionally accorded to ministers of legitimate religion**: Hunt, 'Christianizing the Roman Empire', with Rapp, *Holy Bishops in Late Antiquity*, 236–39.
4. **'Now, Constantia was herself a princess'**: Anonymous, *Passion of Agnes*, 15. The fifth- or sixth-century *Passion of Agnes* text is not currently available in English, but an introduction to the text can be found in Jones, 'Agnes and Constantia'. The Latin text is available in *Patrologia Latina* 17. 813-21 (= *B.H.L.* 156); the English translations here are from an unpublished translation by Hannah Jones and Carole Hill.
5. **'She was swiftly overcome by a sweet sleep'**: *Passion of Agnes*, 15.
6. **'So then, returning to the palace in the best of health, she gave [great] joy to her father'**: *Passion of Agnes*, 16.
7. **'And his character may well be described as blessed'**: Eusebius, *Life of Constantine* 3. 47.
8. **'it is reported by the pagans . . . repented of his evil deeds'**: Sozomen, *Ecclesiastical History*, 1. 5 (tr. Hartranft).
9. **Some scholars argue . . . public relations tour:** Drawing on the

evidence of the Bordeaux Pilgrim's visit to the Holy Land circa 333, Drijvers, *Helena Augusta*, 64–65, argues that Helena's visit was designed to inspect the progress of her son's building programmes in the region – once he had gained control of it.

10. **ideas of harmonious family life**: Clark and Hatch, *The Golden Bough, The Oaken Cross*, 110–18. For references to the scholarly literature on Proba, see Sivan, 'Anician Women, the Cento of Proba, and Aristocratic Conversion', and Cooper, *The Fall of the Roman Household*, 65–68, which I have drawn on for my discussion of Proba here.

11. **Julian's edict banning Christian teachers**: For a well-informed discussion, see Elm, *Sons of Hellenism, Fathers of the Church*, 139–43.

12. **Her grandfather Ablabius**: On Flavius Ablabius, see Barnes, 'Praetorian Prefects', 250–51.

13. **They did not live to raise their daughter**: See Clark, *Jerome, Chrysostom, and Friends*, 108, and Chausson, 'La famille du préfet Ablabius'.

14. **A second Ablabius:** Bernardi, 'Nouvelles Perspectives', 355; Theodosia: On Theodosia, see Van Dam, *Families and Friends in Late Roman Cappadocia*, 55–57, and Bernardi, 'Nouvelles Perspectives'.

15. **'That I might revive souls parched but still producing green growth'**: The words are from one of Gregory's autobiographical poems, 'Concerning his own life'; cited here are lines 599–600 as translated in White, *Gregory of Nazianzus: Autobiographical Poems*, 55; **church dedicated to the Resurrection**: See Snee, 'Gregory Nazianzen's Anastasia Church', at 157–61.

16. **The new emperor's arrival**: On Theodosius' arrival in Constantinople, see Williams and Friell, *Theodosius*, 52–54.

17. **'a certain Elpidius, a Spaniard'; 'the happy yoke of continence'**: Anonymous, *Life of Olympias*, 3; the translation here and below is drawn from Clark, *Jerome, Chrysostom, and Friends*.

18. **'Then by the divine will she was ordained deacon'**: *Life of Olympias*, 6; note that the Greek has the masculine form, *diakonos*. I have emended Clark's translation to reflect this.

19. **'Olympias . . . chose the kingdom of heaven'**: *Life of Olympias*, 3.

20. **John, a priest of Antioch**: Holum, *Theodosian Empresses*, 57; **'attachment to the dynastic faith'**: Socrates of Constantinople, *Ecclesiastical History* 6. 2. 2–3, cited in Holum, *Theodosian Empresses*, 69.

21. **'Do not ignore Him when he is naked'**: John Chrysostom, *Homily on Matthew*, 50 (Matt 19: 23, 24).

22. **a happy collaboration**: Sozomen, *Ecclesiastical History*, 8. 9, describes the beginning of their relationship, in which the new bishop, John Chrysostom, asks Olympias to devote her resources to supporting the poor.

23. **'For no one from the outside . . . Olympias . . . imitated the women disciples of Christ'**: *Life of Olympias*, 8.

24. **Like Olympias, Eudoxia was an orphan. We first hear of her as a ward in the household of Promotus**: Zosimus, *New History*, 5. 3. 2; Her tutor Pansophius: Sozomen, *Ecclesiastical History* 8. 6. 6. The issues treated in this paragraph are discussed in the brief but excellent article by Mayer, 'Aelia Eudoxia (wife of Arcadius)'.

25. **Eudoxia played an important role in organizing the Nicene counter-processions**: Socrates of Constantinople, *Ecclesiastical History* 6. 8. 1–9 and Sozomen, *Ecclesiastical History*, 8. 8.

26. **'She who wears the diadem'**: This sermon (John Chrysostom, *Homilia secunda cum imperatrix media nocte in magnam ecclesiam venisset*) has not to my knowledge been translated into English; the Greek text can be found at Migne, *Patrologia Graeca (Patrologiae Cursus Completus)* 63, 467–72. It is discussed in Holum, *Theodosian Empresses*, 57; I have used Holum's translation here.

27. **All of the early sources agree that the trigger was a sermon preached by John against the vices of women**: Eudoxia's role in Chrysostom's downfall is discussed in Holum, *Theodosian Empresses*, 73–78. Building on (and in some cases challenging) Holum's source-critical work, I have attempted to untangle the complex evidence: see Cooper, *The Virgin and the Bride*, 17–19.

28. **the head of John the Baptist on a plate**: The reference comes from the fifth-century church historian Socrates of Constantinople, *Ecclesiastical History* 6. 18. 1–5; it is discussed in Holum, *Theodosian Empresses*, 76.

29. **'And she did this not only before the plots . . . up to the end of his life she provided for his expenses'**: *Life of Olympias*, 8.

30. **'But he went into the baptistery, and called Olympias . . .'**: Palladius, *Dialogue on the Life of John Chrysostom*, 10 (tr. Moore).

31. **'A flame appeared'**: Palladius, *Dialogue on the Life of John Chrysostom*, 10 (tr. Moore).

32. **'Great fortitude was evinced in the midst of these calamities'**: Sozomen, *Ecclesiastical History,* 8. 14 (tr. Hartranft).

33. **'It is said that during this journey . . . Basiliscus, the martyr, appeared to him'**: Sozomen, *Ecclesiastical History,* 8. 28 (tr. Hartranft).

34. **Eudoxia, who died in childbirth**: Socrates of Constantinople, *Ecclesiastical History* 6. 19. 4–6, discussed in Holum, *Theodosian Empresses*, 77; **her silver statue**: Holum, *Theodosian Empresses*, 53.

Chapter 7: 'The Life of Angels'

In recent years the *Life of Macrina* has begun to receive welcome scholarly attention. Elm, *Virgins of God*, offers a fascinating discussion of the wider context of fourth-century women's communities, with invaluable discussion of the chronology and significance of developments at Annesi in Chapter 3 ('In the Background: Macrina and Naucratius'). Van Dam, *Families and Friends*, and

Limberis, *Architects of Piety*, chart the wider family 'culture of asceticism' of which Macrina seems to have been the leader, though their focus is often on her celebrated brothers. On Gregory's attempt to account for his sister's life, see Krueger, 'Writing and the Liturgy of Memory'.

1. **'When the due time came for her baby to be delivered'**: Gregory of Nyssa, *Life of Macrina*, 962B. Here and below I have used Lowther Clark's translation. Limberis, *Architects of Piety*, 135–37, discusses Emmelia's devotion to Thecla. Corke-Webster, 'Resisting Arranged Marriage', offers an evocative inquiry into what reading the *Acts of Paul and Thecla* might have meant to the ascetic women of Macrina's circle.

2. **Chastity, the refusal to give undue attention to men other than a legitimate husband, was a social necessity**: Many modern writers misunderstand and mistranslate the ancient terminology for sexual restraint. Like the modern English 'chastity', the Latin *castitas* and Greek *sophrosune* refer to virtues of balance and restraint, not outright rejection of sex. By contrast, 'continence' (Latin *continentia*; Greek *enkrateia*) refers to complete renunciation. For further discussion, see Cooper, 'Chastity'.

3. **Constantine had repealed the laws**: See Evans Grubbs, *Women and the Law*, 103–04, for the sources, and Evans Grubbs, *Law and Family in Late Antiquity*, 103–39, for a full discussion.

4. **'She loved the pure and unstained mode of life'**: Gregory of Nyssa, *Life of Macrina*, 962A.

5. **her friendship with Gregory the Wonder-worker**: A native of Neocaesarea in Pontus, Gregory the Wonder-worker was the most influential of the third-century Christian writers from Asia Minor. Remembering his grandmother Macrina the Elder, Basil of Caesarea mentioned that when he was a child she had told stories of the Wonder-worker, and Gregory of Nyssa wrote a life of him, based on these stories, in the 380s; for discussion, see Limberis, *Architects of Piety*, 45–46 and 133–35.

6. **'this name was used only in secret'**: Gregory of Nyssa, *Life of Macrina*, 962 B/C.

7. **'the education of the child was her mother's task'**: Gregory of Nyssa, *Life of Macrina*, 962C.

8. **'when the flower of youth begins to flourish in particular splendour of beauty'**: Gregory of Nyssa, *Life of Macrina*, 4. (Here I have cited the lively translation given by Elm, *Virgins of God*, 43.)

9. **'But Envy cut off these bright hopes'**: Gregory of Nyssa, *Life of Macrina*, 964C.

10. **'And indeed her determination was more steadfast'**: Gregory of Nyssa, *Life of Macrina*, 964C.

11. **'She maintained that the man who had been joined to her . . . was not dead'**: Gregory of Nyssa, *Life of Macrina*, 964C/D (tr. Lowther Smith, with minor amendments).

12. **Macrina came into an inheritance**: The question of property owner-ship in the relationship between Macrina and Emmelia is important. Elm, *Virgins of God*, 82 (and most other scholars) assume that the estate at Annesi was a 'family estate', but if it was owned by Basil it would have passed to the children – not to Emmelia – on his death.

13. **'she helped her mother to bear the burden of her responsibilities'**: Gregory of Nyssa, *Life of Macrina*, 966A.

14. **Emmelia decided to retire to one of the family estates**: On the womanly household of Macrina and Emmelia, see Elm, *Virgins of God*, 39–51 and 78–105; Rousseau, 'The Pious Household and Virgin Chorus'; and the comparative material in Krawiec, 'From the Womb of the Church'.

15. **'unshattered and unshaken'**: For discussion of this episode in the *Life of Gregory the Wonder-worker*, see Woods, 'Gregory Thaumaturgus and the Earthquake of 344'.

16. **accompanied by Peter and Naucratius**: Elm, *Virgins of God*, 97, argues that Peter remained at Annesi until Macrina's death in 379. In 380–81 he was consecrated Bishop of Sebaste in Armenia, but when he was ordained priest is not known; **Caesarea, where Emmelia's brother was bishop**: see Limberis, *Architects of Piety,* 112.

17. **evidence to suggest that Gregory himself was married**: In the 380s or early 390s, Gregory received a letter of consolation from Gregory of Nazianzus on the death of his 'sister' Theosebeia, who was married to a priest called Gregory; Limberis, *Architects of Piety*, 113 argues that Theosebcia was his wife ('sister' was a customary form of address for wives), but it is also possible that she was a biological sister.

18. **'[Naucratius] excelled the rest in natural endowments and physical beauty'**: Gregory of Nyssa, *Life of Macrina*, 966D; **'He took nothing with him but himself'**: Gregory of Nyssa, *Life of Macrina*, 968A. Silvas, *The Asketikon of Basil the Great*, offers a fascinating insight into the geography of the area around Annesi where Naucratius and Basil established their retreats.

19. **'with his own hands he looked after some old people'**: Gregory of Nyssa, *Life of Macrina*, 968B.

20. **'he also gladly obeyed his mother's wishes'**: Gregory of Nyssa, *Life of Macrina*, 968B/C.

21. **'His mother was . . . three days distant from the scene of the tragedy'**: Gregory of Nyssa, *Life of Macrina*, 968D. On the impact of Naucratius' death for his siblings, see Limberis, *Architects of Piety*, 114–15.

22. **'Facing the disaster in a rational spirit'**: Gregory of Nyssa, *Life of Macrina*, 968D/970A.

23. **In the 350s, she was the patron of a major building project**: On the shrine at Ibora, see Limberis, *Architects of Piety*, 137–40.

24. **saints admonishing a child on behalf of an absent parent**: Limberis, 'Holy Beatings'.

25. **'Weaning her from all accustomed luxuries'**: Gregory of Nyssa, *Life of Macrina*, 970C.
26. **'For no anger or jealousy, no hatred or pride, was observed in their midst'**: Gregory of Nyssa, *Life of Macrina*, 970C.
27. **'living in the body and yet after the likeness of the immaterial beings'**: Gregory of Nyssa, *Life of Macrina*, 972A.
28. **'He was puffed up beyond measure with the pride of oratory'**: Gregory of Nyssa, *Life of Macrina*, 966C.
29. **'Macrina took him in hand'**: Gregory of Nyssa, *Life of Macrina*, 966C.
30. **'Indeed, to tell of his life and the subsequent acts'**: Gregory of Nyssa, *Life of Macrina*, 966C.
31. **'Among these was a lady of gentle birth'**: Gregory of Nyssa, *Life of Macrina*, 988C. For a useful discussion of Macrina's ministry to women whom she found 'wandering along the roads in times of famine' (*Life* 26, tr. Elm), see Elm, *Virgins of God*, 92–95.
32. **'Now, when I had accomplished most of the journey'**: Gregory of Nyssa, *Life of Macrina*, 976A; **'I seemed to be carrying martyrs' relics in my hands'**: Gregory of Nyssa, *Life of Macrina*, 976A/B.
33. **'I could not clearly understand the riddle of the dream'**: Gregory of Nyssa, *Life of Macrina*, 976B.
34. **'The band of virgins . . . modestly waited in the church'**: Gregory of Nyssa, *Life of Macrina*, 976C.
35. **'She was lying not on a bed or couch, but on the floor'**: Gregory of Nyssa, *Life of Macrina*, 976D; **'I ran to her and embraced her prostrate form'**: Gregory of Nyssa, *Life of Macrina*, 978A.
36. **'she discussed the future life'**: Gregory of Nyssa, *Life of Macrina*, 978B. Smith, 'A Just and Reasonable Grief' explores Gregory's account as what might be called 'grief work'. See also Krueger, 'Writing and the Liturgy of Memory', along with Gregory's dialogue, *On the Soul and the Resurrection*, which tries to recapture this conversation.
37. **'Meanwhile evening had come'**: Gregory of Nyssa, *Life of Macrina*, 985/86B.
38. **'When she had finished the thanksgiving'**: Gregory of Nyssa, *Life of Macrina*, 986B.
39. **'Grief like some inward fire'; 'my reason no longer remained'**: Gregory of Nyssa, *Life of Macrina*, 986D.

Chapter 8. A World Apart

An engaging introduction to fourth-century women's asceticism can be found in Cloke, *This Female Man of God*. Brown, *The Body and Society*, incorporates a substantial discussion of women, as well as an excellent chapter on Jerome. Leyerle, 'Pilgrims to the Land', offers a useful introduction to Holy Land pilgrimage.

1. **'Often when a daughter yearns to strive after higher things'**: Anonymous, 'Homily: On virginity', (tr. Shaw), 99–101.
2. **'It was from some priests of Alexandria . . . that Marcella heard'**: Jerome, *Letter* 127 (To Principia), 5. Here and below I have used Fremantle's *St Jerome: Letters and Select Works* for translation of Jerome's letters.
3. **'After the death of his father and mother he was left alone with one little sister'**: Athanasius, *Life of Antony,* 5 (tr. Robertson).
4. **'Pondering over these things'**: *Life of Antony,* 5 (tr. Robertson).
5. **three hundred *arourai***: Rathbone, *Economic Rationalism and Rural Society*, xvi, gives one *aroura* as 2760 square metres, or 52.5356 metres square, so three hundred *arourai* would be not much less than a square kilometre (828,000 square metres).
6. **'I . . . was for avoiding the eyes of high-born ladies'**: Jerome, *Letter* 127 (To Principia), 7; 'as the apostle says': a reference to 2 Timothy 4: 2.
7. **'If all the members of my body were to be converted into tongues'**: *Letter* 108 (to Eustochium), 1.
8. **'Noble in family, she was nobler still in holiness'**: Jerome, *Letter* 108 (to Eustochium), 1 and 3.
9. **'Do you pray? You speak to the Bridegroom'**: Jerome, *Letter* 22 (to Eustochium), 16.
10. **'Do not court the company of married ladies'**: Jerome, *Letter* 22 (to Eustochium), 16.
11. **'Women of the world, you know, plume themselves . . .'**: Jerome, *Letter* 22 (to Eustochium), 16; **'Why do you, then, wrong your husband?'**: Jerome, *Letter* 22 (to Eustochium), 16.
12. **'To see them in their capacious litters'**: Jerome, *Letter* 22 (to Eustochium), 16.
13. **'Their houses are filled with flatterers and with guests'**: Jerome, *Letter* 22 (to Eustochium), 16.
14. **'They, meanwhile, seeing that priests cannot do without them . . .'**: Jerome, *Letter* 22 (to Eustochium), 16.
15. **'Read often . . . learn all that you can'**: Jerome, *Letter* 22 (to Eustochium), 17.
16. **'But now that a virgin has conceived'**: Jerome, *Letter* 22 (to Eustochium), 21.
17. **'And thus the gift of virginity has been bestowed most richly upon women'**: Jerome, *Letter* 22 (to Eustochium), 21; **'As soon as the Son of God set foot upon the earth'**: Jerome, *Letter* 22 (to Eustochium), 21; **'Read the gospel'**: Jerome, *Letter* 22 (to Eustochium), 24.
18. **'In her anxiety to be hospitable. . . '**: Jerome, *Letter* 22 (to Eustochium), 24.
19. **'Be then like Mary'**: Jerome, *Letter* 22 (to Eustochium), 24.

20. **'But do you . . . sit at the Lord's feet'**: Jerome, *Letter* 22 (to Eustochium), 24.

21. **'And he will answer: "my dove . . ."'**: Jerome, *Letter* 22 (to Eustochium), 24.

22. **'Ever let the privacy of your chamber guard you'**: Jerome, *Letter* 22 (to Eustochium), 25.

23. **'Emerge . . . a while from your prison-house'**: Jerome, *Letter* 22 (to Eustochium), 41.

24. **the habits and special vocabulary of their way of life**: Sivan, 'Holy Land Pilgrimage and Western Audiences', 66 (note 45) observes that to Egeria even the word 'ascetic' appears new (*Itinerary* 20.5).

25. **'After having travelled fifteen miles from Hierapolis . . .'**: Egeria, *Itinerary*, 31–32 (tr. Gingras).

26. **Egeria, like Lydia the purple-seller, came from a merchant family**: For an illuminating discussion of the evidence for Egeria's family circumstances, see Sivan, 'Holy Land Pilgrimage and Western Audiences'.

27. **'We came to a certain place'**: Egeria, *Itinerary*, 1 (tr. Gingras).

28. **'Here Moses, the holy man of God'**: Egeria, *Itinerary*, 18 (tr. Gingras).

29. **'We said a second prayer after the reading'**: Egeria, *Itinerary*, 18 (tr. Gingras). See Georgia Frank, *The Memory of the Eyes*, 118–33, on the attempt of pilgrims to make the insights of pilgrimage 'stick'.

30. **'At the holy church there is nothing but countless monastic cells'**: Egeria, *Itinerary*, 23 (tr. Gingras).

31. **'there are many cells all over the hill'**: Egeria, *Itinerary*, 42–43 (tr. Gingras).

32. **'The necessities of a journey'**: Gregory of Nyssa, *On Pilgrimages* (tr. Moore and Wilson). For fuller discussion of Gregory's attitude to pilgrimage, see Bitton-Ashkelony, *Encountering the Sacred*, Chapter 1 ('Basil of Caesarea's and Gregory of Nyssa's Attitudes to Pilgrimage').

33. **'if the Divine grace was more abundant about Jerusalem than elsewhere'**: Gregory of Nyssa, *On Pilgrimages* (tr. Moore and Wilson).

34. **'We derived only this profit from our journey . . .'**: Gregory of Nyssa, *On Pilgrimages* (tr. Moore and Wilson).

35. **'You have seen the place of the Nativity'**: Athanasius, *Letter to Virgins who went to Jerusalem to Pray and Have Returned*, 174.91–95 (tr. Brakke). On the writer's emphasis on seeing in this letter, see Frank, *Memory of the Eyes*, 110–11. A well-informed introduction to scholarship on the letter can be found in Elm, *Virgins of God*, 332–39, with further discussion in Bitton-Ashkelony, *Encountering the Sacred*, 165–68.

36. **'I laid the bodies of my parents next to the relics'**: Gregory of Nyssa, *First Homily on the Forty Martyrs of Sebaste* (tr. Leemans).

37. **waves of visitors travelling to his city**: See Bitton-Ashkelony (*Encountering the Sacred*, 62) on Gregory's strained relationship with the Bishop of Jerusalem.

38. **'As regards the chaste deaconess Severa'**: Evagrius of Pontus, *Letter* 7 (to Rufinus and Melania), tr. Elm, *Virgins of God*, 277.
39. **'teach your sisters and your sons not to take a long journey'**: Evagrius of Pontus, *Letter* 8 (to Melania), tr. Elm, *Virgins of God*, 278.
40. **'not the place [topos] where they have settled but the fashion [*tropos*] of their plan of life'**: Palladius, *Lausiac History*, prologue (tr. Lowther Clarke), cited in Bitton-Ashkelony, *Encountering the Sacred*, 170.
41. **'When Poemenia the servant of God came to interview him'**: Palladius, *Lausiac History*, 35 (tr. Lowther Clarke); see Sivan, 'Holy Land Pilgrimage and Western Audiences', 69 (note 58) for references to Poemenia in other texts.

Chapter 9: The Desert Mothers

Benedicta Ward has published a number of useful source collections from the desert tradition, and many of the texts below are from her *Sayings of the Desert Fathers: The Alphabetical Collection*. In addition to the invaluable Elm, *Virgins of God*, there are now a number of useful studies on the women of the desert; particularly interesting, though focusing on a different group of texts to those discussed here, is Krawiec, *Shenoute and the Women of the White Monastery*. Rousseau, *Pachomius*, and Brakke, *Athanasius and the Politics of Asceticism*, offer valuable background, though their focus is not generally on women. The section on Melania the Younger summarizes my longer article, Cooper, 'The Household and the Desert', which gives full references to the relevant scholarly literature.

1. **'We also visited Oxyrhyncus, a city in the Thebaid'**: *Historia Monachorum in Aegypto*, 5. I have drawn the translation here from Parsons, *City of the Sharp-Nosed Fish*, 193, who offers a fascinating discussion of the Christian community in Oxyrhyncus.
2. **'Then, while she struggled with these and other entreaties . . . the letters of the Apostle'**: *Passion of Eugenia*, 2. For further discussion of how this episode sheds light on ancient female readers, see Cooper, 'The Bride of Christ, the Male Woman, and the Female Reader in Late Antiquity'. The anonymous fifth- or sixth-century *Passion of Eugenia* is not yet available in English; the Latin can be found in Migne, *Patrologia Latina*, 21. 1105–22 (= B.H.L. 2666) and *Patrologia Graeca*, 116. 609–52 (= B.H.G. 608). The reference to Thecla exists only in the Greek family of manuscripts, suggesting that if the reference was original, it was suppressed by the translator, but it has not been established whether the Greek or the Latin was written first. Here I have cited the unpublished translation of Hannah Jones and Carole Hill from the Latin version.
3. **'Perceiving your love of equity, my lord praefect'**: *Petition of Aurelia*

Artemis (John Rylands Library, Greek Papyrus 114). The English translation used here, along with an edition of the Greek, can be found in Johnson, Martin, and Hunt, *Catalogue of Greek Papyri in the John Rylands Library, Manchester,* 2, 99.

4. **'which among [the] daughters is worthy of holiness'**: Anonymous, *Pseudo-Athanasian Canons*, 97 and 98 (tr. Riedel and Crum). Discussed in Elm, *Virgins of God*, 231.

5. **another who was able to sleep standing up**: For example, Rufinus, *Lives of the Fathers* 2.15, told the story of the Abba John, who slept standing on the rare occasions when he slept at all.

6. **'There are many who live in the mountains'**: Ward (ed.), *Sayings of the Desert Fathers: The Alphabetical Collection: Syncletica*, 19. On Syncletica, see also the fifth-century anonymous *Life* translated by Castelli (Elizabeth A. Castelli, 'Pseudo Athanasius: The Life and Activity of the Holy and Blessed Teacher Syncletica', in Wimbush, *Ascetic Behavior in Greco-Roman Antiquity*, 265–311). For the Alphabetical Collection, I have used the translations from Ward, *Sayings of the Desert Fathers* here and below.

7. **'She also said . . . "a treasure that is exposed loses its value"'**: *Alphabetical Collection: Syncletica*, 21.

8. **'Choose the meekness of Moses'**: *Alphabetical Collection: Syncletica*, 11.

9. **She told the following story**: 'A devout man': *Alphabetical Collection: Theodora*, 4.

10. **'The same Amma said that a teacher ought to be a stranger to the desire for domination'**: *Alphabetical Collection: Theodora*, 5.

11. **'She also said that neither asceticism, nor vigils nor any kind of suffering are able to save'**: *Alphabetical Collection: Theodora*, 6.

12. **'If you were a perfect monk, you would not have seen us as women'**: Anonymous saying, cited in Elm, *Virgins of God*, 267.

13. **'Once the spirit of fornication attacked her'**: *Alphabetical Collection: Sarah*, 2.

14. **Another time, two old men, great anchorites, came to the district of Pelusium'**: *Alphabetical Collection: Sarah*, 4.

15. **'She also said to the brothers, "It is I who am a man, you who are women"'**: *Alphabetical Collection: Sarah*, 9.

16. **'If I prayed God that all men should approve my conduct'**: *Alphabetical Collection: Sarah*, 5.

17. **'The old man said to me, "Come, brother, let us take the body"'**: *Alphabetical Collection: Bessarion*, 4.

18. **'At one time when Abba Arsenius was living in Canopus'**: *Alphabetical Collection: Arsenius*, 28.

19. **'But with indignation did he raise her up'**: *Alphabetical Collection: Arsenius*, 28.

20. **'And hearing this, she went away troubled'**: *Alphabetical Collection: Arsenius*, 28.

21. **The . . . *Life of Melania the Younger* seems to have been written

by a monk from the ascetic entourage: The author has been identified tentatively as the priest Gerontius. I do not find the attribution persuasive; for discussion, see Cooper, 'The Household and the Desert', 13–15.

22. **'This blessed Melania, then, was foremost among the Romans'**: Gerontius, *Life of Melania*, 1. Here and below I cite Clark's translation of *The Life of Melania*.

23. **the share of piety**: Discussion of the legal arrangements can be found in Cooper, 'The Household and the Desert', 21–23.

24. **Melania had only one brother**: When Publicola (the brother) died, she founded a monastery in his honour in Jerusalem (*Life of Melania*, 49).

25. **'They heard these words with much joy'**: *Life of Melania*, 7.

26. **Palladius tells us that she offered freedom to her slaves**: Palladius, *Lausiac History*, 61. Discussed in Harper, *Slavery in the Late Roman World*, 193, and Cooper, *The Fall of the Roman Household*, 116–17.

Chapter 10: The Queen of Heaven

This chapter is a narrative treatment of themes discussed in three previously published scholarly arguments: Cooper, 'Contesting the Nativity', Cooper, 'Empress and *Theotokos*', and Cooper, '"Only virgins can give birth to Christ"'. These articles offer further detail and documentation for many of the points made here; the first two assess the date and bias of the ancient sources which suggest that imperial women played an important role in developing the cult of Mary as *Theotokos*, while the latter explores the theological issues at stake in the controversy. Holum, *Theodosian Empresses*, and Limberis, *Divine Heiress*, offer lively and fascinating further reading on the themes treated here.

1. **'Stretching out her hands, she prayed thus to the Lord'**: Anonymous, *Passio Sanctorum Gallicani Hilarinini*, in Mombritius, *Sanctuarium* I, 570; I am not aware of a published English translation of this text.

2. **the prayer of Constantia, daughter of Constantine the Great**: Constantine's daughter was actually called Constantina, while he had a sister and niece called Constantia, but the two names are often confused in the ancient sources; see Jones, Martindale, and Morris, *Prosopography of the Later Roman Empire* I, s.v. 'Constantina 2', 222. Jill Harries, 'The Empresses' Tale, AD 300–360', offers a fresh perspective on the women of Constantine's family.

3. **Later, stories circulated that one usurper . . . had penetrated the palace as far as Theodosius' bedroom**: Damascius, *Life of Isidore*, fragment 303, discussed in Holum, *Theodosian Empresses*, 82; **the**

contemporary historian Sozomen expressed astonishment that the boy survived to adulthood: Sozomen, *Ecclesiastical History*, 9. 6. 1.

4. **'Through Mary all women are blessed'**: Atticus of Constantinople, *Homily on the Mother of God*, tr. in Holum, *Theodosian Empresses*, 141. Until the 1930s, this sermon was believed to be a sermon of Proclus of Constantinople; this is why Holum cites a nineteenth-century edition of Proclus, along with the work of Lebon and Brière, who argued for the attribution to Atticus, among his sources for the text.

5. **the 'matronage' tradition**: Brubaker, 'Memories of Helena', with Clark, 'Patrons, not Priests', and Harrison, *A Temple for Byzantium*; **'the place where the *Theotokos* gave birth'**: Socrates of Constantinople, *Ecclesiastical History* 7. 32 (tr. Zenos). Socrates is citing Eusebius' *Life of Constantine* 3.43; the Eusebius passage itself can be found at the beginning of this chapter in Cameron and Hall's translation.

6. **'And in fact Emmanuel submitted to be born for our sake'**: Socrates of Constantinople, *Ecclesiastical History* 7. 32 (tr. Zenos). Socrates is citing Eusebius' *Life of Constantine* 3.43.

7. **A strong popular following was attached to the cult of Mary**: See Herrin, 'Women and the Faith in Icons'.

8. **'Nestorius had an associate whom he had brought from Antioch'**: Socrates of Constantinople, *Ecclesiastical History*, 7. 32 (tr. Zenos).

9. **'While great offence was taken in the church . . .'**: Socrates of Constantinople, *Ecclesiastical History*, 7. 32 (tr. Zenos).

10. **the historical Jesus, born from the line of David**: Young, From Nicaea to Chalcedon, 196: Diodore of Tarsus, for example, was accused of asserting that they were not; **'Has God a mother?'**: Nestorius, *First sermon*, in Loofs, *Nestoriana*, 252: discussed in Holum, *Theodosian Empresses*, 155.

11. **'It was the Logos who was incarnate'**: Young, *From Nicaea to Chalcedon*, 217; **'the suffering of my God'**: Ignatius, *Letter to the Ephesians* 18. 2, discussed in Young, *From Nicaea to Chalcedon*, 217; **'God . . . conceived of Mary'**: Ignatius, *Letter to the Romans* 6. 3, discussed in Young, *From Nicaea to Chalcedon*, 217.

12. **'The virgin's festival . . . summons us today to words of praise'**: Proclus, *Homily 1 (On the Holy Virgin Theotokos, Delivered while Nestorius was seated in the Great Church of Constantinople)*, 1 (tr. Constas, with my revision), discussed in Holum, *Theodosian Empresses*, 155–57.

13. **'She who called us here today is the holy Mary'**: Proclus, *Homily 1*, 1 (tr. Constas), discussed in Limberis, *Divine Heiress*, 86–89.

14. **'Let women come running'**: Proclus, *Homily* 4, 2 (tr. Constas).

15. **'But this ancient city won some divine protection for itself despite the impiety of the age'**: Zosimus, *New History*, 5.6.1 (tr. Ridley, with minor emendation).

16. **'Hail, full of grace!'**: For discussion of the attribution to Proclus of

this homily, see Limberis, *Divine Heiress*, 89, note 149; the translation here is from Limberis, 88–89.

17. **'Let me enter according to my custom!'**: Anonymous, *Letter to Cosmas*, 8, tr. Cooper, 'Contesting the Nativity', 31; see discussion in Holum, *Theodosian Empresses*, 153.

18. **'He [Cyril] worked on the sister of the Emperor, Pulcheria'**: Barhadbeshabba Arbaia, *Ecclesiastical History*, 27, tr. Cooper, 'Contesting the Nativity', 34; discussed in Holum, *Theodosian Empresses*, 163.

19. **'You have . . . with you against me a contentious woman, a princess'**: Nestorius, *Bazaar of Heraclides*, 1. 3 (tr. Driver and Hodgson).

20. **'She resented Nestorius'**: Barhadbeshabba Arbaia, *Ecclesiastical History*, 27, tr. Cooper, 'Contesting the Nativity', 34; discussed in Holum, *Theodosian Empresses*, 163.

21. **'Many years to Pulcheria!'**: *Coptic Acts of the Council of Ephesus*, tr. Holum, *Theodosian Empresses*, 170.

22. **'born from the Virgin Mary, the Theotokos'**: I have cited the Chalcedonian Formula of Reunion here as it is given in Stevenson and Frend (eds), *Creeds, Councils and Controversies*, 353. Price and Gaddis, *The Acts of the Council of Chalcedon*, offer an English translation and valuable commentary on the relevant documents.

23. **'Marcian is the new Constantine, Pulcheria the new Helena!'**: *Acts of Chalcedon*, tr. Holum, *Theodosian Empresses*, 216.

24. **'By showing reverence here to the *Theotokos*, they secured their reign (*basileia*)'**: Leo and Verina's piety for Pulcheria's memory, and for Mary, is discussed in Holum, *Theodosian Empresses*, 227.

25. **'Hail! O unshakeable tower of the Church'**: Anonymous, *Akathistos Hymn*, 23, tr. Limberis, *Divine Heiress*, 158.

Bibliography

Primary Sources

Part I: Texts

(Where the translation cited is a chapter in one of the source collections listed below, only the editor and short title have been cited.)

Ambrose of Milan, *On Virginity*, tr. H. de Romestin, in Schaff and Wace, *A Select Library of Nicene and Post-Nicene Fathers*, Series 2, vol. 10

Anonymous, *The Acts of Paul and Thecla*, tr. Wilson, in Hennecke and Schneemelcher, *New Testament Apocrypha*

Anonymous, *Akathistos Hymn*, tr. Limberis, vol. 2 'Appendix: Akathistos Hymn', in Limberis, *Divine Heiress*, 149–58

Anonymous, *The Chalcedonian Definition*, tr. Bindley, in James Stevenson and W. H. C. Frend (eds), *Creeds,Councils, and Controversies: Documents Illustrating the History of the Church AD 337–461*, 2nd rev. edn (London: SPCK, 1989), 350–54

Anonymous, *The Didache*, tr. Staniforth, in Staniforth and Louth, *Early Christian Writings: the Apostolic Fathers*

Anonymous, *The Gospel of Thomas*, tr. Helmut Koester and Thomas O. Lambdin, in Robinson, *Nag Hammadi Library in English*. Also tr. Layton, *The Gnostic Scriptures*

Anonymous ('Pseudo-Athanasius'), *Homily on Virginity*, tr. Teresa M. Shaw, 'Homily: On Virginity', in Wimbush (ed.), *Ascetic Behavior in Greco-Roman Antiquity*, 29–44

Anonymous, *The Life of Olympias*, in Clark, *Jerome, Chrysostom, and Friends*, 129–42

Anonymous ('Pseudo-Athanasius'), *Life of Syncletica*, tr. Elisabeth Castelli, 'Pseudo Athanasius: The Life and Activity of the Holy and Blessed Teacher Syncletica' in Wimbush (ed.), *Ascetic Behavior in Greco-Roman Antiquity*, 265–311

Anonymous, *The Martyrs of Lyons*, in Musurillo, *Acts of the Early Christian Martyrs*

Anonymous, *The Passion of the Holy Perpetua and Felicitas*, tr. Musurillo, *Acts of the Christian Martyrs*. Also tr. Joseph P. Farrell and Craig Williams in Bremmer and Fornisaro, *The Passions of Perpetua*; Thomas Heffernan, in *idem*, *The Passion of Perpetua and Felicity*; and Allan Menzies, in Roberts and Donaldson, *Ante-Nicene Fathers*, vol. 3

Anonymous ('Pseudo-James'), *Protevangelium of James*, tr. Oscar Cullmann and A. J. B. Higgins, in Hennecke and Schneemelcher, *New Testament Apocrypha*, vol. 1

Anonymous ('Pseudo-Athanasius'), *Pseudo-Athanasian Canons*, in Wilhelm Riedel and W. E. Crum (ed. & tr.), *The Canons of Athanasius of Alexandria* (London: Williams and Norgate, 1904; repr. Amsterdam: Philo Press, 1973)

Anonymous ('Pseudo-Clement'), *The Recognitions of Clement*, tr. Thomas Smith, in Roberts and Donaldson, *Ante-Nicene Fathers*, vol. 8

Athanasius, *Letter to Virgins who went to Jerusalem to Pray and Have Returned*, tr. Brakke, Appendix B: 'Second Letter to Virgins', in Brakke, *Athanasius and the Politics of Asceticism*, 292–302

Athanasius, *The Life of Antony and the Letter to Marcellinus*, tr. Robert C. Gregg (London: SPCK and Mahwah, NJ: Paulist Press, 1980). Also tr. Archibald Robertson, in Schaff and Wace, *A Select Library of Nicene and Post-Nicene Fathers*, Series 2, vol. 4; and tr. White, in White, *Early Christian Lives*

Dio Cassius, *Roman History* vol. 7, Books 56–60, tr. Earnest Cary and Herbert B. Foster (Cambridge: Harvard University Press, and London: Heinemann, 1924)

Egeria, *Itinerary*, tr. John Wilkinson as *Egeria's Travels* (London: SPCK, 1971; 3rd edn, Warminster, 1999). Also tr. George E. Gingras as *Egeria: Diary of a Pilgrimage* (New York and Ramsey, NJ: Newman Press, 1970)

Eusebius of Caesarea, *Life of Constantine*, tr. Averil Cameron and Stuart Hall (Oxford: Clarendon Press, 1999). Also tr. Arthur Cushman McGiffert and Ernest Cushing Richardson, in Schaff and Wace, *A Select Library of Nicene and Post-Nicene Fathers*, Series 2, vol. 1

— *Ecclesiastical History*, tr. Arthur Cushman McGiffert and Ernest Cushing Richardson, in Schaff and Wace, *A Select Library of Nicene and Post-Nicene Fathers*, Series 2, vol. 1

Gerontius, *The Life of Melania*, in Elizabeth A. Clark, *The Life of Melania, the Younger: Introduction, Translation, and Commentary* (Lewiston, NY: Edwin Mellen Press, 1984)

Gregory of Nazianzus, *Autobiographical Poems*, ed. & tr. Carolinne White (Cambridge: Cambridge University Press, 2005)

Gregory of Nyssa, *First Homily on the Forty Martyrs of Sebaste*, tr. Johan Leemans, in Johan Leemans, Wendy Mayer, Pauline Allen, and Boudewijn Dehandschutter (eds), *'Let Us Die that We May Live': Greek Homilies on Christian Martyrs from Asia, Palestine, and Syria* (London: Routledge, 2003), 91–110

—— *Life of Macrina*, tr. W. K. Lowther Clarke, *The Life of St. Macrina* (London: SPCK, 1916). See also Virgina Woods Callaghan (tr.), in *St. Gregory of Nyssa: Ascetical Works*, Fathers of the Church 58 (Washington DC: 1967), 159–191, and Kevin Corrigan (tr.), *The Life of Saint Macrina* (Eugene, Oregon: Wipf & Stock, 2001)

—— *On Pilgrimages*, tr. William Moore and Henry Austin Wilson, in Schaff and Wace, *A Select Library of Nicene and Post-Nicene Fathers*, Series 2, vol. 5

—— *On the Soul and the Resurrection*, tr. Catharine P. Roth (Crestwood, NY: St Vladimir's Seminary Press, 2002); see also William Moore and Henry Austin

Wilson (tr.), in Schaff and Wace, *Nicene and Post-Nicene Fathers*, Series 2, vol. 5

—— *On Virginity*, tr. William Moore, in Schaff and Wace, *A Select Library of Nicene and Post-Nicene Fathers*, Series 2, vol. 5

Jerome, *Letters and Select Works*, tr. W. H. Fremantle, in Schaff and Wace, *A Select Library of Nicene and Post-Nicene Fathers*, Series 2, vol. 6

Justin Martyr, *First Apology* and *Second Apology*, tr. Roberts and Donaldson, in Roberts and Donaldson (eds), *Ante-Nicene Fathers*, vol. 1. See also Thomas B. Falls (tr.), *Saint Justin Martyr* (Washington, DC: Catholic University of America Press, 1948, repr. 1965)

Nestorius, *Bazaar of Heraclides*, tr. Godfrey Rolles Driver and Leonard Hodgson (Oxford: Clarendon Press, 1925)

Palladius, *Dialogue on John Chrysostom*, tr. Herbert Moore, *The Dialogue of Palladius concerning the Life of John Chrysostom* (New York: SPCK, 1921)

—— *Lausiac History*, tr. W. K. Lowther Clarke (London: SPCK, and NY: Macmillan, 1918)

Proba, *Cento*, tr. Elizabeth A. Clark and Diane F. Hatch, *The Golden Bough, the Oaken Cross: The Virgilian Cento of Faltonia Betitia Proba* (Chico, CA: Scholars Press, 1981)

Socrates Scholasticus, *Ecclesiastical History*, tr. A. C. Zenos, in Schaff and Wace (eds), *A Select Library of Nicene and Post-Nicene Fathers*, Series 2, vol. 2

Sozomen, *Ecclesiastical History*, tr. Chester D. Hartranft, in Schaff and Wace, *A Select Library of Nicene and Post-Nicene Fathers*, Series 2, vol. 2

Tertullian of Carthage, *On Baptism*, tr. Allan Menzies, in Roberts and Donaldson (eds), *Ante-Nicene Fathers*, vol. 3

Zosimus, *New History*, tr. Ronald T. Ridley (Sydney: Australian Association for Byzantine Studies, 1982). Also tr. James J. Buchanan and Harold T. Davis, *Zosimus: Historia nova: the decline of Rome* (San Antonio, TX: Trinity University Press, 1967)

Part II: Papyri Cited

John Rylands Library, Manchester, Greek Papyrus 114: Petition of Aurelia Artemis, *c.* 280 CE. In *Catalogue of Greek Papyri in the John Rylands Library, Manchester*, vol. 2, Documents of the Ptolemaic and Roman Period (Nos 62–456), edited by J. De M. Johnson, Victor Martin, and Arthur S. Hunt (Manchester: Manchester University Press, 1911)

John Rylands Library, Manchester, Greek Papyrus 463: Gospel of Mary, Early Third Century CE. In *Catalogue of Greek and Latin Papyri in the John Rylands Library, Manchester*, Vol. 3, *Theological and Literary Texts* (Nos 457–551), edited by C. H. Roberts (Manchester, 1938), 18–23

Part III: Source Collections

Chadwick, Owen (ed.), *Western Asceticism*, Library of Christian Classics (Louisville, KY: Westminster John Knox Press, 1979)

Clark, Elizabeth A. (ed.), *Women in the Early Church* (Wilmington, MA: Michael Glazier, 1983). Contains carefully selected short extracts from a wide variety of sources, including many of those discussed in this book.

Croke, Brian, and Jill Harries (eds), *Religious Conflict in Fourth-Century Rome*, Sources in Ancient History (Sydney: Sydney University Press, 1982)

Ehrmann, Bart D., and Andrew S. Jacobs, *Christianity in Late Antiquity, 300–450 A.D.: A Reader* (New York: Oxford University Press, 2004). Includes extracts from a number of the later texts discussed in this book.

Evans Grubbs, Judith, *Women and the Law in the Roman Empire: A Sourcebook on Marriage, Divorce and Widowhood* (New York and London: Routledge, 2002)

Hennecke, Edgar, and Wilhelm Schneemelcher (eds), *New Testament Apocrypha* rev. edn (by Schneemelcher & Wilson), tr. R. McL. Wilson, vol. 1: *Gospels and Related Writings* (Cambridge: James Clarke, 1991); vol. 2: *Writings Related to the Apostles; Apocalypses and Related Subjects* (Cambridge: James Clarke, 1991)

Hunter, David G., *Marriage in the Early Church* (Minneapolis: Fortress Press, 1992)

Kraemer, Ross Shepard (ed.), *Women's Religions in the Greco-Roman World: A Sourcebook* (New York: Oxford University Press, rev. edn 2004). Originally entitled *Maenads, Martyrs, Matrons, Monastics: A Sourcebook on Women's Religions in the Greco-Roman World*, this exhaustive collection includes extracts of a variety of text types (narrative and documentary texts relating to women from across the ancient Mediterranean), including many of those discussed here.

Layton, Bentley (ed.), *The Gnostic Scriptures: A New Translation* (London: SCM, 1987)

Maas, Michael (ed.), *Readings in Late Antiquity: A sourcebook* (London and New York: Routledge, 2000; 2nd edn, 2010)

Madigan, Kevin, and Carolyn Osiek (eds), *Ordained Women in the Early Church: A Documentary History* (Baltimore: The John Hopkins University Press, 2005)

Meeks, Wayne A., and John T. Fitzgerald (eds), *The Writings of St. Paul: Annotated Texts, Reception and Criticism*, 2nd edn (New York: Norton, 2007). A sure-footed guide to the scholarly consensus on the letters of Paul and his followers.

Miller, Patricia Cox, *Women in Early Christianity: Translations from Greek Texts* (Washington, DC: Catholic University of America Press, 2005). A complete and carefully selected collection of extracts, with a valuable introduction.

Musurillo, Herbert (ed. & tr.), *Acts of the Christian Martyrs* (Oxford: Clarendon Press, 1972)

Petersen, Joan M. (ed. & tr.), *Handmaids of the Lord: Contemporary Descriptions of Feminine Asceticism in the First Six Christian Centuries* (Kalamazoo, MI: Cistercian Publications, 1996). Contains the *Life of Macrina*, the *Life of Melania*, and a number of letters from the circle of Jerome.

Petroff, Elizabeth Alvida (ed.), *Medieval Women's Visionary Literature* (New York: Oxford University Press, 1986). Includes the *Passion of Perpetua* and the *Life of Macrina* alongside a rich tradition of later women writers, many of whom, such as the tenth-century nun Hrotsvit of Gandersheim, were inspired by the women of the early Church.

Roberts, Alexander and Donaldson, James (eds), revised by A. Cleveland Coxe, *Ante-Nicene Fathers: Translations of the writings of the fathers down to A.D. 325*, 9 vols (1951–82); the first edition is available online at http://www.ccel.org

Robinson, James M. (ed.), *The Nag Hammadi Library in English*, 3rd rev. edn (San Francisco: Harper & Row, 1988)

Schaff, Philip, and Henry Wace (eds), *A Select Library of Nicene and Post-Nicene Fathers of the Christian Church* (New York: Christian Literature Company, and Oxford: Parker & Company, 1886–1900 and later editions); the first edition is available online at http://www.ccel.org

Staniforth, Maxwell (ed. & tr.) and Andrew Louth (rev. edn), *Early Christian Writings: the Apostolic Fathers* (Harmondsworth: Penguin Books, 1987)

Stevenson, J., and W. H. C. Frend (eds), *Creeds, Councils and Controversies: Documents Illustrating the History of the Church AD 337–461*, rev. edn (London: SPCK, 1989)

Thiébaux, Marcelle (ed. & tr.), *The Writings of Medieval Women: An Anthology*, 2nd edn (New York & London: Garland, 1994). Includes the *Passion of Perpetua* and the *Travels of Egeria*, along with the cento composed by Pulcheria's sister-in-law, the Empress Eudokia, who lived from *c.* 400 to 460.

Ward, Benedicta (ed.), *The Sayings of the Desert Fathers: The Alphabetical Collection* (Kalamazoo, MI: Cistercian Publications, 1975; rev. edn, 1984) White, Carolinne (ed. & tr.), *Early Christian Lives* (Harmondsworth: Penguin, 1998). Lives of early male saints, including the *Life of Antony*, who influenced fourth- and fifth-century ascetic women.

—— (ed. & tr.), *Lives of Roman Christian Women* (Harmondsworth: Penguin Books, 2010)

Wilson-Kastner, Patricia, *A Lost Tradition: Women Writers of the Early Church* (Washington, DC: University Press of America, 1981). Includes translations of Perpetua, Proba, Egeria, and Eudokia.

Wimbush, Vincent (ed.), *Ascetic Behavior in Greco-Roman Antiquity* (Minneapolis, MN: Fortress Press, 1990). An excellent collection of previously untranslated texts, many of them about women, with high-quality introductions.

Secondary Sources

Adkin, N., *Jerome on Virginity: A commentary on the Libellus de virginitate servanda (Letter 22)* (Cambridge, 2003)

Alexandre, Monique, 'Early Christian Women', in Georges Duby and Michelle Perrot (eds), *A History of Women in the West* (Cambridge, MA: Harvard University Press, 1992), 409–44

Archer, L., *Her Price is Beyond Rubies: The Jewish Woman in Graeco-Roman Palestine* (Sheffield, 1990)

—— 'The Role of Jewish Women in the Religion, Ritual, and Cult of

Graeco-Roman Palestine', in A. Cameron and A. Kuhrt (eds), *Images of Women in Antiquity* (Detroit, 1993), 273–87

Archer, Leonie J., Susan Fischler, and Maria Wyke, *Women in Ancient Societies: An Illusion of the Night* (London: Routledge, 1994)

Arlandson, James M., 'Lifestyles of the Rich and Christian: Women, Wealth, and Social Freedom', in Amy-Jill Levine and Marianne Blickenstaff (eds), *A Feminist Companion to the Acts of the Apostles* (London: T. & T. Clark, 2004), 155–70

—— *Women, class, and society in early Christianity: models from Luke-Acts* (Peabody, MA: Hendrickson, 1997)

Aubin, Melissa, 'Reversing Romance? The Acts of Thecla and the Ancient Novel', in Ronald F. Hock, J. Bradley Chance, and Judith Perkins (eds), *Ancient Fiction and Early Christian Narrative* (Atlanta, GA: Scholars Press, 2003), 257–72

Bakker, J. T., *Living and Working with the Gods: Studies of Evidence for Private Religion and its Material Environment, in the City of Ostia (100–500 A.D.)* (Amsterdam: Gieben, 1994); (Review: D. S. Levine, *Journal of Roman Studies* 87 [1997], 300–01)

Balch, David L., 'The Apologetic Use of the Subordination Ethic by Minority Religious Communities in Roman Society', in David L. Balch, *Let Wives Be Submissive: The Domestic Code in 1 Peter* (Atlanta, GA: Scholars Press, 1981)

—— and Carolyn Osiek (eds), *Early Christian Families in Context: an interdisciplinary dialogue* (Grand Rapids, MI: W. B. Eerdmans, 2003)

—— and Carolyn Osiek (eds), *Families in the New Testament World: Households and House Churches* (Louisville, KY: Westminster John Knox, 1977)

Barnes, Timothy, *Constantine and Eusebius* (Cambridge, MA: Harvard University Press, 1981)

—— 'Pagan Perceptions of Christianity', in Ian Hazlitt (ed.), *Early Christianity: Origins and Evolution to AD 600* (Nashville, TN: Abingdon Press, 1991), 231–43

—— 'Praetorian Prefects, 337–361', *Zeitschrift für Papyrologie und Epigraphik* 94 (1992), 249–60

Bassler, Jouette M., 'The Widows' Tale: A Fresh Look at 1 Tim 5: 3–16', *Journal of Biblical Literature* 103 (1984), 23–41

—— *1 Timothy, 2 Timothy, Titus* (Nashville, TN: Abingdon Press, 1996)

Bauckham, R., *Gospel Women: Studies of the Named Women of the Gospels* (Grand Rapids, MI: W. B. Eerdmans, 2002)

Bauer, Walter, *Orthodoxy and Heresy in Earliest Christianity* (London: S.C.M. Press, 1972)

Becker, Adam H., 'Christian Society', in Michael Peachin (ed.), *The Oxford Handbook of Social Relations in the Roman World*. Oxford Handbooks in Classics and Ancient History (Oxford and New York: Oxford University Press, 2011), 567–86

Bernardi, Jean, 'Nouvelles Perspectives sur la Famille de Gregoire de Nazianze' *Vigiliae Christianae* 38 (1984), 352–59

Bitton-Ashkelony, Brouria, *Encountering the Sacred: The Debate on Christian Pilgrimage in Late Antiquity* (Berkeley and Los Angeles, CA: The University of California Press, 2005)

Boatwright, Mary Taliaferro, 'Plancia Magna of Perge: Women's Role and Status in Roman Asia Minor', in S. B. Pomeroy (ed.), *Women's History and Ancient History* (Chapel Hill, NC: The University of North Carolina Press, 1991), 249–72

Bowes, Kim, 'Early Christian Archaeology: A State of the Field', *Religion Compass* 2/4 (2008), 575–619

—— 'Personal Devotions and Private Chapels', in Virginia Burrus (ed.), *A People's History of Christianity, Volume 2: Late Ancient Christianity* (Minneapolis, MN: Fortress Press, 2005), 188–210

—— *Private Worship, Public Values, and Religious Change in Late Antiquity* (Cambridge: Cambridge University Press, 2008)

Bowie, Ewen, 'The Readership of Greek Novels in the Ancient World', in James Tatum (ed.), *The Search for the Ancient Novel* (Baltimore, MD: Johns Hopkins University Press, 1994), 435–95

Boyarin, Daniel, 'Martyrdom and the Making of Christianity and Judaism', *Journal of Early Christian Studies* 6.4 (1998), 577–627

—— *A Radical Jew: Paul and the Politics of Identity* (Berkeley and Los Angeles, CA: University of California Press, 1994)

—— 'Thinking with Virgins: Engendering Judaeo-Christian Difference', in Amy-Jill Levine and Maria Mayo Robbins (eds), *A Feminist Companion to the New Testament Apocrypha* (Cleveland, OH: Pilgrim, 2006), 216–44

Brakke, David, *Athanasius and the Politics of Asceticism* (Oxford: Oxford University Press, 1995); (Review: Joseph W. Trigg, *Church History* 66 [1997], 308–10)

—— 'The Lady Appears: Materialization of Woman in Early Monastic Literature', *Journal of Medieval and Early Modern Studies* 33.3 (2003), 387–402.

Bremmer, Jan N., 'Magic, Martyrdom and Women's Liberation in the Acts of Paul and Thecla', in Jan N. Bremmer (ed.), *The Apocryphal Acts of Paul and Thecla* (Kampen, Netherlands: Kok Pharos, 1996), 36–59

—— 'Why Did Early Christianity Attract Upper-Class Women?', in *Fructus centesimus: mélanges offerts à Gerard J. M. Bartelink à l'occasion de son soixante-cinquièmeanniversaire* (Steenbrugis–Dordrecht, 1989), 117–34.

—— and Marco Formisano (ed.), *Perpetua's Passions: Multidisciplinary Approaches to the PassioPerpetuaeetFelicitatis*, with text and tr. by Joseph Farrell and Craig Williams (New York: Oxford University Press, 2012); (Review: L. Stephanie Cobb, *Bryn Mawr Classical Review*, 2012.12.16)

Brooten, Bernadette J., 'Early Christian Women and their Cultural Context: Issues of Method in Historical Reconstruction', in Adela Yarbro Collins (ed.), *Feminist Perspectives on Biblical Scholarship* (Chico, CA: Scholars Press, 1985), 65–91

—— *Women Leaders in the Ancient Synagogue. Inscriptional Evidence and Background Issues* (Chico, CA, 1982)

Brown, Peter, *The Body and Society: Men, Women, and Sexual Renunciation in Late Antiquity* (New York: Columbia University Press, 1988)

—— (publishing as P. R. L. Brown), 'Christianization of the Roman Aristocracy' Aspects of the Christianization of the Roman Aristocracy', *Journal of Roman Studies* 51 (1961), 1–11

Brubaker, Leslie, 'Memories of Helena: Patterns of Imperial Female Matronage in the Fourth and Fifth Centuries', in Liz James (ed.), *Women, Men and Eunuchs: Gender in Byzantium* (London and New York: Routledge, 1997), 52–75

Buck, P. Lorraine, 'The Pagan Husband in Justin, *2 Apology* 2: 1–20', *Journal of Theological Studies* 53 (2002), 541–46

Burrus, Virginia, 'Reading Agnes: The Rhetoric of Gender in Ambrose and Prudentius', *Journal of Early Christian Studies* 3 (1995), 25–46

—— 'Word and Flesh: The Bodies and Sexuality of Ascetic Women in Christian Antiquity', *Journal of Feminist Studies in Religion* 10.1 (1994), 27–51

—— and Karen-Jo Torjesen, 'Afterword to "Household Management and Women's Authority"', in Amy-Jill Levine and Marianne Blickenstaff, *A Feminist Companion to the Acts of the Apostles* (London: T. & T. Clark, 2004), 171–76

— and Karen-Jo Torjesen, 'Household Management and Women's Authority', in *When Women Were Priests: Women's Leadership in the Early Church and the Scandal of their Subordination in the Rise of Christianity* (San Francisco, CA: Harper Collins, 1993), 53–87

Bynum, Caroline Walker, *The Resurrection of the Body in Western Christianity, 200–1336* (New York: Columbia University Press, 1995)

Calef, Susan A., 'Thecla "Tried and True" and the Inversion of Romance', in Amy-Jill Levine (ed.), *A Feminist Companion to the New Testament Apocrypha* (London: T. & T. Clark, 2006), 163–85

Cameron, Averil, *Christianity and the Rhetoric of Empire* (Berkeley and Los Angeles, CA: University of California Press, 1991)

—— 'Desert Mothers: Women Ascetics in Early Christian Egypt', in Elizabeth Puttick (ed.), *Women as Teachers and Disciples in Traditional and New Religions* (Lewiston, NY: Edwin Mellen Press, 1993), 11–24

—— 'Virginity as Metaphor: Women and the Rhetoric of Early Christianity' in Cameron (ed.), *History as Text: The Writing of Ancient History* (London: Duckworth, 1989), 184–205

—— (ed.), *History as Text: The Writing of Ancient History* (London: Duckworth, 1989)

Castelli, Elizabeth A., 'Gender, Theory and the Rise of Christianity: A Response to Rodney Stark', *Journal of Early Christian Studies* 6.2 (1998), 227–57

—— *Martyrdom and Memory: Early Christian Culture Making* (New York: Columbia University Press, 2004)

—— 'Pseudo Athanasius: The Life and Activity of the Holy and Blessed Teacher Syncletica', in Vincent Wimbush (ed.), *Ascetic Behavior in Greco-Roman Antiquity* (Minneapolis, MN: Fortress Press, 1990), 265–311

Chadwick, Henry, 'Conversion in Constantine the Great', in Derek Baker (ed.), *Religious Motivation: Biographical and Sociological Problems for the Church Historian* (Oxford: Blackwell, 1978)

Chausson, François, 'La famille du préfet Ablabius', *Pallas* 60 (2002), 17–26

Clark, Elizabeth A., *Ascetic Piety and Women's Faith: Essays on Late Ancient Christianity* (Lewiston: Edwin Mellen Press, 1986)

—— 'Ascetic Renunciation and Feminine Advancement: A Paradox of Late Ancient Christianity', *Anglican Theological Review* 63 (1981), 240–57

—— 'Early Christian Women: Sources and Interpretation', in L. L. Coon, K. J. Haldane, and E. W. Sommer (eds), *That Gentle Strength: Historical Perspectives on Women in Christianity* (Charlottesville, VA: University of Virginia Press, 1990), 19–35

—— 'Friendship Between the Sexes: Classical Theory and Christian Practice', in Clark, *Jerome, Chrysostom, and Friends: Essays and Translations* (New York, 1979), 35–105

—— '*The Lady Vanishes: Dilemmas of a Feminist Historian after the "Linguistic Turn"'*, *Church History* 67 (1998), 1–31

—— 'Patrons, Not Priests: Women and Power in Late Ancient Christianity', *Gender & History* 2 (1990), 253–73

Clark, Gillian, *Christianity and Roman Society* (Cambridge: Cambridge University Press, 2004); (Review: B. Longenecker, *Journal of Roman Studies* 96 [2006], 297–8)

—— *Women in Late Antiquity: Pagan and Christian Life-styles* (Oxford: Clarendon Press, 1993)

Cloke, G., *This Female Man of God: Women and Spiritual Power in the Patristic Age, AD 350–450* (London and New York: Routledge, 1995)

Cobb, L. Stephanie, *Dying to be Men: Gender and Language in Early Christian Martyr Texts* (New York: Columbia University Press, 2008)

Cohick, Lynn H., *Women in the World of the Earliest Christians: Illuminating Ancient Ways of Life* (Grand Rapids, MI: Baker Academic, 2009)

Constas, Nicholas, *Proclus of Constantinople and the Cult of the Virgin in Late Antiquity: Homilies 1–5, Texts and Translations* (Leiden and Boston, MA: Brill, 2003)

Cooper, Kate, 'Approaching the Holy Household', *Journal of Early Christian Studies* 15 (2007), 131–42

—— 'The Bride of Christ, the "Male Woman," and the Female Reader in Late Antiquity', in Judith Bennett and Ruth Mazo Karras (eds), *Oxford Handbook of Women and Gender in Medieval Europe* (New York: Oxford University Press, forthcoming)

—— 'Chastity', *Encyclopedia of Religion*, 2nd edn (Framington Hills, MI: Thomson/ Gale, 2004)

—— 'Christianity, Private Power, and the Law from Decius to Constantine: The Minimalist View', *Journal of Early Christian Studies* 19 (2011), 327–43

—— 'Closely Watched Households: Visibility, Exposure, and Private Power in the Roman *domus*', *Past and Present* 197 (2007), 3–33

—— 'Contesting the Nativity: Wives, Virgins, and Pulcheria's *imitatio Mariae*', *Scottish Journal of Religious Studies* 19 (1998), 31–43

—— 'Empress and *Theotokos*: Gender and Patronage in the Christological Controversy', in R. N. Swanson (ed.), *The Church and Mary* (Woodbridge: Boydell and Brewer, 2004), 39–51

—— *The Fall of the Roman Household* (Cambridge: Cambridge University Press, 2007)

—— 'Gender and the Fall of Rome', in Philip Rousseau (ed.), *A Companion to Late Antiquity* (Oxford: Blackwell, 2009), 187–200

—— 'The Household and the Desert: Monastic and Biological Communities in the Lives of Melania the Younger', in Anneke Mulder-Bakker and Jocelyn Wogan-Browne (eds), *Household, Women, and Christianities in Late Antiquity and the Middle Ages* (Leiden: Brill, 2005), 11–35

—— 'Insinuations of Womanly Influence: An Aspect of the Christianization of the Roman Empire', *Journal of Roman Studies* 82 (1992), 150–64

—— 'Matthidia's Wish: Division, Reunion, and the Early Christian Family in the Pseudo-Clementine *Recognitions*', in George J. Brooke and Jean-Daniel Kaestli (eds), *Narrativity in Biblical Studies* (Leuven: Peeters, 2000), 243–64

—— '"Only Virgins Can Give Birth to Christ": The Virgin Mary and the problem of female authority in late antiquity', in Bonnie McLaughlin and Judith Fletcher (eds), *Virginity Revisited: Configurations of the Unpossessed Body* (Toronto: University of Toronto Press, 2007), 100–15

—— 'The Patristic Period', in John Sawyer (ed.), *The Blackwell Companion to the Bible and Culture* (Oxford: Blackwell, 2006), 28–38

—— 'Poverty, Obligation, and Inheritance: Roman Heiresses and the Varieties of Senatorial Christianity in Fifth-Century Rome', in Kate Cooper and Julia Hillner (eds), *Religion, Dynasty and Patronage in Early Christian Rome, 300–900* (Cambridge: Cambridge University Press, 2006), 165–189

—— 'A Saint in Exile: The Early Medieval Thecla at Rome and Meriamlik', *Hagiographica* 2 (1995), 1–24

—— 'Ventriloquism and the Miraculous: Conversion, Preaching, and the Martyr Exemplum in Late Antiquity', in Kate Cooper and Jeremy Gregory (eds), *Signs, Wonders, and Miracles*, Studies in Church History 41 (Woodbridge: Boydell and Brewer, 2005), 22–45

—— *The Virgin and the Bride: Idealized Womanhood in Late Antiquity* (Cambridge, MA: Harvard University Press, 1996)

—— 'The Voice of the Victim: Gender, Representation, and Early Christian Martyrdom', *Bulletin of the John Rylands Library* 80 (1998), 147–57

Corrington Streete, Gail, 'Of Martyrs and Men: Perpetua, Thecla, and the Ambiguity of Female Heroism in Early Christianity', in Richard Valantasis (ed.), *The Subjective Eye: Essays in Culture, Religion, and Gender in Honor of Margaret R. Miles* (Eugene, OR: Pickwick Publications, 2006), 254–64.

Cunningham, Mary B., 'The Use of the Protoevangelion of James in Eighth-Century Homilies on the Mother of God', in Cunningham and Brubaker (eds), *The Cult of the Mother of God in Byzantium: Texts and Images*, 163–78

Cunningham, Mary B., and Leslie Brubaker (eds), *The Cult of the Mother of God in Byzantium: Texts and Images* (Burlington, VT: Ashgate, 2011)

D'Angelo, Mary Rose, 'Women in Luke-Acts: A Redactional View', *Journal of Biblical Literature* 109 (1990), 441–61

Davies, Steven L., *The Revolt of the Widows: The Social World of the Apocryphal Acts* (Carbondale, IL: Southern Illinois University Press, 1980)

Davis, Stephen J., *The Cult of St Thecla: A Tradition of Women's Piety in Late Antiquity*

(Oxford: Oxford University Press, 2001); (Review: W. Trent Foley, *Church History* 71 [2002], 393–5)

De Boer, Esther, *The Gospel of Mary: Listening to the Beloved Disciple* (London and New York: Continuum, 2005)

Doran, Robert, *Birth of a Worldview: Early Christianity in its Jewish and Pagan Context* (Boulder, CO: Westview Press, 1995); (Review: Robert M. Grant, *Church History* 66 [1997], 312–13)

Drijvers, Jan Willem, *Helena Augusta: The Mother of Constantine the Great and her Finding of the True Cross* (Leiden: Brill, 1992)

—— 'Flavia Maxima Fausta: some remarks', *Historia* 41 (1992), 500–06

Dunn, Peter W., 'Women's Liberation, The Acts of Paul, and Other Acts of the Apostles: A Review of Some Recent Interpreters', *Apocrypha* 4 (1993), 245–61

Edwards, Mark, 'The Clementina: A Christian Response to the Pagan Novel', *Classical Quarterly* 42 (1992), 459–71

Eisen, Ute E., *Women Officeholders in Early Christianity: Epigraphical and literary studies*, tr. Linda M. Maloney (Collegeville, MN: Liturgical Press, 2000)

Elm, Susanna, *Sons of Hellenism, Fathers of the Church: Emperor Julian, Gregory of Nazianzus, and the Vision of Rome* (Berkeley and Los Angeles, CA: University of California Press, 2012)

—— *'Virgins of God': The Making of Asceticism in Late Antiquity* (Oxford: Clarendon Press, 1994)

Emmett, A., 'An Early Fourth-Century Female Monastic Community in Egypt?', in A. Moffatt (ed.), *Maistor: Classical, Byzantine and Renaissance Studies for Robert Browning* (Canberra: Australian Association of Byzantine Studies, 1984), 74–84

— 'Female Ascetics in Greek Papyri', *Jahrbuch der Österreichischen Byzantinistik* 32.2 (1982), 517–24

Epp, Eldon J., *Junia: The First Woman Apostle* (Minneapolis, MN: Fortress Press, 2005)

Evans Grubbs, Judith, *Law and Family in Late Antiquity: The Emperor Constantine's Marriage Legislation* (Oxford: Clarendon Press, 1995)

—— 'Marrying and Its Documentation in Later Roman Law', in Philip L. Reynolds and John Witte, Jr. (eds), *To Have and to Hold: Marrying and Its Documentation in Western Christendom, 400–1600* (Cambridge: Cambridge University Press, 2007), 43–94

Fantham, Elaine, Helene Peet Foley, Natalie Boymel Kampen, Sarah B. Pomeroy, and H. Alan Shapiro, *Women in the Classical World* (New York: Oxford University Press, 1994)

Filson, Floyd, 'TheSignificance of the Early House Churches', *Journal of Biblical Literature* 58 (1939), 105–12

Frank, Georgia, *The Memory of the Eyes: Pilgrims to Living Saints in Christian Late Antiquity* (Berkeley and Los Angeles, CA: University of California Press, 2000)

Frend, W. H. C., *The Archaeology of Early Christianity: A History* (London: Geoffrey Chapman, 1997); (Review: Joan E. Taylor, *Journal of Roman Studies* 89 [1999], 317–18)

—— *Martyrdom and Persecution in the Early Church: A Study of a Conflict from the Maccabees to Donatus* (Oxford: Blackwell, 1965)

—— *The Rise of Christianity* (London: Darton, Longman and Todd, 1984)

Galor, Katharina, 'Domestic Architecture', in Catherine Hezser (ed.), *The Oxford Handbook of Jewish Daily Life in Roman Palestine* (Oxford: Oxford University Press, 2010), 420

—— 'Jewellery: The Archaeological Evidence', in Catherine Hezser (ed.), *The Oxford Handbook of Jewish Daily Life in Roman Palestine* (Oxford: Oxford University Press, 2010), 393

Gillman, F., *Women Who Knew Paul* (Collegeville, MN: Liturgical Press, 1992)

Grant, Robert M., 'Charges of "Immorality" Against Various Religious Groups in Antiquity', in R. van den Broek and M. J. Vermaseren (eds), *Studies in Gnosticism and Hellenistic Religions Presented to Gilles Quispel on the Occasion of His 65th Birthday* (Leiden: Brill, 1981)

—— *Eusebius as Church Historian* (Oxford: Oxford University Press, 1980)

—— *Greek Apologists of the Second Century* (London: SCM Press, 1988)

—— *Gnosticism and Early Christianity* (New York: Columbia University Press, 1959)

Grig, Lucy, *Making Martyrs in Late Antiquity* (London: Duckworth, 2004)

Grossmark, Tziona, *Jewellery: The Literary Evidence* in Catherine Hezser (ed.), *The Oxford Handbook of Jewish Daily Life in Roman Palestine* (Oxford: Oxford University Press, 2010), 382

Guijarro, Santiago, 'The Family in First-Century Galilee', in Halvor Moxnes (ed.), *Constructing Early Christian Families: The Family as Social Reality and Metaphor* (London and New York: Routledge, 1997), 42–65

Haines-Eitzen, Kim, *The Gendered Palimpsest: Women, Writing, and Representation in Early Christianity* (New York, Oxford: Oxford University Press, 2012)

Hall, Stuart G., 'Women among the Early Martyrs', in D. Wood (ed.), *Martyrs and Martyrologies*, Studies in Church History 30 (London: Blackwell, 1993), 1–21

Halporn, J. W., 'Literary History and Generic Expectation in the *Passio* and *Acta Perpetuae*', *Vigiliae Christianae* 45 (1991), 223–41

Hammer, T. 'Wealthy Widows and Female Apostles: The Economic and Social Status of Women in Early Roman Christianity', in G. D. Dunn, D. Luckensmeyer and L. Cross (eds), *Prayer and Spirituality in the Early Church: Poverty and Riches, 5* (Strathfield: Paulist Press, 2009), 65–74

Harper, Kyle, *Slavery in the Late Roman World, AD 275–425* (Cambridge: Cambridge University Press, 2011)

Harries, Jill, 'The Empresses' Tale, AD 300–360', in Carol Harrison, Isabella Sandwell, and Caroline Humfress (eds), *Being Christian in Late Antiquity: A Festschrift for Gillian Clark* (Oxford: Oxford University Press, forthcoming 2013)

—— 'Treasure in Heaven: Property and Inheritance among Senators in Late Rome', in E. M. Craik (ed.), *Marriage and Property* (Aberdeen, 1984), 54–70

—— and *Ian Wood* (eds), *The Theodosian Code: Studies in the Imperial Law of Late Antiquity* (Ithaca, NY, and London: Cornell University Press, 1993)

Harrington, Daniel J., 'The Reception of Walter Bauer's "Orthodoxy and Heresy in Earliest Christianity" during the Last Decade', *Harvard Theological Review* 73 (1980), 289–98

Harrison, Martin, *A Temple for Byzantium: The Discovery and Excavation of Anicia Juliana's Palace-Church in Istanbul* (London: Harvey Miller, 1989)

Hayes, Alan L. (ed.), *Church and Society in Documents: 100–600 A.D.* (Toronto: Canadian Scholars Press, 1995); (Review: E. Glen Hinson, *Church History* 66 [1997], 186–7)

Hazlett, Ian (ed.), *Early Christianity: Origins and Evolution to AD 600* (London: SPCK, 1991)

Heffernan, Thomas J., *The Passion of Perpetua and Felicity* (Oxford: Oxford University Press, 2012)

—— and James E. Shelton, 'Paradise in Carcere: The Vocabulary of Imprisonment and the Theology of Martyrdom in the *Passio Sanctorum Perpetuae et Felicitatis*', *Journal of Early Christian Studies* 14. 2 (2006), 217–23

Hemelrijk, E. A., 'City Patronesses in the Roman Empire', *Historia* 53.2 (2004), 209–45

Herrin, Judith, 'Women and the Faith in Icons in Early Christianity', in Raphael Samuel and Gareth Stedman Jones (eds), *Culture, Ideology, and Politics: Essays for Eric Hobsbawm* (London: Routledge, 1982), 56–83

Hezser, Catherine (ed.), *The Oxford Handbook of Jewish Daily Life in Roman Palestine* (Oxford: Oxford University Press, 2010)

Hickey, Anne Ewing, *Women of the Roman Aristocracy as Christian Monastics* (Ann Arbor, MI: UMI Research Press, 1987)

Holum, Kenneth G., *Theodosian Empresses: Women and Imperial Dominion in Late Antiquity* (Berkeley and Los Angeles, CA: University of California Press, 1982)

Hopkins, Keith, *Death and Renewal: Sociological Studies in Ancient History* (Cambridge: Cambridge University Press, 1983)

Horn, Cornelia B., 'Suffering Children, Parental Authority and the Quest for Liberation?: A Tale of Three Girls in the *Acts of Paul (and Thecla)*, the *Act(s) of Peter*, the *Acts of Nerseus and Achilleus*, and the *Epistle of Pseudo-Titus*', in Amy-Jill Levine with Maria Mayo Robbins (eds), *A Feminist Companion to the New Testament Apocrypha* (New York and London: Continuum and T. & T. Clark International, 2006), 118–45

Horsley, Richard A., *Galilee: History, Politics, People* (Valley Forge, PA: Trinity Press International, 1995)

—— (ed.), *A People's History of Christianity,* vol. 1: *Christian Origins* (Minneapolis, MN: Fortress Press, 2005)

Hultgren, Arland J., and Steven A. Haggmark, *The Earliest Christian Heretics: Readings From Their Opponents* (Minneapolis, MN: Fortress Press, 1996)

Hunt, E. D., 'Christianizing the Roman Empire: The Evidence of the Code', in Jill Harries and Ian Wood (eds), *The Theodosian Code: Studies in the Imperial Law of Late Antiquity* (Ithaca, NY, and London: Cornell University Press, 1993), 143–57

—— *Holy Land Pilgrimage in the Later Roman Empire AD 312–460* (Oxford, 1982)

Ilan, Tal, 'Gender Issues and Daily Life', in Hezser (ed.), *The Oxford Handbook of Jewish Daily Life in Roman Palestine*, 48

—— *Jewish Women in Greco-Roman Palestine: An Inquiry into Image and Status* (Tübingen: Mohr-Siebeck, 1995)

Jacobs, Andrew S., 'A Family Affair: Marriage, Class, and Ethics in the Apocryphal Acts of the Apostles', *Journal of Early Christian Studies* 7 (1999), 105–38

Jensen, Anne, *God's Self-Confident Daughters: Early Christianity and the Liberation of Women*, tr. O. C. Dean Jr. (Louisville, KY: Westminster John Knox, 1996); (Review: Elizabeth A. Clark, *Church History* 66 [1997], 782–3)

Jensen, Robin Margaret, *Understanding Early Christian Art* (New York: Routledge, 2000)

Jones, A. H. M., J. R. Martindale, and J. Morris, *The Prosopography of the Later Roman Empire*, vol. I (Cambridge: Cambridge University Press, 1971)

Jones, Hannah, 'Agnes and Constantia: Domesticity and Cult Patronage in the *Passion of Agnes*', in Kate Cooper and Julia Hillner (eds), *Religion, Dynasty, and Patronage in Early Christian Rome, 300–900* (Cambridge: Cambridge University Press, 2007), 115–39

Kearsley, R. A., 'Women in Public Life in the Roman East: Iunia Theodora, Claudia Metrodora and Phoebe, Benefactress of Paul', *Tynedale Bulletin* 50 (1999), 189–211

Kehoe, Dennis P., 'Law and Social Formation in the Roman Empire', in Michael Peachin (ed.), *The Oxford Handbook of Social Relations in the Roman World* (Oxford and New York: Oxford University Press, 2011), 144–63

King, Karen L., *The Gospel of Mary of Magdala: Jesus and the First Woman Apostle* (Santa Rosa, CA: Polebridge Press, 2003)

—— 'Prophetic Power and Women's Authority: The Case of the Gospel of Mary Madgdalene', in Beverley M. Kienzle and Pamela Walker (eds), *Women Preachers and Prophets through Two Millennia of Christianity* (Berkeley and Los Angeles, CA: University of California Press, 1998), 21–41

Klauck, Hans-Josef, *The Apocryphal Acts of the Apostles: An Introduction* (Waco, TX: Baylor University Press, 2008)

Klutz, Todd E., 'The Rhetoric of Science in the Rise of Christianity: A Response to Rodney Stark's Sociological Account of Christianisation', *Journal of Early Christian Studies* 6. 2 (1998), 162–84

Konstan, David, 'Acts of Love: A Narrative Pattern in the Apocryphal Acts', *Journal of Early Christian Studies* 6 (1998), 15–36

Kraemer, David, 'Food, Eating, and Meals', in Hezser (ed.), *The Oxford Handbook of Jewish Daily Life in Roman Palestine*, 403

Kraemer, Ross Shepard, 'The Conversion of Women to Ascetic Forms of Christianity', *Signs: Journal of Women in Culture and Society* 6 (1980), 298–307

—— 'Jewish Women in the Diaspora World of Late Antiquity', in J. R. Baskin (ed.), *Jewish Women in Historical Perspective* (Detroit, MI, 1991)

—— 'Typical and Atypical Family Dynamics: The Cases of Babatha and

Berenice', in Balch and Osiek, *Early Christian Families in Context*, 130–156

—— *Unreliable Witnesses: Religion, Gender, and History in the Greco-Roman Mediterranean* (New York: Oxford University Press, 2011)

—— 'When is a Text About a Woman a Text About a Woman? The Cases of Aseneth and Perpetua', in A. Levine and M. M. Robbins (eds), *A Feminist Companion to Patristic Literature* (London and New York: Bloomsbury, T & T Clark 2008), 156–72

—— and Mary Rose D'Angelo, (eds), *Women and Christian Origins* (Oxford: Oxford University Press, 1999)

—— and Shira Lander, 'Perpetua and Felicitas', in Philip Francis Esler (ed.),*The Early Christian World*, (London: Routledge, 2000), II, 1048–66

Krawiec, Rebecca, '"From the Womb of the Church": Monastic Families', *Journal of Early Christian Studies* 11 (2003), 283–307

—— *Shenoute and the Women of the White Monastery: Egyptian Monasticism in Late Antiquity* (Oxford and New York: Oxford University Press, USA, 2002)

Krueger, D., 'Writing and the Liturgy of Memory in Gregory of Nyssa's Life of Macrina', *Journal of Early Christian Studies* 8 (2000), 483–510

Lampe, Peter, *From Paul to Valentinus: Christians at Rome in the first two centuries*, tr. Michael Steinhauser; Marshall D. Johnson (ed.), (Minneapolis, MN: Fortress Press, 2003)

—— 'The Language of Equality in Early Christian House Churches: A Constructivist Approach', in Balch and Osiek, *Early Christian Families in Context*, 73–83

—— 'The Roman Christians of Romans 16', in K. P. Donfried (ed.) *The Romans Debate*, 2nd rev. edn (Peabody, MA: Hendrickson Publishers, 1995), 216–30

Leyerle, Blake, 'Pilgrims to the Land: Early Christian Perceptions of the Galilee', in Eric M. Meyers (ed.) *Galilee Through the Centuries: Confluence of Cultures* (Winona Lake, IN: Eisenbrauns, 1999), 345–78

Lieu, Judith, 'The "Attraction of Women" In/To Early Judaism and Christianity: Gender and the Politics of Conversion', *Journal for the Study of the New Testament* 72 (1998), 5–22

—— *Neither Jew Nor Greek? Constructing Early Christianity* (Edinburgh: T. & T. Clark, 2002)

Limberis, Vasiliki, *Architects of Piety: The Cappadocian Fathers and the Cult of the Martyrs* (New York: Oxford University Press, 2011)

—— *Divine Heiress: The Virgin Mary and the Creation of Christian Constantinople* (London: Routledge, 1994)

Lipsett, B. Diane, *Desiring Conversion: Hermas, Thecla, Aseneth* (New York: Oxford University Press, 2001)

Logan, Alastair H. B., *Gnostic Truth and Christian Heresy: A Study in the History of Gnosticism* (Edinburgh: T. & T. Clark, 1995); (Review: Eugene TeSelle, *Church History* 66 [1997], 538–9)

Loofs, Friedrich, *Nestoriana* (Halle an der Saale, Germany: Niemeyer, 1905)

Lüdemann, Gerd, *Heretics: the Other Side of Early Christianity*, tr. John Bowden (London: SCM, 1996); (Review: Kim Haines-Eitzen, *Church History* 67 [1998], 746–8)

MacDonald, Dennis, *The Legend and the Apostle: The Battle for Paul in Story and Canon* (Louisville, KY: Westminster John Knox Press, 1983)

—— 'What Difference Did Christianity Make?' *Historia* 35 (1984), 322–43

MacDonald, Margaret Y., *Early Christian Women and Pagan Opinion: The Power of the Hysterical Woman* (Cambridge: Cambridge University Press, 1996)

—— *The Pauline Churches: A Socio-Historical Study of Institutionalization in the Pauline and Deutero-Pauline Writings* (Cambridge: Cambridge University Press, 1988)

—— 'Reading Real Women through the Undisputed Letters of *Paul*', in Ross Shepard Kraemer and Mary Rose D'Angelo (eds), *Women and Christian Origins* (Oxford: Oxford University Press, 1999), 199–220

—— 'Was Celsus Right? The Role of Women in the Expansion of Early Christianity', in Balch and Osiek, *Early Christian Families in Context*, 157–184

MacMullen, Ramsay, *Christianizing the Roman Empire (AD 100–400)* (New Haven: Yale University Press, 1984)

—— *The Second Church: Popular Christianity AD 200–400* (Atlanta, GA: Society of Biblical Literature, 2009)

Macy, Gary, *The Hidden History of Women's Ordination, Female Clergy in the Medieval West* (Oxford: Oxford University Press, 2008)

Mantas, K., 'Independent Women in the Roman East: Widows, Benefactresses, Patronesses, Office-Holders', *Eirene* 33 (1997), 81–95

Matthews, J., 'The poetess Proba and fourth-century Rome: Questions of interpretation', in M. Christol (ed.), *Institutions, société et vie politique dans l'Empire romain au IVe siècle ap. J.-C: actes de la Table ronde autour de l'œuvre d'André Chastagnol, Paris, 20–21 janvier 1989* (Rome: École française de Rome, 1992), 277–303

Mayer, Wendy, 'Aelia Eudoxia (wife of Arcadius)', in *De Imperatoribus Romanis: An Online Encyclopedia of Roman Emperors* (http://www.romanemperors.org/aeleudoxia.htm)

—— 'Constantinopolitan Women in Chrysostom's Circle', *Vigiliae Christianae* 53 (1999), 265–88

—— 'Patronage, Pastoral Care and the Role of the Bishop at Antioch', *Vigiliae Christianae* 55 (2001), 58–70

McGinn, T. A., 'Widows, Orphans, and Social History', *Journal of Roman Archaeology* 12 (1999), 617–32

McGowan, Andrew, *Ascetic Eucharists: Food and Drink in Early Christian Ritual Meals* (Oxford: Clarendon Press, 1999); (Review: Michael Philip Penn, *Church History* 69, no. 2 [2000], 403–4)

McLaughlin, Eleanor, 'Women, Power and the Pursuit of Holiness in Medieval Christianity', in Rosemary Ruether and Eleanor McLaughlin (eds), *Women of Spirit: Female Leadership in the Jewish and Christian Traditions* (New York: Simon and Schuster, 1979)

McNamara, J., 'Cornelia's Daughters: Paula and Eustochium', *Women's Studies* 11 (1984), 9–27

—— 'Muffled Voices: The Lives of Consecrated Women in the Fourth Century', in J. A. Nichols and L. T. Shank (eds), *Distant Echoes: Medieval Religious Women* (Kalamazoo, MI: Cistercian Publications, 1984–95), 11–29

—— *A New Song: Celibate Women in the First Three Christian Centuries* (New York: Haworth Press, 1983)

Meeks, Wayne A., *The First Urban Christians: The Social World of the Apostle Paul* (New Haven: Yale University Press, 1983)

—— *The Origins of Christian Morality: The First Two Centuries* (New Haven, CT: Yale University Press, 1993)

Methuen, Charlotte, 'Vidua – Presbytera – Episcopa: Women with Oversight in the Early Church', *Theology* 108, no. 843 (2005), 163–77

—— 'The "Virgin" Widow: A Problematic Social Role for the Early Church?', *Harvard Theological Review* 90 (1997), 285–98

Meyer, Marvin W., with Esther De Boer, *The Gospels of Mary: The Secret Tradition of Mary Magdalene, The Companion of Jesus* (San Francisco, CA: Harper San Francisco, 2006)

Meyers, Eric M., 'The Problems of Gendered Space in Syro-Palestinian Domestic Architecture: The Case of Roman-Period Galilee', in Balch and Osiek, *Early Christian Families in Context*, 44–69

Migne, J.-P., *Patrologiae Cursus Completus, Series Graeca* (Petit Montrouge, Paris: Imprimerie Catholique, 1857–66)

Migne, J.-P., *Patrologiae Cursus Completus, Series Latina* (Petit Montrouge, Paris: Imprimerie Catholique, 1844–55)

Millar, Fergus, *The Roman Near East 31 BC–AD 337* (Cambridge, MA: Harvard University Press, 1993)

Misset-van de Weg, Magda, 'A Wealthy Woman Named Tryphaena: Patroness of Thecla of Iconium', in Jan N. Bremmer (ed.), *The Apocryphal Acts of Paul and Thecla* (Kampen, Netherlands: KokPharos, 1996), 16–35

Mombritius, Boninus, *Sanctuarium seu vitae sanctorum* (Milan, 1477; 2nd edn Paris: Fontemoing, 1910)

Moxnes, Halvor (ed.), *Constructing Early Christian Families: Family as Social Reality and Metaphor* (London: Routledge, 1997)

Murphy O'Connor, Jerome, *St. Paul's Corinth: Text and Archaeology*, 3rd edn (Collegeville, MN: Liturgical Press, 2002)

Nathan, G., *The Family in Late Antiquity: The Rise of Christianity and the Endurance of Tradition* (London and New York: Routledge, 2000)

Nicols, J., 'Patrona civitatis: Gender and Civic Patronage', in C. Deroux (ed.), *Studies in Latin Literature and Roman History* (Brussels: Éditions Latomus, 1989), vol. 5, 117–42

Osiek, Carolyn, 'The Family in Early Christianity: "Family Values" Revisited', *Catholic Biblical Quarterly* 58 (1996), 1–24

—— 'Perpetua's Husband', *Journal of Early Christian Studies* 10. 2 (2002), 287–90

—— and Margaret Y. MacDonald, and Janet H. Tulloch, *A Woman's Place: House Churches in Early Christianity* (Fortress Press, 2005)

Pagels, Elaine, *The Gnostic Gospels* (London: Weidenfeld and Nicolson, 1979)

Parsons, Peter, *City of the Sharp-Nosed Fish: Greek Papyri Beneath the Egyptian Sand Reveal a Long-Lost World* (London: Phoenix, 2007)

Parvey, Constance E., 'The Theology and Leadership of Women in the New

Testament', in Rosemary Radford Ruether (ed.), *Religion and Sexism* (New York: Simon & Schuster, 1974) 139–46

Penner, Todd, and Caroline Vander Stichele (eds), *Mapping Gender in Ancient Religious Discourses* (Leiden & Boston, MA: Brill, 2007)

Perkins, Judith, 'Fictional Narratives and Social Critique', in Virginia Burrus, (ed.), *A People's History of Christianity,* vol. 2: *Late Ancient Christianity* (Minneapolis, MN: Fortress Press, 2005), 46–69

—— *The Suffering Self: Pain and Narrative Representation in the Early Christian Era* (London: Routledge, 1995); (Review: Dennis E. Trout, *Church History* 67 [1998], 562–4)

Peskowitz, Miriam B., Spinning Fantasies: Rabbis, Gender, and History (Berkeley and Los Angeles, CA: University of California Press, 1997)

Potter, David, 'Martyrdom as Spectacle', in Ruth Scodel (ed.), *Theater and Society in the Classical World* (Ann Arbor, MI: University of Michigan Press, 1993), 53–88.

Price, Richard, and Michael Gaddis, *The Acts of the Council of Chalcedon: Translated with an Introduction and Notes*, 3 vols (Liverpool: Liverpool University Press, 2005)

Rader, Rosemary, *Breaking Boundaries: Male/Female Friendship in Early Christian Communities* (New York: Paulist Press, 1983)

Rapp, Claudia, *Holy Bishops in Late Antiquity: The Nature of Christian Leadership in an Age of Transition* (Berkeley and Los Angeles, CA: University of California Press, 2005)

—— 'Palladius, Lausus and the Historia Lausiaca' in C. Sode and S. A. Takács (eds), *Novum Millennium: Studies on Byzantine History and Culture Dedicated to Paul Speck* (Farnham, Surrey: Ashgate, 2001), 279–89

Rathbone, Dominic, *Economic Rationalism and Rural Society in 3rd Century AD Egypt* (Cambridge: Cambridge University Press, 1991)

Richlin, Amy, 'What We Need to Know Right Now', *Journal of Women's History* 22.4 (2010), 268–81

Rives, J. B., 'The Decree of Decius and the Religion of the Empire', *Journal of Roman Studies* 89 (1999), 135–54

—— 'The Piety of a Persecutor', *Journal of Early Christian Studies* 4 (1996), 1–25

—— *Religion and Authority in Roman Carthage from Augustus to Constantine* (Oxford: Clarendon Press, 1995); (Review: Gregory T. Armstrong, *Church History* 66 [1997], 543–4)

Ronsse, Erin, 'Rhetoric of the Martyrs: Listening to Saints Perpetua and Felicitas', *Journal of Early Christian Studies* 14 (2006), 283–327

Rousseau, Philip, 'Learned Women and the Development of a Christian Culture in Late Antiquity', *Symbolae Osloenses* 70 (1995), 116–47

—— *Pachomius: The Making of a Community in Fourth-Century Egypt* (Berkeley and Los Angeles, CA: University of California Press, 1985)

—— 'The Pious Household and the Virgin Chorus: Reflections on Gregory of Nyssa's *Life of Macrina*', *Journal of Early Christian Studies* 13 (2005), 165–86

Ruether, Rosemary Radford, 'Mothers of the Church: Ascetic Women in the Late Patristic Age' in Rosemary Radford Ruether and Eleanor McLaughlin (eds), *Women of Spirit: Female Leadership in the Jewish and Christian Traditions* (New York: Simon and Schuster, 1979), 71–98

—— (ed.), *Religion and Sexism: Images of Women in the Jewish and Christian Traditions* (New York: Simon and Schuster, 1974)

Salisbury, Joyce, *The Blood of Martyrs: Unintended Consequences of Ancient Violence* (New York: Routledge, 2004)

—— *Perpetua's Passion: The Death and Memory of a Young Roman Woman* (New York: Routledge, 1997); (Review: Amy G. Oden, *Church History* 67 [1998], 560–62)

Salzman, Michelle R., 'Aristocratic Women: Conductors of Christianity in the Fourth Century?', *Helios* 16 (1989), 207–20

—— *The Making of a Christian Aristocracy: Social and Religious Change in the Western Roman Empire* (London: Harvard University Press, 2002); (Review: Lucy Grig, *Journal of Roman Studies* 97 [2007], 382–3)

Sampley, J. Paul, *Paul in the Greco-Roman World: A Handbook* (Harrisburg, PA: Trinity Press International, 2003)

Satlow, Michael L., *Jewish Marriage in Late Antiquity* (Princeton: Princeton University Press, 2001)

—— 'Marriage and Divorce', in Hezser (ed.), *The Oxford Handbook of Jewish Daily Life in Roman Palestine*, 344

Sawyer, D. F., *Women and Religion in the First Christian Centuries* (London and New York: Routledge, 1996)

Schein, S., 'The Female-men of God and Men Who Were Women: Female Saints and Holy Land Pilgrimage During the Byzantine Period', *Hagiographica* 5 (1998), 1–37

Schottroff, Luise, *Lydia's Impatient Sisters: A Feminist Social History of Early Christianity*, tr. Barbara Rumscheidt and Martin Rumscheidt (Louisville, KY: Westminster John Knox Press, 1995); (Review: Elizabeth A. Clark, *Church History* 66 [1997], 303–4)

Schüssler Fiorenza, Elizabeth, 'A Feminist Critical Interpretation for Liberation: Martha and Mary: Luke 10: 38–42', *Religion & Intellectual Life* 3 (1986), 21–35

—— *In Memory of Her: A Feminist Theological Reconstruction of Christian Origins* (New York: Crossroad, 1983)

—— 'Word, Spirit, and Power: Women in Early Christian Communities', in Ruether and McLaughlin (eds), *Women of Spirit*, 29–70

Schwartz, Seth, 'Ancient Jewish Social Relations', in Michael Peachin (ed.), *The Oxford Handbook of Social Relations in the Roman World* (Oxford and New York: Oxford University Press, 2011), 548–66

Selinger, Reinhard, *The Mid-Third Century Persecutions of Decius and Valerian* (Frankfurt: Peter Lang, 2004); (Review: Christiana Sogno, *Journal of Roman Studies* 94 [2004], 272–3)

Shaw, Brent D., 'The Passion of Perpetua', *Past & Present* 139 (1993), 3–45

—— 'Women and the Early Church', *History Today* 44 (1994), 21–28

Shaw, Teresa M., *The Burden of the Flesh: Fasting and Sexuality in Early Christianity.* (Minneapolis, MN: Fortress Press, 1998); (Review: Virginia Burrus, *Church History* 68 [1999], 680–82)

Silvas, Anna M., *The Asketikon of Basil the Great* (Oxford: Oxford University Press, 2005)

—— *Macrina the Younger: Philosopher of God* (Turnhout, Belgium: Brepols, 2008)

Sivan, Hagith, 'Anician Women, the Cento of Proba, and Aristocratic Conversion in the Fourth Century', *Vigiliae Christianae* 47 (1993), 140–57

—— 'Holy Land Pilgrimage and Western Audiences: Some Reflections on Egeria and Her Circle', *Classical Quarterly* 38 (1988), 528–35

—— 'Rabbinics and Roman Law: Jewish-Gentile/Christian Marriage in Late Antiquity', *Revue des etudes juives* 156 (1997), 59–100

—— 'Who Was Egeria? Piety and Pilgrimage in the Age of Gratian', *Harvard Theological Review* 81 (1988), 59–72

Sivertsev, Alexei, 'The Household Economy', in Hezser (ed.), *The Oxford Handbook of Jewish Daily Life in Roman Palestine*, 229

Smith, J. W., 'A Just and Reasonable Grief: the Death and Function of a Holy Woman in Gregory of Nyssa's Life of Macrina', *Journal of Early Christian Studies* 12 (2004), 57–84

Snee, Rochelle, 'Gregory Nazianzen's Anastasia Church: Arianism, the Goths, and Hagiography', *Dumbarton Oaks Papers* 52 (1998), 157–186

Snyder, Graydon F., *Ante pacem: Archaeological Evidence of Church Life before Constantine* (Macon, GA: Mercer, 1985, repr. 2003)

Soren, David and Noelle, *A Roman villa and a late Roman Infant cemetery: Excavation at Poggio Gramignano, Lugnano in Teverina* (Rome: L'Erma di Brettschneider, 1999)

Spencer, F. Scott, *Salty Wives, Spirited Mothers, and Savvy Widows: Capable Women of Purpose and Persistence in Luke's Gospel* (Grand Rapids, MI: W. B. Eerdmans, 2012)

—— 'Women of "the Cloth" in Acts: Sewing the Word', in Amy-Jill Levine and Marianne Blickenstaff, *A Feminist Companion to the Acts of the Apostles* (London: T. & T. Clark, 2004), 134–56

Stark, Rodney, *The Rise of Christianity: A Sociologist Reconsiders History* (Princeton: Princeton University Press, 1996)

Stratton, Kimberley B., 'The Rhetoric of "Magic" in Early Christian Discourse: Gender, Power, and the Construction of Heresy', in Todd Penner and Caroline Vander Stichele (eds), *Mapping Gender in Ancient Religious Discourses* (Leiden & Boston: Brill, 2007), 89–114

Swan, Laura, *The Forgotten Desert Mothers. Sayings, Lives and Stories of Early Christian Women*, (Mahwah, NJ: Paulist Press, 2001)

Thurston, Bonnie Bowman, *The Widows: A Women's Ministry in the Early Church* (Minneapolis, MN: Fortress Press, 1989)

Tilley, Maureen A., 'The Ascetic Body and the (Un)Making of the World of the Martyr', *Journal of the American Academy of Religion* 59 (1991), 467–79

Torjesen, Karen Jo, *When Women Were Priests* (San Francisco, CA: Harper, 1993)

Tuckett, Christopher, *The Gospel of Mary* (Oxford: Oxford University Press, 2007)

Van Bremen, Riet, 'Women and Wealth', in Averil Cameron and Amelie Kuhrt (eds), *Images of Women in Antiquity* (London: Routledge, 1983), 223–42

Van Dam, Raymond, *Families and Friends in Late Roman Cappadocia* (Philadelphia, PA: University of Pennsylvania Press, 2003)

Wegner, Judith Romney, *Chattel or Person?: The Status of Women in the Mishnah* (New York: Oxford University Press, 1988)

White, L. Michael, *Building God's House in the Roman World: Architectural Adaptation among Pagans, Jews and Christians* (Baltimore, MD: John Hopkins University Press, 1990)

Wiles, Maurice. 'Orthodoxy and Heresy', in Ian Hazlett (ed.), *Early Christianity: Origins and Evolution to AD 600* (London: SPCK, 1991), 198–207

Wilken, Robert, *The Christians as the Romans Saw Them* (New Haven, CT: Yale University Press, 1986)

Williams, Daniel H., *Ambrose of Milan and the End of the Nicene–Arian Conflicts* (Oxford: Oxford University Press, 1995); (Review: Charles M. Odahl, *Church History* 66 [1997], 310–12)

Williams, Michael Allen, *Rethinking "Gnosticism": An Argument for Dismantling a Dubious Category* (Princeton: Princeton University Press, 1996)

Williams, Stephen, and Gerard Friell, *Theodosius: The Empire at Bay* (New Haven, CT: Yale University Press, 1998)

Willis, Wendell Lee, *Idol Meat in Corinth: The Pauline Argument in 1 Corinthians 8 and 10* (Chico, CA: Scholars Press, 1983; repr. Eugene, OR: Wipf & Stock, 2004)

Winter, Bruce W. *Roman Wives, Roman Widows: The Appearance of New Women and the Pauline Communities* (Grand Rapids, MI: W. B. Eerdmans, 2003); (Review: Susan A. Calef, *Journal of Theological Studies* 66 [2005], 930–31)

Wire, Antoinette Clark, *The Corinthian Women Prophets: A Reconstruction through Paul's Rhetoric* (Minneapolis, MN: Fortress Press, 1990)

Witherington, Ben, *Women in the Earliest Churches* (Cambridge and New York: Cambridge University Press, 1988)

Woods, David, 'Gregory Thaumaturgus and the Earthquake of 344', *Journal of Theological Studies* 53 (2002), 547–53

Wypustek, Andrzej, 'Magic, Montanism, Perpetua and the Severan Persecution', *Vigiliae Christianae* 51 (1997), 276–97

Yarborough, Anne, 'Christianisation in the Fourth Century: The Example of Roman Women', *Church History* 45 (1976), 146–64

Yarborough, Larry O., *Not like the Gentiles: Marriage Rules in the Letters of Paul* (Atlanta: Scholars Press, 1985)

Young, Frances M., *From Nicaea to Chalcedon: A Guide to the Literature and Its Background* (London: SCM Press, and Philadelphia: Fortress Press, 1983; 2nd rev. edn, London and Grand Rapids, MI: Baker International, 2010)

Index

Acknowledgements

Many kind friends took time to read drafts of chapters as I was writing them, and both the kindness and the criticism have made all the difference. Georgina Capel and Rebecca Carter were the muses who helped me to conjure the project into being. Sarah Chalfant, Susan Charlton, James Corke-Webster, Carole Hill, Richard Millbank, Alex Poots, and Suzi Rabinowitz each read through the whole manuscript at one or another stage of its development, and helped me, successively, to discover its shape. Others – Stephanie Cobb, Kent Cooper, Emily Davies, Jen Ebbeler, Kevin Gustafson, Amalia Jiva, David Frankfurter, Bettany Hughes, Will Jackson, Hester, Hildelith, and Conrad Leyser, Candida Moss, James Rives, Jo Sadgrove, Jamie Wood, and Katie Wood Peters – offered invaluable reactions to specific sections, as did my students – Laura Almond, Elif Karaman, Ursala Knudsen-Latta, Ciara Ó Nualláin, Victoria Palazzo, and Emily Spencer – who helped me to tell the difference between what was obvious and what wasn't. Ron Cameron, John Gager, Helmut Koester, Vasiliki Limberis, and Margaret Miles helped me to find my way into the world of the first four centuries many years ago, and they have been an inspiration ever since.

The book was written during my mother's last illness, a bittersweet time during which a real band of angels, Celeste, Andrea, Mariana, Mercedes, and Rosanna – came into our lives, bringing warmth and laughter. With my father, Kent, I am grateful beyond words for this priceless gift. My cousins, Carol, Fran, Hank, Robb, John, Tina, Tom, Stuart, Langston, Brian, and Kayla, did more than they know to lighten our spirits. To Conrad, Hester, and Hildelith, I owe thanks for everything and nothing at all.

A Note on the Author

Kate Cooper is Professor of Ancient History at the University of Manchester. Her academic titles have explored the role of virgins in early Christianity (*The Virgin and the Bride*) and of women and the family during the decline and fall of the Roman Empire (*The Fall of the Roman Household*). Born in Washington, DC and educated at Princeton, Harvard, and Wesleyan universities, she is a Rome Prize winner and Fellow of the American Academy in Rome.